Praise for *The Complete Idiot's Guide to Buddhism, Second Edition*

"Gary Gach has done a genuine service in presenting this knowledgeable and accessible overview of Buddhist teaching and wisdom."
—Jack Kornfield, author of *The Wise Heart: The Universal Teachings of Buddhist Psychology*

"Let this book guide you practicing the Buddha's teachings, and surely you will become less idiotic, more educated at least, and well on your way to Enlightenment."
—Maxine Hong Kingston, author of *The Fifth Book of Peace*

"This book is not for idiots. It tells us what smart people want and need to know about Buddhist wisdom, history, theory, and its practice today. Gary Gach has done a fine job here, in lending a helping hand to lift ourselves toward the spiritual goal of awakened enlightenment."
—Lama Surya Das, founder of the Dzogchen Center, author of *Awakening the Buddha Within*

"Gary Gach is like that teacher you always wanted—easygoing, full of information, able to communicate in humorous and meaningful ways, and a little bit wacky. So he's the perfect author for *The Complete Idiot's Guide to Buddhism* ... Gach brings it all together with a light touch and an enthusiasm that makes you want to get up and do something Buddhist."
—Brian Bruya, Eastern Religion Book Reviewer, Amazon.com; translator of *Zen Speaks, The Tao Speaks*, and *Confucius Speaks*

"The best of its kind."
—Chevy Chase, comedian

"With great integrity and critical insight, Gary Gach immeasurably enhances authentic interfaith understanding and fellowship. *The Complete Idiot's Guide to Buddhism* is an exquisitely organized and comprehensive introduction to Buddhism that honors the intellect, illumines the spirit, and ennobles the human sojourn."
—Reverend Dorsey Blake, The Church for The Fellowship of All Peoples

"At last! *The Complete Idiot's Guide* makes Buddhism as accessible as Volkswagen repair. (Or is it the other way around?) It's so easy even a woman can do it. Not only that. Even a *man!*"
—Susan Moon, author of *The Life and Letters of Tofu Roshi*, co-editor of *Being Bodies* and *Not Turning Away*

"It is difficult to resist sitting down by the fireplace with book in hand and reading all 390 pages in one sitting. ... user-friendly ... a good overview for students ..."
—*MultiCultural Review*

"What allows *The Complete Idiot's Guide to Buddhism* to transcend the genre of introductory books is its openness. Gach lets the one taste of the dharma flow right through every page, and succeeds where other introductions fail by bringing Buddhism to life, to this very moment. It's well informed, broad-minded, richly textured, and, finally, *useful*. The whole tapestry of Buddhism in one book. What's not to like? If you're looking for one basic book on Buddhism, this is it."
—Franz Metcalf, author of *What Would Buddha Do?*

"Since we are a species of idiots, this book is for everyone. The Buddha's wisdom is timeless, and it's your time, now."
—Wes Nisker, author of *The Essential Crazy Wisdom* and *Crazy Wisdom Saves the Day Again*

"Gary Gach gives a tremendously useful overview of the basic history and practices of Buddhism combined with first-hand insights gathered from decades of personal practice. This is a highly readable, no-B.S. guide to Buddhism. Gach's good solid scholarship is fused with a likable, down-to-earth style that makes Buddhism easy to understand without watering it down. You don't need to be an idiot like me to appreciate his approach!"
—Brad Warner, Zen Soto priest, author of *Zen Wrapped in Karma Dipped in Chocolate*

"… Surprisingly enlightening and wonderfully accessible … this book truly shows how the complex ideas of one of the most ancient philosophies in the world can be adopted into anyone's life."
—Neela Banerjee, *AsianWeek*

"Ever balanced between the poet and the pragmatist, Gach guides, prods, and inspires readers, and stirs old souls and young from their sleep state to awaken to Buddhism's wisdom.
—Perry Garfinkel, *New York Times* contributor and author of *Buddha or Bust*

"It's like a college seminar on Buddhism distilled into Cliff's Notes."
—Leza Lowitz, *The Japan Times*

"Gary Gach knows his stuff. Just as importantly for this book, he writes sharply, cleanly, and well. Gach's writing is elegant and sparse and the message is boiled down, never dumbed down and never, ever boring or dry."
—*January* magazine

"I loved this book. All my adult life, I have studied world religions, and Buddhism often has overwhelmed me. Gary Gach uses the *Complete Idiot's Guide* format, and uses it well …. I have gained a greater appreciation for Buddhism and realize that much of what I do daily actually is Buddhist in nature. I highly recommend *The Complete Idiot's Guide to Buddhism* to any seeker, beginning or advanced."
—Lynn Allison, *Whole Living Journal*

"What I liked best about this book is its ability to get across the incredible richness and diversity of the Buddhist experience without losing sight of the details. Enjoy!"
—Anthony Flanagan, host, Buddhism.About.com

Buddhism

Third Edition

by Gary Gach

ALPHA

A member of Penguin Group (USA) Inc.

To the well-being of all beings.

ALPHA BOOKS

Published by the Penguin Group

Penguin Group (USA) Inc., 375 Hudson Street, New York, New York 10014, USA

Penguin Group (Canada), 90 Eglinton Avenue East, Suite 700, Toronto, Ontario M4P 2Y3, Canada (a division of Pearson Penguin Canada Inc.)

Penguin Books Ltd., 80 Strand, London WC2R 0RL, England

Penguin Ireland, 25 St. Stephen's Green, Dublin 2, Ireland (a division of Penguin Books Ltd.)

Penguin Group (Australia), 250 Camberwell Road, Camberwell, Victoria 3124, Australia (a division of Pearson Australia Group Pty. Ltd.)

Penguin Books India Pvt. Ltd., 11 Community Centre, Panchsheel Park, New Delhi—110 017, India

Penguin Group (NZ), 67 Apollo Drive, Rosedale, North Shore, Auckland 1311, New Zealand (a division of Pearson New Zealand Ltd.)

Penguin Books (South Africa) (Pty.) Ltd., 24 Sturdee Avenue, Rosebank, Johannesburg 2196, South Africa

Penguin Books Ltd., Registered Offices: 80 Strand, London WC2R 0RL, England

International Standard Book Number: 978-1-59257-911-2
Library of Congress Catalog Card Number: 2008941490

12 11 10   8 7 6 5 4

Interpretation of the printing code: The rightmost number of the first series of numbers is the year of the book's printing; the rightmost number of the second series of numbers is the number of the book's printing. For example, a printing code of 09-1 shows that the first printing occurred in 2009.

Printed in the United States of America

Note: This publication contains the opinions and ideas of its author. It is intended to provide helpful and informative material on the subject matter covered. It is sold with the understanding that the author and publisher are not engaged in rendering professional services in the book. If the reader requires personal assistance or advice, a competent professional should be consulted.

The author and publisher specifically disclaim any responsibility for any liability, loss, or risk, personal or otherwise, which is incurred as a consequence, directly or indirectly, of the use and application of any of the contents of this book.

Most Alpha books are available at special quantity discounts for bulk purchases for sales promotions, premiums, fundraising, or educational use. Special books, or book excerpts, can also be created to fit specific needs.

For details, write: Special Markets, Alpha Books, 375 Hudson Street, New York, NY 10014.

Publisher: *Marie Butler-Knight*
Editorial Director: *Mike Sanders*
Senior Managing Editor: *Billy Fields*
Executive Editor: *Randy Ladenheim-Gil*
Development Editor: *Julie Bess*
Senior Production Editor: *Janette Lynn*

Copy Editor: *Christine Hackerd*
Cover Designer: *Bill Thomas*
Book Designer: *Trina Wurst*
Indexer: *Heather McNeill*
Layout: *Ayanna Lacey*
Proofreader: *John Etchison*

Contents at a Glance

Contents

Foreword

The complex and varied cultural and textural manifestations of Buddhism are bewildering to many modern Western readers. A living religion that has spanned half the globe over 2,500 years is not easy to encapsulate. You may feel like a complete idiot when confronted by the variety of forms and teachings of one of the world's great religions. All of the different strands of Buddhism are simultaneously being introduced to the West at this very moment. A trivial example is the color of Buddhist robes. In Southeast Asia, saffron robes are worn; in the Tibetan traditions, red; Korean Buddhists wear gray; those from the Japanese tradition wear black.

The need for a guide through this vibrant thicket is clear. Gary Gach has taken up this difficult challenge in *The Complete Idiot's Guide to Buddhism, Third Edition*. Pointing out the similarities and differences in the complex weave of teachings of the cultures and practices called Buddhism, he puts them into a comprehensive context. It may be a guide for the complete idiot in that it assumes little, yet it avoids the traps of over-simplifying and dumbing down the subject. The book explores and presents simply and creatively the practical and theoretical, the mundane and the sacred, of Buddhism.

I suggest that you keep in mind the following words of Eihei Dogen, the thirteenth-century founder of Soto Zen in Japan, from his famous essay, *Genjo Koan*, when trying to come to grips with Buddhism:

> To study Buddhism is to study the self
> To study the self is to forget the self
> To forget the self is to be awakened by all things
> And this awakening continues endlessly

You can study Buddhism as an external object, but it is also an internal exploration. "To study Buddhism is to study the self." Not the study of old and antiquated artifacts, but of something alive and kicking. "To study the self is to forget the self." When you study the self, Buddhism as a separate object disappears. When you study and focus on yourself as a discrete object, the self loses its boundary. "To forget the self is to be awakened by all things." To let go of your habits and preconceptions is to experience things as they are, not as you have grown to expect them to be. "This awakening continues endlessly." By letting go of your conditioning, awakening is present in each moment. Thus, wisdom and compassion naturally arise.

I would like to close with an old Zen caution: "Don't mistake the finger for the moon." Buddhism, Zen, Christianity, Islam, Taoism, Judaism, Confucianism, and so on are all useful fingers. Teachings that point the way to fully actualizing ourselves and benefiting others are pointers, but not the end itself. All religious teachings are about what is, but if we focus on the teachings as objects we miss the point. Enjoy this book, and allow your natural light to inform your reading.

—Michael Wenger

Dairyu Michael Wenger is a Soto Zen priest and Dean of Buddhist Studies at the San Francisco Zen Center (SFZC) in San Francisco, California, where he has been a member since 1972. Dharma heir of Sojun Mel Weitsman, Wenger is also a former president of the SFZC. He received his M.A. from the New School of Social Research in New York, New York. He is author of *33 Fingers: A Collection of Modern American Koans*; editor of *Wind Bell: Teachings from the San Francisco Zen Center, 1968–2001*; and co-editor with Mel Weitsman of *Branching Streams Flow in the Darknesss: Zen Talks on the Sandokai* by Shunryu Suzuki Roshi. He's also a modern master of the art of *zenga* (Zen calligraphy, fusing imagery and words).

Introduction

It is a great honor, indeed, to present the message and practice of Buddhism to you. And it's a particular honor to do so in the time-tested *Complete Idiot's Guides* format. A few people may scoff that this is sacrilegious, or something. I can think of no better reply than the words of British writer G. K. Chesterton, when he said, "Angels can fly because they take themselves lightly." Not that my heels are more than an inch off the ground, mind you.

Now, if you're already a fan of *Complete Idiot's Guides*, like me, you'll know they're highly organized, which was one reason I thought it a perfect fit for introducing Buddhism, which is itself a highly organized system. So this book covers a whole lot of territory, and in a developmental, step-by-step manner. Presenting the teachings of the Buddha in this way, I only hope you find them no less stimulating and nourishing—and sacred—than they have continued to be for me, and hundreds of millions of others.

There's nothing to convert to, here. I'm not trying to sell anything, but I can't repress my enthusiasm. If you're only curious, that's fine: curiosity is my religion, too. I wouldn't claim you can become enlightened by a mere book, but I'd hope you might draw a little more than information from this well. I think you might find yourself looking at things in ways you might not have done before. The merits of Buddhism penetrate beyond abstract intellectuality. Here are a few more practical possibilities, based on common testimony. People who practice Buddhism notice being less stressed, for one thing. Sharper concentration and attentive focus also tend to come with the terrain. One can more fully deal with each encounter, and live in closer intimacy with life—a more genuine life, perhaps.

Buddhism encourages people to accept, understand, and make do with What Is rather than grasp after illusion, and thus experience their life to the fullest. This engenders a compassionate wisdom, compassion for others, but also oneself. It nourishes a more open mind and receptive heart, and thus a gentler and more relaxed attitude. You might find yourself getting more of a handle on difficult emotions. You might also notice other people giving you nicer vibes than before. If they remark that you have a halo, or a brighter aura, well, I don't know. These are all already yours from birth. Anyway, those are some potentials of this smart person's guide. Of course, you can't will any of these good things into effect, any more than you can will enlightenment. When the right causes and conditions have been cultivated, they seem to come more as an accident. May this book make you accident-prone!

(Please see for yourself.)

How to Use This Book

If you were to learn only four aspects of the Buddhist path, they'd cover …

1. *Buddha*, the awakened, teaching us the Way.

2. *Dharma*, the teachings of the Buddha, and all they pertain to.

3. *Sangha*, the practice and practitioners of the teachings.

4. Discovering potentials of the Buddha Way in daily life.

The first three are the nitty-gritty of Buddhism. So I've made them the blueprint for the whole first half this book. "Buddha, Showing the Way" looks at the Buddha and the spread of his teachings. *Dharma: Truth, and the Way to Truth* explores the essentials of his teachings (Dharma). *Sangha: Joining the Path* introduces the practice of Buddhism and surveys primary communities of practice (Sangha). Then, *Buddhism in Action: Applications in Everyday Life*, the whole second half, puts Buddhism in further perspective, from various walks of life. You could say the first half is about living Buddhism; the second half is about Buddhist living. (This book is two in one: a two-fer.)

Just as you can choose here from a shorter and a longer table of contents, here's a more detailed version of our map. **Part 1, "Buddha, Showing the Way,"** starts out with a short-story biography: the life of the Buddha. Then I'll sketch the fascinating history of how the Buddha's teachings spread and adapted to different lands. Next, we'll compare and contrast Buddhism with major religions. (It's compatible with them all, actually, as well as atheism.) And we'll explore Buddhism's emergence in the West. It's here to stay, yet "how" may take decades before anyone can say, as it continues to take shape (hence, in part, this third edition). I'll point out some directions in which it's already headed.

Having introduced you to the Buddha, I'll offer a guided tour of what he taught. In **Part 2, "Dharma: Truth, and the Way to Truth,"** you'll find all the essential teachings in plain, everyday language. It begins with what's known as the Three Jewels: Buddha, Dharma, Sangha (again, that's the ground plan for our book's first half). Then comes the core teachings, the Four Noble Truths: four profound, powerful facts of life, succinctly conveying the Buddha's unique vision. The last of the four opens up into an eight-part path, which we'll tour step by step. After that, I'll present the compassionate wisdom underlying Buddhism. And the contents of the final chapter, on conscious conduct (ethics), might look familiar at first glance, but it's no less vital and unique.

All that's left is how to put it into practice. In **Part 3, "Sangha: Joining the Path,"** I'll introduce you to meditation, in two chapters. Then, I'll spotlight four major schools of practice in the West (rather than just one particular lineage, as most books do). I don't want to make Buddhism seem like a supermarket ("Attention, shoppers! Zen bread-tasting in Aisle 4!"), yet one of the unprecedented aspects of Buddhism today, particularly in the West, is the variety of schools coexisting and coevolving for the first time side by side. The lineages we'll examine will be Insight Meditation (Vipassana), Zen, Pure Land, and Tibetan (Vajrayana)—like four basic food groups, but each fully nourishing.

From there, you might consider the book's last part, the entire second half, a kind of buffet: a broad, salad-bar selection of ways in which the Way can be tasted and tested out in the world at large. Having explored living Buddhism, we move on to Buddhist living. In **Part 4, "Buddhism in Action: Applications in Everyday Life,"** we'll survey real-world interchanges with Buddhism, starting with our primary relations—from cradle to grave. Then we'll look at two more aspects of everyday life enriched by Buddhist views: work and food. In the next pair of chapters, we'll explore Buddhism and the arts (popular and fine), including sports, gardening, music, movies, photography, and writing (even your own). Then, we'll see how Buddhism harmonizes with the shift in view (paradigm) taking place in the sciences. Having begun this smorgasbord of applications of Buddhism in daily life, with our closest relations, our final chapter shows Buddhism in our relations in the world at large, be it through volunteering to serve others or engaging in modern issues that Buddhism is addressing in its own gentle but firm, transformative way.

Buddhism is amazing. It's composed of utterly simple things. In the appendix, you'll find the basics all on one page. Put them together, they're a whole greater than the sum of their parts: equal to life itself. Also in the appendix is a glossary and an annotated book list. Throughout, you'll find numerous meditations and tips you can try out for yourself. After you finish this guide, its main points will stay with you. Use them as the spirit moves. May they serve you in good stead.

Our Buddhist Bulletin Board

Part of the added value and fun of any *Complete Idiot's Guide* are the boxed notes, called sidebars. (Until I wrote this book, I always thought they were called "little doohickeys.") For your enhanced learning and reading pleasure, I'll incorporate four such little doohickeys, like violets doodled in the margins:

Along the Path

... reserved for various and sundry sayings and thoughts commenting on the text. Often, they mingle East and West or different traditions, inviting further study. (Do all roads lead to Om?)

 Hear and Now

... for the voice of notable folks who illuminate some gist or pith. However near or far, they speak to us as contemporaries and neighbors, here and now.

 This Is

... to highlight and define key words and phrases. Don't mistake a finger pointing to the moon for the moon itself. Or, like it says in the Foreword (and as semanticist W. I. Korczybyski put it), "The map is not the territory." Meaning: a word can leave you at the gates, but it can't bring you across; it's up to you to make it real.

 Leaves from the Bodhi Tree

A tree sheltered the Buddha during the meditation that led to his supreme enlightenment. This sidebar is for leaves from that living tree of awakening: anecdotes and meditations illuminating this growing tradition. (Even the one about the priest, the rabbi, and the guru ...)

The Way of the Buddha can be understood, realized, and expressed through the most subtle or simple concept or fact. Putting just one into practice can eventually lead to all the others. Enjoy the journey.

Acknowledgments

I thank my parents, family, sangha, teachers, and friends. Of innumerable invisible hands here for which I'm grateful are my publisher Marie Butler-Knight and editor Randy Ladenheim-Gil; marketing maven and publicist Dawn Werk; Julie Bess, Christine Hackerd, Jan Lynn, Bill Thomas, Trina Wurst, patient, cheery, brilliant production pals, all a great pleasure, honor, and blessing to work with; Michael Wenger and Lewis Lancaster, prefacer and technical editor, respectively; my literary representative, Jack Scovil; and agencies, administrators, executives, and saints too numerous to name, although I'd be remiss not to give special thanks for this edition to Alex Arrais, Simone Biase, Reverend Dorsey Blake, Bill Bushell, DC, Margery Cantor, Bryan Caston, Swami Chaitanya, Venerable Rubina Courtin, Lyn Fine,

Ian Grand, Rick Hanson, Reverend Heng Sure, Jane Hirshfield, Matthew Jacobs, Dr. Ping-Qi Kang, Ko Un SSN, Rabbi Lawrence Kushner, Stephen Levine, Sally McAra, Reverend Ryuei Mike McCormick, Katherine Massis, the Mechanics' Institute reference librarians, Raymond Mondini, Susan Moon, Ganden Thurman, Michael Robbins, Gent Sturgeon, Scoop, Su Ong and Su Co, Piya Tan, Stephen Toole, Karma Tenzing Wangchuk, J. R. Willems, Judith Wing, and all the readers writing me with constructive feedback. Any residual errors remain wholly my own.

Special thanks to *Urthona: Buddhism and Art*, where my text on cinema appeared in a slightly different form. *Dream Deferred* by Langston Hughes, from *The Collected Poems of Langston Hughes*, copyright © 1994 by The Estate of Langston Hughes. Used by permission of Alfred A. Knopf, a division of Random House, Inc. Wordless poem by Paul Reps from *Sit In: What It Is Like* (Zen Center Press, copyright © 1975, Zen Center); reprinted by permission. *The Red Wheelbarrow* by William Carlos Williams, from *Collected Poems* 1909–1939, Volume 1, copyright © 1938 by New Directions Publishing Corp. Reprinted by permission of New Directions Publishing Corp. Best efforts have been made to locate all rights holders and clear necessary reprint permissions. If any acknowledgments have been omitted, or any rights overlooked, it is unintentional and forgiveness is requested. Any oversights will be rectified for future editions upon proper notice.

Special Thanks to the Technical Reviewer

The Complete Idiot's Guide to Buddhism was reviewed in this and its two previous editions by an expert who not only checked the accuracy of what you'll learn in this book, but who also provided valuable insight to help ensure that it tells you everything you need to know about Buddhism. Our special thanks are extended to Professor Lewis R. Lancaster.

Professor Lancaster was born in Virginia, and earned his B.A. from Roanoke College, his M.Th. from USC-ST, and his Ph.D. from the University of Wisconsin. As a distinguished Professor at the University of California, Berkeley, he co-founded its Buddhist Studies program and served on committees and boards of numerous programs, departments, and extramural nonprofit organizations, including the American Academy of Religion, the International Association for Buddhist Studies, the Pacific Neighborhood Consortium, and Scholars Engaged in Electronic Resources. He is adjunct faculty at the Graduate Theological Union, the Institute of Buddhist Studies, and University of the West (President Emeritus). He's been resident faculty at the University of Michigan, Dartmouth College, Peking University, Rissho University, and Korea University.

A renowned speaker at national and international panels, workshops, conferences, and symposia, he's produced nine scholarly Buddhist books, and his essays have been published in dozens of anthologies and journals. He's been a pioneering contributor to the electronic publication of a six-CD collection of such definitive texts as 45 volumes of the Pali Canon, 11,000 pages of Sanskrit texts, 70 Chinese Zen texts with bibliography, 8,000 pages of archival materials on Korean Buddhist history, and an interactive database on Korean Buddhist thought. He is founder and Director of the Electronic Cultural Atlas Initiative (ECAI), an unprecedented international collaboration guided by the paradigm of the historical atlas. Research data is indexed at ECAI by time and place, and is retrievable on a map-based interface, allowing comparisons across discipline, region, and time (www.ecai.org). That he's taken time from such endeavors to focus such considerable expertise and care to this book is an immeasurable honor and aid, indeed. Thank you, Lew.

Trademarks

All terms mentioned in this book that are known to be or are suspected of being trademarks or service marks have been appropriately capitalized. Alpha Books and Penguin Group (USA) Inc. cannot attest to the accuracy of this information. Use of a term in this book should not be regarded as affecting the validity of any trademark or service mark.

Part 1

Buddha, Showing the Way

Let's begin with "Who?" Such is the start of various primary questions as "Who wrote the book of love?" "Who's in charge here?" and "Who am I, really?" (And "So who wants to know?")

Our "who" is the one who can show us the Way in this world. I'm referring to the Buddha, and also the buddha within—within you, me, and everyone.

No matter one's country, creed, or car, the Buddha can have an important influence in anyone's life. And it's good merely to understand the teachings he embodies. So without further ado, it's a privilege and a pleasure for me to introduce to you everyone's good old buddy … the Buddha.

Chapter 1

The Teachings of a Smile: The Life of the Buddha

In This Chapter

- The Four Signs
- The Renunciation
- The Middle Way
- Supreme Enlightenment
- Teachings

This life story is itself a teaching. It's both simple and sublime. The tale has been known by upwards of a third of humanity. A sacred story, you can hear at least four levels at once in its multilayered tapestry: in *historical, imaginative, mythic,* and *personal* dimensions. It's fact that there was such a person, living amid a crucial historical turning point. Reconstruction of his thoughts, feelings, and decisions call upon the imagination ... our inner life ... and the depth and wonder in being human. His story also teaches in mythic terms. Myth invites us to perceive timeless truths beyond the limitations of its words, behind its symbols. Of all myths, scholar Joseph Campbell has said, "The closest we have to planetary mythology is Buddhism. In it all things are potentially Buddha things."

And we might find this story speaks to each of us, if we but change his name to ours; look in the mirror, and reflect. This is the personal dimension. I leave it to each reader to participate in any or all of these levels as they wish. I guarantee this is a story well worth hearing. It's the story of a smile, still felt today.

Are You Ready?: Waking Up to Yourself, Waking Up to Buddha

We can read the story of the Buddha simply as a biography, but how do we know he was a real person? As Buddhist scholar Professor Lewis Lancaster points out, Europeans at first believed his story was a myth. But when archaeologists started to dig at the key spots matching his biography, they found the oldest examples of writing in India. Within about a century and a half from the time of Shakyamuni, King Ashoka dedicated pillars saying that "This is where the Buddha was born," "This is where he reached Nirvana," and so on. Few ancients have so precise a biographical identification with places so soon after their lifetime. Prof. Lancaster feels this suggests people's personal memory of the Buddha was passed along from the great-grandparent generation. Many of us today have memories passed on to us belonging to our parents, grandparents, and great-grandparents. Prof. Lancaster concludes, "So the timing, the pillars, the collective memory gave scholars good reason to assume that there was a historical person who had a life history close to the lore that had been passed down three generations at the time of Ashoka."

Yet even if he'd never lived, his teachings are still viable today. Whoever invented bread, I salute his or her achievement, which in one stroke enhanced all our lives. I liken this vital relevance of discovery—sometimes called bootstrapping—with the Wright brothers' pioneering of flight. They stepped forth into the unknown and flew, and we still use their extensive calculations for flight today. Indeed, what the Buddha achieved can likewise boot us up to a higher plane (pun intended). Just reading the story of the Buddha encourages us to achieve peace—a wakefulness, a heightened sense of goodness, and the full potential of life.

Are you ready to meet a person who charted a priceless, complete, commonsensical guide to true happiness? His discovery is universal, available to every human being. It's right in front of our faces. But, as he would also discover, something so simple might not be for everyone. Why not? Well, for one thing, the Buddha only said he was teaching what worked for him, and invited others to try it and see for themselves. He was a guide but not a god, and some people prefer to wait for God or priests to tell them what they can find out for themselves or what they already intuitively know. (Might this be you?)

Moreover, some people prefer to imagine their happiness will last forever. (Could *this* be you?) Others have a hard time letting go of the accumulation of wounds and labels that have stuck to them throughout life, tenaciously clinging to sorrows as a ballast, rather than letting go and sensing the innate and ineffable lightness of life; rather than appreciating how the luminous blue sky, solid brown earth, and tender green plants are always present for enjoyment. (Is *this* you?) If you can see yourself in this portrait gallery (and who can't?), then "Welcome to the club!" It's commonly called The Human Condition. Right there, in a nutshell, you have it. We spin around in our self-created rat cage when all along the cage door is unlocked.

But so long as there are people living their life as if sleepwalking through a kind of bad dream, and even choosing to perpetuate their daze, there'll always be a chance for awakening. That's what *Buddha* means, in essence: someone or even something that awakens, and awakens us … not just physically. Just 'cause your eyes are open doesn't mean you're awake. We're more than physical bodies. We can awaken—really awaken—in body, heart, and mind.

Try this right now: pause, be attentive, listen, and look. A buddha voice or a buddha sight might be right at hand. It's in every ray of sunshine, every snowflake, every drop of rain, every laugh of a child, every wonder around you! (Please consider, too, how you can always pause, throughout your day, as simply as that.) Now, if all things are potentially buddha, then we have great reason to consider and learn from, if not honor, the original Buddha.

> **This Is**
>
> **Buddha,** derived from the Sanskrit root *budh*, means "to awaken." Buddha, like King or Christ, is not a name, per se, but a title. As such, it means "Awakened One," "Supremely Awakened." At its root, the word refers to the awakener, the awakened, and the awakening … and all three as one.

The Buddha once said, "If you want to really see me, then look at my teachings." The reverse is equally true. That is, his life is itself a teaching.

The Buddha teaches that living without worry and fear, becoming intimate with life, becoming awake, is to awaken to ourselves, to our fullest potential as human beings, and to the Buddha within all of us. It's as important as life and death, and as easy as drinking a cup of tea. (You'll see.) It starts like this …

The Birth of a Sage, Siddhartha Gautama

One full-moon night in May, around 560 B.C.E., a woman gave birth. Her name was Mahamaya, and she'd been on a journey to her father's house, about 50 miles from her home, to lie in waiting, as was the custom in India. Now she headed back to the foothills of the Himalayas, on the border between what's now India and Nepal, to present to her husband his new son. This would be no ordinary son. Mahamaya was a queen, married to King Suddhodana, the *raja* (ruler) of the Shakya clan. Her son would be prince of their small but prosperous independent nation-state. They named him Siddhartha, meaning "every wish fulfilled" or "aim accomplishment."

As was also the custom, a soothsayer was brought in to make a prediction at birth. He declared Siddhartha would either grow up to rule the world if he remained in the palace, or he'd become the Supremely Enlightened One.

 Along the Path

> Sometimes it seems like this one guy had a string of aliases. Here's the lowdown: Gautama (*goh-tah-mah*) was his family clan name, and Siddhartha was his personal name. He's also sometimes called Shakyamuni, meaning the sage of the Shakya tribe. Interestingly, he's called Buddha from the time he went forth from home on his quest.

The Life of a Prince

The king adored his son and wanted him to inherit the throne, and so he kept him cloistered within the strong, high palace walls—not unlike the way we can wall ourselves in, get set in our ways, and unquestioningly go about our lives. Moreover, the father went so far as to create an environment as artificial as a Hollywood soundstage, wherein sick people, the elderly, and even dirt and withered leaves were all whisked from view. But, for the persevering seeker, the truth is always out there.

The prince proved to be a prodigy; he soon knew more than his teachers, the finest in the land. He was unequalled in literature and math. He surpassed everyone in swimming, running, archery, and fencing. He could strategize, command respect, and win any battle. In a huge athletic competition, he won the hand of one of the most beautiful maidens, Yashodhara (Keeper of Radiance), who became his bride. Not only a whiz kid and a champ, he also got along with everyone and proved a compassionate and loving husband.

Delighted, Siddhartha's father gave his heir three different palaces, one for each of India's three seasons: hot, cool, and wet. There, the prince was lavished with endless fun and games, beautiful attendants, fleets of horses, fabulous feasts, live concerts at the snap of his fingers, and the whole bit. But Siddhartha started to chomp at that bit.

What Is This!?: The Four Signs

Siddhartha was curious and wished to explore the outside world: the real world. So does anyone who wants to lead an authentic life. To keep his son happy, the king granted his wish, yet made sure everything outside was as controlled as it had been inside.

Everywhere Siddhartha went, he saw prosperity and happiness until, somehow, a decrepit form passed through all the young, healthy people the king had arranged for him to see. Siddhartha asked his servant Channa "What is this!?" The faithful servant told him that although he had white hair down to his knees, this was an old man using a staff to walk, and that this is what eventually happens to everyone. All the way back to the castle, Siddhartha brooded, and when the king heard about this, he increased the budget for Siddhartha's lavish lifestyle.

A second time, however, on another excursion, Siddhartha chanced upon a maimed fellow with bloodshot eyes, groaning through a frothy mouth. "What is this!?" Siddhartha asked, and his faithful servant told him that this was a person who'd become ill, but that Siddhartha needn't worry because the prince ate a good diet and exercised. Siddhartha returned home brooding, and so the king plied him with even still more luxuries and opulence.

On a third outing, reality bit yet again. This time, Siddhartha chanced upon a funeral procession, mourners sobbing and waving their arms in all directions, while at the head of the procession a body was being carried, utterly still, as if sleeping. The faithful servant explained what death is, that nothing could be done for it, and that it happens to everyone. No point in worrying, he said, just hope for a long life.

What a shock! Old age and sickness were bad enough. But now this! The inevitable, ultimate destination of us all. Is there anyone for whom an encounter with death isn't one of the most unforgettable, difficult moments of their life?

Each of these encounters was but a glimpse, but perhaps their having been withheld for so long made them even more of a revelation. In any event, Siddhartha saw they were a matter of his own life and death, and, by extension, of everyone he loved—and indeed, all mortals. Was there no way out?! Meanwhile, when the king saw his beloved boy brooding more darkly than ever before, and found out why, he despaired. He didn't want to lose his only beloved son and heir. But did he level with him? No, he pampered him all the more. Yet life's truth pierced through again, a fourth and final time.

Journeying outside the palace walls, Siddhartha happened to see a man with a shaven head, clad only in an orange sheet the color of liquid sunshine, walking very slowly, holding only an empty bowl, and his entire manner radiating majestic tranquility and serene joy. "What is this?" Siddhartha asked, and he was told that this was a monk who'd renounced the world in search of spiritual truth. This silent monk seemed to be telling him, yes, there is an answer to the questions burning inside him since he'd so starkly witnessed human suffering for himself. He'd never find this answer as long as he numbed his mind with endless sensual indulgence. Well, when all this got back to the king, he was beside himself.

Hear and Now

Dream Deferred

What happens to a dream deferred?
Does it dry up
Like a raisin in the sun?
Or fester like a sore —
And then run?
Does it stink like rotten meat?
Or crust and sugar over —
like a syrupy sweet?
Maybe it just sags
like a heavy load.
Or does it explode?

—Langston Hughes

Just then, as fate would have it, Siddhartha's bride bore a child. Siddhartha probably was torn, as we can see from the name he gave his son, Rahula, which means "chain." The king took the occasion to stage a blowout celebration to keep Siddhartha close to hearth and home. But after the sumptuous feast, as Siddhartha was being entertained by the finest dancing girls in all the land, he yawned, laid down on his cushion, and closed his eyes. As there is no point entertaining someone who isn't paying attention, the dancing girls stopped, laid down, too, and napped. When Siddhartha opened his eyes again, he saw these women who just moments ago had been the quintessence of beauty, now sweaty and sprawled in awkward positions, their once lovely mouths now drooling or gnashing their teeth in their sleep. So much for the pleasures of the material world … and what a cue for an exit!

He got up and tiptoed out. Passing by his wife's chambers, he took one last lingering look at his sleeping beloved ones, then was gone—gone in search of an answer to the human riddles of disease, decay, and death, in search of the ultimate meaning of life.

Renunciation and Going Forth

Time out. Before we follow Siddhartha on his quest, we might pause for a moment to consider his break with his past, his renunciation. For one thing, it was extreme: a prince renouncing the wealth and power of his birthright. In today's terms, he could have been a trillionaire. Actually, it was respectable for noblemen of India to investigate ultimate truth, but only in their retirement, after they'd fulfilled family and social obligations. But for Siddhartha, truth couldn't wait.

True, Siddhartha was also walking away from his responsibilities as a father as well as a prince. He was aware of the pain he'd cause others by leaving, but suffering seemed the ever-present essence of this ultimate enigma he intended to resolve, once and for all. Once he'd found the answer, Siddhartha would return, bringing it back to his people and all the land.

So we acknowledge the courage, the fearlessness necessary to stand up for his dream, his ideals, and his quest to seek sovereignty over his own life rather than over a kingdom. It's also interesting to notice that Siddhartha was leaving behind inherited ideas, as well as inherited privilege. I think a message here, for all of us, is to look at life with our own two eyes, regardless of what Simon says, without asking "Mother, may I?" to see for ourselves, beyond the high, strong palace walls of what we've learned to call self … to renounce habit and hand-me-down ideas, in search of the genuine.

Into the Forest: Finding Out

Siddhartha gave his royal robes and jewels to his faithful servant. Before giving him his sword, he shaved his head (an act repeated by those who become Buddhist monks and nuns today), leaving only a top-knot, severing his ties with not only his family but also his royal caste—and thus the whole hereditary caste system. (If India were a body, the peasants were the feet, the merchants and craftsmen were the legs, the warrior and noble class—from which the Buddha hailed—were the arms, and the priestly Brahmins were the head.) He went forth into the wilderness.

Now, in those days, India's wild mountains and forests were dotted with a variety of truth-seekers, abundant with as many as 63 discernible schools. Siddhartha studied under one renowned forest teacher after another. In relatively no time, he learned all his teachers knew and was even offered jobs carrying on their work, but that wasn't what he was looking for. True, he'd learned to transcend his senses and thoughts, his materiality, and even his own consciousness. But while these techniques transcended reality, they didn't unlock it. They didn't resolve the riddle of birth and death. They offered temporary bliss, but not permanent peace. They couldn't answer the deep frustration, the pain still burning in his heart.

Siddhartha's achievements had drawn to him a handful of companions. With them, he tried the *ascetic* path of self-denial, to the point of self-mortification, as a means of attaining self-control and liberation. He lay on a bed of nails. He progressively reduced his diet until he was down to one grain of rice a day. Soon, overachiever that he was, he came to the brink of self-annihilation.

> **This Is** _____
>
> **Ascetic,** from Greek, originally meant "hermit," such as a person practicing austere self-discipline for religious purposes. Besides seclusion, common forms of asceticism are fasting, celibacy, and poverty. These self-disciplines are believed to sharpen the mind, heighten awareness, and free the practitioner from mundane attachments.

Just skin and bones. This sculpture depicts Buddha's extreme asceticism. His veins bulge over his ribs, through his blackened and withering skin. If he rubbed his tummy he could feel his spine. His eyes stare from their sockets like stale water from a deep well. Yet he does not waver on his quest.

(Sikri, Pakistan [Gandhara], second century C.E., 83.8 centimeters, Lahore Museum)

The Middle Way

At this point, a young girl from the village passed by with food her mother had given her as an offering to the forest gods. She saw Siddhartha, nearly unconscious, and put some rice milk to his lips, and he drank. By so doing, he renounced not only asceticism but also extremism.

There are two things going on here worth noting. First, there's the wonderful recognition of the importance of our bodies and their relationship to our happiness. So many spiritual paths have rejected the body as evil. Siddhartha realized he couldn't achieve his goal if his mind was in a trance and his body too weak to grasp and carry on the truth. Indeed, realizing the mind-body connection, he saw he couldn't have a sound mind without a sound body.

Moreover, he realized something simple yet sublime, now known as the *Middle Way*. We all meet with varying forms of extremism in ourselves and others. The Buddha would say to listen to all sides, then find a harmonious middle road. Don't tear the ground out from under your feet, nor chase after a spring dream. If the guitar string's too taut, it snaps; too loose, it won't play. Find the mean and, *Ping!*, it sings.

This Is

The **Middle Way** is an expression of the Buddha's direct, nondualist outlook. Dualism divides: good vs. bad, self vs. other, mind vs. body, life vs. death, all or nothing. Buddhism embraces all sides, seeing their interrelatedness, and seeks the mean. Look beyond extremes, and see for yourself. (A school of Buddhism studying the Middle Way is called *Madhyamika.*)

As he realized self-denial didn't free him from attachment, he also came to see self-denial as but another kind of attachment, another attachment to self, no different from his princely self-indulgence. Looking deeper, he began to truly wake up to how identification with "self" is always a set-up for ultimate disappointment, because it implies a dualist opposition: self and its desires ("in here") vs. world and its rewards ("out there"), This *versus* That. So, with no attachment to self, no dualism. No longer debating this versus that, he could experience directly.

Well, meanwhile, his eating food blew his credibility with his five self-appointed disciples, for sure. They wandered off before he could explain his realization. And so he went at it alone. At some point, we all must. But the girl returned and offered him food every day. With the recovery of his health came fresh perceptions, which led to new insights, which would lead to wisdom and, ultimately, enlightenment.

Enlightenment

Meditating in a healthy body allowed him to see things around him with clarity; really see. Whether looking at the food the girl offered before he ate it, or sitting under a tree and looking at its leaves, he saw how each was not independent. Food might come from a leaf. And the leaf? The leaf came from the sun above, from the Earth beneath, and from the water in a cloud. Where did each of these come from? They were all interconnected … interdependent … interacting … inter-reacting. He saw, too, how self-denial could never liberate him from the intricate, vast web of life, of which he was a part. Nor is the web of life at fault. Indeed, there is no fault, anywhere … only boundless goodness.

Looking further, he saw how nothing lasts in the dance of life. The cloud passes away in the sun. The leaf falls to Earth. Similarly, he, too, was part of not only the interdependence but also the impermanence of all life. Seeing clearly now, these realizations made him appreciate each moment. And why not? Why not fully live each moment when each moment occurs only once, yet contains the potential of all of life in each instant?

Now he felt he was really getting somewhere. Now he was cooking! The meaning of birth and suffering and death was becoming clear at last. Before sundown, looking at the evening star beside the full moon of May, he felt that tonight he'd make his final, ultimate breakthrough.

Sitting beneath the sheltering leaves of a fig tree (the Indian *banyan* variety), he endured thunderstorms, some say even demonic temptations waged by tempter Mara. First Mara surrounded the Buddha with the most seductive women imaginable, but the Buddha remained composed. Then Mara unleashed the most bloodthirsty warrior demons upon him, but he had no fear. Finally, Mara tried to tempt him away from his meditation by challenging his motives, saying, "Aren't you really doing this for selfish reasons? Who are you to claim enlightenment!? And if you really have transcended this realm, then why don't you just leave! But even if you did attain enlightenment, who'd believe you?" Looking at Mara, the Buddha touched the ground with one hand, taking the earth—and all of creation—as witness of Enlightenment.

The Buddha calls upon all the earth, all beings, as witnesses of Enlightenment.

(Sukhothai school, fourteenth or early fifteenth century, bronze, 101.6 centimeters, National Museum, Ayuthya)

In the dark of night, gazing into his heart and the heart of creation, he saw into the mystery of life, that we are bound to die and thus bound to suffer. Mortality ensures cravings never to be fulfilled—and perpetuates with them the false mind-sets of self that only produce more suffering. He saw clearly now the jail, which we ourselves construct, in which we entrap ourselves, and which we ourselves police. But whatever is constructed will deconstruct. He saw, too, the happiness of being free.

He understood that what we call our life is but a wave, not the ocean. He became one with that ocean, and all the rivers and raindrops flowing into it. He saw the morning star in the sky as if for the first time, his mind as clear as a mirror, and his heart as wide now as the world, almost overflowing with understanding and love. The luminous, joyous starlight matched the smile on his lips. This was it. He had found out. Now he was fully awake.

Supreme Awakening.

After Enlightenment: Teach!

Imagine Siddhartha sitting there, at the culmination of a seven-year quest, a fully self-realized being. So happy! He had finally found complete freedom from all unnecessary mortal suffering. He'd experienced the greatest awakening and attained supreme enlightenment. He now directly perceived ultimate reality, free of all limitation, and his compassionate awareness and sublime wisdom was one with all that is.

After some time, he stood up and took his first steps, just walking lovingly around the tree that had sheltered him. He felt the solid earth supporting his bare feet and the fresh wind caressing his cheek, as if he and the world had been born together this instant. When the young girl brought food that day, she could feel his transformation in her own heart.

It's interesting to consider how he might have remained beneath the tree in perfect nirvana, supreme peace, for the rest of his days. Yet his enlightenment showed him how the seeds of enlightenment are within the hearts of everyone. His awakening to life's ultimate meaning was bound up, part and parcel, with his love for all beings and compassion for their needless suffering. So he returned to the companionship of his fellow human beings.

Now when his five former followers in the forest saw Siddhartha coming, they turned their backs. They remembered him as having copped out on the rigors of the ascetic path. Yet as he drew nearer, they could recognize in their own hearts that he was transformed. Supreme Enlightenment was evident just from his presence. They let go of judgments and preconceptions, and welcomed him.

That night he gave his first talk, known today as *The Turning of the Wheel of Truth*. Explaining his discovery, he introduced four premises, known as the *Four Noble Truths* (discussed in Chapter 5), defining the origin of and liberation from suffering, with a practical, personal program for such liberation, known as the *Eightfold Path* (Chapter 6). While some were mulling it over, one of the companions got it and awoke on the spot. There was nothing to memorize or take on faith. Instead he awoke to the truth resounding within himself.

Buddha was a traveling teacher (peripatetic), on a perpetual pilgriage. Thus did his teachings spread by foot. The traditional topknot of his hair is elongated to represent his enlightenment. His fingers are tapered to symbolize his ability to reach deep within. His gesture of one hand up means "Have no fear"; the other hand offers a boon. The design displays an amazing balance of motion and rest.

(Sukhhothai, 3.53 centimeters × 2.35 centimeters)

It was decided these teachings would be called *Dharma*, the path. Those on this path would be called *Sangha*. Siddhartha would become known as *The Buddha*, the one who shows others the path in this world. Thus began the Buddha's course for the rest of his life—teaching to not only his growing order of disciples but also whomever would listen—young and old, rich and poor, male and female, and even the so-called untouchables, the outcasts below the peasant class (Nirvana knows no borders)—as he walked around the vast delta of the Ganges River, with an annual retreat during India's three-month heavy rains. All told, it was to be a journey lasting the next 45 years.

This Is

> **Dharma,** from Sanskrit (Dhamma, Pali), has a number of meanings, depending on the context: "teachings," "system," "path," "reality," and "truth"; also "calling," and "fruit." We can say it refers to truth and the way to the truth, the Buddha's teachings and that to which they pertain (everything in life).
>
> **Sangha** means "assembly," or "host." Generally, it refers to the Buddhist community; more specifically, it refers to its monastic order, one of the oldest in the world.

Tales Heard Around Buddha's Campfire

The Buddha was and is a brilliant teacher. Here follow a few examples. Disciples didn't write down his talks (generally called *sutras*), until later. He also taught by his presence, as example; always a good method. ("Don't do as I say, be as I am.") His teachings can be typified as nonauthoritarian (noncoercive), empirical (see for yourself), real-time (present-moment), and pragmatic (practical), as well as supremely compassionate and wise.

It is said the Buddha was a genius for matching his teaching to the person, an art called *upaya* (skillful means), as seen throughout this guide. His clarity can be judged not only for the truth of his message but also the simplicity, inclusiveness, realism, persuasiveness, and care with which he presented it. For example, a woman named Kisa Gotami was a young bride of an arranged marriage. Not having given her in-laws an heir, they grew cold to her and began looking for a more suitable mate for their son. When she did give birth, the boy infant died. She'd heard the Buddha was a miracle worker who'd transcended the bonds of death. Weeping, she came with her infant, wrapped up in a blanket, and implored the Buddha to restore her son to life. (If you were the Buddha, what would you do?)

The Buddha smiled compassionately, giving her hope. She felt reassured in his warm, calm presence, and trusted the lucidity of his wise smile. "Before I do anything," he told her, "go to the nearby village and bring me a handful of mustard seed. But, please, make sure the seed comes only from a home where death is unknown." And so Kisa Gotami hurried to the village, and knocked on the first door. When the owners of the house saw her, clutching her dead child, they invited her in and said they'd be glad to give her some mustard seed. But when she added the Buddha's stipulation, the woman of the house wiped away a tear as her husband told Kisa Gotami of the death of his father. Second house, third house, everywhere: the same thing. Kisa Gotami returned to the Buddha's enclave in the forest, buried her child, and asked to learn the Dharma.

Amazing story. He hadn't told her to learn to forget and be happy. No, he showed her a way to reach deeper into her grief, a way through that also enabled her to see something larger than her own loss, something in which she could take refuge: the universality of impermanence.

 Along the Path _____

> In Asia, _Buddhism_ is an alien term, because it merely refers to reality, _Buddha-Dharma_. What else to call it? Because the Buddha wouldn't address certain basic metaphysical questions, his path isn't technically philosophy. Likewise, because his teachings aren't built around God or an afterlife, they aren't precisely a religion. His teachings about self as an illusory construction makes it tricky to categorize as psychology. Some people prefer to call it a science, an education, or a way of being.

Beyond the Dualism of Words: Parables and Silence

The Buddha frequently used vivid similes and apt parables. Explaining skillful means, for instance, he said one uses a raft to get to the other shore (Nirvana) but then leaves the raft behind. Meaning, don't mistake a finger pointing at the moon for the moon. The map is not the territory.

Sometimes Buddha answered profound imponderables with a parable. He'd say, for example, that asking where the universe began was like the man struck by a poison dart who won't allow himself to be taken to a doctor until he knows exactly who fired the dart, just what poison he used, precisely how the dart was made, and so on.

Other times, the Buddha taught by silence. Such was the case when asked questions typically not open to direct, personal experience. "It does not further" (meaning "time is too precious to go down that road"), a disciple might say when asked about God, whether space is infinite, whether the universe is eternal, whether the soul is immortal, and whether body and mind are identical. (Had the Buddha heard of stand-up comedy, he might have replied with one-liners, like Woody Allen: "If man were immortal, just think of what his laundry bills would be!" Ba-dum!)

The Buddha wasn't necessarily being irreverent about the ineffable, but he sure didn't try to catch the wind. Some say that, being omniscient, the Buddha actually knew the answers to questions of infinity and eternity, divinity and immortality, but kept silent realizing how the rest of us would get tangled up in words and views, wanting to argue all night but never getting anywhere. Rather, he's like a noble fireman who doesn't debate the metaphysics of the origin of fire with children who don't realize they're trapped in a burning building.

The Final Teaching

The end was unexpected. Some food he'd been given as alms was bad. Eventually, he had to lie down. Just as he'd taught meditation while sitting, standing, and walking, now he taught while on his side (as in the first picture in Chapter 21). Naturally, many in the community feared they couldn't go on without him, but he reassured them it wasn't necessary for him to be there for them to practice his teachings. "The Dharma is the best teacher," he said.

"Even if I were to live for eons," he told them, "I'd still have to leave you because every meeting implies a departure, one day." With his faithful disciples by his side, he died the way he'd lived, an exemplary spiritual teacher beyond compare. It is said that, as with his birth and his enlightenment, his final nirvana (extinction) was on the night of a full moon, in May.

That's but a quick sketch of the rich tapestry of the Buddha's life: a life that is, itself, a teaching. (Even if you don't believe the story 100 percent, the teachings remain true 100 percent.) From the very first, the Buddha, and each of us, was born with the capacity for a good life of tranquility, joy, harmony, love, energy, clarity, and excellence. This capacity is a gift. And it is yours ... just by being.

The Least You Need to Know

- ◆ The Buddha realized the Middle Way: directly knowing the practical mean between extremes.

- ◆ With wisdom and compassion, the Buddha realized suffering's origin and its end. In so doing, he also realized that just as he could attain enlightenment, so can we.

◆ Supreme enlightenment is called Nirvana. It may be more useful to think of enlightenment as a process of transformation, as a way of enlightened living, rather than as a thing.

◆ The Buddha was noncoercive, nondogmatic, and nonauthoritarian—a guide not a god. Pragmatic and scientific, he invites us to see for ourselves.

◆ Extensively, Buddha can mean whoever or whatever awakens us to greater intimacy with life.

◆ When asked about God, Heaven, and the immortality of the soul, the Buddha simply remained silent because these theoretical matters didn't affect his teachings: the nature of suffering and freedom therefrom.

Different Flavors, One Taste: The Teachings Travel to Different Lands

In This Chapter

- Life after Buddha's death
- An awakened king
- Adoption and adaptation in various lands
- Evolution of camps and schools
- Modern times, and an overview

The Buddha's teachings have now traveled around the planet. In so doing, Buddhism became the first world religion, not confined by geography, language, race, or cultural origins. It's like a spacious boat: as it reaches various shores, it docks and people mingle, on board and offshore. As it adapts easily within various cultural contexts, it naturally adopts characteristics of each locale.

In this respect, Buddhism's like tofu. It picks up the flavor of the food around it while retaining its own subtle taste: the taste of freedom. Here are some international recipes.

Mother India

The Buddha designated no single heir, no centralized religious structure, no Head Office. Instead, he left a map of the Path, and said, "Listen up, everyone. Here's the Way. Mindfully work on your own enlightenment."

Forming one of the world's first monastic communities, his *Sangha* (gathering) of *bhikkhus* (monks) and *bhikkhunis* (nuns) vowed to follow the *Dharma* (his teachings) and to become *arhats* (those who free their mind through perfect understanding, at one with ultimate reality).

The Sangha pledged to live a life of simplicity, meditation, teaching, and monastic upkeep. But their door was open to people who did work, the laity, the sangha-at-large. Sympathetic merchants and noblemen may not have become "full-timers," joining the monastic order, but they partook of the teachings, and donated money or land. Monasteries thus formed in capitals of big, new kingdoms, such as Vaisali in Kosala and Rajagaha in Magadha, whose kings sought out the Buddha for advice.

Buddhism offered a simple and pragmatic alternative to a culture of stress, offering values other than material, in cities newly emerging under rulers keen on territorial and economic expansion. And Buddhism was more direct and tolerant than the Brahman religion, which was hierarchical and often arcane, and whose constant demand for animal sacrifice strained both city-dwellers and farmers. Monks were sometimes requested to establish monasteries in cities and play a role in the community, not only as spiritual teachers but also as educators and even physicians. By the time of the Buddha's death, the Dharma had been heard over some 50,000 square miles, spanning some seven nations of central India. Considering that Buddha and his followers traveled on foot, this was no mean feat (no pun intended).

The year the Buddha died, 500 arhats assembled for a summit conference to collate and agree on his teachings and the codes of monastic discipline. Disciples recited from memory all the Buddha's teaching. If such a feat of memory seems remarkable, bear in mind that oral culture and the art of memory were highly developed in pre-modern civilizations. (And it helped that the Buddha created a very cohesive, complex system out of very simple elements, sometimes including bullet points and numbered lists.)

Further councils of elders were convened. A second one, a century later in 383 B.C.E., met to clarify such practices as the use of money (though they knew that *change* must come from within). Money had become a common medium of exchange, enabling long-distance trade. Some merchants investing in caravan expeditions were Buddhist and helped set up monasteries close to trading posts (this approach may also have served as a model for later Muslim caravansaries).

Along the Path

> The Buddha's lifetime is a prominent example of a pivotal era of world history dubbed the *Axial Age,* spanning from roughly 800 to 200 B.C.E. It included the Upanishads and the Jain religion in India; Confucius and Lao-tzu in China; Heraclitus, Plato, and Socrates in Greece; Zarathustra in Persia; and Hebrew prophets Jeremiah and Ezekiel. Radical reformers in their day, Axial thinkers all shared common characteristics, foundational to civilization ever since.

A Great Buddhist King and a Center of Learning

Two centuries after the Buddha, the Sangha remained relatively small. Within a mere 50 years more, it bootstrapped up from a sect to a major force, thanks to a king named Ashoka.

Reigning from 272 to 236 B.C.E., Ashoka held vast power in his hands, ruling from the southern tip of the Indian subcontinent on up to part of Persia. After a long but victorious battle, Ashoka was repulsed by the violence he'd witnessed firsthand. He hung up his sword and took up the Dharma, learning from a disciple of the Buddha.

Ashoka replaced hunting expeditions with pilgrimages; military parades now became devotional processions. A tree-hugger, he ordered forests be preserved. He not only invested in hospitals but also saw that animals be given medical care. Wells were dug along roads and rest houses were built for wayfarers. Egalitarian, his citizenry could call on him anytime, day or night—whether he was on the throne, in his carriage, in the dining room, or in the boudoir. Buddhism now appealed to the common people, emulating their emperor.

Moreover, he sent envoys all around the Indian subcontinent and beyond, as far as Syria, Egypt, and Macedonia. Following the Buddha's example, these ambassadors of Dharma didn't try to convert anyone, only inform—no coercion, no inquisition. Spreading Buddha's truth (Buddha-Dharma) would be rather like telling someone that the sum of a triangle's angles equals 180 degrees. And if the speaker has a good vibe and a lovely aura, people would likely want to check out where he or she is coming from. Subsequent Buddhist kings included Menander I (Milinda) and Kanishka, but thanks largely to Ashoka's seminal patronage, Buddhism flourished in India for a millennium, and the Buddha ultimately became a lasting worldwide influence, rather than a mere footnote to history.

Another factor contributing to the transmission of Buddhism was education. In the fifth century C.E., Buddhist monastics established one of the world's first universities, in the city of Nalanda. Along with Buddha-Dharma, courses included the primary spiritual texts of the time (*Upanishads* and *Vedas*), plus grammar, logic, philosophy, politics, and medicine. Campus libraries held some nine million scriptures alone. With free tuition and residence, it attracted students from around the country and as far east as China and Korea, as well as neighboring Tibet and Sri Lanka. Peak enrollment was about 10,000 students, with thousands of faculty. It continued for seven centuries, until destroyed by military general Bakhtiar Khilji (who conquered Bengal the next year) and was said to burn for months.

Has the Buddha Left the House?

Until recently, Buddhism as a distinct path all but died out in its land of origin. How did this happen? For one thing, the destruction of Nalanda was like a blow to the head. Nalanda was as much of a central body as Buddhism ever had, and with that much of the Sangha destroyed, the practice never quite recovered. But the body itself had already been weakened by blows from Hun marauders from the Steppes, about eight centuries earlier.

We must note, too, how *Hinduism* survived both of these attacks, and prevailed. Buddhism had drawn upon 7,000-year-old traditions predating the religion brought by the Aryans who'd invaded India a millennium earlier. Buddhism had always drawn the ire of their priests, who were glad to help squash it. Aryan Hinduism had integrated into the lives of common people, at the village level, whereas Buddhism relied on aristocratic patronage. And Hinduism included devotional rites and deities, which Buddhism often lacked. When the raiding Huns ended the Gupta Dynasty, funding for Buddhist monasteries evaporated. Moreover, Buddhism's critique of Hindu philosophy helped spark a revitalized, self-critical, nondualist reformulation, known as Advaita, starting in the eighth century C.E. and still going very strong today. So by the time of the destruction of Nalanda, Hinduism had reasserted itself as the dominant religion.

This Is

> **Hinduism** refers to the spirituality originating with the Aryans who came to India thousands of years before Christ. Defined sects didn't appear until around the time of the Buddha. The word "Hinduism" itself is a modern, Western invention, though universally accepted—more correct would be "Brahmanic traditions," referring to a common belief in *Brahma* (God); "Vedic traditions," referring to primary teachings of the *Vedas;* or "*Sanatana Dharma*" (Eternal Way). Most familiar in the West are techniques for physical and mental cultivation that are a part of yoga.

King Ashoka's lion is part of the national emblem of modern India, and the Buddha's Wheel of the Dharma is on the flag. Today, it's reemerged in India as a distinct path, fueled by: (1) the ordaining of former *dalits* (untouchables), (2) the influx of Tibetans with the Dalai Lama going into exile here in 1959, and (3) adoption by a new class of wealthy elite in India. The latter factor brings us back full circle with, as in the time of the Buddha, patronage of an emergent affluent class seeking relief from the regimentation and stress of material culture. The Wheel of Dharma proves to be a living law.

Camps and Schools: Don't Sweat Over Any Isms or Schisms

Buddhism is what *you* make of it. It's a personal affair. There's no one-size-fits-all "Buddhism" to take home, plug in, and awaken you. There are as many "Buddhisms" as there are people. Each reader comes to this book for a different reason (I don't know what). Paying attention to a variety of schools practiced in the West, it would be appropriate to pause to mention the initial division into schools.

It is said that 10 years after the Buddha's death, there were 16 schools of practice, and more than 500 by the first century C.E. Overall, there seemed to be two collections of schools—not so much different Buddhisms, different truths, but rather different approaches to One Dharma. Traditionally, the two are typified as "Old School" and "New School." But some branches of the "Old School" were formed well after those of the "New School." And recent scholarship suggests the divergence was essentially present from the early days of the Sangha.

On the one hand, some emphasized the Buddha's first, original teachings as central ("original" Buddhism). Their ideal was the individuated, monastic *arhat* (worthy) attaining nirvana. On the other hand, there were those who emphasized the ideal of the *bodhisattva*, whose aspiration for enlightenment is, from the very beginning of practice, for the benefit of all.

This Is

A **bodhisattva** (*bodhi*, Sanskrit for "awakened," "wisdom," and "way"; *sattva*, meaning "essence," or "being") means literally an "enlightened being" or "essence of the Way." A bodhisattva's enlightenment, whether attained or aspired to, is for the benefit of all. And not just all people, but all sentient beings; some even define "sentient beings" to include all beings (period), since everybody and everything is sacred, imbued with inherent *buddha nature*.

Historically, the division reflected various factors. Laypeople, for example, who'd often donated quite a share, deservedly wanted more representation. And fewer people aspired to arhatship. Laypeople weren't intrigued by the idea of monastic life, and wanted a more immediate sense of kinship between themselves and the Buddha. This led to inclusion of deities embodying the Dharma, approachable and active in daily life. Plus, doctrinal aspects of the traditional teachings seemed to call for clarification. Add the bodhisattva ideal, and this became known as the "great" camp, as in inclusive.

Interestingly, this evolved in Indian regions with the most foreign influences, so it became highly adaptable for export. Indeed, this approach would prevail in China, Korea, and Japan to the east, and Nepal, Tibet, and Mongolia to the north. The more traditionalist schools, on the other hand, developed in relatively isolated regions in the southeast.

Their generic names reflected factionalism. First, it was the *elders* and the *majority*. The latter became known as *Mahayana* (Great Way), *yana* meaning "vehicle," or "path." Mahayana called the other camp *Hinayana*, "Narrow Way." "Narrow" had a pejorative spin; as in lesser, inferior, even dirty. We say *Theravada* (pronounced "tair-ah-vah-duh," meaning "teachings of the elders"), without implying that others were newcomers or naïve.

A further factor came via the Mongols. Though short-lived, the Mongol Empire had a deep impact. Following their encounter with the Mongols, Southeast Asian nations adopted a "new" Theravada. This new Theravada had neither nuns nor arhats. So if Mahayana accuses Hinayana of only being interested in arhatship (individual attainment), it no longer pertains, because the latter hasn't produced any arhats for a thousand years. The distinctions can get murkier still considering that in Vietnam the two paths often coalesced, and considering that Tibetan Buddhism said it was uniting the two within a third, *Vajrayana* (Indestructible Path).

Our approach is to focus on what's widely practiced in the West, space permitting. The most common Western Theravada practices are called *Vipassana* (pronounced "va-PAH-sa-na," literally meaning "insight"). We spotlight Mahayana traditions of *Zen* and *Pure Land*, and *Vajrayana* (Tibetan Buddhism), the latter being like Mahayana with a tantric twist. But don't fret over any schisms or isms. We'll fill you in on the common basics, as well as different spins, so you can decide how you wish to put it all together, which is what Buddhist practice is all about.

Southeast: The Wisdom of the Elders

The tropical island of Ceylon (Sri Lanka) has enjoyed the oldest continuous Buddhist tradition in the world. In 250 B.C.E., Ashoka's prince and princess, Mahinda and

Sanghamitta (both arhats), personally introduced Buddhism to Ceylon's King Tissa. Besides establishing a monastery and a nunnery there, they brought a sapling from the bodhi tree, still growing today. A century and a half later, Buddhist scripture was committed to writing here, in a language called Pali, similar to Sanskrit. (In the Buddha's time, India had no single common language.) The canon became known as the *Tripitaka* (three baskets), around a hundred volumes, each about 600 pages long. The three baskets are:

♦ *Sutras* **(Buddha's talks).** Beginning with his explanation of the Dharma to his five ascetic companions at the deer park, there are now a couple of hundred sutras and several thousand volumes of commentaries.

♦ *Vinaya* **(ethical monastic conduct).** Ethical guidelines were established in the Buddha's Sangha on a case-by-case basis, as various situations arose. So the *vinaya* illustrates each rule with the story of its origin.

♦ *Abhidharma* **(special dharma).** This includes cosmology, natural science, philosophy, in-depth psychology, plus a thesaurus.

(Don't worry, you won't be quizzed. Buddhists aren't "people of the book.") The Tripitaka guided the Theravada tradition of southeast Asia—branching through Ceylon (Sri Lanka) to Burma (Myanmar), Siam (Thailand), Cambodia, Laos, and southern Vietnam. By the tenth century, the Ceylon monastery conferred kingship; up until the nineteenth century only a Buddhist could be king.

Burma originally had a mix of Hinduism, Mahayana, and esoteric practices. When King Anawrahta unified the nation in 1044, he swore allegiance to Theravada and he had thousands of monasteries and temples built in Pagan, his capital, earning Burma the nickname "Land of Pagodas."

This Is

The word **sutra**, from Sanskrit, means "a thread," such as for stringing jewels or prayer beads. It also carries the connotation of the word "story," the way we hear "tale" in the word "yarn." It comes from the same root from which we derive the word *suture*, meaning "to sew," "to connect," and "to heal wounds."

The native Mon people of Siam had practiced Buddha's way ever since Ashoka sent missionaries, and continued to as the Thai people of southwestern China were driven in by the armies of Kublai Khan. In some Thai Buddhist temples, you might see some traces of Hinduism as well as *animism* (the belief that all things have souls). While there are temples in cities and towns, many practitioners still study in caves and tropical forests, perpetuating the forest tradition of Buddha's own time. Thailand is the only country to make Buddhism its national religion in its constitution. Young men are often ordained as monks as a rite of passage.

Before the Internet: The Silk and Spice Routes

Sheer information has become a hot item these days, as are the means of getting it (such as HDTV, Internet, and, oh yes, books). Back in the Buddha's day the hot item was silk, as were the means of getting it. Chinese silk was a status item as far west as Rome and Egypt. Even Cleopatra had to have it.

Not too far from the Buddha's stomping grounds emerged a zone—just north of India, south of Central Asia, and west of Tibet—that was a hotbed of interchange. Present-day Afghanistan (then Greek Bactria) forms part of this fertile crossroads of the world, as well as Pakistan and China's Xinkiang region. In this relatively small niche, a mix of people settled: Tokharians, Kapisans, Soghdians, Bactrian Greeks who'd come with Alexander, and Kushanas (Indo-Scythians). From this emerged a robust culture of international trade.

Thousands of years before FedEx and UPS, a 6,000-mile road evolved now known as the Silk Route. Silk left China along this route, through Central Asia, passing from way station to way station. Meanwhile, from the other direction, caravans with gold, silver, and wool rode in. Always an exchange; roads travel in two directions. And along for the ride came Nestorian Christians … and Buddhist scholars and monks. Thus did Buddhism make its way across Central Asia and on to Russia, and east to Mongolia and China. Eventually way stations included outposts of Buddhists, monastic centers with libraries and schools, as well as hotels and hospitals.

Alternatively, there was transport by ocean, between India and the Arabian Peninsula, along what would become known as the Spice Route. Merchant expeditions often had Buddhist monks aboard as a good luck charm and a calming influence during storms. Borderless, the Spice Route probably saw even more trade than the Silk Route, but traffic across watery ways leaves no traces.

The Silk Route also furnished another potent vehicle for the Dharma—namely, art. The Buddha had insisted no images be made of him. The first devotional images of him were abstract, such as a wheel, or footprints, or a throne. Now, Hellenism (devotion to Greek culture) had taken root in Northern India, following Alexander the Great's campaign there (fourth century B.C.E.). Under the influence of Greek art, sculptors made bas-reliefs of Buddhist patrons and of the Buddha. One early example looked like Apollo in a toga accompanied by female lute players and floating cherubs. On the other hand, the Buddhist fresco paintings in the caves of Dun Huang (a Silk

Route terminal to outermost western China) display a mix of styles—from semi-abstract to elegant visionary.

Word gets around.

(*Map: Gary Gach*)

The Middle Kingdom: China

We come now to this rare historical encounter: two supreme civilizations of Asia finally meet thanks to their smiling mutual friend, the Buddha.

The Silk Route gave Buddhism the horse (or camel) power to traverse the blazing, barren deserts and perilous, precipitous peaks from India to China. Culture was a mighty obstacle to overcome. Indian culture had more in common with Europe than China. Plus there's China's strong national identity and insular culture—just consider the Great Wall! (In calling herself "Middle Kingdom," China implied she's the center of the world.) Indeed, maybe if Buddhism could make it here, it could make it anywhere. It took centuries, yet Buddhism evolved from being a practice of foreigners to a path at the forefront of Chinese spirituality.

Emperor Ming had invited Buddhist envoys from India in 67 C.E. China also had contact with Buddhists of Central Asia. Two lucky similarities played out in favor of the Buddhists. One, Buddhism seemed to answer questions that *Confucius* couldn't (such as the nature of human suffering, and liberation therefrom). Two, Buddhism clicked with *Taoism*, which happened to be brewing. Curiously, both Confucius and the father of Taoism, Lao-tzu, were born roughly around the same time as the Buddha, and all three were, at bottom, key reformers of old ways. Tao and Confucianism composed the double helix of Chinese culture. Confucianism, like Buddhism, can be seen as more of an educational system than a religion.

This Is

The Tao ("dow") means "the Way." Its chief writer was Lao-tzu (b. 604 B.C.E.). **Taoism** holds that (1) what's really real is that which never changes, and (2) we're each innately a part of this reality. **Confucianism** is a comprehensive ethical and social system. Lao-tzu seems a carefree, terse mystic next to Confucius (K'ung Fu Tzu, 551–479 B.C.E.), a deep-thinking, wide-ranging humanist force who became China's "philosopher king" (his philosophy became imperial ideology).

Emphasis was placed on Buddhist teachings stressing Confucian filial piety and enlightenment as being of benefit to society. Monks translated Sanskrit Buddhist terms with Chinese words already in vogue through Taoism. Plus, since Taoism's chief proponent Lao-tzu had, in old age, headed west fairly recently and never come back, the notion arose that Buddhism was the result of Lao-tzu's teachings abroad, his "conversion of the barbarians." This way China wouldn't be importing anything—merely welcoming back a native tradition they'd exported in the first place. (That works!)

During the political chaos with the collapse of the Han Dynasty (221–589 C.E.), Buddhist monasteries and temples were permitted and flourished across the land, and Buddhism integrated itself into daily life.

In general, Chinese religion often resembles a salad bar, or a Lazy Susan in a Chinatown restaurant, everyone picking what they like in various proportions. So, too, have the Chinese concocted their own mixes of Confucianism, Taoism, Buddhism, ancestor worship, and folk cults.

China's Golden Age: The T'ang

Buddhism's peak years in China roughly coincided with its Golden Age, the T'ang Dynasty (pronounced "tong"; 618–906 C.E.). Of the ten prominent Buddhist schools then, *Pure Land* would become the most popular school in China, Japan, and Vietnam today, emphasizing faith in the boundless compassion of Amitabha Buddha. Most widely publicized in the West is *Zen* ("*Ch'an*" in Chinese), which literally means "meditation." Indeed, it's been called a synthesis of India and China. Certainly, it's proven to be historically resilient.

China (brilliantly) recognized *Kwan Yin* as a feminine manifestation of the genderless Buddhist deity of compassion named Avalokiteshvara (pronounced "ah-vah-loh-key-teh-shvah-rah"). Not only simpler to pronounce, Kwan Yin's presence in the Buddhist pantheon also drew women practitioners to the Path in great numbers. Kwan Yin would become like Buddhism's Virgin of Guadalupe (patron saint of Mexico), for men and women alike. (Canon, Japanese maker of cameras, printers, and photocopiers, is named after her [*Kannon*, in Japanese].)

This is the era when Xuanzang made a 17-year pilgrimage to India, bringing back Buddhist scripture, as recounted in his classic travel memoir, *Journey to the West*. The devoted Chinese translators of Buddhism are worth a chapter unto themselves.

In 868 c.e., Chinese monks disseminated the *Diamond Sutra* as the first printed book, sharing the Dharma and earning good karma merit thereby. More copies, more merit. (A century earlier, Korea had produced the first printed document, a one-sheet sutra. In the fourteenth century, Korea would invent movable type, for Buddhist scripture, a century before Gutenberg. It was then just a matter of time before the printing of, ahem, *Complete Idiot's Guides*.) China became a hub of Buddhism in the East. As some countries would learn Latin to learn of Jesus, others were learning Chinese to learn of Shakyamuni Buddha.

What Goes Up Must Come Down

Members of the Chinese elite had, from the very get-go, lifted an eyebrow at the sight of Buddhist monks without sons to perpetuate the honor of their parents, contrary to Confucian values. And you didn't need an abacus to see the strain on the economy the temples would cause. By the middle of the ninth century, China's Buddhist monasteries were richer than the Emperor's court. Indeed, the empire looked with alarm at the possible economic crash this could cause. Farmers were leaving the fields to help construct monasteries and temples. (Who'd feed the country?) The monks produced no revenue. (Who supported them? Members of the royal court and wealthy aristocrats, who could've been underwriting Imperial projects instead.) And what value had gold or silver now that those ores were being used to cast Buddhas and other accoutrements of an essentially foreign craze? So the empire struck back.

Monasteries and temples were shut down, or choked off under strict government supervision. State Confucianism was encouraged instead.

Buddhism in China today has been re-emerging from a 50-year shadow, in both state-sponsored and back-alley temples. In 2006, China hosted the first World Buddhist Forum. Three relatively recent international Chinese Buddhist organizations are Tzu Chi, *Fo Guang Shan* (Mountain of Buddha's Light), and Dharma Drum, all based in Taiwan.

Other Gardens of East Asia

From China, Buddhism went further east to Korea, then Japan; and south, to Vietnam. In each land, it mixed with local culture.

Korea: Land of Morning Calm

Early Korean Buddhism blended with the indigenous shamanist religion. *Shamanism*, per se, dates back to the Neolithic. A shaman contacts and mediates with natural and supernatural forces, combining duties of priest, doctor, psychologist, psychic, weatherman, and family counselor. Monasteries were often built on mountains patronized by an unseen immortal old man accompanied by a tiger deity from heaven.

Korea had learned Buddhism from China in the fourth century. This led Korea to learn Chinese to know about Buddhism; today, almost half their vocabulary is Chinese. Yet, over time, Korean Buddhists would attain such mastery that China would send emissaries to study with them, for clarification and guidance as to fine points. After refining it for a century, Korea brought Buddhism to Japan.

Leaves from the Bodhi Tree

Korean monk Wonhyo (617–686 C.E.) set out for China to study Buddhism. On the road one night, he took shelter in a cave. He found a gourd of pure water, which he drank. Content, he then fell asleep. At dawn, he awoke startled to discover he'd spent the night in a tomb and that he'd drunk putrid water from an old skull. It came to him in a flash that "mind creates all things, all things are products of the mind alone." Realizing this, he turned around, as there was no longer any need to study in China. He studied his own mind instead and went on to become one of Korea's greatest Buddhist teachers and scholars.

Buddhism led in national influence for a millennium, through two dynasties: the Silla (668–935 C.E.), under which the peninsula's three kingdoms were unified, and the Goryeo (1140–1390 C.E.), the Golden Age from which Korea takes its name.

Korean Zen (*Son*) emerged as dominant practice. Then, as with China, institutional Confucianism took the upper hand in the royal court, beginning in the thirteenth century, and the influence of Buddhism waned. For two centuries, neither monk nor nun could so much as set foot in any major city. But following a vacuum in the nineteenth and twentieth centuries, Buddhism is again strong. A modern development is a school called *Won*, with a simple circle for its symbol.

Japan: Land of Eight Islands

After arriving via Korea, Buddhism mingled with or formed alliances with local Japanese beliefs, such as the indigenous *Shinto* cults. Japan later sent emissaries to China and eventually learned all the Chinese Buddhist schools. Japan developed its own version of Vajrayana, called *Shingon*, and of Pure Land, called *Amidism*.

The Japanese adaptation of Ch'an, called *Zen*, emerged during the Kamakura Era (1185–1333 C.E.). Seizing power from a decadent imperial aristocracy, *samurai* (the military elite) established the *Shogunate* (military government) at Kamakura. Imagine a well-heeled, swashbuckling soldier of fortune strutting down the street and encountering some mere monk on his path, sitting in open-eyed meditation. The samurai draws his sword and bellows, "Out of my way, wretched dog, or I'll test this new blade on your bald scalp!" (Those swords could slice through flesh and bone like so much cheese.) The monk looks up with an unflinching, implacable expression of "So!?" as if merely brushed by a breeze—totally present to each instant, and nothing else. Naturally, the samurai wanted such absolute fearlessness for themselves and so studied Zen.

> **This Is**
>
> In Japan, indigenous spirituality is **Shinto**, centered on the *kami* (spiritual essence) present in gods, human beings, animals, and even inanimate objects. "Shinto" is an umbrella term for hundreds of different customs, and was coined in the sixth century when Japan felt it needed to distinguish its own native beliefs and practices from new foreign concepts such as Confucianism and Buddhism.

When Kublai Khan sent two envoys to Japanese soil, dictating terms of surrender, *Kwaaatz!*, they were beheaded on the spot by samurai Zen swordsmen. Soon thereafter (1281 C.E.), these Zen warriors defeated the Khan's attack by sea (one of the largest naval forces in history, about 100,000 men). Little wonder that Zen temples were given the finest plots of land and the finest teachers imported from China to coach them. Amidism, on the other hand, appealed to the common person. Also in the

Kamakura arose the *Lotus Sutra Schools: Nichiren Shu, Nichiren Shoshu,* and such modern offshoots as *Soka Gakai International* (SGI) and *Rissho Kosei-kai* (RKK). Buddhism so imbued Japanese life that every branch of culture found a way to express Buddhism (the Way of Tea, the Way of the Sword, the Way of Flower-Arranging, and so on).

Meeting Place: Vietnam

Vietnam is somewhat equidistant from China to the north and India to the West, and has been enriched by both cultures, a fertile meeting place where Theravada and Mahayana practices became unified in modern times. Buddhism from India came via the Spice Route, in the first century C.E., at least three centuries before it reached China. Subsequently, Vietnam brought Buddhism to parts of southern China, and was later enriched by Mahayana Buddhism from China, particularly Zen ("Th'iĕn") and Pure Land.

At the Roof of the World: Tibet

With Tibetan Buddhism, we come back full circle to India. Himalayan Buddhism went north from India, to Nepal, Bhutan, Mongolia, Siberia, and Tibet, without stopping in China first. It arrived in Tibet 1,300 years after the time of the Buddha, bearing elements called *tantra*, diffusing throughout both Hinduism and Buddhism in India at that time. The story goes that the Buddha—having used skillful means to modulate his teachings so as to reach the many different kinds of people he encountered— introduced a final system, toward the end of his life, incorporating tantra. Texts of tantra teachings were hidden away, to be dug up long after.

Though close to India, Tibet is separated by the Himalayas, and has a different climate (India is subtropical; Tibet is 12,000 feet above sea level). Indian civilization is largely agricultural; Tibet's is pastoral.

Moreover, there was also a wall of cultural resistance from the native shamanist religion called *Bon*. Furthermore, Tibet wasn't fully unified. When King Songtsan Gampo inherited a newly centralized authority, he traveled around his new nation and brought back a Buddhist Nepalese bride from over the border. Eventually, he made Buddhism a state religion, but Bon put up strong opposition. Then, in the eighth century, King Trisong Detsan enlisted Padma Sambhava (Lotus-Born) from Nepal to aid him.

Besides winning Bon magic over with his tantric mojo, Padma Sambhava translated the Dharma for the common Tibetan. Interestingly, Tibet had been pre-literate, but devised an alphabet to learn the Buddha's way. Like India of Siddhartha's time, Buddhism was a nation builder, here not just a state religion but a basis of a theocracy (rule by divine sanction)—or more properly a Buddhocracy. In the sixteenth century, Tibet became the first country in the world with a monk on the throne, the *Dalai Lama* (teacher whose wisdom is as great as the ocean).

Tibet's original school was called *Nyingma* (Ancient Ones), from which comes *The Book of the Dead* and *Dzogchen*, a form of practice recently becoming popular in the West. After Nyingma became established, and following the Huns' pillaging of monasteries in India, Indian Buddhist adepts brought texts to Tibet for preservation. Because Buddhism had developed further in India by then, Tibetan Buddhism amassed the world's largest collection of Buddhist scripture. Two more schools then arose in 1000 C.E. One new school was *Sakya* (Grey Earth), a scholarly group that unified teachings of the sutras and of the tantra. Another school was called *Kagyu*, which counted among its ancestors such celebrated teachers as Naropa (1016–1100 C.E.), Marpa (1012–1097 C.E.), and Milarepa (1052–1135 C.E.).

The fourth major school, established in the fourteenth century, is called *Gelug* (Way of Virtue). Gelug was a reformist movement combining elements of the other three schools, while returning to original Indian sources. The Gelug became the largest school and initiated the office of the Dalai Lama. Contemporary master Chögyam Trungpa established an international, nonsecular lineage called *Shambhala*, now headed by his son and spiritual heir Sakyong Mipham.

Buddha's Way in Asia Today

Buddhism has been adapting to modern times as well as foreign lands—weathering invasions, wars, revolutions, and exile. Buddhism often provided the glue, as it were, for nation-building. No war has been fought in the name of Buddhism, earning it the nickname "the gentlest religion," although some Buddhist nations do know problematic domestic politics. Today, Buddhism in Asia faces erosion from waves of Christian evangelists.

Overall, has the transmission of Buddhism been worthwhile? Well, Buddhism has educated and even enlightened masses of human beings, fueling literacy, self-reliance, and tolerance. Additionally, Buddhism has helped to peacefully establish or unify nations and empires. And when each nation looks back, it often finds its great periods coinciding with Buddhism's flourishing. Buddhism has touched all of Asia and is one common heritage uniting the peoples of Asia today. (What else? Well, rice!)

The Middle Way fostered the development of medicine and other sciences, sparked such agents of change as the printed book with movable type, established a precedent for interfaith understanding, and continues to teach personal liberation from needless suffering. The promise of these gifts remains yet to be totally fulfilled, but then history is a golden book whose next chapter we always anticipate, living through it ourselves in our current events.

In this guide's next chapter, we'll see how Buddhism interfaces with the world's religions: interfaith. Then we'll conclude Part 1 with the most recent development in Buddhist history. For the first time in over a millennium, the Lotus is opening a new petal … in the West.

The Least You Need to Know

- Buddha's teachings (Dharma) are common to all of Asia, and continue to flourish through its growing community (Sangha).

- Buddhism adapted to the different cultures of various lands, but all its forms have a fundamental essence—the taste of freedom.

- Two main branches, or collections of schools, developed: Theravada and Mahayana. In the West, Theravada's most popular manifestation is Vipassana (Insight Meditation); Mahayana's are Zen and Pure Land, plus the Lotus Sutra schools (Nichiren, SGI, RKK, and so on).

- Tibetans speak of three branches of Buddhism: Theravada, Mahayana, and Vajrayana, though the latter might also be considered Mahayana with a tantric twist.

- Buddhism has often played a part in nation-building, and its flourishing has coincided with the golden ages of many nations.

- Tolerance has been one of Buddhism's leading social characteristics. (Quick, how many Buddhist wars can you name?)

3

Interfaith: Same Mountain, Different Trails

In This Chapter

◆ Oneness (not sameness)

◆ Buddha and God, atheism, or agnosticism

◆ Buddhism, Hinduism, and Taoism

◆ Buddhism and the children of Abraham

◆ Buddhism and other creeds

As we've just seen, Buddhism blossomed beyond the matrix of India's native soil to become the first world religion. The teachings have thrived beyond the confines of cultural context, geography, language, and so on. You could even say it thrives "beyond religion," because (whether or not it's a religion itself) Buddhism interfaces well with whatever spiritual path you may already subscribe to. It can deepen your roots within a pre-existing tradition and lend you a new pair of wings. Or it could be the only path for you. Plus, it can also provide a lens of insight into the creed of others. Let's compare notes.

What's Universal?: Commonality Within Diversity

Let's begin with a general orientation. Tenzin Gyatso, His Holiness (HH) the four-teenth Dalai Lama, says his religion is kindness. Period. Just be a good person. For one thing, it will liberate so much energy in you! Buddhism's hardly for members only. Anyone can benefit. And you don't have to give anything up, except maybe a rigid sense of self, like a shoe that's too tight. Is it asking much to be generous ... to breathe consciously ... to make friends with your mind ... to consider the conse-quences of your actions ... to live in the present? Of course, if everyone did this, and became awakened, would Buddhism exist anymore? No, Buddhism depends on non-Buddhism, just as non-Buddhism depends on Buddhism. Nothing is separate. And to make our study doubly interesting, Buddhism is universal. Buddhism is a model for spirituality without borders; it's interfaith. To quote King Ashoka, who had his edicts inscribed on monumental stone pillars still standing today: "There should be growth in the essentials of all religions .... Whoever due to excessive devotion praises one's own religion and condemns others only harms one's own religion."

 Hear and Now

> "Aware of the suffering created by fanaticism and intolerance, we are determined not to be idolatrous about or bound to any doctrine, theory, or ideology, even Buddhist ones. Buddhist teachings are guiding means to help us learn to look deeply and to develop our understanding and compassion. They are not doctrines to fight, kill, or die for."
> —The Order of Interbeing, First Mindfulness Training: Openness

Interfaith is more than comparative religion. The rapidly growing interconnections in our globalized world call for cooperation. Institutions are learning what it means to have more than one faith under their roof (multifaith), as are households and indi-vidual human hearts. A 2007 survey found 70 percent of Americans agree salvation can be reached through more than one faith. Underscoring the importance of that news, Reverend Patrick McCollum states, "People are just beginning to see that there's a tremendous shift in one of the most significant areas of human history and humanity: religion. The change is taking place right now." Healing and holy resources both new and old are flourishing, cross-fertilizing each other, and revitalizing what it means to be human. Our challenge is to understand and respect their diversity, while cherishing and realizing our oneness: one humanity; one earth. And, since we're more than mate-rial beings: one heart; one love.

Sure, maybe by now you've heard what the yogi said to the hotdog vendor: "Make me one with everything!" But it's true.

Let's do some basic Interfaith math. Judaism says God is one: *Adonai echad.* Christianity says the Father, the Son, and the Holy Spirit are one in God. Islam says *La illaha il'allah:* there is no God but God. Hinduism says our *Atman* (innermost identity) is one with *Brahman* (Supreme Identity). Same mountain, with different slopes for different folks. Different travel itineraries to the same destination: this timeless moment, this sacred space. Certainly it's your personal means of approach—as well as companions, crew, and scenery—that help mold the journey. Differences matter. (Oneness isn't sameness.) Yet to truly appreciate difference, we must also experience commonality; nondualism. Otherwise, we're like the blind men confronting different parts of an elephant, each insistent his point of view is the only one. In my book, Buddhism, Confucianism, Taoism, Sikhism, Christianity, Unitarianism, Native Spirituality, Zorastrianism, Jainism, Judaism, Islam, Bahai, and Hinduism—all set forth the Golden Rule. All the rest is commentary.

Hear and Now

"It seems to me that the world's religions are like siblings separated at birth. We've grown up in different neighborhoods, different households, with different songs and stories, traditions and customs. But now we've been reunited, and, having found each other after so many years apart, we look into each other's faces and can see the family resemblance. We're back together again, and it's very good."
—Reverend Richard Watts

All religions are one. The question is: which one? The Middle Way steers clear of extremes. Some religious leaders, even Buddhists, might say to shun any other path but theirs. I think this is like a hospital asking your religion before surgery; kind of scary. (I like Joe Gould's answer: "In the summer, I'm a nudist; in the winter, I'm a Buddhist.") Instead, the very first thing I do when I wake up in the morning is ask myself: Who am I? And the answer that invariably comes is I don't know, but I'm awakening. (And the second thought? It's a good day. 24 brand-new hours. Be happy!)

Continuing a medical metaphor, consider how many different kinds of remedies people turn to these days. It's not uncommon to find an herbal extract alongside a pharmaceutical in a medicine cabinet. So can it be with one's spiritual path. When people warn that a variety of traditions makes a salad out of spirituality, one answer is: So what's wrong with salad?! The danger is like digging a number of shallow holes in the ground when you're trying to reach water. A well requires boring down. So whatever you practice, go all the way.

Do Buddhists Believe in God?

To answer a question with another question, Buddhist folksinger Suzanne Vega asks, "Did you hear about the agnostic dyslexic insomniac who lies awake at night wondering if there really is a dog?"

Certainly, Buddhism is ranked as a religion, for its role in the world. Yet there's no creator deity, no supreme being—and with that comes also the critical difference of Buddhism's locating the origin of suffering and the means of alleviating it as within each of us. There's Buddha nature in each and every one of us, and the Way encourages us to let our natural Buddhahood shine. So it's Do It Yourself (DIY). As for God or gods, atheism or agnosticism, Bring Your Own (BYO).

The gold standard for truth here isn't theoretical or theological, but experiential and practical (what you can observe, experience, and test in your own life). This may be one reason Buddhism is so popular today (yet, at the same time, why it may never become universal). Of all the Buddha's sayings, his most commonly looked-up quotation on the Internet is from his talk to some citizens known as the *Kalamas*, when he tells them, in effect:

> "Don't believe a teaching just because you've heard it from a man who's supposed to be holy, or because it's contained in a book supposed to be holy, or because all your friends and neighbors believe it. But whatever you've observed and analyzed for yourself and found to be reasonable and good, then accept that and put it into practice."

Both the Buddha and the Bible say, "O taste and see!" This fits in squarely with what's been an open secret since the end of the last century: namely, a mass movement of people making real for themselves their relation to the sacred, rather than repeating what they've learned by rote.

Me, I've had a Buddhist outlook as long as I can remember. So, when my rabbi would call God "The Most High," I was fine with this, taking it as a place-marker signifying the highest anyone can conceive of when on the highest peak of awareness. (Worked for me.) Your Buddhist practice can put you in touch with the heart of creation; whether or not that's the same as the heart of your creator is up to you. The Buddha's answer: silence.

Roots: Buddha Was Born a Hindu

Being born in the culture of Buddha's motherland, India, is like being Jewish or Italian—it's as hard to change after being immersed in India's culture as it is for a zebra to change its stripes. So, naturally, this culture flows like a wide, long, deep river through his teachings. Buddhist-Hindu comparison and contrast can be interesting and instructive. (I use the word *Hindu*, until more correct terms become more commonplace.)

Inheritances and Contrasts

The Buddha and Hinduism share common aspects of *dharma* (truth, reality, the natural way of the universe). Informing their mutual, ethical awareness of the impermanence and needless suffering of life are such concepts as karma, the round dance of life, and interconnectedness. *Karma* is a kind of moral cause and effect. Everything has its effect, causing something else in turn. While this creates a cyclic dance of life, it can also appear fatalistic. Indeed, for centuries prior to the Buddha, it was taught that karma was part of divine will (not unlike God's will, which some comedians point out is still in probate). Buddha differed, and taught we're all each responsible for our own destinies. "As ye sow, so shall ye reap."

With karma, the Buddha also inherited the Indian concept of the circularity of life, which contrasts with our typically Western approach to thinking linearly, and isolating each thing in its own separate compartment, like ice cubes. In the West, we are naturally predisposed to efficient, mechanistic thought: therefore and thusly … insert big toe into Slot B and twist. Root Western symbols of life include the procession, the ladder, the chain, and next month's credit card bill. In India, an archetypal symbol is the wheel, reflecting cyclic thought. A seed that becomes a flower will decay into mulch so as to fertilize a new seed. Round and round we go, as with a merry-go-round or a spinning top. And it makes for playful thinking.

While Western traditions think of the universe as a measurable thing—God's creation, signed in the lower right-hand corner—in Indian culture the universe is more of a play. for example, the deity Shiva is often depicted in a dance that simultaneously creates, maintains, and destroys the universe, while also waving grace to his devotees and simultaneously concealing and revealing all of it. (Olé!) Life's a ballroom, and we and everything around us are part of a never-ending cosmic pageant of energies (called gods), boogying among themselves and with us … a cosmic square dance with interpenetrating light shows, where everything gets mixed and reshuffled, you do-si-do with your partners, and you play endless hide-and-seek. In a sense, it's like the limitless, undifferentiated God of the Bible creating our universe and us humans so that He might know Himself in us. (And, now and then, a word from our sponsor ….) The Eastern mode sees we and He (or She) as One Self-Awareness throughout all eternity, once we see the unchanging truth through the veils of illusion's dance.

This makes for interconnectedness, as seen in the *advaita* (nondualist) motto "Thou Art That." We're all part of a cosmic dream dance of the gods, with everything we see as but foam and wave of the same vast ocean of which we're all made. So, although we identify with our masks and roles in the awesome pageant we call life, life itself is part of a vaster, cosmic unfoldment—the universe playing peek-a-boo with itself. This theme crops up again with the idea that we're all buddhas, only we don't know it (such idiots we mortals be!) until we wake up to our place in the process of truth (dharma). Another variant you'll also hear is that everyday reality mirrors cosmic reality. An ordinary radish is a manifestation of the cosmos, and so are you. To paraphrase Indian medical doctor and mystic Deepak Chopra, we are the universe pretending to be individuals, the cosmos using our nervous system to localize itself.

The Buddha agrees that a small sense of self (me, me, me) stands in the way of seeing reality. Such self is a convenient fiction, called ego. We get caught up in and identify with our moment in the cosmic dance, making of it instead a soap opera revolving around one's self; we become addicted to the drama. ("Don't touch that dial! We'll be back with scenes from next week's all-new episode, starring … you!") Just drop it. Let it go.

Ultimately, what's now called Hinduism incorporates enough of Buddha's influence—and vice versa (most so in Tibetan Buddhism)—that the idea of separating the two today might be like a married couple filing for divorce on their 60th anniversary. But we must bear in mind Buddha's unique slant. The priests mediated individual experience of the sacred, saying, "You have an immutable, inmost identity (*Atman*) that is one with the Supreme Identity (*Brahma*)." Small self equals Timeless Self. The Buddha broke with the power of the priests, saying instead: there's no self, no identity—or rather, don't identify. With one eternal God, comes one eternal soul. The Buddha says nothing is eternal but change and interrelatedness; our identity is as diverse as creation, and ultimately as open as the sky.

The Buddha criticized the Brahmans' demand for animal sacrifice as superstition and a waste of precious life, *all* life being precious. Moreover, tradition said the caste system was God's plan. If you were born into a lowly caste, that was due to your unresolved bad karma in a previous life. (That didn't explain, however, why the elite could pass their caste along to their children.) When Siddhartha shaved his head and went forth to become the Buddha, he not only renounced his own caste but also the whole caste system. Rejecting the priestly class (Brahmans), he said the seeds of enlightenment are innate in everyone. What he'd experienced anyone else could, too, through self-discipline rather than priestly prescribed ritual.

Yoga: The Mindful Body, the Embodied Mind, As One

Buddhism and *yoga* often seem as close as twins. In Tibetan Buddhism, advanced practice is even called yoga. In the West, some practice ashtanga yoga, also known as *raja* (unifying body and mind with contemplative practices); others, *bakhti* (devotional). The most familiar branch of yoga is hatha yoga, with its asanas (postures, beginning with sitting), some of which are mentioned in Chapter 10.

> **This Is** _____
>
> **Yoga,** at root, means "yoking, union, as between individual and Godhead." Indeed, religion's etymology means the same: to "reconnect." Before his Enlightenment, the Buddha tried various forms of yoga techniques of energy, concentration, and meditation. Perhaps inspired by the success of Buddha's monastic system, a master named Patanjali systematized yoga practices in the Yoga Sutras, in which key teachings seem to bear the influence of the Buddha's own teachings.

As both yoga and Buddhism grow ever more popular in the West, some teachers offer both. After all, when we see the Buddha sitting in the lotus position, it's a basic yoga position (*padmasana*). Yogis no longer have to sneak across the hall to Buddhist meditation workshops if their yoga teacher doesn't open their wisdom eye (that is, to see deeply and understand), though all asanas are opportunities for observing the mind. Conversely, Buddhists can practice yoga postures as mindfulness practice, in and of itself, not just as a warm-up before meditation. Yoga enhances whole body stability and flexibility, focus, penetrative attention, and mindful awareness.

A cornerstone of meditation, as detailed by the Buddha in his *Satipatthana Sutra*, observes awareness of the body *in* the body. Indeed, physical energy and sensation, as well as mental and emotional awareness, are sources of insight. Just as there's *pranayama* (meditation on breathing) in yoga, so does the Buddha devote an entire sutra to breath: *Anipanisati*, "Mindfulness of Breathing," the enlightenment of breath. (Does breath belong to any single creed?) In short, the Bodhi Tree is inseparable from the banks of the great rivers of India that nourish it.

China's Version 1.0: Buddhism + Taoism

A keystone of interfaith awareness is the *Tao Te Ching* (pronounced "dow deh jing," *The Book of the Way*), a mere 5,000 words in Chinese. It's a simple but profound account of how to live in harmony with the Unchanging amidst the 10,000 things of whatever's happening at any given moment. ("Whatever's happening" is, in a way, what never changes. 'Twas ever *thus*.) As we've noted, Buddhism had a cousin when it came to China, a fundamental link called *Tao* (the Way), which finds full expression in *Ch'an* (literally, "meditation"; *Zen*, in Japanese). It's as if Ch'an is born of the marriage of Indian philosophizing and Chinese practicality. Both are imbued with the spontaneity and playfulness of a newborn kitten, the intuitive wisdom of finding the light switch in the dark, the commonplace simplicity of a glass of water, and the completeness of swallowing the whole world in a single gulp.

Like Buddhism, Taoism says that beyond realms of contingency and form, we're each embedded in what's ultimately real (called the Tao, the Way) through our innate, individual character. One way to realize our connection to the Tao would be through *tso wang*, sitting with blank mind, forgetting our transient self, and finding *hsin tsung*—the heart within the heart, the mind of the mind, the still point within the turning world, the ground of our consciousness within the cosmic processes. There's a similarity here to the idea of perfecting the self through selflessness, the Hindu yoking (*yoga*) of *Atman* and *Brahman*, and this technique is similar to the Buddhist practice of sitting meditation to enrich our innate buddha nature.

Like Zen, the Tao is beyond words, and any attempt to pigeonhole it is to miss the point. To speak of the Tao is not the Tao. Or as Louis Armstrong said of jazz, "If you got to ask, you'll never get it." Yet it has a very instructive symbol, the *tai chi* yin-yang, a Taoist diagram of the Middle Way.

This Chinese symbol of the Ultimate Principle of All Things (Tai Chi, often referred to as "yin-yang") seems to resemble two fish each forever trying to catch the other's tail in its mouth. (Ain't life like that?!)

Here we see the origin of all polarities—male and female, light and dark, outer and inner, self and other, chocolate ice cream and vanilla, hot and cold—and their unity. The two are clearly distinguishable, yet clearly interdependent. One defines the other. There's no buying without selling, no selling without buying. There's no me without you, and this book is proof: no writers without readers. The more extreme my position is, the more it embraces my worst enemy's. The more I try to control and pin everything down with labels, the more everything turns to goo. And the more I let everything just flow, the more everything reflects an uncanny, inherent, natural order—like the fractal formula for the pattern of a seashore, which matches that for the outline of a cloud and the outline of cauliflower.

Each contains its mate within its own heart. Within the heart of darkness there's a bright spot, and vice versa. But the most direct path between the two isn't necessarily a direct line (it's nonlinear). Try and walk across this map via any "straight narrow path" and you step in black and white equally. The Middle Way isn't some statistical mean; it is a very dynamic process. The contact between the two equal halves isn't fixed or static (like a fence, or words); rather, it is fluid and flowing (like a river, or a dance).

Here's another fundamental difference between Eastern and Western mind-sets. The Western mind-set is typically *dualistic*, the individual split asunder from nature (to, say, put up a parking lot), body separated from soul, self from the cosmos, humanity from God (the list goes on, as is the nature of dualism to perceive). The Eastern mind-set, on the other hand, sees humanity embedded in nature, interconnected and intertwined (for example, see the Mu Chi landscape in Chapter 12).

But if you say *yin-yang* is a symbol of two things, you're not quite right, because it's one picture. If you say it's one picture, wrong again, because it clearly shows two different things. Buddhism recognizes heads and tails as two sides of the same coin—without attachment to either the oneness of the coin, nor the two-ness of the sides. Zen says: "Not one, not two." So, again, how we reach the One depends on the road map.

 Leaves from the Bodhi Tree

> Who can judge good from bad? In a Taoist story, a farmer's horse once ran off into foreign lands. The neighbors all said this was terrible, but the farmer shrugged, "Maybe, maybe not." Later, the horse returned with a foreign horse of fine breed. The neighbors all said this was wonderful, but the farmer shrugged, "Maybe, maybe not." The horses mated, and the farmer eventually became a wealthy horse trader. One day his only son was riding and fell and broke his hip. The neighbors all said how horrible, but the man shrugged, "Maybe, maybe not." Next year, foreigners invaded. All able-bodied young men were drafted. Almost all died in battle. The army had taken all the man's horses, but his son, because of the broken hip, was spared.

Benedictine Buddhists, Zen Judaists, Sufi Yogis

Westerners born into an Abrahamic religious heritage typically look to Buddhism for one of two things: new roots, because the spiritual tradition of their parents or ancestors had become wounded or inaccessible; or they'd been raised in an active, vibrant spiritual heritage, which Buddhism further strengthens and vitalizes. A good fit, either way.

Christian Followers of the Way: Onwards (and Inwards)

Had Jesus and Shakyamuni met, I know they'd be two good buddies. (What religion was Jesus? Was he a Christian? What religion was Shakyamuni? Was he a Buddhist? Was Freud a Freudian? Einstein an Einsteinian? As Gandhi asks, what religion is God?) Some even say that Buddhists from the Silk Route were present in Galilee during Jesus' time, so maybe their minds did meet. Today, Buddha and Christ are still conversing, and the ongoing dialogue is making for many good hearts. Amen.

Jesus said, "I am the Way." The Buddha said, "Here is the Way." Lest we forget, both were inviting us to emulate their teachings, to live their meaning—to *be* the Way—rather than lose our way by studying their words like a lawyer. Yet it is interesting how their teachings tabulate, in divine double-entry bookkeeping fashion. Seek and ye shall find, the Buddha said. Jesus said, "He who would may reach the utmost height, but he must be anxious to learn." And Jesus once said, "Regard the lilies of the field." The Buddha once gave a sermon in which he just held up a flower.

Students of the apocrypha point out how, in the remarkable *Gospel of Thomas*, Jesus speaks in terms of illusion and enlightenment rather than sin and redemption. Scholar Elaine Pagels notes how in this text "he comes as a guide who opens access to spiritual understanding. But when the disciple attains enlightenment, Jesus no longer serves as his spiritual master: the two have become equal—even identical." Lists of Buddhist-Christian correspondences are numerous, though the real places of convergence aren't in books but in living hearts and minds.

Different paths can lead to a common destination. These images of Buddha and Christ seem to have been drawn by the same person, though one was made by a Tibetan artist, the other by a Russian. From 1981 to 1992, these images hung on the sign outside the School of Sacred Arts in New York City, the Buddha facing east, Christ facing west.

*(Buddha by Tupten Norbu
Christ by Vladislav Andreyev)*

A Tibetan Buddhist meditation called *tonglen*, on giving and receiving, has affinity to Jesus teaching his disciples to wash each others' feet, and teaches how to love one's enemy as oneself. Buddhist recitation and mantra resonates with early traditions of Christian prayer, such as recitation of *Kyrie Eleison*, and the Jesus Prayer (Hesychasm) still practiced by Eastern Orthodox Christians. You don't need to finger out the similarity between Christian and Buddhist rosary beads: the center, which is everywhere (and nowhere), is circular.

Through meditation of mindful breathing, many Christians are rediscovering what St. Paul meant by praying without ceasing (1 Thessalonians 5:17). Buddhist meditation on sunyata (emptiness) also parallels what Paul had spoken of as kenosis (emptying out), an active recognition of the utter mystery of God; also referred to in Christianity as "the cloud of unknowing," this parallels the "Don't-Know Mind" of Zen discipline. For Simone Weil, a Jewish Catholic who also studied Buddhism, prayer is nothing other than paying attention. (Listening to God in silence, we hear God also listening, in silence.) Honorary Catholic bodhisattva St. Francis said, "Preach the Gospel always, and use words if necessary."

 Along the Path

"Be still and know that I am God." (Psalm 46)

"'Be still' means to become peaceful and concentrated. The Buddhist term is *samatha* (stopping, calming). 'Know' means to acquire wisdom or understanding. The Buddhist term is *vipassana* (insight or looking deeply). When we are still, looking deeply, and touching the source of our true wisdom, we touch the living Buddha and the living Christ in ourselves and each person we meet."

—Thich Nhat Hanh

A Personal Note

Interfaith dialogue breaks down isolation. I can testify from my own experience. Growing up Jewish, I'd felt distanced from Christianity. When my Hebrew school made a field trip to the Catholic church across the street, it seemed, alas, mostly a lesson in deportment. Interestingly, for me, it was through Buddhism that I came to deeply understand and appreciate Jesus. When I'd touched "the peace that passeth understanding" for myself, through my Buddhist practice, then I understood the Kingdom of Heaven within reach of all. The seeds of enlightened living are within all of us. As the Quakers ask, "Where shalt thou turn if not to the light within?"

When I understood the Buddha's teaching on the inevitability of suffering and how to deal with that as instrumental in finding true happiness, I began to understand how Christians could worship an image of a human being suffering so horribly, on a cross—the ultimate sacrifice and universal redemption. Both Buddha and Christ offer a message of love having participated in the sorrows of the world, out of compassion for the human condition.

When asked to pick up Jesus' cross for myself, I'm touched to recognize my own sorrows, and transform them into fertilizer for my own flowers of peace, and to bear witness to the needless sorrows of others. In the bodhisattva ideal, pain is overcome by bearing it for others, with others—vowing to save all beings. (Those who try to split the hair of difference between enlightenment and salvation will miss my point.)

Jubus (and Bujus): Where Mount Sumeru Greets Mount Sinai

Today, there's a word for Jews who bring Buddhist insight to their Jewish practice, Jubus (pronounced "joo boos"), and another word for full-time Buddhists who are Jewish on their parents' side, Bujus. However you slice it, it's interesting. For one thing, there are proportionately more Jews than Christians along the Buddha's way. For example, Jews comprise less then 3 percent of the American population, yet make up 15 to 30 percent of its non-Asian Buddhists. One obvious reason is the fact that one third of all Jews in the world were systematically mass-murdered, leaving the souls of so many survivors and their descendants deeply scarred and seeking spiritual renewal. Yet where to turn? The vast majority of rabbis and teachers of ancient oral tradition had been singled out for annihilation. Thus, too, the fear that Jews who even mention Buddhism are diluting an already imperiled religion.

> **Leaves from the Bodhi Tree**
>
> A Jewish mother traveled to Nepal to seek an audience with a guru. When she arrived at the monastery, she was told that she could have an audience with him, but visitors could only utter five words to him. So she passed through the outer doors and entered the inner sanctum. She approached the guru, put down her bags, and said, "So, Sheldon, come home already!"

Bu-ju, Jubu: it's an interesting interrelationship. Where is the line between living fully in God's presence and living fully in the present? Jewish and Buddhist wisdom see no separation between the material and the divine, the sacred and the everyday. There need be nothing mystical about goodness; one can progress daily on a basis of practicing goodness, whether it's called *mitzvot* or *metta*. Neither are Buddhism nor Judaism an object, but rather living traditions, defined by each generation through processes of perpetual renewal. In our time, Buddhism has provided remarkable influence on Jewish renewal.

For instance, Rabbis Zalman Schachter and Shlomo Carlebach saw the emergent availability of Hindu and Buddhist spirituality in the 1960s as both a gift from the Nameless Source of All Being (for the Jews now unable to make connection through their own heritage) and as a call to restore and revitalize the indigenous meditative paths in Judaism's backyard. Shlomo (of blesséd memory) had said of the extinction of so much mystical lineage in World War II that it's hard to learn from so many corpses. Plus, Jewish meditative practice, never a core commandment, wasn't typically taught until a studenthad mastered Hebrew biblical studies of Torah, Talmud, and Mishnah; was never available to women; and even then often proved unsystematic and vague.

What's interesting is not that so many Jews went to Hindu or Buddhist spirituality to contact spirituality without orthodoxy or catechism, but that so many then returned to their roots, bringing back what they tasted elsewhere. (Some tarry, some linger, and some stay. The garden is always open.) It's no secret that Judaism has, since its inception, borrowed religious ideas from along its travels, as now evident in the Asian influence on a contemporary movement called Jewish Renewal. It's ironic how much post-Buddhist Jews discover is already there in their own backyard, such as a traditional weekly spiritual retreat, called *shabbos* (Sabbath). And, yes, there are various words in Hebrew for meditation, but try just this one: prayer.

In recent years, there's been a renewal of interest in the indigenous Jewish meditation practice of silent communion and union with God (*hitbodedut*), with an intuitive process akin to Zen. There's a tradition in Jewish mysticism (*Lurianic kaballah*) of repairing the brokenness of creation and restoring oneness to the world (*tikkun ha'olam*), whose participation in the co-creation of the universe is not unlike the bodhisattva path for the awakening of all beings, for the sake of all creation. There's a common emptying of self in Jewish wisdom akin to Buddhist *anatman* (nonself)—(after which, some still remember their zip codes, some don't; Jews are still debating this issue). The kaballist interplay between something (*Yesh*) and nothingness (*Ayin*) matches the Buddhist equation of phenomena (form) and blank essence (emptiness); after all, divine creation brought something out of nothing. (Such a deal!) And the pure devotion of literalist Jews who don't doubt the Messiah could come riding into town tomorrow on a donkey resonates perfectly with the devotion of the Buddhist Pure Land school, where self-power and other-power rhyme well with the "I and Thou" teachings of twentieth-century Jewish philosopher Martin Buber.

As with Buddhism, there's really no catechism, no head office to Judaism, so there's a pluralist dynamic between tradition and adaptation in both. Hear Shimon ben Zoma's voice, from almost 2,000 years ago: "Who is truly wise? One who learns from all people." Interestingly, when Abraham Maimonides—son of one of Judaism's stellar commentators and philosophers, Moses Maimonides (1138–1204)—began studying the mystical Islamic path of Sufism, Moses wrote that any Jew who did so needn't be formally initiated back into the fold because the two paths were monotheistic. (And Maimonides himself had learned much of his Aristotle through Arabic sources.) Thus do many Jews seeking the mysticism of Dharma discover its utter wholesomeness and practicality, then return (never having really left). Some Jews stay in the Dharma, at home there. Not Buddhist Jews, they're Jewish Buddhists (Jubus).

But interchange is never one-sided. (The Silk Route traveled in at least two directions, or more.)

At a summit on Tibetan-Jewish dialogue, in Dharmasla, India, Rabbi Zalman Schachter-Shalomi responds to the Dalai Lama's question about angels.

(Photo: Rodger Kamenetz)

Make Room for Rumi

Of interfaith, it is written in the Quran: "To you be your way, and to me mine." Buddhists and Muslims naturally share a long history of interchange as Buddhism was the world's most popular religion at the time of the prophet Muhammad. When he refers to "the Fig and the Olive and Mount Sinai and Mecca," some commentators interpret the fig to refer to the fig tree associated with the Buddha's enlightenment. And when the Quran refers to Muslims as "the Middle Nation" and advises they avoid extremes in life, would that be the shared wisdom of the Middle Way, or a case of great minds thinking alike? And is there a difference in devotion when Pure Land Buddhists remember and recite the Buddha-name and Muslims remember and invoke the names of Allah (the latter practice called *dhikr*)?

Buddhist-Muslim interchange is recorded in such places as Egypt, Jordan, the Central Asian Islamic Republics of the former Soviet Union, Mauritius, Turkey, and Zanzibar, to name a few. For example, in the southeast Asian country of Java, predominantly Islamic, there's a native spiritual tradition called *Kejawen* (the state of being Javanese), which mixes Buddhism and Hinduism with Sufi-influenced mystical Islam. Java is also home to a Buddhist temple called Borodubur, one of the wonders of the world, where local Jesuit priests use the sculptures on its walls as topics for interfaith dialogue.

In southwest Asia (the Middle East), architects from India helped build Baghdad, in the eighth century, when the Islamic caliphs made it their capital. Buddhist as well as Hindu translators came along and practiced there, learning the local language and rubbing elbows with the local Christians, Zoroastrians, Jews, and Muslims. Mention might be made, too, of Mani (210–276), who synthesized Buddhist, Christian, Muslim, and Zorastrian doctrines in what became known as Manicheasm. To remind us how difficult it is to limit such immensities as is any spiritual path, it's always good to consider such mystic poets as Kabir (1398–1448), whose bridge between Islam and Hinduism transcends both in its pure love, and Rumi (1207–1273), who says, "Grapes all want to turn to wine," inviting us to celebrate the path of all freelance mystics, the path that circles back to our own heart.

> **Hear and Now**
>
> "When we are face to face with truth, the point of view of Krishna, Buddha, Christ, or any other prophet, is the same. When we look at life from the top of the mountain, there is no limitation; there is the same immensity."
>
> —Hazrat Inayat Khan (1887–1927)

Native Spirituality: Everything's (a) Relative

There are as many religions as there are people. Forgive me if I've omitted yours. I wish, last but not least, to note the Buddha's appreciation of the spirituality of first peoples. (I wouldn't say primitive, unless that recognizes primary connections, in all their vitality and elegance.) Buddha's Way easily combines with indigenous spirituality, beginning with his own native Harappan civilization (itself practicing seated meditation, belief in karma, and a path of renunciation), and then with indigenous Taoist, Shinto, Bon, and shamanic, nature-based Native practices around the planet. They all nurture an appreciation of our place on earth, reverence for all life forms, and a quiet attentive mindfulness.

There's perfect harmony between the Bodhisattva Vow to awakening with and for not just all human beings but all beings, and the Lakota prayer *Mitakuye Oyasin* (pronounced "mee 'tak kwee ay o 'ya sin"), meaning "all my relations" (people, animals, birds, fish, insects, trees and plants, and even rocks).

With such mutual, nondual nature awareness comes shared wisdom as to the interconnectedness of all things, and their impermanence. This resounds in the famous 1854 speech of Squamish Chief Seattle, affirming: "Whatever we do to the web we do to ourselves. All things are bound together. All things connect." And to survive all things must change. Chief Flying Hawk, an Oglala Sioux, testifies: "If the Great Spirit wanted men to stay in one place, he would make the world stand still; but He made it to always change, so birds and animals can move and always have green grass and ripe berries, sunlight to work and play, and night to sleep; always changing; everything for good; nothing for nothing."

 Hear and Now

"It has seemed natural to seek out Aboriginal law holders and actively explore the affinities and resonance between two spiritualities, Aboriginal and Zen, as they meet in the place where I am [Australia]. The meeting can't be hurried along, but if the rain falls, the Earth can't help getting wet. Some intimacy with an Aboriginal sense of being here, and some tending of that awareness, can only green Zen practice here in the ancient red continent, can only make it more Zen."

—Susan Murphy

To my knowledge, the Buddha hasn't been translated into Kiswahili nor Creole … yet. But, as I said at the outset, there wouldn't even be Buddhists if there weren't non-Buddhists. To say that once more, another way, Buddhism isn't only Buddhism if it is truly Buddhism. Or, as all faiths are now saying, in a word: interfaith.

The Least You Need to Know

♦ Interfaith dialogue is one of the vital and more crucial topics of our times. Buddhism has much to say in dialogue with all creeds. It can also provide a neutral, objective context for interfaith dialogue in general.

♦ Buddha was part of the culture of his time and place. So Hindu practices such as yoga are a natural part of his heritage. Many of his teachings are present within Hinduism today.

♦ China's reception of Buddhism was influenced by the preexistence of Taoism, which in turn influenced Zen, thus melding Chinese and Indian philosophy.

♦ Buddhism offers mutually rewarding dialogue with the Abrahamic faiths, Judaism, Christianity, and Islam.

4

The Newest Petal of the Lotus: Western Buddhism

In This Chapter

- ◆ Buddhism and modern thought
- ◆ Conditions conducive to East–West interchange
- ◆ Teachers, translators, scholars, and the Internet
- ◆ Issues and themes in Western Buddhism

Toward the end of his life, when asked to single out the most significant event of his times, historian Arnold Toynbee (1889–1975) remarked, "The coming of Buddhism to the West may well prove to be the most important event of the 20th Century." Indeed, for the first time in more than a millennium, the lotus of the Dharma is opening a new petal … on Western shores.

Here's a tour of the gardens of the Buddha's wonderland in the West. (Cuttings and seeds welcome! Bring some, take some. This great, growing park's for everyone.) You might even glimpse the Buddha himself along the trail, grafting and pruning, or just relaxing in a hammock in a hilltop teahouse (taking a break after teaching for 2,600 years).

Preparing the Ground and Mulching the Cultural Soil

Even as you're reading these pages, Western Buddhism is still taking shape. (Set this book aside a moment to take a few conscious breaths, and it takes further shape.)

How broad-based is this growing movement? Rather than knock on doors and attempt a census, we note a few facts. Item: more people in France today say they're Buddhist than Protestant. Item: in 2005, the Swedish government sent a questionnaire to every high school child in the country. One question was, "If you had to follow a religion, which religion would you choose?" 60 percent said Buddhism. Item: while there may currently be anywhere from three to six million self-identified Buddhist adherents in America, an insightful survey by Cadge and Wuthnow discovered one in eight Americans (approximately 30 million) are aware of, receptive to, and influenced by Buddhist teachings in their life. (You don't have be Buddhist to enjoy Buddhism.) Connecting the dots, we see the "Big Sky Mind" of awakening now being enjoyed beneath the skies of Russia, Australia, British Columbia, and Brazil. (In the latter nation, it's called a humanistic philosophy, rather than a religion. Does that alter its importance in any way? Or is it convenient nomenclature?) Like the wind, the Dharma now encircles the globe.

We've seen how different lands adopted and adapted the Buddha's teachings of awakening and awareness, as well as how they enter into dialogue with other creeds. There's ample time before anyone can say for sure how this will all shake out. It took several centuries in China. Meanwhile, why wait to come back in a hundred years and see? For now, here's a survey of those thriving thus far, plus elements influencing future growth. Having started with a gardening metaphor, let's continue. Gardening, like Dharma, is a living process. Cultivate soil. Plant seeds at the right time. Nourish them. New life comes to fruition, and in turn yields new seeds. It's very nice. Buddhism here in the West is just such a process. Here's a tour of the gardens of the Buddha's wonderland in the West.

Consider our soil and similar conditions. Since the Renaissance, secularism has been crucial to philosophy, culture, society, and government, as we know them today in the West (think: separation of Church and State). This outlook, still-evolving, goes well with the nontheistic outlook of Buddhism, wherein belief in God is optional. Fast-forward to the dawn of the twentieth century. We see secularism as modernism, shifting focus from divinity, fixity, and permanency, and transferring attention to the relativity, worldliness, and fluidity of reality and the many ways we can interpret it. You don't have to agree with Einstein, Darwin, Freud, or Marx to recognize their influence in modern civilization, and the Buddha takes his place alongside such tall trees of the West.

Pilgrims to the Western Lands

Buddhist practice took hold in America earlier than in Europe. China nicknamed the United States "Gold Mountain," after the Gold Rush of 1848. In 1853, they established America's first Chinese Buddhist temple in San Francisco. It's interesting to consider that while Emerson and Thoreau were waxing rhapsodic in New England about an Eastern spirituality they'd never actually seen firsthand, literally hundreds of Chinese temples of actual practice were springing up in California like mushrooms after a good rain, some with Buddhist priests, and others with Taoist masters or Confucian scholars. Then America passed the Chinese Immigration Exclusion Act in 1882, denying any further immigration of Chinese workers. In 1888, the Act was extended to include Chinese women except merchants' wives. Gold Mountain suddenly became steeper than Mount Everest.

Early Eastern spirituality in the West, in daily life, seen from the outside: the entrance to Kuan-yin Temple, Spofford Alley, Chinatown, San Francisco, on a summer day sometime between 1895 and 1906. (Note the mix of traditional and modern attire, such as the hats.)

(Photo: Arnold Genthe)

In 1899, two Japanese priests came to support the Buddhists among the Japanese immigrants in America who were resistant to conversion to Christianity. Ordained in the Jodo Shinshu Pure Land tradition, they became America's first permanent resident Buddhist clergy. It should be noted, as well, that their order was renamed Buddhist Churches of America (BCA) after WWII. Following Pearl Harbor, Buddhist priests, suspected of being spies, were among the first Japanese Americans to be interned and placed in internment camps. Eventually, the majority of Japanese Americans were interned in such civilian camps during the war; over half were Buddhists, mostly Jodo Shinshu. Some, forbidden to return to the west coast, established temples on the east coast.

In 1924, a national immigration act limited immigration by an annual quota of two percent from any country. After these restrictions were relaxed in 1965, immigration from Thailand, Laos, and Kampuchea, for example, then increased roughly a hundredfold in just three decades. Thus, some rural North Americans discovered acreage adjacent to their farms being bought and settled by monks in orange robes. Of the three to four million Buddhists estimated in America at the dawn of the twenty-first century, a minority 800,000 (plus or minus) were white.

Journeys to the East

Early Western pilgrims to the East were like advance scouts returning to their campfires to tell of what they'd seen over the mountains. Here are a few examples. Russian noblewoman Madame Helena Blavatsky (1831–1891) teamed up with Colonel Henry Steel Olcott (1832–1906) and founded the Theosophical Society in 1875. They traveled in south and southeast Asia from 1879 to 1884. In Ceylon, in 1880, she and Olcott became the first Europeans to formally take vows of Theravadan Buddhism. It wasn't until 1966 that the Theravada tradition would have a home in America, with the establishment of the Washington Buddhist Vihara, in the District of Columbia. All good things all in good time.

In 1923, Alexandra David-Neel (1868–1969), well-versed in Sanskrit, became the first European woman to enter Tibet's forbidden city of Lhasa. She stayed in Tibet for 14 years. Her subsequent books helped somewhat to dispel the romantic myths spun by the fiction of James Hilton, Talbot Mundy, and H. Rider Haggard. One of her visitors there, Ernst Lothar Hoffmann (later known as Lama Anagarika Govinda) stayed in the East for 30 years, before becoming a venerated teacher in the West. But it would take another half-century before Tibetan teachers would establish their own bases in the West.

Following WWII, a few priests in Japan were surprised to discover white pilgrims coming to their temples requesting instruction in Zen, such as Philip Kapleau and poet/ecologist/anthropologist Gary Snyder. In the late 1960s and early 1970s, veterans of the U.S. Peace Corps returned from South Asia, sharing their inspiration with their peers and fueling a subsequent wanderlust for trekking to India, Burma, Thailand, and Ceylon. Lama Surya Das, Daniel Goleman, Joseph Goldstein, Jack Kornfield, Wes Nisker, and Sharon Salzberg are some of the pilgrims to the East who became first-generation pale-faced teachers of Buddhism in America.

Living Dharma: Living Teachers

Up to the dawn of the twentieth century, Buddhism in the West had been based mostly on book learning. But learning about North Dakota from a book ain't the same as talking to a North Dakotan. A harbinger of change was the World Parliament of Religions, held in conjunction with the 1893 Chicago World's Fair, the first formal gathering of representatives of Eastern and Western spiritual traditions. Teachers included Anagarika Dharmapala (founder of the Maha Bodhi Society, from Ceylon), and Zen Master Soen Shaku accompanied by D. T. Suzuki, Nyogen Senzaki, and Shaku Sokatsu, each to become important Western Buddhist pioneers. There were also representatives of Jodo Shinshu, Nicheren, Tendai, and Shingon schools, as well as Jains and Vedantists. Former abstractions now had a human face. Along with Buddha and Dharma, the West was learning the value of Sangha: the living, contemporary expression of the teachings.

American Zen teacher Mel Weitsman recalls his teacher would say, "I can't give you anything but my Zen spirit." Pilgrim from the East, founder of the San Francisco Zen Center (first Zen monastery in the West), Shunryu Suzuki Roshi (1904–1971) has been arguably the single most influential figure in the adoption of Zen practice in America. Maybe his smiling gaze will begin to tell you why.

(Photo: Robert S. Boni)

Buddhist teachers from the East arrived in three waves in the twentieth century. First, the 1920s saw the introduction of insight meditation (Vipassana) in the West. Zen's popularity began in the early 1960s. Tibetan Buddhism began to become widely known a decade later.

With former Western students of teachers in the East returning to Western soil, new generations of Western seekers don't necessarily have to cross the great waters for training. Moreover, teacher and student can now speak the same language. This brings up the interesting question of *translation*, which we can explore next.

Pioneer from the West (born in Philadelphia, 1917), author of over a dozen books, peace activist, and Zen Master Robert Aitken has stated "All of my guides have passed away, but they are alive in my mind and body." Though this is only a photograph, this lineage can be seen as far back as to the Buddha (Guan Yin gazing over his shoulder, the Heart Sutra resonating in his space of peace). What it is, is up to us.

(Photo: Robin Scanlon)

Translators, Scholars, and the Internet

We've noted how translation of the Buddha's teachings was so important in the dissemination of Buddhism throughout Asia. Translation is equally essential for Westerners, who often can't read a foreign menu without a trained diplomatic interpreter (also known as a waiter).

In 1879, Sir Edwin Arnold (1832–1904) published his book-length retelling—in Victorian blank verse—of the life and teachings of the Buddha, titled *The Light of Asia*, going through 80 editions and upward of a million copies, helping make Buddhism a household word of the time. It wouldn't be until after WWII that American universities would offer intensive study in Sanskrit and Chinese (as well as Pali, Tibetan, Japanese, and Korean), whose impact on our culture might well be comparable to Greek and Roman in the European Renaissance.

Buddhist studies in the West could well be considered a contemporary Buddhist monastic tradition of sorts: "Buddhology," if you will. It is certainly cognizant of its roots, Western universities being modeled after the Buddhist caravanseries and missions, and Nalanda. Anglo-German, Franco-Belgian, and Leningrad schools of Buddhist Studies developed first. Buddhist studies came to America during the 1960s and proves a viable discipline today. American Buddhists tend to be well-educated, with campuses a fertile Dharma garden for many, where more and more Buddhist scholars are themselves practitioners and thus an important emerging factor in our understanding of the Way. There are now private schools with Buddhist-centric curricula such as California Institute of Integral Studies, Institute for World Religions, Naropa Institute, Soka University of America, and University of the West. Schools can also be found online, at such centers as AshokaEdu.net.

 Along the Path

Compare:

"Words are just like a man carrying a lamp to look for his property, by which he can say: This is my property."
—The Buddha, *Lankavatara Sutra*

"Seeking Perfect Total Enlightenment / is looking for a flashlight / when all you need the flashlight for / is to find your flashlight."
—Lew Welch, *Difficulty Along the Way*

We've noted how Buddhist innovation influenced the communication device now known as books. The Dharma has a distinct presence in our new media technology as well. (A subject for another book might be how Eastern spirituality looms in the legendary early days of personal computing. Did you know Peter Norton, the founder of Norton Utilities, is a former Buddhist monk? Why do you suppose Mitch Kapor named his groundbreaking company Lotus? And exactly what did Stephen Jobs see when he backpacked around India in the 1970s?)

The ocean of Dharma texts is now digitized (be they in Pali, Tibetan, Japanese, Chinese, or Korean), their huge canonical treasure chest available for keyword search, structural analysis through algorithms, or cross-indexing with other databases. (In a word: "Nerdvana!") For the rest of us, new media takes us back to the Buddha's original means of teaching: orally, be it CD, DVD, podcast, or audio/video archives. As we all know, the Internet is so-named because of its amazing capacity for *internetworking* interconnected networks; as such, it makes for a dynamic example of interbeing. As the Buddha said, "It is called a net because it is made up of a series of interconnected meshes and each has its place and responsibility in relation to other meshes." For much of the planet, as for Buddhism, it is the Silk Route of our times. As of this writing, widely visited Buddhist sites, such as BuddhaNet and The Buddhist Channel, average 28,000 "unique visitors" a day, five to six million per year. As it evolves, possibilities of global collaboration and interpersonal contact give new dimensions to the meaning of Sangha.

Stay Tuned: Topics to Watch in Years to Come

Buddha's roots are more than two and a half millennia old. They've spread like that fig tree beloved for sheltering the Buddha in the forest. A fig tree grows broad roots that support long branches. And it renews itself by planting those long branches in the soil, using them as new roots. The branches now reach every major continent. Conditions for Buddhism's flowering in the West have, as we've just seen, proven very, very good: fertile soil, receptive environment, and loving gardeners.

It's far too soon to predict what the outcome of all this might be. It took Buddhism 300 years to find its way in China. But Western Buddhism has thus far manifested at least six interesting, distinguishing issues and themes: acculturation, feminism, egalitarianism, integration into daily life, ethnicity, and ecumenism (greater dialogue and cooperation among Buddhist schools). As is the case of Buddhism, no component stands alone; chunks overlap.

East? West? West Meets East in the West, and Vice Versa

Buddhism has always adapted to native conditions, finding the Middle Way between tradition and change. It's interesting that the path traditionally associated with preserving the original teachings (Theravada) is, in the West, the one having the greatest latitude as to their lineage, having little emphasis on religion, and most likely drawing upon different schools' teachings—Buddhist and non-Buddhist (such as psychology). Indeed, in such adaptations as emotional intelligence, full catastrophe living, and mindfulness, even Buddhism itself seems to disappear. Zen in the West is allowing adaptation of its tradition, but gradually, generation by generation. Pure Land has a much longer tradition in the West, largely Asian-based until now, and is confronting how it wants to proceed. And Tibetan Buddhism, the most recent arrival, keeps its traditions the most intact.

Acculturation raises a commonly asked question: Can Westerners adapt to an Eastern practice? So while we speak of oneness, it's always important to realize differences count, too. For example, someone once said all human beings basically see the same world the same way. Psychologist Richard Nisbett conducted a study to test this out. He showed a decorative fish tank to some Westerners, then some Easterners, and asked each to write about what they saw. The Westerners began by describing the fish.

The Easterners began by describing how much water there was, the rocks that lined the bottom, and so on. Each got the whole picture, but with different ways of getting at it, with different emphases.

Frankly, I'm a complete idiot when it comes to knowing where East ends and West begins (or vice versa). In just whose backyard is it? In between Ankara and Constantinople? Or Buda and Pest? Is it so difficult for Westerners to follow a path with Eastern origins (besides Judaism, Christianity, and Islam)? Hardly. I find "karma" and "guru" in my *American Heritage Dictionary*. Many Asian American Buddhists can count a Western heritage spanning many generations. And there are European American Buddhists, born and raised at Buddhist monasteries in the West, for whom "Eastern thought" isn't applicable to anything—to them, it's Western. Without implying stereotypes, Michael Wenger has noted that up until now, the East has looked to the past, and the West toward the future. As East and West come together now, we arrive fully at the present moment. In this wonderful moment, we're seeing how much really is universal, and what's unique.

In defining Euro Dharma and New World Dharma, it's good to question whether there's an attraction to a pasture seemingly greener on the other side of the fence, the mango more exotic than the apple. Exoticism can be as much of an illusion as attachment to ego. But Buddha shows there's no fence, no "other," no dualism. So why not a Buddha in a baseball cap? Or a beret?

Along the Path

> "Many Westerners have gotten involved in the chopsticks, tatami mats, flower arrangements, green tea, etc., thinking them to be Zen. This is a terrible shame. The Japanese made use of their own forms to express meditation, and there is just as much Zen in golf or car driving or jogging ... We must let Zen permeate our daily lives, not graft on a foreign artificial lifestyle. Remember the Buddha did not eat with chopsticks and never in his whole life chanted in Japanese."
> —Jitsudo Baran and Isan Sacco

Many look to Western Buddhism for minimal dogma, for a "spirituality without religion" as it were, sometimes to such a degree as if spirituality were free-range, without lineage or tradition. At issue here is the question of transmitting a coherent body of doctrine and discipline, past to present to future, generation unto generation. How much dogma and ritual is necessary? Tibetan Buddhism's continuity of ritual makes some compare it to Catholicism. American Lama Surya Das, on the other hand, teacher of the direct path of Dzogchen, had a business card with three images: a Buddha, a Sanskrit mantra, and a toaster.

American Zen Buddhist monks and nuns at Shasta Abbey no longer use Japanese names for monks as they did for the first 10 or 15 years. They use an adaptation of Gregorian chant for most of their morning service scriptures, and other types of music for invocations. They drink Western teas and coffees, as well as Asian teas if they are donated. Reverend Shiko Rom, Prior, states "We have kept the spirit and heart of Soto Zen (Serene Reflection Meditation) and have changed some of the forms which were cultural." Charlotte Joko Beck trained under two Japanese masters and teaches Zen, but without affiliation to other Zen groups or religious denominations, the Awakened Way being universal. Formally ordained as a Zen Master by Roshi Philip Kapleau in a lineage tracing itself back to the Buddha, Toni Packer decided to sidestep all the ritual and trappings. So, rightly, she calls her work "meditative inquiry" rather than Zen.

Historically, we've noted how the West met living teachers of Eastern spirituality for the first time in any big way at the Parliament of World Religions. Now, you might not think anything similar could be presented in the East. Yet representatives of Western civilization assemble in the East quite frequently, only they've been called business summits. So while the West has been playing catch-up with Eastern holistic thought and spiritual cultivation, the East has been doing likewise with Western materiality (though not necessarily individualism). (Personally, I've never liked the term "underdeveloped country," because it depends on what the criteria for "development" are.)

Footprints travel in two directions. Consider this: Thoreau was influenced by the East, and his writings influenced … Mahatma Gandhi, who in turn influenced … Martin Luther King, Jr., whose speeches have also been studied around the world. All of these individuals have there own separate stories. So an intriguing aspect of Western Buddhism is the effect our adaptations can have, in turn, on the East, because of the West's influence today. Consider women, for example.

Women Buddhas Giving Birth to Western Buddhism

For Buddhism to take hold in the West, it absolutely has to accommodate certain basics Westerners come to expect of their own culture: women's rights, for example. Just as the adoption of Guan Yin by Chinese Buddhism had an incalculable effect, so are women very influential today in the creation of Western Buddhism, yet often in striking contrast to Eastern traditions. Yes, you'll read that the Buddha was wary of women in his order, but I think that's the filter of the ingrained sexism of its author, not the Buddha. Old habits die hard.

In the Buddha's time, it was forbidden for women (and slaves) to read Hindu scriptures; nor could women even pray on their own. In defiance of the Brahmins, the Buddha ordained nuns, starting with his own stepmother and then his former wife. His order of nuns is one of the earliest women's associations in the world. Today, there are dozens of Western women Buddhist priests and teachers. Because it hasn't always been this way, many eyes in Asia are turned toward the various ways Buddhism adapts in the West; for instance, Buddhist women in Asia lobbying for full ordination.

Women also seem to have a great eye for picking up on social imbalances, perhaps in part due to their own historic exclusion from so many situations of power. Women priests have often replaced hierarchical models with more communal approaches, sharing power with a free flow of responsibilities and roles back and forth from periphery to center. Which brings us to democratic organization.

The Cherry Branch Grafted onto the Hickory: Buddhist Democracy

The premise of democracy is that everyone can make their own choices about their lives. Buddhism is similarly based. All beings carry the seeds of their own enlightenment.

It's a good match. That is, the Buddha fits in well with the Yankee spirit. After all, he's a do-it-yourself self-starter. (When I think of self-reliance, not only Emerson's essay of the same name comes to mind, but also Frank Sinatra saying, "Don't tell me—suggest it to me!") The Buddha was the kind of pragmatic, no-nonsense, can-do, no-limit guy that appeals to Americans. What he said, essentially, was "Hey! I tried this! Worked for me. But don't take my word for it. See for yourself." That emphasis on independence and personal experience is at the heart of America's most cherished ideals. So we must consider and pay homage to our own national karma, our blessings of freedom. (It's interesting to note when Thomas Jefferson wrote "All beings are endowed with inalienable human rights to life, liberty, and the pursuit of happiness," in 1776, he'd originally written "property," before changing that to "the pursuit of happiness." So Thomas Jefferson said you have a right to study Buddhism.)

Along the Path

"In Europe, intellectualism takes precedence over tradition; in the East it is the reverse. In Dharma terms, the European has an excess of *panna* (intelligence) over *saddha* (faith), and he tends to reject what he cannot understand even if it is true; the [Asian] has an excess of *saddha* over *panna*, which leads him to accept anything ancient, even if it is false."

—Nanavira (1963)

Buddhism offers a dynamic Middle Way of balance between authority (the teachings) and egalitarianism (the community). The Western model favors shared power, with less emphasis on hierarchy and more on democracy. While some people may want to all face one master, others will prefer to all face in the same direction, teaching and learning from each other. We'll continue awakening, whether in formal temples or in a neighbor's living room, which brings us to the next element …

Integration into Ordinary Workaday Life

A key characteristic of Western Buddhism is that it's primarily lay, rather than mostly monastic as in the East. This means that many Western sanghas allow a member to hold an outside job and pay rent, plus bypass celibacy and maintain a family life, while still undergoing the full training course of a monk or nun.

And why not? Well, monastic tradition ensures stability. This might be one reason why many lay Buddhist centers pack up their tents and fold, lacking a strong succession of teachers and administrators. There's a lesson here for "convert" Buddhists (European Americans) to learn from "ethnic" Buddhists (Asian Americans). Asian American sanghas are entering their second century in America. Though many have no monastic orders, one reason for their stability is their emphasis on community and continuity, which European Americans are often still discovering. Can Buddhism sustain itself just by newcomers and walk-ins alone, every generation?

Another upshot of the lay emphasis in Western Buddhism is its concerns for "worldly" affairs. The whole second half of this book, in fact, is devoted to practice applied in the world, with the last chapter devoted to an important Western Buddhist trend, "engaged" Buddhism (engaged in affairs of society), although we're touching on some of those issues here, such as the rights of women, and …

Diversity, a Tapestry of Many Threads

A sign that Buddhism has arrived in the West is diversity. At Soka Gakkai International (SGI), there might be one or two white people in a sangha composed of members from Hispanic, Latino, and Asian heritage. Some Theravada monasteries in the West have Thai and Caucasian monks, side-by-side. Actually, of the three to four million Buddhists in America, Caucasian "converts" count for less than a million, perhaps the largest group being Unitarians (U.U.Bu). While converts tend to emphasize individual practice, largely meditation, "ethnic" Buddhists tend to practice together as families in congregational activities taking place alongside meditation (basketball Buddhism, for example). Dialogue between the convert and ethnic Buddhist communities is still tentative. Thus Pure Land, the most widely practiced school, is still under-recognized by convert Buddhists in discussions of Western Buddhism. Pure Land temples, conversely, are re-examining their tradition in the West in terms of opening it up more to others.

Koreans aren't Japanese. And Asian Americans are Americans. Bridge-building and dialogue is evolving between those for whom Buddhism is new and those for whom it is integral. An evolving Western Buddhism will necessarily be nourished by the cultural traditions of Buddhists red, white, yellow, and brown (and purple?). What we have in common is our diversity.

Western Buddhism has many faces. Jan Willis grew up with racism (the Klan burned a cross on her lawn in Alabama), and encountered an antidote to hatred in the teachings of Tibetan Buddhists. She knows ultimate liberation is possible, and in this lifetime. An Indo-Tibetan scholar, author, and Vajrayana practitioner, she is one of the leading spiritual innovators of our time.

(Photo: Marlies Bosch)

Nonsecularism: Buddha at the Salad Bar

Western Buddhism certainly engages interfaith practice. You don't have to be Buddhist to be nourished by its influence. It's also diverse as to intrafaith, offering a blend of Buddhist traditions. In the East, a corner store might stock a bar of soap by Kleenexes and batteries. A Western supermarket displays seven brands of soap on a big shelf. For better or worse, so it is with spirituality, at the risk of shopping-cart spirituality. ("Attention, shoppers! Krishna's playing flute in Aisle 9!" "Macrobiotic food samples next to the Vitamin Bin!") In Asia, religious pluralism can be as rare as an overweight postman. In the West, this is one of the most dynamic and exciting aspects of Buddhism. Vipassana teacher Joseph Goldstein calls it One Dharma.

For the first time, different schools of Buddhism that might never even know about each other back home in Asia are now rubbing elbows, opening new possibilities as to what it might mean to follow the path of the Buddha. Indeed, this book is a tangible example of the trend (if I may toot my own horn), the first to survey and spotlight different major paths of practice all within the same covers. (Who woulda thunk it? Or why did it take so long to happen?!) A gray-robed Korean Buddhist monk might have never seen a saffron-robed Sri Lankan one, much less study the other culture's practice, in translation. It's been a striking difference between East and West, weakening with the trend toward globalization.

With its nonsectarian approach, Western Buddhism carries minimal dogma, is open to inquiry and innovation, emphasizes personal experience and meditation, and is conversant with such Western modalities as psychology. This ecumenical, nonsectarian approach is important to recognize, too, in terms of Western living teachers, who're naturally more inclined to embody a pluralism within their approach because they have often studied more than one tradition. Stephen Batchelor, for example, is an Englishman who'd lived in Asia and studied Tibetan Buddhism for nine years, then Korean Buddhism for four. In retrospect, he's said his Korean training enabled him to drill straight down within himself, vertically as it were, while his Tibetan training covered the terrain in a more horizontal expanse through separate rituals. He's also an example of the creative approaches to adaptation in the West, exemplified by his phrase "Buddhism without beliefs," coined for his own "agnostic" teachings. (Christianity, Judaism, and Islam asks us to believe their tenets, whereas the Buddha asks us to practice his findings.)

Hear and Now

"In the final analysis, there is no entity called 'Buddhism' which travels from one culture to another. The insights and values of Buddhism are transmitted solely through their being realized in and communicated through the lives of individual women and men. And we can no more create a Western form of Buddhism than we can manufacture a fairy tale or a myth. For Buddhism achieves its cultural expressions in a mysterious and unpredictable way over many generations; in a way that no one of us can possibly foresee."

—Stephen Batchelor

Study different teachings. The second Bodhisattva Vow reminds us that Dharma doors are endless, inviting us to enter them all.

No new petals had blossomed from the Lotus for a thousand years, until now. Passport stamped, Buddha the Gardener has headed West, and is hoeing his row with us. This is a wonderful time.

The Least You Need to Know

- The influence of the Buddha upon the West is comparable to Einstein, Darwin, and Freud, and continues. It may take generations before anyone can say what Western Buddhism definitively is (it took centuries in China).

- There are Buddhist practices in the West where Buddhism is never mentioned: emotional intelligence, mindfulness, stress reduction, and so on.

- Early Western Buddhists naturally include Asian immigrants, whose practice now extends across many generations.

- Study of Western Buddhism calls for attention to such topics and themes as acculturation (adaptation), ecumenism (different schools), feminism, organization, integration into everyday life, and pluralism.

Part 2

Dharma: Truth, and the Way to the Truth

The Buddha taught for nearly 50 years, yet all his teachings are but one Dharma ... one truth ... one taste. The taste is that of freedom: freedom *from* endless disappointment, needless suffering, and repeating the same-old unsatisfying round; freedom *to* fully realize the authentic experience of your finest capacities, life's richest gifts.

The seeds of such freedom are inherent within us all. It's our innate ability ... our birthright ... our buddha nature. It only takes waking up to it. (You know it when you see it.)

There is nothing here to be learned by rote, or taken on blind faith. Rather, one can recognize, work with, and make real for oneself the Way It Is. Here's the essential harvest of the Buddha's teachings about life. The Dharma. The Way.

Gem of Refuge, Ennobling Truth

In This Chapter

♦ The Triple Gem

♦ Taking refuge

♦ The Four Noble Truths

♦ Liberation in practice

What is important? In prehistoric times, our life harmonized with the universe. Our ancestors might have pictured the universe as a giant buffalo, if buffalo was the animal that provided them with hide for clothing and shelter, meat for food, bone for tools. And they knew to take no more than they needed. But now buffalo are nearly extinct. Gone, too, is a common frame of meaning for why we're alive. Contemporary life often seems out of balance, fragmented, incoherent. (Press 5 for more options.) Sometimes it's hard to find any meaning except in what we bring to the table.

Did the Buddha offer us bedrock? Yes! True, he intentionally left no central church and nothing was written down. He trusted the autonomy of each person to listen to his teaching, and select, test, and self-actualize his findings for herself or himself. 2,600 years later, the bedrock remains—a triple gem, a fourfold truth—same as it ever was, available to all. And it's really quite simple …

The Triple Gem

The first three of the four parts of this book are structured around these three basics (the fourth surveying their applications in our world). Known as the Three Treasures, the Triple Gem, or the Three Refuges, they are as follows:

- **Buddha** From the Sanskrit root *budh*, "to awaken." This is the title given Siddhartha, because he attained Complete Enlightenment. More generally, it could refer to any self-realized being.

- **Dharma** Sanskrit for reality or truth (also phenomena, calling, fruition). It refers to the teachings of the Buddha. More generally, it can also refer to all that the teachings pertain to, and all that leads to the truth, as a falling leaf teaches impermanence.

- **Sangha** Sanskrit for gathering or assembly. It refers to the monastic order established by the Buddha, plus lay followers; communities of practice. By extension, it also refers to the practice of the Way.

This Is

> The Tibetan language has no word for "**Buddhist,**" using instead *nangpha*, roughly meaning "a person who looks within." In fact, "Buddhism" isn't used in Asia. The closest word is *Buddha-Dharma*, roughly meaning "facts of an enlightened life," "awakened life-truth," or "the nature of reality" (as Buddha pointed out). (It's at our feet, right here and now.)

We've imagined the origin of these three words when five forest companions of Siddhartha became his first disciples, after he'd returned from the Bodhi Tree. They sensed a penetrating peace in his step … an all-inclusiveness in his glance … a glowing wisdom in his presence. After he spoke to them, they declared themselves to be "Sangha," a community, a body of seekers and teachers along the path. "Dharma" became their word for the path itself, and "Buddha" for the one who finds and shows us that path.

Why jewels? Jewels may not evoke the power they did 2,600 years ago. (Things change.) But we're not talking about synthetic diamonds nor healing crystals. The meaning also goes beyond a beautiful adornment. It includes being rare … priceless … flawless. As gold once was, these jewels are a touchstone, a standard of value. Unlike the price of rice, or the stock market, their worth never fluctuates.

Slang for jewel is "rock." Here is that connotation of the solidity missing from a life adrift. Here's the rock of Buddhism … a touchstone … the diamond dormant in a lump of coal … secure bedrock. As the gift of a rare jewel can lift us out of material want, so can these jewels liberate us spiritually. Some think of magic, a wish-fulfilling jewel for their deepest aspirations.

Just like a wish and other good things come in threes, so are only three jewels enough. Touch one deeply, you touch all three—one truth, one heart, one mind.

This is not abstract. Rather, it's so personal and immediate, abiding and real, you can take refuge in it.

 Hear and Now

"I've given Buddhism another name. I don't call it Buddhism. What do I call it? I call it People-ism (the religion of the people). Why? Because people become Buddhas. It isn't that the Buddha becomes a person, but the people can become Buddhas. So Buddhism can be called People-ism."

—Venerable Tripitaka Master Hsüan Hua

Safe Harbor: Taking Refuge

Drivers sometimes keep an image of a saint on their dashboard. If you were lost at sea, sailing a ship in a high storm, the North Star is the light by which you'd steer your rudder. Our mother's womb was our refuge when we were but tiny buds. Refuge is our true home.

Taking refuge is like coming home; affirming one's appreciation of and trust in something abiding, always there. Using the analogy of healing, the Three Jewels are like a doctor's care. The mere existence of some medicine or a doctor or a hospital doesn't guarantee health. If your doctor gives you a prescription but you haven't taken the medicine yet, then you still haven't taken refuge in his or her care. Taking refuge in the Three Jewels means you've evaluated and decided this is good healing. If the Buddha's like a doctor, the Dharma is his medicine, and the Sangha is the clinic. You can put your life in these hands. Taking refuge in the Buddha, we commit ourselves to our own capacity for freedom. Through Dharma, we bring the path of awakening to life. In Sangha, we acknowledge our interconnectedness.

Triple Gem in Everyday Life

You can appreciate Buddha and buddha nature in your everyday life without having to formally take refuge. Author and teacher Franz Metcalf came up with a wonderful *mantra* (a phrase to focus your mind in positive energy). He saw a book titled *What Would Jesus Do?* and decided to write one of his own titled *What Would the Buddha Do?* It's a question you can ask all the time—in crisis or at calm or just anytime. What would the Buddha do? The more you think of the Buddha, the more you might think like a Buddha. Meditating on the Buddha, you start to meditate as a buddha.

Similarly, you can appreciate the presence of *dharma* in your everyday life without formally taking refuge. I take refuge in it wherever I find it. It might not be capital "D" Dharma, something the Buddha specifically spoke of, but you never know. The Buddha never took a bus, but his Great Vehicle carries us all. Just the other day, in fact, I was waiting at a bus stop during the after-work rush hour. The bus was very late, and a large crowd had formed, growing anxious and tense. When the bus finally arrived, it was already like a sardine can, crammed with people who'd accumulated in the long wait at previous bus stops.

Hear and Now

"Associations with wise and compassionate people help sustain the practice. To reflect on the *Sangha* of past, present, and future can give further inspiration. We develop appreciation for this expansive network that contributes to living with love. The *Sangha* has no particular religion, no dogmatic standpoints, no flavor of being a cult or sect. It is found inside and outside religion. Wherever we find wisdom and compassion, we find the *Sangha*."

—Christopher Titmuss

At the front of our palpably uncomfortable crowd, I saw a lady of rather large girth. She'd undoubtedly seen her share of trouble in life, including boarding crowded buses. Way behind schedule, the driver opened his doors, and completely out of patience, yelled at us all, "Hurry up! C'mon, get on! C'mon, c'mon, move to the rear of the bus!" But the woman just stood there and waited. No one could get past her, right in front of the open door. So we all waited. Finally, the driver sensed something was happening outside his bus, turned, and saw her. When they finally made eye contact, she just said one thing to him: "Please! Please don't make me get angry at you. Because then we'd be liable to say or do something for which we'd *both* be sorry!" The driver lifted his hands from the wheel and bowed his head in apology. Everyone calmed down, inside and outside the bus. People already on board looked around and very kindly made room for us. The drive was otherwise uneventful.

The dharma of the story?

- **Emotional intelligence.** It takes two to fuel anger. Fighting anger with anger only generates more anger. If one person refrains, then the other might, too.

- **Awakening of mind can happen anywhere.** A teacher doesn't have to hold beads or wear robes. The voice of the Buddha is always clear, if you have ears to hear.

- **We're always in relation, ever in sangha, even in the Rush-Hour Sangha of life.** Right now, you're a member of *The Complete Idiot's Sangha*—you and me and all fellow readers of this book past, present, and future.

Me, I'd been waiting for the bus to take me to my sangha, for Buddhist study practice, until a stranger showed me I'd already arrived. Study and practice had already begun. Actually, we all embody the sangha of the universe through the earth in our bones, the wind in our lungs, the ocean in our bloodstream and cells, and the fire in our metabolism. When I sit in meditation, I do so with the whole universe (and vice-versa).

Hear and Now

"We take refuge in the Buddha because he is our teacher. We take refuge in the Dharma because it is good medicine. We take refuge in the Sangha because it is composed of excellent friends."

—Dogen (1200–1253)

"To realize the very heart of essential nature is to take refuge in the Buddha. To cultivate the garden of realization is to take refuge in the Dharma. To share the fruits of the garden is to take refuge in the Sangha."

—Robert Aitken

Different Schools, Different Facets

The major currents within Buddhism complement and reinforce each other in how they emphasize the Three Jewels. Traditionally, Theravadins refer to Buddha as the historical Buddha; the Dharma as the Tripitaka (the Pali canon) recorded his teachings; and the Sangha as those who've attained enlightenment, more generally the monastic community, and the wider community of lay practitioners.

Mahayana perspectives are typically interpretive and innovative. For example, if you prefer, the Buddha is realization, Dharma is truth, and Sangha is being in harmony.

Members of the Zen Peacemaker Order take refuge in:

- Buddha, the awakened nature of all beings.

- Dharma, the ocean of wisdom and compassion.

- Sangha, the community of those living in harmony with all Buddhas and Dharmas.

Along with the Three Jewels, Mahayanans often take refuge in the path of the Bodhisattva, vowing to liberate all needless suffering. Tibetan Buddhists take refuge in an additional triplet, called "the refuge tree": the *lama* (*guru*, teacher, living embodiment of the Buddha), *yidam* (personal deity, an enlightened being whose attainment we wish to emulate), and dharma protector (similar to a guardian angel). Whether or not you take a pledge, the Three Jewels are timeless, the solid timeless handshake between ourselves and the universe whenever we appreciate, understand, and live the path of the Buddha in the twenty-first century.

From the Ultimate Dimension

I've said, "One thing on which all Buddhists agree is the Three Jewels"—even though this one thing appears to be three. No contradiction. Not unlike the Christian trinity, they are a unity. (Indeed, early Western interpretations of the Three Jewels reflect the interpretation of Christian missionaries. The Buddha was called the Savior, the Dharma was called the Scripture, and the Sangha was called the Church. But let's not forget the monastic order of the Buddha predates that of the Christ by several centuries.)

The Three Jewels are so interconnected as to be one, and each contains all the others. The Buddha is his teachings, the Dharma. After all, the Buddha's teachings are what enabled him to become Buddha. The Dharma is thus the essence of the Buddha. And Sangha depends on Buddha and Dharma to show people the way. Conversely, if the Buddha hadn't established the Sangha, then his teachings wouldn't have been kept alive. Buddha and Dharma depend on Sangha to be actualized. If there were no people, there'd be no Buddhism.

Buddha, Dharma, and Sangha are ultimately one.

The Basic Lesson: Four Noble Truths

The Three Jewels are the root structure of Buddhism. The root teaching is known as the *Four Noble Truths*. These are the first teachings of the Buddha following his enlightenment—so here's how the Buddha *became* the Buddha. How a person named

Siddhartha became The One Who Woke Up, and in so doing invited the whole world to join in.

The Buddha said, "I teach one thing and one thing only, suffering and the end of suffering." Interesting, he didn't say these are two things. Once you get it, you'll see it's one truth (a fourfold truth, if you will), and one truth only. If you're like me and can't count past two, this is a great relief. Everything else is, as it were, an elaboration on this core teaching. So, without further adieu, here's the deal. Plain and simple.

Awakened Facts of Life: In 4 Words, 25, or 750

If you can remember the Sanskrit, it's just four words: *dukkha*, *trishna*, *nirvana*, and *maggha*. ("Dukkha" is pronounced "dookha," and is easily remembered as sounding like doggy doody, or doodoo.)

This Is _____

The Sanskrit word **dukkha** literally means "an axle that doesn't quite fit into the hub of a wheel," so the state of being is always askew, or out of joint. It's usually translated as suffering, but could also translate to bumpy road, sour, unpleasant, or unsatisfactory. Also: disappointment, frustration, stress, emotional difficulty, anxiety, anguish, angst, depression. (Any *Ick!* grimace is extra.)

Nirvana is the state of ultimate perfection, beyond dualism, beyond words. The Sanskrit word literally means "extinguishing": the extinction of dukkha, difficulties; extinction of the *Three Fires* (or poisons) of ignorance, greed, and anger; liberation from samsara, the wheel of endless rebirth based on the karma of our actions, perpetuating self-delusion. Sometimes called "the other shore," yet it's here and now.

In 25 words or less: (1) there is needless suffering (dukkha), (2) needless suffering has a cause (trishna), (3) needless suffering can end (nirvana), and (4) there's a way to end needless suffering (maggha).

(1) Needless suffering is called *dukkha*, after the Sanskrit for an axle that doesn't quite fit the hub of a wheel. So, to use contemporary plain speech, life's invariably a bumpy road. We get schooled in hard knocks. You can easily remember the adage of the jogger's mantra: "*Pain is inevitable, suffering is optional.*" (Common Misconception 1, dispelled: the Buddha didn't say it's all suffering. What a downer that would be! Were that so, why then is he smiling?)

(2) The cause of suffering is … grasping. The Sanskrit here, *trishna*, can be remembered as being the root of our word for thirst—thirst in the sense of craving, clinging,

grasping. The common colloquial expression here might be: "Let it go." "Let it be." Pleasure, pain, and indifference—"this too shall pass." In shorthand, everyday slang: to try to hang on to life is to get all hung up; a real hang-up. An easy-to-remember motto for the Second Noble Truth comes from mystic poet William Blake: "*He who bindeth himself to a joy doth the winged life destroy; but he who kisses the joy as it flies, lives in eternity's sunrise.*"

This Is _____

The Sanskrit word **trishna** can be translated as "desire." It's the root of our word for thirst. Like the thirst of a person alone in a desert, it seems unquenchable. It can also be translated as attachment. Another good translation, in this context, would be clinging, grabbing, grasping. The colloquial term for excessively hanging on is apt here: being hung up, having a hang-up.

This grotesque creature's called a "hungry ghost" (preta, Sanskrit; li mei, Chinese), this one being of the Japanese variety called gaki. Its belly is immense because of its gnawing hunger, but its throat's only as wide as a soda straw, sometimes only the eye of a needle. And so it's emaciated because it can't get enough food to nourish itself, let alone slake its ravenous appetite. It symbolizes a human craving for more than it can ever have. (When's the last time you felt that you were in a somewhat similar condition?)

(Drawing: Gary Gach)

Common Misconception #2, dispelled: the Buddha didn't say to have no desires. That would be death. Everything that lives has desire. A plant desires to be watered, to have sunshine, to grow in nice soil, to have a bee stop and tarry, and so on. Rather, don't grasp onto and identify yourself with your desires. For instance, the first lick of ice cream can be a set-up to thinking, "Ice cream! This is what makes me happy! More, more, more!" Thus we create fictional stories that don't always mesh with the reality of our lives. It's like trying to catch the wind, rather than appreciating each taste and living in the present, just as it is.

In Buddhism, grasping (the root of all ills) can stem from an unholy trinity, known as the *Three Poisons* (sometimes, the *Three Fires*): ignorance (delusion about how things are), anger, and greed.

(3) In seeing into the nature of needless human suffering, you can glimpse how it needn't always be that way. Pain is inevitable, but suffering is optional. It's your call. You can drop it. Give it up. Let it go. Let it be. This state of liberation is nirvana, and is beyond conceptual framework. The Sanskrit word means, literally, "blown-outness." It's the peace after the fires are out, except there's no need to put on coveralls and a big mask and go at life with an enormous hose, like a fire-fighter (overkill). Rather, what's needed is more like a lookout on a mountain peak. The fires (of delusion—fear, anger, and greed) will burn out and die, if no longer fed. Without fuel, of causes or conditions, needless suffering can be extinguished. Gone.

Poor guy, seems like he'll just never learn. He's laboring under a common misconception that Buddhism means eliminating desire. But desires are a natural part of being alive. The Buddha said, "Don't hang on to them, and thus get hung up." Meanwhile, this poor dunce tries to learn this fact by repeating the words, rather than understanding their true meaning, and living it. (When's the last time you felt like this?)

(Drawing: Robert Crumb)

Common Misconception #3, dispelled: Buddhism is not nihilism (nothingness; the idea that nothing matters). No, the end of needless suffering isn't a vacuum, devoid of life. Rather, Suzuki Roshi says it is following each thing through to the end. It's life itself, with nothing missing

(4) The Sanskrit word *maggha* (also *margha*) means road, or path. A theory or idea may sound well and good, like the Golden Rule. Now try living it. But there *is* a Way, a practical path. Remember: the journey of a thousand miles begins with a single step. Another saying which pertains here, by Yogi Berra: "In theory, there's no difference between theory and practice: in practice, there is." Remember: even an 8-year-old knows the Golden Rule, but an 80-year-old may still be trying to live it.

We've been living for so long according to routines of animal instincts, social conventions, and hand-me-down ideas for so long it takes some training to truly see the truth, act on it effectively, and make it real. So there's a set of steps we can consider, an enlightened way of proceeding along life's trail. Just as the Gem has three facets, and the Noble Truth has four aspects, this Life Path breaks out into component parts, eight in number. But it, too, can be folded into a sharp summary. Count the main themes on the fingers of one hand: wisdom, virtue (ethics, conscious conduct), and meditation. In a word: enlightenment. Or, more accurately, it is an enlightened way of going about this process called living. There is a better way. Life is good.

Common Misconception #4, dispelled. You don't have to be "a Buddhist" to enjoy the beneficial influence of its gems, its fourfold truth, its eight-spoke wheel, or any of it. There's nothing to convert to, no formal ceremony necessary. Whatever fits in your own life, please, take it as a gift. Take it to heart. This is your time. And that's, in 750 words or less, the basics of the Four Noble Truths.

P.S. The four truths are called noble because they enable us to reclaim or retain our sovereignty over our own lives, to awaken from habit and live in full awareness.

A Traditional Twelve-Phase Program for Practice

The entire next chapter tours the eightfold path. But why wait?!

Consider the following traditional program of practice for the four ennobling truths you've just heard. Each truth can be considered in terms of (1) seeing, (2) studying, and (3) realizing and understanding. Or consider each in terms of (1) statement (theory), (2) prescription (weighing, trying it out, practicing with it), and (3) result (development, transformation, fruition).

I'll give you a personal example. I was to teach the Four Noble Truths, but that morning I had an accident. I fell. Seemed okay, but by the time I got off the train my knee had swollen so I could barely walk. Excruciating pain, inevitable; suffering, extra. But I had to remind myself of the Four Noble Truths. First, I stopped saying I. Rather than me, me, me (*ouch!*), I'm in such agony, and so on, I rephrased my situation. There is pain.

Immediately, this opened up space. Rather than entertaining additional suffering, I disidentified with it, and the suffering became constructive. I was seeing the moment as an example of the first truth, that there is pain. It is. It was no longer mine alone but a fact among others, one organ in pain among various parts of life. Moving from a clinging-based outlook of desire (wanting the pain to cease), to a breath-based view of the present (moment to moment), I could see the pain, though sharp and intense, wasn't always steady. It was good to observe and realize that, like my breath, it wasn't all the same but rather varied.

With each breath I widened the space between me and the more-and-more impersonal pain, moving from personal to universal. I included in my sense of pain all the people in pain this very moment, imagining them in larger and larger groups. Progressing from people at the train station, to the town, and so forth, it was quickly obvious there were people out there—this very moment—in worse suffering than me. There were individuals whose suffering was quite real, and who had far less hope of cessation anytime soon. They were not separate from me. Noble truth: we all experience this. The recognition of pain, the first noble truth, can be not only solace but also motivation. In this case, it motivated me to see it as an opportunity to deepen my wisdom and widen my compassion, rather than suffer needlessly.

By the time I slowly limped into the classroom, I'd gone from the phase of seeing to studying. I don't mean study in the sense of intellectual pursuit of abstract ideas, but rather utter practicality, which is the Buddha's way. In Sanskrit the word "study," *seuksa*, means "to see one's self by one's self." Clearly, I could see this was what I was there to teach that night. I was a living example of it. And so as the class saw me mount the single stair to the podium with extreme difficulty, yet with a smile, it was clear that I wasn't going to be teaching some metaphysical principle floating around in limbo, but rather sharing what I was realizing for myself.

Seeing, studying, realizing. Applying these stages to each of the four truths yields a rich, flexible pattern of twelve interlaced phases of potentially great healing.

Further Variations on a Noble Theme

Your own life can teach you about the Four Noble Truths. To assist your lifelong learning, here are a few more variations on our theme. Another traditional one stems from the likening of the Buddha to a great doctor. Here, then, is his medicine. Consider (or memorize) the four truths as (1) symptom, *dukkha*, suffering; (2) diagnosis, *trishna*, grasping; (3) prognosis, *nirvana*, liberation is available; and (4) prescription, *margha*, the Eightfold Path.

Short and sweet. Like something jotted on those little prescription pads doctors use. Only it doesn't require anything external, like a drug. Rather, it's something to take home to study and use to cultivate our own natural curative powers. So this is a holistic approach, cultivating our own natural, curative, innate health. It's all-natural. And it's a whole plan of treatment (like a balanced diet, exercise, and meditation, in addition to medication) addressing the whole person: body, spirit, and mind.

Yet another approach might be to phrase the four truths as questions. If you're familiar with the contemporary mystic Byron Katie, you'll hear how the four truths asked as questions resonate with the Work she teaches. Questions are really just a form of seeking. Once we've grown up, we often forget how questions were integral to reality for us as children. Some of that reality, we learn, is unprofitable craving. "Why can't I have that red _____?" "Can I eat just dessert?" But other kid questions are really profound, like, "What is that?"—and "Who says?!" Questions are a wonderful way of finding what's overlooked, amplifying what's really juicy and eliciting answers already within us. Ask yourself:

> Am I suffering? What's the situation? (Be brief.)
>
> What keeps me from being happy? What am I attached to about my suffering? How do I identify myself with it? Is it real? Does it have a life of its own? Is it physically present here and now? Is it in my mind? Is it permanent?
>
> What if I let go of my attachment to all in the situation that's not immediately present, and the self-image I identify with that situation? Then would I be happy?
>
> How can I cultivate a better way of living that doesn't let me fall into the same patterns I fell into all over again?

Try writing your answers; really process them within yourself. And have fun with it.

One fun method of processing vital new information is called Jukebox Mind. Think about song lyrics echoing the four truths. Can't get no satisfaction? (*Dukkha* is often translated as "unsatisfactory.") You try and you try? (Unless you get to the root, dissatisfaction will keep cropping up.) You can't always get what you want (by craving for stuff), but if you try (remember the teachings and test them in your own life) you can get what you need (nirvana).

Similarly, we've also used everyday speech to drive the truths home. Noting how the Tibetan word for attachment, *shenpa*, means getting hooked, Tibetan Buddhist teacher Pema Chodron suggests, "Don't bite the hook!" You could visualize this as a cartoon of a school of fish, being taught by a mama fish. She points to a picture on a black-board of a giant fish hook, saying to them, "Don't bite the hook!" And last, but not least, there are always jokes, of course. (Question: Why don't Buddhists vacuum in corners? Answer: They don't have any attachments!)

Buddhism in one word: nongrasping.

If life is filled with suffering, then why are these two people smiling? (Maybe they can't help but smile being in each other's presence.) Each seems to have looked deeply into the heart of life. They invite us to do likewise. Each, in their own way, reminds us, "Life is good. Enjoy!"

*(Leonardo da Vinci, Mona Lisa [c. 1505–1514], Paris, Musée du Louvre.
Buddha in Meditation, Gongxian style, grey limestone, 95.3 centimeters, Northern Wei Dynasty [386–535], Honolulu Academy of Arts, Gift of Mrs. Charles M. Cooke, Sr. 1930 [3468]).*

The Least You Need to Know

- All Buddhists agree on the core value of the Three Jewels and the Four Noble Truths.

- The first is the basic structure of Buddhism. The second is the basic teaching of Buddhism.

- The Three Jewels are the Buddha, the Dharma, and the Sangha.

- The Three Jewels are so valuable and solid, timely and true, we can take refuge in them.

- The Four Noble Truths deal with (1) the existence of suffering, (2) the origin of suffering, (3) the cessation of suffering, and (4) the way to live without needless suffering.

Chapter 6

Buddha's Way: The Eightfold Path

In This Chapter

- ◆ Touring Buddhism as a path, step by step
- ◆ Putting theory into practice for awareness, happiness, and well-being
- ◆ Joining body, spirit, and mind through conduct, wisdom, and meditation
- ◆ Understanding and practicing all eight aspects of the Path

After Enlightenment, the Buddha decided not to slip away and meditate alone for the rest of his life. Sharing his awakening, his first talk is known today as his "turning of the wheel of the Dharma." How come? Well, for one thing, the wheel of the Dharma (with four spokes for the Noble Truths; sometimes eight, the Way) is a handy visual icon. Its simplicity reflects how he opened the way to Enlightenment for all, even today.

On a deeper level, we remember Dharma means "reality," and also "teachings." The Buddha taught ultimate reality in his first talk using his listeners' own present-moment lives as example, as an integral manifestation of the timeless Dharma. So turning the wheel is an apt image. Like a river, that wheel keeps rolling on. The difference between merely existing and living life transformatively is a different spin on things … a turning …. So Dharma is not only a statement of fact but also a calling: go on, give it a whirl! And it's also fruition: to be on this Path is itself the goal.

The Path

Sometimes a journey of 10,000 miles begins with a leaky tire or a broken fan belt. Sometimes it begins with just one step. Everyone comes at it differently. Each takes away something different. Each step on this path leads to all the others. To quote the sage adage of Cambodian Buddhist teacher Maha Ghosananda: "Slowly, slowly, step by step."

🪷 Hear and Now

"The spiritual journey does not consist of arriving at a new destination where a person gains what he did not have, or becomes what he is not. It consists in the dissipation of one's own ignorance concerning oneself and life, and the gradual growth of that understanding which begins the spiritual awakening."

—Aldous Huxley

We've glimpsed the Buddha's core teaching, a way beyond suffering. Pragmatic and noncoercive, it's all there in his Fourfold Truth for you to observe, understand, and realize in your own life, day by day. Now we follow up his probing diagnosis and optimistic prognosis with a closer look at his gentle but powerful prescription. It's called a path, yet it's also known as a wheel. Same difference? To quote Sri Lankan Buddhist peace leader Ari Arayatne, "We make the road, and the road makes us." Here's a program—a travel itinerary—for finding our way in the world. It's a treasure map to freedom, within the depths of our own heart. This path has proven the way for over a third of humanity. To quote the Buddha: "Come and see!"

The Path is eightfold:

1. Right View
2. Right Thought
3. Right Speech
4. Right Action
5. Right Livelihood
6. Right Effort
7. Right Mindfulness
8. Right Concentration

This may be the only teaching the Buddha ever wrote down, perhaps sketching it in the dirt with a stick and eight pebbles. A wheel is a very skillful means of traveling. The spokes can be memorized in linear sequence, but a wheel is circular, with no top nor bottom. No beginning, middle, end. All eight spokes are needed to navigate the whole journey.

The Eightfold Path.

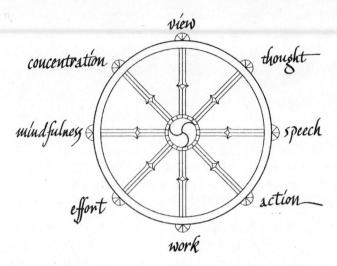

Don't worry. "Right" is only the traditional translation of *samma* (from which we get our word summit), literally "perfect" in Sanskrit, or "optimal," or "tops." So here *right* doesn't imply there's also a *wrong*. There is no judgment. Good and bad may apply to what to do, or what not to do, but Buddhism prefers *skillful* and *unskillful*, referring to *skillful means*, or what's conducive to enlightened living. (Right on.)

I like considering right as a verb … *right* as in "to restore," as in restorative health. (A fellow author I know will reply when asked what he writes: "I right wrongs.") *Right* is "perfect," as in "to perfect." The steps could also be framed as questions, such as "Am I viewing okay?" and "What would the Buddha do?" However you read them, they're yours to study, test, claim, and make real for yourself … one by one.

We'll tour all eight, within three broad, traditional groups: *wisdom* (or, if you will, spirit), *conduct* (the body), and *meditation* (mind), ultimately treating body, spirit, and mind as one. (When the Buddha speaks of mind, he isn't referring to intellect. As the word in East Asian calligraphy conveys, our mind is one with our heart. When you experience a change from a dark mood to a light one, ask yourself what changed.) We'll cap our tour with ideas for practice in everyday life.

Wisdom: Getting It Right, from the Get-Go, on Out

Start anywhere. Why not begin with clear view, like a sky with unlimited visibility? The sky's the limit. Don't grasp after limiting concepts, preconceptions, or misconceptions; don't bite the hook.

This is the character for "heart" in Chinese and Japanese. It depicts a human heart, with its chambers and aorta. It's also the character for "mind." So here we see mind and body as one. The equivalent word in Tibetan has the same sense. (On the left, a block-style version; on the right, a more flowing, cursive version; both are straight from the heart.)

(Calligraphy: Kazuaki Tanahashi)

Abstractions, removed from what's immediately at hand, can obstruct our directly seeing for ourselves things as they really are. So the Buddha's telling us like it is: don't mistake the forest for the trees, or mistake definitions or names of trees for the trees, or any of that. Keep your vision clear.

Wisdom. On the left, a block-style version; more flowing, cursive version on the right.) One interpretation of the Chinese word reveals the upper component as a broom, and the middle as a hand taking hold of the broom and sweeping the heart (mind), below. In this view, understanding or wisdom isn't an accumulation of knowledge, but rather the shedding of ignorance … cleaning and clearing away … clean sweep; an open mind.

(Calligraphy: Kazuaki Tanahashi)`

"Wholesome understanding" is another definition of *view*, or *open outlook*. View means constantly re-*viewing* the Fourfold Truths. With perfect view, each moment is complete and sufficient, as it is. Every seat is always the best seat in the house, right in front of wherever we are.

Along the Path

Take a blank sheet of paper and write on it with big, clear letters, "Are you SURE?" (Or "Think again.") Tack it up on a wall where you'll see it regularly, such as at work. If the ringing of your phone sounds like an alarm, then you might answer nervously. Are you sure it's a danger signal? Prevent unnecessary anxiety and pain by examining your attitude.

The companion to *view* here is *thought*. The wisdom here tells us that how we think about our path colors our journey. The Buddha says, "Please check in your mental luggage at the door before you embark upon this Path." Other words for *thought* could be *aspiration*, *attitude*, *motive*, and *commitment*. The simplest way might be to consider thought not so much as your intellect, but rather as your spirit, or your heart. It's what's really important, your inmost aspiration.

Hear and Now

"Mind is forerunner of action, foremost of deeds. Everything's made up of mind. If your mind is polluted, sorrow will follow, as a wagon wheel trails the hoof of an ox …. If your mind is pure, happiness will ensue, the way your shadow trails along wherever you go."
—The Buddha

Telling it like it is, the Buddha asks you to check out where you're coming from. Don't set yourself up for disappointment later on. Get clear. There's nothing to *get* from this Path: it's simply your life, in all its beauty. So if you think the teachings are a cosmetic personality makeover, it's best to realize from the very start this kind of transformation isn't about changing what you look like but rather how you look at yourself and the world. To repeat, there's really nothing here to attain: wherever you go, there you are. You'll always be you (perfect—who else could you be?!), only with room for a bit of improvement—possibly gaining more acceptance, more conscious awareness, more generosity, a little more wisdom, more maturity, more kindness (to yourself and to others), and more compassion.

This is perennial wisdom, if not widely preached. Recall that the Buddha opposed the hierarchy of priests of his day, the Brahmins, because the Path is already there at everyone's feet. It's a kind of counter-wisdom, if you will, reflected throughout human culture as well as diverse spiritual traditions. French novelist Marcel Proust writes, "The real voyage of discovery consists not in seeking new landscapes, but in having new eyes." Thoreau echoes this when he says, "Only that day dawns to which we're awake."

Tip: From time to time, we stop and return to the fundamental wisdom of understanding our motive for Buddhism. We might catch ourselves seeking enlightenment, which is a set-up for a fall; it's a conceptual dualism separating self from enlightenment, as if we didn't have innate buddha nature already.

Attitude is all. While my ultimate goal is enlightenment, I can only attain it by dis-identifying myself with concepts, conditionings, and cravings, having no attachments to them so that enlightenment may happen on its own. That is, I can't enlighten myself any more than I can surprise myself. Rather, through the discipline of the path I am laying a strong foundation, with ample space and wholesome conditions for that chance to take place. Only then can I (continually) discover that I've already arrived.

Thought as attitude: you can almost hear the heroic cogitation in the Rodin sculpture, grasping at thinking with every muscle right down to his very toes. And thoughts without a thinker: the Buddha or bodhisattva sits up, enjoying his breathing; whatever thoughts may come are welcomed, like hearing the chirp of a happy bird. (What do you think thinking is?)

(Auguste Rodin, The Thinker *[1880], 79 inches × 51¼ inches × 55¼ inches, The Rodin Museum, Philadelphia, Gift of Jules E. Mastbaum.* Bodhisattva Maitreya in Pensive Pose, *Korean National Museum, Seoul, Silla Period, early seventh century, Gilt bronze, 90.8 centimeters.)*

Conscious Conduct: Do the Right Thing

The next three spokes of the wheel locate awakening in our daily lives: *action*, *speech*, and *work*. Sometimes grouped under the term *virtue*, I prefer a less loaded word, because virtue can imply vice, original sin, and all that. Also called *ethics*, these aren't philosophical abstractions. They get down to where we live, as human bodies. Here's where the pedal meets the metal, the real nitty-gritty.

Perfect action means acting out of love, not causing suffering by our acts, for any beings. A fuller definition is a series of road signs, known as precepts (or "mind-trainings")—conscious conduct, if you will—as we'll explore in Chapter 8.

Say the Word and It Will Happen: Perfect Speech

Watch what you say: it colors our thoughts, which shape our deeds, which in turn influence our predispositions. So *speech* is an action. Habits to observe, learn from, and refrain from, include lies, harsh words, slander, and frivolous speech. How often do we put people down, put people off, or put people on hold through our speech? How often do we gossip about things for which we don't have any firsthand evidence? Just consider: whatever we say about others, applies to us well.

More Than a Job: Wholesome Work

*Work*wise, Buddha cautioned against dealing in arms, intoxicants, slavery, prostitution, or animal slaughter. That would seem to leave a pretty clear field for whatever's left. Or does it? Modern choices haven't gotten any easier. For instance, is it breeding an animal for slaughter when animals are used for medical experimentation that might save lives? Sure, it's all well and good to say, "Don't harm the ecosphere, live green!" but in today's globalized economy we all seem to be part of the pollution. The point is that contemporary life's interwoven complexity asks us to be no less aware of traditional values, in whose mirror we can be more conscious of our conduct. Livelihood is always rich (pun intended) with opportunities for fulfillment and transformation. (More in Chapter 16.)

Meditation: What We're Presently Aware of Is Reality

For many, meditation is the number-one attraction in Buddhism, so much so that it's now often practiced outside of traditional Buddhist contexts—often renamed "relaxation response," "emotional intelligence," or "mindfulness." As the fourteenth Dalai Lama says, "There are four billion people on the planet. One billion are Buddhists, but four billion are suffering." Chapters 9 and 10 are given over to basic Buddhist meditation; meanwhile, we can enjoy its grounding in some primary teachings. The Path speaks of meditation in terms of three interlocking spheres: effort, concentration, and mindfulness. (I've intentionally reversed the traditional arithmetic order of the last two.)

We've seen wisdom as a blend of attitude (*thought*) and understanding (*view*). Similarly, meditation can be presented as *concentration* (attention) and *mindfulness* (awareness), each working (*effort*) in tandem. *Effort* says get started and keep at it—you can get there if you really try. This positive energy counterbalances our understanding that we can't just will our own awakening. Trying to make enlightenment happen is like a snake trying to swallow its tail. Yet a plant won't take root and grow just by holding it against a rock and waiting for something to happen. Causes and conditions need to be present. There needs to be a space for the chance to take place. Seeds need to be planted and nourished.

This Is

> The Sanskrit word for **mindfulness,** *smriti,* means "to remember." We become intimate with life when we remember to be aware, to be here and now. Mindfulness is being fully attentive to things as they are, in and of themselves, moment to moment. And if this awareness feels splendid, even miraculous, remember it's your birthright.

As a practice, each school might have a little slogan for their slant on it. Insight meditation (Vipassana) says, "Look within." Zen says, "Just do it." Pure Land says, "Say the name." Tibetan Buddhism (Vajrayana) says, "Honor the resistance." Whatever their approach, these are all invitations to effort, to practice. Among the Buddha's last words were, "Seek your enlightenment with diligence." (Meaning: "You can do it, too—so get busy!" Don't waste time.) And if the Buddha were alive today, he'd be that person sitting over toward the back and to one side in the meditation hall … still sitting, practicing ….

And what is meditation? In addition to effort, it's concentration plus mindfulness. Of course it's really an experience, rather than a tangible thing, or subject, so putting meditation into words can be subtle. Indeed, there are at least a dozen distinct translations for the Sanskrit root for concentration here, *samadhi*. Call it one-pointed concentration, meaning paying undivided attention to what's in front of your nose. Like a hammer hitting the nail on the head, this one-pointedness is fixed on neither hammer nor nail alone but on both as well as the intense concentrated *thwack!*, straight through in a single stroke. Hammering a nail while thinking about dinner, on the other hand, can be an invitation to a swollen thumb.

Utterly present-moment, this kind of concentration can provide a stability often lacking in our modern multiplexing and stress-maxed lives. Attentiveness to what's happening "in the now" can restore us to a steady feeling of calm silence and wellness, like the tranquility of a forest pond silent beneath the surface ripples. Original buddha nature is always present, the vast ocean beneath waves. One way to practice returning to buddha nature through samadhi is to practice stopping. Think of the tree that sheltered the Buddha: it wasn't going anywhere. Take a moment to stop, feel breath, bone, blood, and attention in the present moment, free of any plots our mind might be hatching. (Please, try it right now.) It's a coming home to our original nature, our buddha nature. So total samadhi can mean stopping, cessation, stillness, silence, steadiness, stability, calm, tranquility, equanimity, and peace.

Who could ask for anything more, right? Well, the Buddha had learned samadhi techniques during his years in the forest, and mastered each, but he found none unlocked the enigma of human suffering. As he stuck to his quest, he came to a radical, unique form of meditation we know as *mindfulness* (*sati*, in Pali). Mindfulness can be described as an intelligent alertness. We may not change our behavior, but with mindfulness we can change our mind, which can transform everything.

Meditation = undivided attentiveness (concentration) + energetic awareness (mindfulness) + practice (effort). Concentration and mindfulness work together like the bright, broad beam of a steady light illuminating a lens through which we can see deeply, directly into our nature—our true, original nature, as it is, rather than the temporary story we tell about it. Looking deeply, we see our human nature as all nature: impermanent, interconnected, and selfless. Another analogy is to a laboratory. Mindfulness provides an ideal practical environment in which to test (in real-time) the wisdom of clear view and superb attitude in our daily actions.

Hear and Now

"Concentration and mindfulness go hand in hand in the job of meditation. Mindfulness directs the power of concentration .... Concentration furnishes the power by which mindfulness can penetrate into the deepest level of mind .... Too much awareness without calm to balance it will result in a wildly over-sensitized state similar to abusing LSD. Too much concentration without a balancing ratio of awareness will result in the 'Stone Buddha' syndrome."—Venerable Henepola Gunaratana

And what's the laboratory's special formula, the magic catalyst? Available to all at all times: it's *breath* ... the easiest of tools for focusing our attention on the here and now.

It's one of the first things we notice when we practice stopping. Through conscious breathing, we can also see an immediate, personal example of the impermanence of life's flow … and our interconnectedness with our environment, without any self of its own (more on this in Chapter 8.) Breath acts as a kind of hinge between body and mind, like a mirror of our awareness. What a great gift!

If self-awareness is a trait distinguishing us from animals, being aware of awareness is a step of yet another order of magnitude, a major evolutionary leap. We may still only be at the crossroads here, as a species. As author and meditation teacher Wes Nisker spryly puts it, "mindfulness is the opposable thumb of consciousness." So meditative effort could be nicknamed "evolutionary sport." Many long-time players swear it's the only dance there is. So pay attention. Slowly, slowly, breath by breath.

The Way doesn't await you. You *are* the Path. Enjoy the journey.

 Leaves from the Bodhi Tree _____

> A passing stranger encountered some Buddhist monks in a forest. He asked what they were doing. A monk stopped to explain that they were Buddhists and that he and his fellow monks were cutting wood. "Wait. I cut wood, too, for my fire," said the man. "I don't see anything extraordinary about that." "Well, sir," the monk replied, "when we cut wood, we know we're cutting wood. We don't cut wood to build a fire. We cut wood to cut wood." The monk smiled, and added, "If we can't cut wood, how then can we build a fire?" Then he resumed his work, and the man went on his way.

Travel Tip: Step by Step

Remember: you don't have to give anything up to let the healthy influence of these teachings nourish you. Actually, the Buddha said, "All living beings, whether they know it or not, are following this path." If anything here resonates in your own life, then, by all means, give it a try. And if you keep at any one of these eight steps, you'll find each will lead, sooner or later, to all the others.

Exercise: Take a blank sheet of paper and fold it into eighths. (Fold it in half, then in half the other way. Then fold it in half yet again. *Voilà!*) Having thus divided the page into eight boxes, write the name of one spoke of the wheel in each box. Keep the document with you, in your wallet or purse. Be alert to situations throughout your day (and night) that might present themselves to you as particularly thematic, an issue, in terms of one of the eight steps. Before you go to bed, copy your day's mental notes in the appropriate boxes. It might be a key word or phrase for a hindrance or an aid, a habit or a goal. For example, under "speech" you might jot down "gossip," under "thought" you might note "look deeper," and under "concentration" you might write "not reading while eating." Eventually, you'll notice all eight in your everyday life.

Reminder: each aspect of the Path isn't a destination, out there somewhere for us to align ourselves. Rather, each spotlights important innate abilities to cultivate, already within ourselves.

Sangha has been compared to a clinic, where Dr. Buddha prescribes medicine (Dharma). Here we've seen his prescription, a *whole* plan of treatment for healing, not unlike the way a doctor might recommend a balanced diet, enough exercise, and rest. Otherwise, prescribed medication or surgery may not have lasting effect. Head, heart, and spirit all work in tandem. Body isn't divorced from spirit or mind. It's all connected. Meditation grounds our wisdom in personal experience, which in turn better informs our conduct. With our actions grounded in harmony, our wisdom is based in our day-to-day, and confirmed through meditation. The way the steps interrelate is dynamic, keeping it turning. Start anywhere. It's a wheel, without beginning, middle, or end. It all comes around again, full circle and rolling on like a river to the sea.

Hear and Now

"It is the nature of life that all beings will face difficulties; through enlightened living one can transcend these difficulties, ultimately become fulfilled, liberated, and free .... The way to realize this liberation and enlightenment is by leading a compassionate life of virtue, wisdom, and meditation. These three spiritual trainings comprise the teachings of the Eight-Fold Path to Enlightenment."

—Lama Surya Das

So: "Slowly, slowly, step by step." If your doctor recommended eight ways to change your diet—for instance, no fried food, less sugars and caffeine and red meat, and so on—you'd gradually modify your diet, so as not to throw your metabolism into a state of shock. (Spiritual as well as physical crash-courses might result in a kind of adrenaline rush at first, but without sustained benefit.) Instead, by gradual adjustment, all steps eventually become integrated and second nature—buddha nature. Come and see!

The Least You Need to Know

- Buddhist practice (the Eightfold Path) and Buddhist theory (the Four Noble Truths) mutually support each other.

- The eight steps are easy to memorize, and can be grouped in three: *wisdom* (view [understanding] and thought [intention]), *conduct* (speech, action, livelihood), and *meditation* (effort, mindfulness, concentration).

- Meditation is only one aspect of Buddhist practice, along with wisdom and conscious conduct (ethics). All three build upon and feed into each other.

- You needn't practice the steps in any order, nor all at once. Gradually but steadily develop each element.

- Each step is an end unto itself. Indeed, in everything you do, just do that—fully aware of your doing that and nothing else. And enjoy!

Take Karma, Make Dharma: Key Points

In This Chapter

- ◆ Karma: moral cause and effect
- ◆ Interconnectedness, the web of life
- ◆ Impermanence, a cause for celebration
- ◆ Nonseparateness: selflessness
- ◆ Nirvana: freedom
- ◆ Emptiness (infinite openness) and suchness

This chapter guides you through the essential ideas in Buddhism. Let me preface by saying the Buddha didn't preach abstruse, abstract metaphysics. No misty woo-woo here. Rather, the Dharma is totally on the dime, realistic, and impeccably accurate as an analytic system, as well as amazingly perfect as a program for enlightened living. It's also multidimensional, with infinite interpretations and applications. So be open to see the world in new ways. New words open new worlds. And remember: these aren't ideas taken from a jar on a shelf—they're realities you can test for yourself (please) in your own world. There's enough here for a lifetime (which, who knows?, may be not that much longer than all of eternity … or this present moment). "Slowly, slowly, step by step."

Buddhism in Seven Words or Less

A friend once complained to the poet Jane Hirshfield, a longtime Zen practitioner who had spent three years in monastic practice at Tassajara Zen Mountain Center. He was supposed to write a book covering all of Buddhism, but had only been allowed 40,000 words. She replied, "40,000, for all of Buddhism? That's either way too few, or way too many. Really, you only need seven." He asked, "What might they be?" Hirshfield's answer: "Everything changes; everything is connected; pay attention." There you have it. Buddhism in a nutshell.

Actually, Buddhism is often boiled down to two words (in the same breath): wisdom and compassion. Venerable Master Sheng Yen expresses very well their interrelationship. "Cultivate wisdom, which is the absence of self-centeredness. You can only be free from self-centeredness, however, if you have compassion: an awareness of the suffering of all sentient beings. Compassion allows you to give selflessly. If you are selfish, you will not have much compassion—or wisdom! Therefore, wisdom and compassion are inexorably linked; if there is only wisdom, your practice is incomplete."

Here, in 7,000 words or less, are variations on that theme. The compassionate wisdom of the Buddha is as viable and vital today as it ever was.

One Thing Leads to Another: Karma

Up ahead are five key compassionate, wise concepts central to Buddha's teachings: (1) karma, (2) interconnectedness, (3) impermanence, (4) nonself, and (5) thusness. These are interconnected. So though I lay these out in linear fashion (one by one, along sequential page numbers), these simple truths subtly overlap and combine to create a beautifully intricate, effective system or whole (Dharma). This is true to life, which isn't necessarily a prescribed series of steps, but rather a whole dance. Let's take karma as a point of departure.

Karma is as simple as pie. It's the notion of moral cause and effect. Your yesterday affects today, and what you do today affects tomorrow. The idea of karma predates the Buddha by several centuries, and in his day, was often seen as dependent upon divine will. (But God's will is in probate, some say. Badum!) The Buddha said we are responsible for what happens to us. Of course, certain things—causes and conditions—are inevitably beyond our immediate control. But we hold in our own hands the power of transformation. The seeds of awakening are within all.

Karma literally means "action" but it needn't be an overt act ("… lizard scrambles off rock …"), but an *intention* (which prompts an action, which then colors our disposition, in turn eliciting a new intention). Scientists can now rig up a prosthetic limb operable by mere thought. Thought (and feeling) influence action, as does speech. Even if I don't act on a thought, bad intentions and guilty consciences influence action and affect others, as do good intentions and pure consciences. For example, if you look at someone who's compassionate, generous, kind, and wise, I think you'll see someone who attracts good friends. Or look at someone who's angry all the time, bickering, loud, and abrasive, and you'll see how angry feelings, thoughts, words, and deeds help shape a person people avoid. You can take karma and make *samsara* (vicious cycles). Or take karma, make Dharma. Quoting Paul McCartney: "And, in the end, the love you take / Is equal to the love you make."

This Depends on That: Interbeing

Pay attention: it's all connected. Have you heard the word? *Interbeing!* It wins my vote for entry in the next edition of the dictionary (karma's already in.) Venerable Thich Nhat Hanh coined it as a handy alternative in English for the more tech-sounding dependent origination. (Tech-talk: that which makes complete idiots of us all!) It's the web of karma, of life—and it's not static (everything's changing).

Interbeing says nothing exists independent of anything else. Everything is every thing dependent on every other thing—inextricably interdependent, relational. This is because that is. An illustration is the yin-yang diagram in Chapter 3: no yin without yang; no yang without yin.

The wheel shapes the path; the path shapes the wheel. This is how we can see karma as continual interaction and interreaction. What we think in turn affects what we feel, which affects what we say and do—along with causes and conditions themselves dependent upon other causes and conditions. With karma, we help make or co-create our world. Simple, it's also complex and all-embracing, because it is so inherent in everything, all the time. Karma choice-points are everywhere. They create ripples that will create further ripples; the seeds of an apple (cause) become apples (result) and then become a new cause. So we imagine the vast web of all the threads of karma as more complex and precise than any supercomputer (or even human brain). The mere rub of our sleeve on a stranger's in passing is accounted for (by Dharma). In 1963, Dr. Martin Luther King Jr. said of karma's web, we are all "inescapably caught in a network of mutuality." Interbeing is that network.

Sometimes personal experience helps bring an idea home, so I'll share with you my own initial, vivid, personal intimations of interbeing. People ask me, "When did you become a Buddhist?" I smile, remembering a vision that came to me as a boy. Our teacher was giving us "busy work" before the lunch bell, asking us to raise our right hand, then our left hand, and so on. Instead, I followed the beat of a different drum.

Across the street, a crew was hammering at a wood frame that would one day be a two-story house. The weather was that for which Los Angeles is famous. (Comedian Fred Allen quipped that California is a fine place to live, if you happen to be an orange. Well, it was that kind of a day.) Warm, crisp, tawny light drenched the land-scape. Listening to the rhythm of the hammers, looking at the sun pouring down through the tree-lined street, my mind suddenly went on a riff.

It all came to me in an instant. Narratively, it went something like this: A house was going up ... out of wood ... as from the trees lining this very street. Trees are nour-ished by sunshine, just like today's ... the same sun also helped make the cereal that the workers had eaten that morning for breakfast before coming to the work site. I could see the foreman had blueprints made of paper, which was made of wood ... the blueprints drafted by some man, who'd eaten cereal ... *all* nourished by the sun—the man, his ideas, the blueprints, the wood, the building. (*Hammer, hammer.*) Wow, see the pattern to it all!? (*Hammer, hammer, hammer.*) Chlorophyll, sun energy, human energy, blueprints ... and because there were blueprints, a pattern, and patterns within and to patterns ... then there must be some grand pattern to all the patterns—

Aha! Seeing that with my own two eyes was an awakening, an illumination. It was like seeing the face of God (or at least touching the veil). I think everyone's had this rec-ognition, sometime or other, seeing one's self as part of the stream of life and sensing one's connection with whence it comes, and where it's going.

Along the Path

"All things are interwoven with one another; a sacred bond unites them; there is scarcely one thing that is iso-lated from another. Everything is coordinated, everything works together in giving form to the universe."

—Roman Emperor Marcus Aurelius (121–180)

We don't always see this connection, though perhaps we know of the split-second relays of modems and satellites conducting a single currency transaction ... the 84 separate steps that food takes to get from a farm to our fork ... the flapping of a butterfly's wings in an Amazon rainforest affecting the weather in our own backyard ... "the web of life."

Western civilization has proven very good at mea-suring and dividing the universe up into separate, isolated, units, like ice cubes in a tray. The East has proven very good at looking at the totality of life as a dynamic interplay, like waves at the ocean's shore.

The Buddha once taught by just holding up a flower. (Imagine if he'd done that at some Ivy League university, as guest lecturer, or better still, as a commencement address.) But when we stop our hurried, isolated way of perceiving and bring mindful awareness to a flower, we can *see* it's a messenger of the cosmos: the *water* cycle coursing through its cells, breathing fresh *air*, harnessing the sun's *fire* through chlorophyll, and *earth* supporting and nourishing its thriving. A flower buddha, teaching dharma. And so pretty! Thich Nhat Hanh, having coined the word *interbeing*, likewise speaks of it vividly. He points out that when we see that sun and cloud are present in this page, interbeing's the word for that. This page depends on a tree, which depends on the earth and a rain cloud and the sun. Tree, earth, cloud, and sun inter-are in this page. Any one thing is interdependent with another.

 This Is _____

> **Interbeing** can be illustrated by Indra's Net. Imagine a net so vast our cosmos is but a part of it (perhaps created by Hindu deity Indra, to entertain his daughter, who knows). At each node on the net, there's a jewel. To look closely at just one jewel is to see reflected there all the other jewels of the infinite net. And in each jewel reflected within this one jewel is also reflected all the other jewels, *ad infinitum*.

When I saw interbeing, God was the only word I had for it. So I kept my vision tucked away like a gold nugget at the bottom of my pocket, until I was 15 and learned about Buddhism, finding there the apt articulation for what I'd experienced. And interbeing does not depend upon a sacred story about the creation of the universe (cosmology). There are no great debates here about First Cause or Unmoved Prime Mover. The entire universe coexists with all that is, sufficient within this present moment. (Ain't it grand?!)

The Four Noble Truths can be clearly reviewed in this light. Understanding the nature of the arising of suffering includes the nature of the cessation of suffering. Suffering arises; therefore, suffering falls away. Coming into being and going out of being "inter-are." Whatever is dependent upon causes and conditions has no intrinsic identity of its own. Remove conditions, and the unconditional remains, often called nirvana.

Bouquets of Interbeing: *Avatamsaka*

The Lotus Sutra schools devote special attention to the unimpeded interpenetration of all things, as does another school, allied with the Pure Land tradition, called *Hua Yen* (*hwah yehn*, Chinese; *Kegon*, Japanese), the Flower Garland School. This school is based on the largest sutra in Buddhism, the *Avatamsaka*. It teaches *mutual identity* (unity) and *mutual intercausality* (universal interdependence). The motto here might be "One in all, all in one." All the seas are but one drop of water, and in every wave is the entire ocean.

To review, Buddhist teachings treat causality in terms of karma. Karma's web teaches us intercausality. Next we'll see how the provisional, relational (interrelational) nature of all things teaches us the impermanence of life. Without any separate and enduring identity, identity (self) is more or less a convenient fiction, giving way to a wider, deeper view.

It Was That, Now It's This: Impermanence

Along with the Four Signs that Siddhartha saw when he went beyond his palace walls, he saw other clues. One early morn, for instance, he'd seen garden leaves all covered with gorgeous, clear, bright little gems, radiant in the dawning sun. But when he came back to admire them in the afternoon, the magic gems were all gone. His faithful servant explained that it was dew, and that it's natural for all things to pass away like dew. Along with dukkha (and its cessation, nirvana), it's a *mark* of all existence. What's known as a *Seal of Dharma*.

I pause in my writing to see if this is true in my own life, right now. Here, near Chinatown, cherry trees have been blossoming. I, like my neighbors, have a few branches at home. Of all plants, it is said the cherry and the plum teach us about the floating, fragrant fragility of life, its ineffable perfume. I'll keep them here for a day or two after the flowers start to lose their freshness, when there are just a few pink clumps where not long ago there were dozens, all eventually brittle and brown. For me, that's part of their teaching, too. It's no less difficult to accept than the reality of dukkha. In fact, *impermanence* is practically dukkha's middle name.

Hear and Now

"Everyone knows that change is inevitable. From the second law of thermodynamics to Darwinian evolution, from Buddha's insistence that nothing is permanent and all suffering results from our delusions of permanence to the third chapter of Ecclesiastes ('To everything there is a season …'), change is part of life, of existence, of the common wisdom. But I don't believe we're dealing with all that means. We haven't even begun to deal with it."

—Octavia Butler, *Parable of the Sower*

Heraclitus, a Greek philosopher contemporary with the Buddha, said, "You can't step into the same river twice." (I'm a complete idiot: I say you can't step into the same river ... once.) It's a timeless theme, but with a lesson often learned late. We know it's natural for life to make way for more life, but it's human nature not to easily accept that fact. Thus the Buddha's teachings can go against the grain of our common social and even instinctual conditioning. The First and Second Noble Truths teach us to recognize, accept, and see through the suffering that impermanence seems to prompt. Actually, impermanence doesn't cause our sorrow, it's our mistaken attitude, trying to build sandcastles at the seashore. To grasp onto (or avoid) what has no lasting being is like trying to clutch (or push) a river. In so doing, we set ourselves up for disappointment, dissatisfaction, suffering, and the whole playbook of needless human sorrow.

Everything changes. Physician/poet Dr. William Carlos Williams reminds us, "What does not change is the will to change." Chögyam Trungpa Rinpoche affirms, "Impermanence is indestructible." Thich Nhat Hanh goes a step further by rejoicing: "Long live impermanence!" Why? Without impermanence, a flower wouldn't blossom. Waves wouldn't break upon the rocks. This week's issue of *Star* wouldn't be replaced by next week's all-new sensational never-before-revealed sizzle. Our hearts wouldn't beat. Our lungs wouldn't pump. We'd be like statues. (Now *that's* scary!) Change is essential to life, and adapting to change is essential to survival. The Four Noble Truths are excellent coaching for such inescapable, essential conditions.

Who said "forever"? Yet we pursue goals we think are permanent and will bring us lasting happiness, until we remember that things change. Seeking happiness in things that are, like ourselves, impermanent is like trying to put out a fire with kerosene. *Kerblam!* It's a perpetual house on fire. But when we accept the simple fact of things as they are in the wonderful present moment, when we let go and go with the flow ... *Ahh!* Suffering can go, too.

 Hear and Now

> Three Haiku by Basho
> *falling the camellia spilt rain
> held till vanishing into
> warm tears ... autumn frost
> a roadside hibiscus ...
> my horse ate it*

Neither Mine nor Thine: Selflessness

To review, as the web of karma is relational and interconnected, so life is in continual flux (flow). To try to grasp onto and freeze the flowing results is dukkha. Okay, so now we come to the kicker, in a way. Just as an ice cube (whatever we grasp onto) is really part of a vast cosmic process called water (rain one moment, lemonade the next), so are we. Our real address is ultimately temporary—and relational; relative; moment-to-moment. Certainly, ownership is dubious (mail me the ice cube, or equally absurd, mail me the self that owns it). Within the unimpeded interpenetration of all things, self of any kind (yours, mine, or its) is like a reflection in a web of jewels, infinitely reflecting sets of their interreflections—without any self-nature or own being. Period. (To say "I" don't "have" a "self" is an embossed invitation to metaphysical word games, horse feathers; instead, the point is to see into the nature of human suffering, and its liberation.)

Consider, again, the life of the Buddha. His enlightenment began when he left the fortress walls of a palace called self-indulgence and self-absorption. Then, seeing his self-denial was just another attachment to self, he discovered the Middle Way. And this differed from the spirituality of his day. He'd already tried freeing "inner self" from "the bondage of the flesh" and reuniting it with "the OverSelf." But he discovered, hey, the body isn't necessarily the slave-driver. The real culprit is building a fortress around an illusion, and is called self. Freed from that illusion, it then didn't matter whether you sought to recognize godhood within a more superconscious state. The path is to be free of self, and then see.

Hear and Now

"The more a human being feels himself a self, tries to intensify this self and reach a never attainable perfection, the more drastically he steps out of the center of being, which is no longer now his own center, and the further he removes himself from it."
—Eugen Herrigel

"Selflessness is not a case of something that existed in the past becoming nonexistent. Rather this sort of 'self' is something that never did exist. What is needed is to identify as nonexistent something that always was nonexistent."
—The Dalai Lama

Selflessness is further cause for celebration. It may just take some getting used to. Self is merely a point of view, one out of innumerable. It is interdependent on everything else, which is nonself, or selflessness, and it is ultimately as blank as wide-open space. Here's where the Buddha sheers off from his Indic brethren, who said there's an eternal soul or *atman* (self) who's one with *Brahma* (God). Buddha rejected any eternal "me"-ness (*an-atman*, "nonself"). There's neither a higher personal identity nor Ultimate Identity. Rather there's only this present moment, in which what we call self is really a passing trick of the light, one instant within a multidimensional kaleidoscope, a unique combination of elements (matter, sensations, perceptions, mental habits, and cognizance—collectively called *skandhas*, or "the five heaps," a good name for a rock band). It's a radical departure from not only the Brahmanic but also any viewpoint based on monotheism (the classic two-fer—one God, one eternal soul per lifetime). Yet no self of its own is one of the essential stamps of existence, along with impermanence and interconnectedness, dukkha and its release (nirvana).

Reviewing the Four Noble Truths, we can see this notion of a permanent and locatable self as grist for the mill of needless suffering. Think, for instance, of all the times when we eat past when we're satisfied, leaving the table a bit full, or even bloated. When I bite into a pizza, my (ignorant, deluded, conditioned) tendency is to say (all-in-one-instant), "*Yum!* This makes me happy! And I crave happiness! So as long as I eat pizza, I'm happy!" In other words, Mr. Pizza Fancier is a (false) separate self, set up by craving (in turn, set up by ignorance), creating a karma that—if it keeps pushing at the wheel of samsara—can result in eating disorders, further sorrow, consolation in the form of more pizza, and so on. So instead, pay attention. Appreciate the moment-to-moment pizza of life, slice by slice. Slowly, slowly, bite by bite.

This links back to an idea only touched upon earlier: *no karma*, in distinction from good karma and bad karma. Bad karma, of course, is to be avoided. But good karma can likewise be a trap. Just think of all the times we or someone else we've known has played Do-Gooder only to pat self on the back. Indeed, playing the proud role of Do-Gooder can become a starched uniform, or a suit of armor, certainly an over-rigid identity. By lifting just one grain of dust here, who knows what ramifications I cause elsewhere; so by trying to save the world, all the time I may only be making matters worse. No-karma means getting with the program, the Eightfold Path grounded in the immediate, elusive, interconnected, incomparable moment; it's hitting the nail on the head, *Blam!*, without any thought of nail, hammer, carpenter, or craft. The action is done without creating any further karma, and no self is attached to be reborn in the next go-round. Nirvana, essential mark of all existence, is freedom from vicious cycles, or labels (selves) of any kind.

"Everything changes; everything's connected; pay attention." Recently, Jane Hirshfield has been suggesting that seven words might be too many, and the last two words are enough—if you pay attention, all the rest follows. I agree. To really pay attention, then, is to notice how the one who's paying attention is likewise interconnected with all things, with everything else, and is always changing, all within karma's vast inter-woven web. It's an awesome recognition, and it inspires compassion. Impermanence certainly does, too. So, by definition, selflessness and compassion are practically identical.

Hear and Now

"What is this story that many of us tell ourselves and hold on to almost all the time? It goes something like this—I'm here and you are over there, my life is separate from yours, the objects of my awareness are external to me. This story is almost instinctive. Once it arises, it is almost impossible not to grasp it as real. Attaching to it as real is the origin of our suffering. With this story we are well equipped with anxiety but not well equipped to face it, so we embark on a career of trying to avoid anxiety and blaming it on others instead."

—Reb Anderson

Compassionate wisdom shows us how clinging to and identifying with the concept of a lasting, separate self is at the root of our suffering. But don't worry. This self you're so familiar with doesn't quit its day job and vanish overnight. Buddhists still have driver's licenses. And what is this self, anyway, for which you might fear, if you think you'd lose it? (This is a question for meditation.) It's another form of interbeing, or impermanence. Selflessness is almost spatial; it is impermanence, and it is temporal. Once you were a child and could only imagine adulthood. (Where is that child now?) A beginner at Buddhist practice (like the rest of us), you're only imagining enlightenment. Better to commence by saying "I don't know, let's see" than by trying to attain what you're only imagining, which perpetuates self-illusion. (You'll find there's nothing to attain; by merely being, you're already part of the ocean, you just didn't realize it. And that ocean is nirvana, as we'll see next.)

You're IT: Nirvana *Now*

No self, no problem. *Freedom.* The third mark of all existence is *nirvana*, the peace that passeth understanding. At one with all, nirvana is the ultimate recognition that self and universe aren't separate.

This is both freedom *from* and freedom *for.* It is freedom from ignorance, fear, isolation, and suffering; and it is freedom for peace, love, compassion, and wisdom. Nirvana is true happiness; it is oneness. There's no self that has to attain this boundless ocean of freedom, called nirvana, any more than a wave has to attain wateriness. We already *are* it. It's our true home.

We're an ocean that manifests as a wave that then imagines itself as separate and permanent. (Ha ha ha! *Ker-splash!*) When life's no longer filtered through the lens of self, and the dualism of self/nonself falls away, there's no "I" that attains this enlightenment. There's unfiltered, direct awareness of what limitlessly is. There's nowhere to go, and no way to get there. You're right where you are, right now.

Hear and Now

"Nirvana is everywhere. It dwells in no particular place. It is in the mind. It can only be found in the present moment…. It is empty and void of concept. Nothing can comprise nirvana. Nirvana is beyond cause and effect. Nirvana is the highest happiness. It is absolute peace. Peace in the world depends on conditions, but peace in nirvana is unchanging …. Suffering leads the way to nirvana. When we truly understand nirvana, we become free."

—Maha Ghosananda

We've come more than a long way. From karma and interbeing, to the three seals. What else is there to say? Well, *nothing*, really …

It Is and It Isn't: Emptiness (Total Openness)

Beyond self, we can see the Middle Way in a new light. Between the palace of self, with its pageants of drama, and the forest of self-denial, on the brink of annihilation, there is a middle path. Between existence and nonexistence. Life and death.

Consider a rainbow. It's a result of environmental karma, it is completely impermanent, and its elements inter-are. With sun and no rain, no rainbow. Rain but no sun, no rainbow. But put them all together, and … *Ahh!* Or, if you happen to be a night person, there's the moon in the water. On a clear full-moon night, it's rippling, dancing, and doing somersaults in a pond, a teacup, or even a dewdrop.

Now, rainbows and the moon in a dewdrop are splendid metaphors for *sunyata* (fertile void). Empty of any durable, solid, separate existence of their own, they represent *emptiness.* Don't be put off by the lingo. Empty, in Buddhism, is shorthand for "empty of any independent, permanent, tangible existence."

Emptiness is not exactly nothing. Like impermanence, emptiness is actually a positive idea, only (1) it is *verbally* expressed in the negative, and (2) it requires explanation as to what emptiness is empty *of* (lasting, substantial, independent existence). As a realm of limitless possibility, there's all the more reason for words not to get in its way. If *no boundary* seems better than *empty*, try that. Try *boundless, blank essence, without limit, infinite oneness, openness, transparent, spacious,* or *fertile void.*

Because everything's contingent—interrelated, continuously interacting, and inter-reacting, with everything else—if just one thing had its own separate, airtight, lasting identity, 100 percent pure of any outside ingredients or conditioning, forever and ever, then nothing would ever come to be.

Just as we can say "Long live impermanence!" so, too, can we give thanks to emptiness. Impermanence allows events to keep happening. Emptiness permits being to inter-be, and create existence. The spokes of a wheel depend upon and revolve around the emptiness at the hub. A potter sculpts a bowl by centering it around emptiness. Things wouldn't exist without this fertile void. (Think of it as a cosmic cornucopia.) Right now, there's this book and everything-that-is-not-this-book. That everything-else, from the edge of this book to the furthest stretches of the universe, is the fertile void of emptiness out of which this book came and whence it eventually returns. Buddhist scholar Edward Conze once said, "Emptiness is not a theory, but a ladder that reaches out into the infinite. A ladder is not there to be discussed, but to be climbed." And, like a ladder, it is not only practical but unfolds successive stages of meaning.

Misconception 19: Buddhism's gotten a bad rap, I think, because of all its Sanskrit terminology phrased in the negative: nonpermanence, nonattachment, nonself, and so on. *Dukkha* is often misconstrued to mean that Buddhism is pessimistic and believes in eternal suffering. That's like mistaking a closed door for the wall that enables it to be. Nirvana, likewise, is actually very here-and-now, not hither-and-yon. Absence of suffering reveals fundamental goodness. So, too, emptiness isn't *nihilism* (nothing matters). If a bank error added some zeroes to your account, would that be nothing? And none of this denies individual uniqueness by one hair, as we'll see next.

Emptiness, Unique and Full: Suchness

Imagine, what might the flip side or twin of Buddhist emptiness be? Not *separate identity*, because sunyata shows how there's no such animal. *Somethingness* would be closer. What really fits emptiness like yang to its yin is *suchness* (*tathata*, Sanskrit; also translated as "is-ness" and "thus-ness"). "Like so."

 This Is _____

> Scholar Christmas Humphreys defines **tathata** (suchness), equivalent to buddha nature, as "… the ultimate and unconditioned nature of all things …. It cannot be called the One as distinct from the Many, for it is not distinct from anything. Nothing can be denied or affirmed concerning it, for these are modes of expression which exclude and thereby create opposition. It can only be understood by realizing that one can neither find it by searching nor lose it by trying to separate oneself from it. Yet it has to be found."

We've all experienced suchness. Just think of a precise moment that was … well, indescribable. "You had to be there," is all you can say. It's the way the cat jumped off the refrigerator onto the kitchen counter and got a paw stuck in the empty jam jar. Or consider a new, unopened ball of twine, fresh out of the box. Or that moment in early winter when you feel a hush and a new chill in the air and then, suddenly … raindrops. (Just *this*.)

Like a nonstop Ferris wheel, the fertile void is continually giving birth to unrepeatable interpenetrations of impermanences, each time just *this*: balls of twine, kitty-cat dances, clouds about to rain, white chickens beside a red wheelbarrow. Each is empty of separate, solo, lasting identity so each is *just so*, like the patterns of a mobile … the swirl of cream poured in a cup of coffee … the sound of wind in trees. (As it is.)

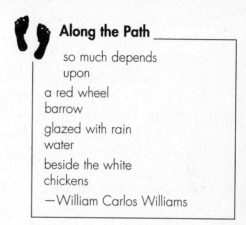

Along the Path

so much depends
upon
a red wheel
barrow
glazed with rain
water
beside the white
chickens
—William Carlos Williams

I've said emptiness and suchness dance with each other like the interplay of yin and yang. There's a Buddhist motto close to this: "*Form is emptiness; emptiness is form.*" ("Is" here could also be expressed "no different than.") Form refers to matter, also phenomena, and the way matter takes unique form, or suchness. Think of form as a *wave*, exquisite as it swells, curls, and rises to its majestic height and then spills down and merges, pebbles scuttling along beneath, and so on. Think of emptiness as the *ocean*, limitless, vital, the womb of life, with no fixed center. Waves equals ocean; ocean equals waves. Emptiness is the vast ocean of pure being and (quoting American poet Charles Reznikoff) its "ceaseless weaving of the uneven waters." Or as Einstein put it, $E = mc^2$; energy becomes matter, and matter becomes energy. Final analogy: "The clear breeze wipes away the bright moonlight. The bright moonlight wipes away the clear breeze."

No Thing: Even Emptiness Is Empty

Besides suchness, some landmarks of our experience of elusive but essential sunyata are as follows:

- Spaciousness
- Consecutiveness
- Cycles

- Illusions
- Combinations
- Relativity

> Varying approaches to the Buddha's way illuminate emptiness. Zennists drink from a handcrafted tea cup (an instance of suchness, kin to emptiness). There are ancient Tibetan bowls made of human skulls (a reminder of impermanence, kin to emptiness). Theravada compares things to empty vessels. Mahayana says there really are no vessels.

Focusing awareness on breathing and nothing else, we become aware of blank space that's neither in-breath nor out-breath. As we free ourselves from the "traffic jam of discursive thought," as Chögyam Trungpa Rinpoche puts it, thoughts continue to flicker, but we become conscious of the space in between them, the spaciousness in which they take place. And we experience things as they are: open, transparent, bright, all there ever is. Instead of living in a cubicle called self, it's like living large, on the whole block. It's a great relief, but it's not the same thing as being spaced out. Many have described sunyata as our true home, like finally coming home.

We've already seen a *cycle* in simultaneous karma. Effect can become cause; that is, a seed becomes a flower that bears new seeds, and neither has any permanent, individual essence. Examples of *combinations* are the composite pencil, the rainbow, and the moon in water. Or consider the calligraphy for "wisdom" and for "listen" in the previous chapter, or the calligraphy a little further on here: things in combination express something else that is really intangible. The ultimate meaning (sunyata) exists in between the things and in between the words.

Consecutiveness is like a movie, a compilation of short strips of film, themselves made up of consecutive frames. We think a movie's real, but is it? It is and it isn't. Breathing is consecutive, too. In between an in-breath and an out-breath, there's sunyata.

Big Misconception 32: people are mistaken who think Buddhists say "Everything is an *illusion*." Rather, everything is *like* an illusion. Our lives are empty of any permanent, tangible, separate identity, the way dreams interweave in our consciousness just before falling asleep, and just before waking up. Who am I? Who am I really? "Gary Gach" is a label. I'm not an illusion, but I don't identify with my identification cards, my Internet passwords, and my bills (ah, yes, that reminder of the relative amid the transcendental). Like a pencil or the rainbow, "Gary Gach" is a series of moments, states, events, and cycles. It is a composite, and all composite things decompose. (That's what happens to musicians when they die, you know—they decompose. *Ba-dum!*) Irish poet W. B. Yeats expressed the illusion of self (sunyata) when he sighed, "Ah, body swayed to music, ah, brightening glance, / how can we know the dancer from the dance?"

Relativity was described by the Buddha in advance of Einstein's Theory of Relativity ($E = mc^2$). But thanks to Dr. Einstein, we're accustomed to thinking in Buddha's terms. When we say, "One man's meat is another man's poison," that's relativity, also an example of sunyata. Another example is words. Words vary according to context. A nun's habit isn't the same as an alcoholic's. As Groucho Marx says, "Time flies like an arrow, fruit flies like a banana." The word *emptiness* depends on context, and so is itself empty (of any lasting, unique, single meaning), which brings us to a final aspect worth noting …

Nothing. (Or, better, *no-thing* … not anything … because the idea of nothing conjures up a vacuum, whereas no-thing is just blank like a movie screen or a blank piece of paper.) Emptiness itself is empty, meaning don't get attached to any concept of it. Even saying it's ineffable or indescribable already puts a label on it. You can't pin it down. The ultimate is uncategorizable. Even the Buddha is empty: not a concept, not a thing. It's better to remain open. Personally, I find emptiness is a reminder that I *don't know.* It's a reminder to keep watching, mindfully observing, and being energetically attentive.

So I'll say nothing more about that which can't be said, except to recount that, some time ago, when some priests and monks from Westminster Abbey were visiting a Japanese Zen temple for the first time, they paused at a large, framed piece of beautiful calligraphy of the word *no-thing* and asked what that was. Rather than explain the whole nine yards, the Zen guide just whispered, "God," and moved on.

The Chinese pictogram to the left shows a clearing, as made by a natural forest fire. To the right, the fire is burning. Together, they present no-thing (wu, Chinese; mu, Japanese).

(Calligraphy: Chungliang Al Huang)

Living It: Meditations in a Floating World

Karma, impermanence, interbeing, nonself, emptiness (openness), and suchness are five key concepts, as in keys that can open doors. If you only understand the Buddha's teachings intellectually and don't practice them, then Buddhism's just books and websites. (A carpentry manual's not a guide to living in a house.) Here are a few hints and prompts for encountering these teachings in your daily life. Like the Buddha going beyond the castle walls of defined reality, be open for signs of what you haven't seen before.

Devote a few days to noticing *karma*, yours and others'. Be aware of the consequences of your actions. Notice who seems attracted to material things; observe whether they seem truly happy. Observe this potential in yourself. When you notice anger, in yourself and others, see how it creates more anger or confusion. When you notice calm, see how it attracts more calm.

Devote a few days to noticing examples of *interbeing*. Consider how many ingredients and steps went into each thing you encounter. Enjoy intimacy with it, in a new light, the light of its interbeing with the universe, a sufficiency with which you, too, are equally engaged.

Devote a few days to noticing *impermanence*. Notice how impermanent, yet complete, just one breath is. Notice seasonal changes. Do beginnings in your life seem easier than endings? If you sense attachment or surging feelings, make a note of those, too. Consider your own impermanence.

Devote a few days to observing how you define your *self* and its boundaries. Set aside some quiet time to look at your hand. As you look, try to remember how your hand looked when you were little. Then see if you can see your parents' hands within the patterns of your hand … the shape of the pads of your fingers, the fingerprints, the pattern of pores on the back of your hand. When you're done, put your two palms together and notice your breath. See if you feel compassion for your parents, and for you.

Devote a few days to noticing examples of *sunyata* and *suchness*. Take a blank piece of paper. Pin it up where you can look at it for a few days. Notice its texture, color, how it catches light and casts a shadow (its suchness), and how you could write anything on it (its sunyata). Also see in it the tree it came from, and the rain and cloud that nourished it (its interbeing). Feel the interrelations of these views so they're real for you, rather than philosophical concepts.

Just as we need a mirror to see our face, so can we use the heavens to see our mind. Weather permitting, go out and look up at a clear sky from a comfortable position as high up as can be. Notice variations in light and color, and how far the sky extends. Imagine to yourself, "I am this." Let your mind slowly grow as blank, bright, and vast as the sky you're looking into. If thoughts come, think of them as passing birds, and let them pass uninterrupted. When you're ready to end the meditation, notice how the sky seems both endless and without any particular location anywhere. Then stay with the presence of "big sky mind" for a few minutes and let your "busy daily routine mind" find its way back on its own. Notice if it's clearer … calmer.

Devote a few days to considering *no-thing*. Notice how automatically you label and categorize things. Look at things as if you've never seen them before. Practice admitting "I don't know" to yourself and others.

Think of song lyrics that illustrate any of these concepts, for example: "I Got Plenty of Nothing" (nothing's plenty for me) by the Gershwin brothers and DuBoce Hayward, or "Tomorrow Never Knows" by The Beatles; songs of suchness, like "The Way You Look Tonight," "My Favorite Things," and "Love Is a Many Splendored Thing;" and romantic farewell songs about impermanence. Make up lyrics of your own.

Devote a few days to just thinking about the Buddha and all he taught. Consider your mind as part of Buddha's mind. All human beings are related, with common ancestors; concentrate on him as your relative. Thinking of his name, consider that you're invoking his presence in your life. See if this makes you feel happier, and your surroundings seem more pleasant. (Nirvana now!)

Set aside a space in your thoughts for mental notes or observations. Check into it from time to time. See what works well, and what doesn't.

And remember: compassionate wisdom is a third of the Path, along with meditation and virtuous action (conscious conduct, as we'll see next), spokes of the Wheel moving as one. All can be life-changing—and lifelong. So enjoy!

The Least You Need to Know

- Karma doesn't mean predestination. We control our words, deeds, thoughts, and feelings, which cause reciprocal effects. Effects likewise become causes.

- All things are interdependent, interacting, inter-reacting, and interpenetrating. This can be summed up as interbeing.

- Things change. Impermanence seems a primary cause of sorrow, but without it life wouldn't be possible and so it's really a cause for happiness.

- Sunyata (void) means emptiness of any permanent, tangible, separate self. Nonrecognition of this fact perpetuates suffering but, like impermanence, it's positive, enabling things to come into being, each thing just so (suchness). It points to the boundless, open, transparent nature of all things, including the self.

- We have no permanent, solid, separate identity. Self is as much a product of transient, contingent conditions as a rainbow.

- Nirvana is the nature of What Is. We don't need to attain it. We are it. It is the liberation from needless suffering the Buddha taught. (Thank you, Buddha.)

Conscious Conduct: Precepts for a Path with a Heart

In This Chapter

- Reverence for life
- Trustworthiness and generosity
- Sexual respect
- Loving speech and deep listening
- Mindful consumption
- Defining guidelines

The previous chapter touched on wisdom; coming up, meditation. No less important, here's the third of the Eightfold Path known as ethics, virtue: conscious conduct. Trainings for Buddhas-In-Progress. Having sensed the selfless, loving Way of the Buddha, wouldn't you want guidelines for happily living that way in the world?

Well, early on, Buddhists laid down an ethical framework of guidelines based on their own experiences, for daily, active cultivation, called *precepts*. These teachings all boil down to but one, the Golden Rule. These precepts are cast from that same universal gold. Yet, while the basic principles underlying them resonate with the Perennial Philosophy, you might notice different emphases you could apply to your own root tradition, your own working guideline of do's and don'ts. Learn them. Practice them. Meditate on their dynamic impact. And see for yourself. The precepts reveal how deeply interwoven we are with our environment. They each lead to enlightenment, to enlightened ways of living. They pave the path with a heart.

To Not Kill: Reverence for Life

Not killing applies not only to human beings but all beings. Such deep regard for life in all its myriad forms is evident in the folk literature of ancient India, illustrating aspects of Buddhist ethics, known as the Jataka tales, featuring talking animals (and, oh yes, humans, too); you may have already heard those retold by Aesop. When we widen our horizons to embrace all creation, not-killing expresses positive affirmation: what Albert Schweitzer, as a missionary physician stationed in Africa, termed "reverence for life." In a word, compassion.

This Is _____

Central to spirituality in India is the concept of **ahimsa** (Sanskrit, meaning "to do no harm," non-violence). Jain monks filter water so as not to consume microbes. Mohandas Gandhi applied ahimsa to the political sphere, with the nonviolence of **satyagraha** (truth-force).

Look: a lion with lamb, leopard and cow, living together! This is the first of many paintings by Quaker minister Edward Hicks. It depicts the peaceable kingdom prophesied by Isaiah (11:6–9), and can be seen on certain hot days when otherwise antagonistic species share shade together.

(Edward Hicks, American [1780–1849], The Peaceable Kingdom. *Oil on canvas, 47.6 cm × 59.7 cm. The Cleveland Museum of Art, 2001, Gift of the Hanna Fund, 1945.)*

Every "Shalt-Not" Has Its "Shall": What "It" Is, Is Up to You

The precepts offer both negative and positive response to the human condition. Do's and don'ts. One reason they're phrased restrictively recognizes that humanity is prone to and already has a head start on bad habits. We're so invested in habit that we might be amazed to see how noticing and refraining from negative habits can free up incredible energy. No less remarkable is our natural potential for real good, naturally manifesting in our behavior. So precepts may sound at first like restrictions, but actually they promote freedom. True happiness, beyond variable pleasures. And the benefits go beyond the personal. If I refrain from harmful behavior, everyone will be much happier, myself included.

While every "Shalt Not" has its "Shall," there aren't any preprinted road maps. Each is up to you to determine. To do so, you'll accentuate the positive and eliminate the negative, like the song says, and also latch on to the Middle Way. Find your own balance between extremes.

At the Grill: Are All Buddhists Vegetarians?

It's up to you. If you eat mindfully, attentively, communing with a beet or carrot, for example, it can tell you what it means to live deep inside the fragrant, dark earth, growing so moist, compact, and sweet. And that it had no mother or father who'll miss it if you eat it.

Carnivores who might cringe at this reminder have the option of choosing the healthiest meat, allowed to range around and feed freely instead of being cramped up in a pen, pumped full of chemicals in a factory farm. Killed compassionately, instead of being chained on an assembly-line kill floor, sensing its fate, adrenaline of fright flooding its bloodstream, which you'd in turn consume. By now, you've probably guessed my own personal dietary preferences. But the precepts aren't exactly set in stone. You'll meet Buddhist vegetarians and carnivores. Buddhists were vegetarian in Japan, as in China and Korea, until the nineteenth century when the Meiji Emperor (1852–1912) tried to eradicate Buddhism, and made monks eat meat. Thus many Japanese monks today still eat meat. In Tibet, the climate simply precludes year-round agriculture. Tibetan Buddhists began to reconsider their diet when they came to India, predominantly vegetarian. Many stuck to meat, since an animal wasn't slaughtered expressly for them. But in America, there were cases where students switched from tofu to lamb to please a Tibetan Buddhist teacher. So you see here how the precepts are not edicts, from on high. See for yourself. The Middle Way always applies: don't go to extremes.

To Mourn the Unborn

Sooner or later, abortion comes up in any extensive discussion of the first precept. Dharma can compassionately see the suffering either way. And stillbirth is still birth. Japanese Buddhists have evolved a unique practice, which can alleviate grief. Many temples conduct a special funeral service *(mizuko kuyo)* for an aborted or stillborn fetus (in Japanese "water baby"). Zen teacher Robert Aitken notes, "It's given a posthumous Buddhist name, and thus identified as an individual, however incomplete, to whom we can say fare-well. With this ceremony, the woman is in touch with life and death as they pass through her existence, and she finds that such basic changes are relative waves on the great ocean of true nature which is not born and does not pass away."

Jizo is the Japanese Buddhist patron saint of children and travelers. These stone Jizo images in Chichibu, Japan, are accompanied by umbrellas, shawls, and toys to express compassion for deceased children and the unborn, as well as prayers for their well-being in the world beyond.

(Photo: William R. LaFleur, from Liquid Life: Abortion and Buddhism in Japan (Princeton University Press, 1992)

To Not Steal: Trustworthiness and Generosity

The second precept trains us to be aware of our relation to literal "stuff." Living in the material world. You can easily see that to live monastically, communally, life together would get quite messed up rather quickly if someone stole stuff from the common pot. Out in the secular world, if someone were to entrust you with a big suitcase full of cash, would you be tempted? What do you think you lack? More generally, where do you hold back, and where do you yield? So you see you don't have to be a thief to consider this precept's relevance in your own life. (As for that suitcase, it's not only about being trusted by others, but also learning to trust our own wonderful potential, life's natural abundance.)

Becoming a buddha (and remembering how much so you already are) is like perfecting an art. It's a practice, a perfecting of the compassionate wisdom of selflessness. Consider charity. The Buddha said, "If you knew what I know about the power of generosity, you would not let a single meal go by without sharing it." This is not about just the act of giving, but also the cultivation of generosity. Training mind and heart. In giving, we let go. Over time, we learn unconditional generosity, in which there's no separation between giver and taker; only gift. (Is that why some say the present moment is a present?) In such experience of Dharma, we too give thanks as we are thanked. If nothing else, in giving we can give thanks for the opportunity to practice compassion.

This is not to belittle donations and such, but how often do people offer charity out of a sense of superiority, inflating a sense of pride, reinforcing a tenacious but illusory sense of enduring separate selfhood. To give, we must first stop, in and of itself a requisite of meditation, *samadhi*. We renounce our assumption of having no time for some mere ragamuffin on the street. Stopping, we realize our sense of one-track purpose may blind us to everything else along the way. Practicing generosity can loosen up and expand a thin and tight, rigid and brittle sense of ourself, giving our mind and heart a larger space in which to function fully. Opening our boundaries gives our heart a nice compassion workout. Being stingy to others, we short-change ourselves as well. When we say we have no time, we don't realize that time is all we have, really. Our spare time, if not change, may be just what a houseless person is really asking for. Being generous to others, we notice how generous they are to us, in return. The delusion of dualism might be summed up as mine versus thine. Because I have this apple, you don't. Very simple.

But what if you do happen to have an apple right now? What then? Well, there must be other people who don't have the apple that you and I do—the whole world, in fact. So, like I say, if you have an apple, I don't. Suddenly, world hunger stares us straight in the face. We have apples; they don't. The problem is blunt: the poor don't have enough—and the rich have more than enough. It's interesting how money and property make the interconnectedness of all things more vivid to our imagination. Given this awareness, the challenge is to live simply, consuming less needless stuff, cherishing what one already has, and being generous.

I know, all this might imply that everyone should immediately donate all their stuff to the poor. Might even be true. But if everyone did that, the poor would have things that everyone else would no longer have, and the cycle of poverty wouldn't be broken. That would violate the Middle Way of harmony and balance. So we learn to not take more than we need, and not to take what's not ours, and to share what we have with those who don't, without going in want ourselves.

This logo commonly means "recycling station" or "recycled product." The arrows represent the Three R's: Recycle, Re-use, and Reduce waste. The concept was first introduced to America by kids. As you can see, it introduces us, as well, to interconnectedness and cultivation of practice in daily life. Take karma, make Dharma.

Sexual Respect: Intimacy and Responsibility

We'll start with the Shalt Not. Without naming names, every religious order has proven vulnerable sooner or later to sexual misconduct. But is it any surprise?—given the power of priesthood, the trust in taking refuge, the intimacy of living body-spirit-mind as one, and the joyful friendliness of spiritual community. This doesn't make it any less unconscionable. Behind any lurid details, of scandal or cover-up, a seemingly simple act of nature can take generations for the deep wounds it inflicts throughout the community to heal.

Pardon my French, but in common parlance the Thou Shalt Not here means to not screw around. That is, don't mess with the sexual surge that shaped us, and surges and quivers within us still. It's as elemental a force as the intertwining of yin and yang. Daily, we interact with subtle energy fields which are sexual, although we don't usually call them such. This precept, then, acknowledges the fundamental yin-yang dance of male and female energies and calls us to be mindfully aware, to let that energy flow skillfully.

Love is not a drug, not a toy. Our forefathers' veil of secrecy and hypocrisy about sex has been discarded, yet society can swing to the other extreme, to obsession, glorification, and sensationalism. The advertisers' motto is "Sex sells"—from face cream to cars. Since advertisers aren't known for hiring models that look like my Aunt Ida in Jersey, some American women have tried to starve themselves silly to emulate shadow-thin models. And when a husband and wife look at each other in bed and don't see glorified fantasy models, how often do they roll over and lick their wounds of suffering self—and go out the next day and invest in something unessential, or harmful, out of disappointment, dukkha. Conversely, one can seem to have a great sex life and still be unhappy.

Hear and Now

"… our social conception has managed to supply shelters of every sort, for, as it was disposed to take love-life as a pleasure, it had also to give it an easy form, cheap, safe and sure, as public pleasures are …. For one human being to love another: that's perhaps the most difficult of all our tasks, the ultimate, the last test and proof, the work for which all other work is but preparation."

—Rainer Maria Rilke

Respecting life, all life forms, we live within the heart of creation, enjoying a greater intimacy with life. Respect sees Self and Other as no different. From respect comes true intimacy, with ourselves, and with life itself, as well as each other.

To Not Lie: Deep Listening and Loving Speech

The Ten Commandments address lying, in terms of bearing false witness. The Talmud (Hebrew books of biblical commentary) says no one should talk one way with his or her lips and think another way in his or her heart. This is so universal it hardly sounds any different in, say, Taoism: "Do not assert with your mouth what your heart denies."

To lie is to automatically be dishonest about everything—to be indifferent to the truth. The Buddha is very clear about this. He says, "A person is born with an axe in his mouth. He whose speech is unwholesome cuts himself with an axe." (Talk about having a sharp tongue!)

As we've noted, speech is one spoke of the wheel of the Way. Now we can explore it further. Consider, for example, how the Buddha says the blade of unwholesome speech wounds ourselves. There's a profound truth here, if difficult at times to face. What we say of others, is true of ourselves (how else could we have noticed it?). To cease criticizing others (and ourselves) is to discover how much energy we free up, because we invest an amazingly large amount of time in picking apart and putting down. The reverse is true, too. When we say "love" in all sincerity, we actually bring love into the world.

True, Buddhism knows the inability of mere words to describe the truth we are. Yet, from a nondual approach we can find our Middle Way within silence and speech.

Leaves from the Bodhi Tree

Once four intimate friends promised one another to observe seven days of silence in quiet meditation. On the first day all were silent, and the meditation went according to schedule. But when night came, the oil-lamp they were using ran out of oil and started to flicker. A servant was dozing off nearby. One of them could not help but say to the servant: "Fix the lamp." The second friend was horrified to hear the first one speaking. "Hush," he said, "We are not supposed to say a word, remember?" "Both of you are very stupid. Why did you talk?" said the third. Very softly, the fourth muttered, "I was the only one who didn't say anything."

—Venerable K. Sri Dhammananda

To Not Bear False Witness, Simply Bear Witness

Speaking implies listening. Deep listening hears what's unsaid, as well as what's said. To do so means leaving behind preconceptions or expectations. Listening without judgment. Inhabiting silence, as it were.

To be unconditionally present to the present moment is simply to witness it. Right now, I pause. I listen to my breathing. I *bear witness* to the freshness of the foggy morning breeze in my nostrils. The flowerlike quality of the moment at hand, in my heart and in the back garden. I bear witness to how the misty morning fog makes the garden's flowers and vegetation, the stone fence and the buildings look more vivid. I bear witness to unseen birds in a tree, outside my window, their song mimicking the morning's mood and my own. To bear witness means to show by your existence that something is true.

This Is

"When you go to **bear witness,** it means that you go with no preconceived notions about what you'll see and what will happen .... Bearing witness means to have a relationship .... Out of bearing witness, out of that relationship, a healing arises. In what form, through what activity or event, through what person, I have no idea."

—Bernie Glassman

I'm sure you've felt when someone "sucked the air out of the room." It's as if they were obsessively committed to speaking without listening, setting up an almost physically palpable energy imbalance. You feel a kind of relief or release when they're gone. And how often have you heard two people talking as if playing verbal tennis, talking *at* each other? It's as if their ears were in their mouth, not their heart.

I once participated in a liberating workshop in which Zen teacher Joan Halifax introduced an exercise in bearing witness that provided a welcome alternative. We broke up into twos and sat facing each other. My job was to make myself as transparent as I possibly could, dropping all my masks and just manifesting my deepest, truest nature to my partner. As I did so, my partner did the same for me. In silence, looking into each other's open face, we gave our undivided attention to the buddha nature we sensed. Then we each took turns telling the other what we experienced, with the same awareness. Then we took turns telling the group, and listening to everyone else. There grew a common feeling of compassion and mutuality.

Loving Speech

The compassionate wisdom of the Path, of Right Thought, tells us thought gives rise to speech, speech gives rise to action, and action creates habits which form our personality. Case in point: I was once honored to be guest of an enlightened local talk show host who once told me, during our interview, how he gave up a national daily program because one day he came to work and just could no longer calmly read the daily news items about rifle murders or suicides as if he were a numb blank. A great guy, with a good heart, a real pleasure to be with, with devoted listeners.

Speech and listening form a common karma. See for yourself. Pay attention to how the very words we use imply certain values and color our outlook. Right View.

In my own profession, I substitute "due date" or "tight time frame" instead of "deadline." (During the Civil War, at the jail at Andersonville, a borderline was formed of prisoners who'd tried to run away and were shot.) Nor do I wish for my writing to "knock 'em dead." (I'd prefer my readers might just levitate an inch or two off the ground now and then.) Another speech toxin my profession's prone to is gossip: who's up, who's down, who fired who. Maybe you've indulged in it, too. Gossip's a common red flag indicating that loving speech is absent. My dictionary defines gossip as trivial rumor. Even positive gossip can be secondhand information, and about someone not here and now in the room. (Be here nowness), as are all the precepts.

A survey found, alas, working couples spend four minutes a day talking to each other with concentrated attention; a typical parent and child engage in meaningful conversation for only 20 minutes a week. (What if they looked at it as an opportunity to practice mutually beneficial meditation?) You don't have to be in a relationship to be aware of loving speech, as words are daily reminders of our interrelation with all things. Poet and Zen teacher Norman Fischer points out how in words we reach out toward the Unnamed, the limitless: so, when we pay attention, prayer is just what comes out of our mouths. Loving speech can be a prayerful meditation. Listening to … and saying … each … word … with … love.

Mindful Consumption: A Diet for Transformation

In a traditional sense, this precept means no alcohol. Period. Alcohol not only inter-feres with personal practice, it can also threaten the community. Releasing inhibitions while clouding the mind could lead a practitioner to break the other precepts—killing, rape, and so on.

What does the Middle Way say here? Recognition that abstinence forgoes pleasures on the one hand, but harmful possibilities, on the other. There's awareness too of karmic implications. If I drink only a drop at dinner, I may still be a role model for someone, who might not be able to stop at just a drop, or is unable to "hold their liquor." It's like the opposite of the minimal amount of food the Buddha first ate following his asceticism. Here just a few drops may not nourish but rather destroy. Turning "not drinking" into a positive formulation, sobriety is another word for awareness. Awakening. Let's explore where the Eightfold Path meets the Twelve-Step Program, then further open the precept out.

The Eightfold Path Meets the Twelve-Step Program

Ask anyone who knows an alcoholic or drug addict. They'll tell you. It's a symptom only, of something deeper, underlying. What, they may not know yet. The root in Buddhist terms is the poison of craving, here manifest graphically, as addiction; the personification of a separate, enduring self blindly identifying with one's craving. Addiction is, by definition, self-perpetuating; from a Buddhist view, it perpetuates an illusory self, regardless of the consequences (further suffering) of such illusion (liter-ally drunken delusion). Understanding the nature of suffering, its root, its arising, we see the way out.

Of course, this is a culture so rife with toxins and addictions, we're all addicted in one way or another. Money. Prestige. Self-image. Ideology. Food binges. Shopping sprees. Noise (music). One can divide any roomful of people in half: those in denial ("denial is more than a river in Egypt"), and those in recovery. So we're all in the Recovery Movement, in some way. But I'm also aware how much more gripping and deeply dangerous actual physical addiction to alcohol or drugs can be, which hijacks metabo-lism along with mind-set and morality.

Buddhism alone isn't a one-stop panacea, yet can be a potent boon, a healing ally. Like the Twelve Steps, Buddhism asks for personal responsibility, paying attention, taking one's own life as teaching. Buddhist practice gives positive feedback and sup-portive mindfulness and compassion. The idea of samsara furnishes a skillful model of vicious cycles, and the Four Noble Truths nourish the empowerment to break free, without playing the Blame Game of shame or guilt. For those with issues around God, the Third Noble Truth's awakening of faith can correspond to the eleventh step of Alcoholics Anonymous, a Power Greater Than Self (consonant too with Other-power in Pure Land).

Tip: Just as the recovery movement is steering away from the phrase "self-help," neither should Buddhism be considered a safe, quick-fix, self-help, per se (show me the self that's in need of help: where is it?!). To consider Dharma as a therapeutic system risks minimizing or fetishizing its essence. Then even Buddhism can become an addiction.

Medication or Meditation?

In San Francisco, back in the mid-1960s, invariably somebody high on LSD from the Haight-Ashbury neighborhood would think they'd attained *satori*, Zen enlightenment, and so would trek down to the newly opened Zen monastery nearby, bang on the door, and try to engage in some verbal Dharma dueling, for which Zen is famous. ("What is the sound of one hand clapping?") Yet numerous folks have earnestly embarked on the Buddhist path following chemical experimentation, now ready to discipline themselves to access their minds without psychedelics. (*Psychedelic* means "mind manifesting.")

Are drugs helpful or harmful to the Way? Some say intoxicants means toxic substances only. In the Buddha's time, people knew of camels but never smoked them; there's nothing in the precepts about tobacco. But we know tobacco is toxic. So smoking would fit into the Fifth Precept defined as "no intoxicants." But remember skillful means: if a raft takes you to the other shore (nirvana), you don't carry the raft with you once you get there. As Alan Watts put it, in this context: "Once you get the message, you hang up the phone." Similarly, someone may attend a weekend retreat and come back with a new hair-do, a new name, saying they're a totally new person. (An altered state may not result in an altered trait.) Transformation is a personal process, not a product like a pill. It's spontaneous, not at-will. It takes discipline ("trainings") to be an integral part of daily life. And one doesn't come down from Supreme True Enlightenment, which is continuous.

Media Consumption

Buddhists say we ingest media, and they too become part of our make-up. Cynicism and violence plant seeds that can harm ourselves and our environment.

I confess, I'm an accredited member of the media, whose Golden Rule is "The one who owns the gold, rules." The bottom line. Unfortunately, they've found the lowest common denominator spikes circulation. And so a common motto dominating mainstream print and broadcast media (besides "Sex Sells") is: "If it bleeds, it leads," (leads, as the Number-One Story). Now we're stuck with this Frankenstein monster of media on steroids. (CRASH! Boom!! Splat!)

The mainstream media seldom reports the good news, the three million unreported inspiring stories happening each day.

And it's interesting to recognize how it's programmed. Have you ever noticed how TV's seem to talk to you? ("Don't touch that dial! We'll be right back!") It's highly manipulative. Anyone media-savvy knows how in a dramatic thriller, a scene of kids playing is often a set-up for an act of senseless violence to follow. When HH the Dalai Lama was in America once, he'd been in a room where a television was on. Glancing over at the screen, he'd see a pretty image, like children dancing in a field of flowers. He'd looked away, but when he looked back just a moment later, there was a terrible image, such as a man threatening a woman with a chainsaw. Positive image, then negative image, he discovered, and so it went, on into the night. He concluded that watching TV must make Americans really exhausted!

Of course, we don't notice how we're being manipulated—that's part of the agreement. We develop antibodies and/or grow desensitized. And it's addicting (author Marie Winn calls TV "the plug-in drug"). But consider this: by the time an average American is 18 years old, they'll have seen 16,000 simulated murders, plus 200,000 other acts of violence. (Ever have to remind your kids, or yourself, "It's only a movie!"?) I'm not proposing a ban or crusade. We ourselves hold the switch. Food for thought, in this precept as in all these mind trainings, for a good heart.

Practicing the Precepts

We've explored how extensive, personal, and interrelated each precept is. Now we'll consider how to put them into practice. As Venerable Master Hsing Yun points out, we might consider three aspects to practicing the precepts: *form, practice,* and *spirit.* Form means grasping the idea. But once you understand the words, you must put them into practice yourself. Then you'll see the inner spirit of the precepts, and can internalize them for yourself, and see how they're integral to meditation and wisdom.

Step by step. You might take refuge only in those precepts with which you're comfortable. This is in accord with the Buddhist tenet of weighing everything against your own life experience. Listen within. Use your intuition. And, as mentioned, to touch just one precept deeply is to touch the others. Lying (denial) can lead to addiction, such as addiction to sexuality, which can lead to violence, and violence to greed, greed to disrespect for life, and all of this to unhappiness. Reverence for life leads to generosity and consideration for others, which makes for happy relations, and peace.

To practice all the precepts might seem to require monasticism. Yet you can follow them and still carry on with regular, rent-paying everyday life. That seeming impossibility, however, is important to note. It's an aspect of another Buddhist tenet that asks us to consider the seemingly impossible … a snowball of purity in a blazing furnace … the sound of one hand … what the One returns to. (If that seems "illogical" it's only to our dualistic mind-set.) Such is a Zen approach.

Zen recognizes three levels to the precepts. The first level is *straightforward:* Don't do harmful things, such as killing. The second level asks us to recognize that we're killing *all the time* (crushing microbes, blowing out flames, eating vegetables, and so on). Being aware of this keeps us from being too *self*-righteous. The third level asks us to recognize the *impossibility of killing.* Matter is never created nor destroyed. Destroy something here, and it pops up in another form elsewhere. This threefold approach applies for all the precepts.

Precepts: A Mindfulness Meditation

In my own experience, the precepts reinforce my mindfulness, and my mindfulness illuminates my understanding of the precepts. A beautiful coexistence. Your ordinary mind is buddha mind, as you discover when you do one thing at a time, mindfully. This takes discipline, and inspires it. The precepts cultivate conditions to further that goal. It's not an imposition from the outside but rather a means of realizing that no one owns your mind but you, an opportunity of learning how to live that freedom well.

Building upon an insight meditation exercise taught by author and Vipassana teacher Jack Kornfield, I'd like relay (in my own words) his wonderful invitation for you to make this Precept Mindfulness Month. (Actually, a five-week month.) For one week, just notice the influence of the first precept in your life. Vow to bring *no harm* to any living creature through word, deed, or thought. Yourself included. Notice all the living beings in your world you might normally ignore. Weeds poking up through pavement. Bugs. Birds. Cultivate a sense of care and reverence for them. Houseplants are buddhas, too. Stones, too.

Next week, observe the *material things* in your daily life, including money. How do you handle objects that cross your path—yours and others? Do you recycle? Do you waste water in the shower? Are you energy efficient? Are you tempted by what's not yours? And you might practice random acts of spontaneous kindness. Act on your friendly, benevolent impulses. At the end of the week, measure your wealth in non-material terms. How many sunsets or dawns did you watch? How many times did you play with kids? Did you smile enough?

During Week Three, notice how often *sex* arises in your consciousness. Each time, ask yourself what it's associated with. Power? Loneliness? Compassion? Stress? Self-esteem? Pressure? Pleasure? Nature? You might be surprised. You can extend this into an additional week of observing your sensuality, sensing your senses, and seeing what pulls you in. Yet another week could be devoted to relationships. Do you view others as objects? Where do you withhold, where do you yield? Where do you respond as an equal?

Hear and Now

"At first, precepts are a practice. Then they become a necessity, and finally they become a joy. When our heart is awakened, they spontaneously illuminate our way in the world. This is called Shining Virtue. The light around someone who speaks truth, who consistently acts with compassion for all, even in great difficulty, is visible to all around them. Better than perfume, its fragrance rises to the gods."
—Jack Kornfield

Next, devote a week to *deep listening* and *loving speech*. Listening, see if you can completely give yourself over, without preconception or judgment. Listen with an open mind, an open heart. Are you … trying to show what a good listener you are … or rehearsing what you'll say? Speaking, listen to yourself. Do you see and mean each word? Try envisioning every noun, verb, and adjective in your mind's eye. Note how often you make frivolous, cynical, and negative comments. And how often do you speak of things about which you really don't know firsthand?

Last, spend one week observing what you *consume*. Does what you consume preserve peace, well-being, and joy? When you have an urge for a little dose of poison, see what motivates your impulse. Notice your addictions (compulsive habits) and observe what beliefs they satisfy. Habits are of course habit-forming, so note those you'd like to foster and those you'd like to leave behind.

Owning the Precepts, as Your Own

The heart-mind trainings of the precepts have preserved the continuity and vitality of the Sangha over millennia. Indeed, formal initiation (ordination) into many Buddhist sanghas occurs with transmission of the precepts; along with the Three Jewels, you can take refuge in them. Some monastics observe 254 precepts; some schools have 58; others, 16. These are different ways to cut up the ethical pie. As mentioned, just practicing one deeply will ultimately lead you to all the others.

Some sanghas and people adapt and personalize the precepts. This doesn't mean you make up your own. Don't act like your own defense attorney. Rather, hear them deeply, within yourself, as your own inclinations worthy of bringing out through mindful conduct. Thich Nhat Hanh's extended sangha, the Community of Mindful Living, for example, uses a traditional Buddhist phrase for the precepts—"mindfulness trainings"—since "precepts" can sound daunting and judgmental. Not moral absolutes—they're guidelines for conscious conduct. They're each an opportunity for contacting positive impulses and qualities already within ourselves, rather burdensome obligations. They reflect our own innate capacities for keeping our appointment with life. Blueprints for real happiness. Enjoy! The Path is right at your very feet ....

The Least You Need to Know

- In tandem with meditation and wisdom, the precepts are an essential part of the Way of the Buddha. Precepts are ethical guidelines for conscious conduct along the Path. Not absolute, they aren't restrictions but rather a structure for living in harmony and peace, equanimity and joy.

- To not harm implies reverence for life, all forms of life. To not steal implies generosity and trustworthiness. To not lie implies deep listening and loving speech.

- Sexual restraint implies respect, intimacy, trust, and responsibility in human relationships.

- Abstinence from alcohol implies sobriety as well as freedom from addictions, and mindful consumption, both physical and mental.

- The precepts relate to your own experience. Listen to how they resonate within your life.

- Choose precepts with which you feel comfortable. Practicing just one precept fully will eventually lead to all the others.

Part 3

Sangha: Joining the Path

Here, we put Dharma, the Buddha Way, into practice. The proof is in the pudding. Fortunately, it's not like trying to learn to swim by diving into the middle of the ocean. The community of practice, *Sangha*, will always keep your boat afloat. Here, you're always in the company of best friends.

Plain and simple, we'll review the nuts and bolts of Buddhist meditation, and then spotlight four major schools of practice. But, really, it's all One Dharma. So please don't sweat any –isms that might crop up along the way. It's how *you* practice that's the important -ism. (Feel free to consider this book a guide to youism ….)

Chapter 9

Stepping into Freedom: Establishing a Practice

In This Chapter

◆ Establishing a practice: the path is the goal

◆ Taking time and making space

◆ Stocking up on a bit of gear (skillful means)

◆ Practicing together

◆ Maintenance tips

"In theory, there's no difference between theory and practice. In practice, there is." Most of what's been covered thus far may make perfect sense to you, headwise and heartwise. If so, the only missing ingredient is to make it real for yourself, like driving a car out of a showroom. In a word, it's all about how you put the teachings into *practice*—seeing, understanding, and actualizing the Dharma (the way things really are) in your daily life. Wisdom and ethics are practice; here, we'll hone in on the practice of meditation. This chapter and the next are about cultivating an everyday Buddhist meditation practice. (Repeat every day, until it's second nature.) Before the recipe steps (next chapter), here are essential ingredients, material and otherwise.

How's Your Practice?: The Path Is the Goal

Start with your viewpoint. Why practice? Well, our minds are a bit limited, as are words, so we naturally want firsthand experience of concepts, especially regarding the limitless. Practice clarifies whatever doesn't quite click yet, and enables us to discover what we don't know yet, so we can walk the walk as well as talk the talk. So practice is obviously practical.

Calling Buddha's way "a practice" may seem a bit of a misnomer. The word usually implies repeating something to be performed or enacted in the future, like athletic warm-ups or musical scales. Well, yes, it is consistent and persistent—and very basic. In other words, it's just like your life. Indeed, practice is your life, where you are, keeping your appointment with life. So the path (the practice) is itself the goal. If I repeat this slogan often, it's because it's so fundamental, it can take time to sink in. To be *on* this path is to commit to the Eightfold Way, and this path's *goal* is to keep at it. In this way, you can see your life as life itself.

We Westerners easily get obsessed with goals, and so can miss what's right at our feet: the present moment, the only moment ever available to us. So practice here's all about being in the present. True, you're already present. But you're missing it when you're busy reviewing or rehearsing, assessing the past or anticipating the future, or grasping or longing. Like the sign says at a Las Vegas casino, "You Must Be Present to Win."

The goal? An enlightened way. This means letting go of any concept of goal, relinquishing any attachment to outcome. Spiritual practice is about being present to your life, leading an authentic life, being genuine. Life is indeed a present—the greatest there is. We meditate to remind ourselves. Practice means really being intimate with our life. Go step by step, and practice consciously, fully, virtuously, wisely, and mindfully—with body, energy, and mind as one. Here follow steps to consider, getting set for meditation as a way—*your* way.

 Leaves from the Bodhi Tree _____

> Sharon Salzberg had been following the Way of the Buddha for 14 years when she became a student of U Pandita. She'd practice six days a week and, when she'd describe her meditation experiences to him, he'd just say, "Well, in the beginning it can be like that." No matter what, he'd say the same thing. After weeks of this, it finally dawned on her that he was saying it's good to be a beginner, not burdened by expectations or preconceptions based on past experiences. When she understood this, he stopped saying that.

Getting Started: Beginner's Mind

I'll let you in on a big, open secret. Maybe you've seen various books with titles like *Buddhism for Beginners*. Well, guess what!? Buddhists *are* beginners. It's actually a common habit of the wisdom paths. Socrates was declared wise because he knew that he did not know. Fourteenth-century Christian mystic Meister Eckhart called it "learned ignorance." Have you seen the bumper sticker?: "Minds, Like Parachutes, Must Be Open to Function." (A bumper sticker: a teaching along the Way.) The words *expert*, *professional*, and *specialist* have a commanding ring of authority to them. But they also have a reputation at stake, and so grow timid, learning to like wearing blinders, and to repeat their specialty like a one-trick pony. The word *amateur*, on the other hand, has a slightly disparaging ring today. But listening to its Latin root—*amare*, "to love"—reminds us of its original meaning: having a fondness for everything. Beginners' minds are equally willing to scale the highest peak, or to break for peanut butter and jelly sandwiches. As Suzuki Roshi put it so well, "If your mind is empty, it is always ready for anything; it is open to everything. *In the beginner's mind there are many possibilities; in the expert's mind there are few.*"

The popularity of this very book's series title is an interesting example: *The Complete Idiot's Guide*. So many of us just don't know! Examples of beginner's mind mantras in daily speech are: "Who knows!?" "You never know!" and "I'm new here." In my own life, pounding the pavement looking for day jobs taught me how a lack of prior experience can be a plus. You're not set in your ways; you're not going to say, "But that's not the way we did it where I used to work." Similarly, beginner's mind doesn't have any preconceptions of nirvana. Beginner's mind trusts itself to know when it gets there.

Leaves from the Bodhi Tree

A learned professor knocked on the door of the local Zen temple. He had a thousand questions. The resident teacher bowed and invited him in to sit down on a mat and share a pot of freshly picked tea. The tea steeped, and when it was ready, the host poured it into his learned guest's cup first. He poured and he poured and he poured, until the professor shouted, "What?! Stop!! It's overflowing! There's no more room!" The host put the teapot down and replied, "Exactly. Like this cup, you're full of your opinions and preconceptions. How can I show you Zen unless you first empty your cup?"

There are many examples of beginner's mind in everyday life. Many people have experienced beginner's luck in sports or games, such as with a perfect first golf swing, or an initial lucky bet. Everything's new when you're on vacation and playing tourist. And one reason I think we enjoy spending time with children is they have all of life ahead of them. They're absolute beginners.

These examples reflect how the mind given to us at birth, our beginner's mind, is still here beneath all the labels and decals and passwords, still impeccable, bright, open, and fond of everything. Returning to that mind is like coming home and reclaiming our buddha nature … the boundless clarity of the mind at peace … our nonself, our not-knowing … our *mu*, no thing … and all the priceless freedom that affords.

No Time Like the Right Time, and the Right Time Is ... Now

"The path is the goal" also leads to the question "If enlightenment is when you meditate, where is it the rest of the time?" *Answer*: Meditation is continuous with living. There's not the least iota of boundary line between your meditation and you. There's no separation. It's like asking, "If The Sacred is in a church on Sunday, where is It the rest of the week, in the rest of the world?" So why not have a taste of practice right here? Please try this:

1. Close your eyes.

2. Notice your breath.

3. Don't change anything. Just notice.

4. If you'd like, when you're done, take a mental snapshot of yourself at that point in time.

You can keep your mental snapshot in your mental wallet and take it out and look at it from time to time. In time, compare it with newer ones (like looking at photos of loved ones). Stopping and taking time for your practice, a few breaths throughout the day, is essentially as easy as that.

Time and Times for Practice (Besides All the Time)

Five or even ten minutes of meditation may only get your toes wet. It usually takes 15 minutes or so to begin to taste the depth and clarity of the practice. Scientifically, it takes about this long for our primitive fight-or-flight hardwiring to dim down and allow more evolved awareness to arise, but see for yourself. A good rule of thumb: meditate until you feel like you don't want to stop. You'll know when you've arrived.

It's coming home to our true home, arrival in the here and now. Favored times are morning and evening: morning, first thing after brushing your teeth (before the day starts unfolding its patterns); evening, either an hour or so before or after dinner, or before going to bed. Meditating right after a meal can be distracting when your blood sugar changes and digestion sees peak traffic.

Varying your daily practice period, you'll see how times of day feel different. Christian mystic Thomas Merton noted how wonderful 5 A.M. is. No one owns it. No one's making claims on you or the universe. I can feel how at five in the morning the first rays of the sun are striking my part of the planet, whereas at five in the evening I can feel the sun making way for noble nighttime. Autumn equinox likewise feels different than spring equinox or winter solstice.

More important than when and for how long is doing it regularly. That's a foundation. See if you can practice once if not twice a day, six days a week. Making it part of your ordinary life, for one thing, helps eliminate the idea of getting anywhere and instead opens up your familiarity with the range and phases of your mind. Buddha mind isn't off just out of reach; rather, it's available in everyday mind, so don't be a stranger. In fact, you might think of meditation as if you're reconnecting with the best friend you have in the world (you), with whom you haven't spent enough quality time.

A Retreat Needn't Be a Step Backward: It's a Treat!

A retreat is common today to a variety of organizations. During the muddy, three-month rainy season in India, the Buddha used to retreat with his disciples to the shelter of one of their monasteries and they would practice together until the monsoons stopped howling. The three-month retreat is still observed as a special time. A retreat can be of any length, as little as one day. There are retreats lasting from a day to a week. In Zen it's called a *sesshin* (touching/gathering/conveying the mind).

You can enjoy a one-day retreat in your own home. *Try this*: a day of mindfulness. Set aside a full day. Clean house and do any necessary shopping the day before. Unplug the phone. Use words sparingly. From the time you wake up to the time you go to sleep, you'll go slow, go light, and notice your breathing. Vow to be mindful of whatever you're doing. Practice sitting and walking meditation at various times of the day. One day can inspire and inform practice throughout the week. This tradition is core to the Abrahamic traditions: Sunday, the Christian Sabbath; Saturday, the Jewish *shabbos*; Friday, the Muslim *jumma*.

Any retreat is an excellent opportunity for solidifying, clarifying, and deepening your practice, and encouraging you to fit what you find there into daily life. It's as if the mental snapshot of yourself in meditation becomes that much more vivid. It's as if you're forming a deeper groove, which is then easier to dip into, within shorter periods.

Got Time? Time Is All We Have

The time it takes is the time you make. I've gotten mail from readers saying they only have five minutes a day for meditation. Well, it's a question of priorities, of course. If you think you only have five minutes for something of such lifelong value, then maybe it's just not for you, or maybe you'd better look again at your life. For busy beavers who think they don't have time, let me respectfully relay my dear teacher Lew Welch's pronouncement: "That's not a valid excuse. Time is really all we have. If we decide it's necessary, there's time for it." The Buddha tells us no one owns our mind but we ourselves. The same is true for time.

It might take some getting used to the fact that time is eternally present. The Chinese have an adage expressing it quite well: "Life unfolds on a great sheet called Time, and once finished it is gone forever." Time's like a river, everywhere at once: at the waterfall, at the docks, in the mountains, and flowing out to sea; always present tense. As always, the Middle Way pertains: nothing extreme. Stillness is inherent in activity, and vice versa. Western society glorifies doing over being. The Buddha, on the other hand, found the highest attainment in the mind at rest. And in terms of nirvana, there is no time—no past, no future. *Question:* Without looking, what time is it? *Answer:* It's now.

The question of not having time reminds me of this haiku by Shou: "Birds sit and sing among the flowers, laughing at human beings who have no time to sing."

Buddha's in the House, Inviting Practice to Take Place

Now it's time to talk about place. Practice isn't confined to a weekly or monthly meeting place. Start with where you are. You're never alone; there is sangha wherever you are. The other morning, as rays of the dawn sun slowly brightened the wall, I practiced along with the eucalyptus tree out back and the finches thereabouts. The temple is everywhere, and everywhere alive with living beings; there's even a film of microorganisms invisibly flowing across the floor and objects of our immediate environment. Like you and me, all beings are seeking happiness.

Setting Aside Some Breathing Room

Like a comfortable sofa, everyone can designate a spot in their dwelling as a literal space in their lives where meditation can take place. Setting aside some breathing room is a great gift to give one's self, and one's family.

It needn't be a room all its own, just wherever you won't be disturbed. It could be an area just large enough to lay a small mat for a cushion upon the floor. Preferably, it might be near an open window, so the air's fresh. It might be shaded, so bright light won't distract you. And this area could be relatively quiet. Nothing more elaborate than that is needed. If it's all you have, you could fold your blanket and sit on it on your bed.

> **Hear and Now**
>
> Standing Outside my pointed-roof hut,
> Who'd guess how spacious it is inside?
> A galaxy of worlds is there,
> With room to spare for a zafu.
> —Shih-wu (1272–1352)

Just knowing I have that space where I can always go gladdens my heart and calms my mind. I take refuge there, renew my vows, and practice. So every now and again, I celebrate my growing buddhahood and place a flower (from the park near my house) in a simple glass of water, beside my mat, near the window. This little living buddha is sharing the light and air with me and my practice, and I with it.

Home Altars: Seeing the Buddha Within and Without

For growing buddhas, regularly nourishing and inviting essential buddha nature is cause for celebration, no? It's celebrating our life, which is our practice. One way of doing this is setting aside a place at home (and work) as a sacred space, an altar. Whatever you put on that shelf or mantel is a reminder of your promise to live your fullest potential—renewing vows. Naturally, Buddhists place an image of the Buddha on an altar. Except it's not an idol; it's merely a formal representation of the true nature of our heart and mind, our wisdom and compassion. It's a mere image of the experience of meditation.

So is bowing to a statue of the Buddha idol worship? Vietnamese Buddhist monk Thich Tanh Thien explains, "You stand in front of Buddha, not to a statue, but to buddha inside yourself. It's important to know that, otherwise you're bowing to a piece of wood or metal. When you look inward to the buddha nature, you feel peace in your heart. You give thanks to Buddha because without his teachings, you would not have found this way of understanding and loving." And so Buddhist ritual (in general) is not done because something *is* so: the ritual act *makes* it so.

Zen teacher Mel Weitsman points out that when you bow at something, it bows back. (Have you noticed?) The Buddha image I have in my home is a small statuette. So my small Buddha gives me a small bow in return (more than that I might have trouble with, on a day-to-day basis).

You might nurture your own buddhahood, nourish your growing link with the awakening of the Buddha and his teachings, on a home altar. It could be an image or statue, on a windowsill or shelf. You might add a flower, a candle, incense, or a small bowl of fresh water. Some altars have precise symbolic details, depending on the practice; others are free-form. Portable altars have been an early fixture of Buddhist devotion, and the practice continues in Pure Land, Tibetan, and Nichiren Buddhism. Some home shrines include cherished seekers and enlightened leaders. Some include pictures of relatives and teachers and close friends, a place where a practitioner goes to share personal news with them. For many, an altar's a way of deepening the meaning of home, and making the divine personal.

Along the Path

Seen against a Judeo-Christian background, an altar can smack of graven images and idolatry (*avoda zara* in Hebrew). Yet within Buddhism there's a parallel, almost identical warning: "If you see a Buddha along the road, kill him." Don't bind yourself to an image or concept. As Quakers say, seek the living light within yourself.

Hear and Now

"… a butsudan … is a beautiful little cabinet. Inside you put things that represent the necessities of life: little candles for light, incense for smell, water, fruit, and so on. And you hang your gohonzon in there, too—a scripture, rolled up on a scroll. The butsudan looks like a little altar; but the idea is not that you're *worshipping* this piece of paper or anything. These things allow you to focus, to be in the right frame of mind to receive, and they are a form of respect."

—Tina Turner

The meaning of an altar or shrine grows over time. A devotional image or artifact is like that snapshot of a loved one that someone keeps in their wallet or on their desk. To us, it's just another face, but to the one who knows that person and looks at the picture at various times of the day, the image is a doorway to love. Remember: "Thou art *that*."

Gear: Clean Socks—What Else?

During his ascetic stint, the Buddha slept out in the open, naked. Had he attained Enlightenment that way, this section might have been devoted to information on bug bites and poisonous plants. Anyway, you should feel comfortable when you meditate. No need for tight watches or collars, glasses or belts that constrict circulation, or starchy or scratchy clothes. Colors in Zen temples are blacks or grays, so as not to distract anyone. Tibetan Buddhists, on the other hand, favor bright colors, generating the glow of inner warmth.

Some people sit with a blanket over their knees because circulation slows down during meditation, and it's important not to catch cold. Clean socks? Many temples ask that shoes be removed when sitting in the main hall.

In seated meditation, posture often calls for elevating your fanny slightly higher than your knees and feet. A rolled-up blanket can do. A more formal amenity would be a pillow. There's one designed for sitting meditation called *zafu* in Japanese. A mat placed under it is called *zabuton* in Japanese. Even in non-Japanese practices, zafus and zabutons are familiar fixtures.

Meditation sessions often begin with a bell (usually a bowl, really). A higher-sounding bell signals the end—time to str-r-r-retch! Some people call that sound the voice of the Buddha, calling us home, home to the present time, home to our true selves. Some people carry two small brass cymbals in their pocket or purse, called a *tsingsha*, a portable bell of mindfulness. In my practice, before actually sounding a bell, I give the bell a little preliminary nudge, a soft tap, a mere touch, inviting the bell to speak.

A handy (skillful) item for home practice is a *meditation timer*, available in dharma catalogs and online. Meditation is a time for stepping back from the push-pull of the calendar and schedule, so glancing at a clock runs counter to the whole point. ("Am I meditated yet?") Enjoy the beautiful awareness of now, which is timeless.

Did you ever wonder about the name for worry beads? They're supposed to help dis-solve worries, not create them. Sanskrit for a string of beads, *japa mala*, literally means "rose beads," from which the word *rosary* comes. They could be as small as a bracelet, or as large as a necklace with 108 beads, for the traditional 108 varieties of ignorance that hearts are prone to (in Buddhism, there's a numbered list for everything—but don't ask me why this happens to be the same as the number of moves in Tai Chi *and* the number of stitches on a baseball). A mala can count recitations of a mantra or of the Buddha's name, or just keep attention focused. Meditating on breath, out-and-in or in-and-out, can count as one bead. And there's one big bead, the teacher bead, where you turn around and go the other way. The beads can also be simply relaxing to feel (and play with).

Some people time their meditation to the length of one stick of good incense. (Bad incense, on the other hand, might only give you a headache, and be carcinogenic.) There's Japanese, Tibetan, powder, rope incense, and so on. Sandalwood was used by Buddha's disciples to help them concentrate during heat waves. When the Buddhist monks from India took to the Silk Route, they brought along their incense. Like the fragrance of the Dharma, suffusing its ineffable fragrance everywhere, incense burns away impurities and refreshes body and mind, stimulating a feeling of alertness and calm, like a cup of fresh green tea.

And nothing warms the heart like a candle. Lama Anagarika Govinda observes how its gentle light is "a means of recalling and being mindful of the light of enlightenment that has shone within every one of us without any recognizable beginning, even though darkened by the self-built walls of the ego, which it is necessary to tear down." These can all be skillful means, not to be mistaken as ends in themselves. Dharma isn't a thing, like a stick of incense, but rather what you make of its fragrance. Don't mistake all the various lamps along the real journey's trail.

Community of Practice: Friends Along the Path

A practice is, by definition, something you do. It's one thing to do it solo, yet another when in community. There's a limit as to how much you can learn on your own. True, it all depends on you. So you can certainly try and see if you can reach enlightenment solo. You might find it to be like trying to teach cats to dance. Even if you think you can, how would you know you're not just building yourself up, trying another way of making a sandcastle at the water's edge (a lonely enlightenment of self-delusion)? Practicing together can be likened to potatoes bumping around together boiling in a pot, rounding out each other's rough spots. As Zen priest and scholar Michael Wenger explains, "[F]or the enormity of all that transforming yourself to Buddha is about, you realize that you can use all the help you can get." I'd add that if you don't yet grasp that enormity, a sangha helps you realize it.

True, the Buddha attained enlightenment sitting beneath a tree, after seven years. But he had a head start, being a prodigy with kingly training in all things, including meditation. And on the night in question, the Buddha called all of creation as his witness, the sangha of all beings. For nearly 50 years thereafter, he practiced in the company of his friends along the path, and the tradition continues, expressed in a way appropriate to right now. Nothing can replace practice with others.

"Go as a Sangha." Some people have that taped to the inside of their front door, as they go out into the world. The quote is from the Buddha. What he's saying is: when you step out onto a path, you can go alone, or with the whole universe. Listening to the sound of the wind through the trees, we can hear the voice of the Buddha teaching the Dharma. In the sunlight on a hill, we can see the body of the Buddha teaching the Dharma.

With whom—with which best of friends—shall you joyfully join in? Of all the e-mail I'm so happy to receive, the most common question has been, "Where can I find a group to practice with?" For those with 'Net access, I posted a page with links online (word.to/sangha.html). The backs of Buddhist magazines also have directories.

Here are two tips for beginners:

1. To practice sitting quietly in stillness in community, see if any Quaker groups meet in your area (often called "Religious Society of Friends" in the phone book). Make a visit, and see.

2. To become comfortable about posture, see if there's any Zen sangha that meets in your area, and find out when they offer an introduction for beginners. They usually take great care to go through posture in detail, which is invaluable base camp training.

Sangha reinforces good habits of practice—beginning with just doing it in the first place. As editor and publisher of *Tricycle Magazine* (a Buddhist review) James Shaheen attests, "Sometimes showing up for others is easier than showing up for yourself." Personally, I find myself sensing a larger, group energy generated that I vibrate with and enjoy when I practice with others. You may well have experienced similar human communion. Anyone speaking or performing in front of an audience, for example, feels a "living link," an impalpable group mind. And there's a noticeable difference between getting up in front of a dozen people and a thousand people. Consciousness is aware of other consciousness. This awareness is magnified in sangha. We're all part of one big living being.

Sangha's buoyant as an ocean. My practice is upheld by the sangha as a boat upon water, as I uphold it by my practice. Sangha's also a community resource center. Sangha members are there for each other. Sangha is refuge, it's true security, and it's healing. Following meditation one rainy afternoon, a dear member of my root sangha told us of his terminal cancer. He'd tried and given up on the painkillers. *"This,"* (meaning our being together) he said, "is the only thing that helps."

What and How Much Are All Up to You

You don't have to go for ordination and be a monk or a nun. Nor do you need to begin your practice by taking refuge in any sangha. Maybe Buddhist practice will enrich an already grounded religious practice, in which case you already have the sangha of your fellow congregants. But for the Buddhist practice, you still need a teacher and a sangha. There's a range of options.

Picking and Choosing Wisely

As we've noted, Western Buddhist practice spans an unprecedented range of traditions and hybrids—certainly more than different kinds of Christianity. What'll yours be? Zen Pure Land? Native American Tibetan? Taoist Zen Islam? There's no one-size-fits-all practice. As R. H. Blyth, scholar of Buddhism and haiku, once said, "For every person there's a religion. And for every religion there's a person." (Maybe you.) This holds true for the Buddha's way, as well. It's said there are 84,000 Dharma doors (entrances to the Way) because there are at least 84,000 different kinds of suffering. But remember: the Dharma has but one taste, the taste of liberation.

Sometimes the path comes with the teacher, as when you like a particular teacher and so will naturally learn of her or his lineage. Or you may start with a sense of what lineage you'd like, and then find an appropriate teacher.

Leaves from the Bodhi Tree

The master of a monastery interviewed a new monk. "Who'd you study with before?" he asked. After the monk answered "So-and-So," the master asked what he'd learned. "Well, I'd asked him what's the meaning of Buddhism, and he said, 'The Fire God comes for fire.'" The master said, "Good answer! I guess you didn't understand it." The monk replied, "But I did understand! If the Fire God asks for fire, that would be like my asking about Buddhism, because I'm really a buddha already." The master shook his head, and said, "I knew it. You missed the point completely." "Well, how do you handle it?" The master said, "You ask me." So, the monk asked him, "What's the meaning of Buddhism?" "The Fire God comes for fire," replied the master, and the monk got it.

Don't Sweat the Isms

The more experience you have of the variety of the Buddha's way, the more you'll appreciate *your* way. As you move through Buddhaland, don't be shy. Listen to and learn from Hinayana, Mahayana, Vajrayana … and even Swami Beyondananda.

Understanding the essentials is always a good critical tool (*criticism* coming from Greek *kroinos*, "to choose"). Major paths of practice are spotlighted in the following chapters. They're doors. The one true Way is underneath your feet.

When the Student Is Ready, the Master Appears

American author Erma Bombeck once said something very appropriate here: "Never go to a doctor whose houseplants have died." That is, you could really like a teacher, but look around and look within. If, deep down, you don't feel comfortable, then they're not right for you. Don't worry. Another will turn up.

Just like you, each teacher's a unique human being. Some might have thick black lines around themselves, clearly marking off their lineage and demands. Others might be eclectic and free-form. Just as each teacher's different, so will each student take what they need, differently. A good teacher optimizes the conditions for your own practice. How you respond and what you make of it all goes to make up the wonderful mystery of you.

Along the Path

Each practice emphasizes its teacher-student relationship differently. In traditional Tibetan practice, the teacher (*guru*) must be worthy of unconditional trust, and the relationship will often be lifelong. In Korea, on the other hand, teachers (*sunim*) rotate, so monks eventually study under four teachers. Some Western sanghas might host an array of guest teachers, supplementing its core.

This Is

In Thailand, a Buddhist teacher is called *ajahn* (from the Sanksrit *acharya*, "teacher"). Theravada teachers are considered a *kalyana mitra* (spiritual friend) and act as mentors. In Japanese Zen, a teacher's called *roshi* (Japanese for "old master"), and in Korean it's *sunim* (pronounced "soo-neem"). Here, as in Tibetan practice, a student works closely, one-on-one, in addition to receiving guidance from monastic or lay meditation teachers. A Tibetan teacher is a *guru*, *lama*, and *rinpoche* (pronounced "RIHN-poe-shay"); a *geshe* (pronounced "geh-shee") is a scholar.

Often you can feel a special affinity, right off. Along with your deep-down feeling, here are six road signs to observe in choosing a teacher:

1. Does the teacher communicate in a way you can readily understand? Or do you have to mentally translate a great deal of foreign-sounding information?

2. Does the teacher smile? Light's important, but so is warmth, compassion.

3. Do the teacher and the sangha seem harmonious and happy? Do they teach or emphasize the precepts?

4. What do you hear from other students? Avoid gossip, but listen to wise counsel and experience. Check credentials. What was this teacher's relationship to their teacher?

5. Do they use threats, or fear? Do you sense authoritarianism, dogmatism, coercion, or salesmanship? Do they make lofty claims or promise easy enlightenment? Has a cult evolved around the teacher? Do other students copy his or her speech patterns?

6. Remember, too, that teachers are only human and have quirks and foibles.

A Few Drops of Compassionate Wisdom

Before proceeding to basic meditation, I'd like to pass along a few general tips (like beginner's mind) to dot an "i" in our *intention* (correct thought) and *view* (perfect understanding), and to cross a "t" in our *effort* (stick-to-it-iveness).

Why Meditate?

For practice, take a sheet of paper, and write these two words at the top: *Why meditate?* Then give it some perfect thought. Look below the surface. Ask yourself, "What are my inmost urgencies? My highest aspirations? My deepest wish? What would be nice side benefits as well?" You might frame your answers as verbs or adjectives, rather than as nouns. For example, from a list written by a poet named Suvanna: "… to practice noticing … to understand simple things … to face inevitable difficulties … to make a conscious choice … to welcome my feelings … to learn without words … to unlock my heart …"

What you write will be like the mental snapshot of where you are, from the beginning of this chapter. Review where you're going from time to time. You might well find the reasons you take up practice are different from why you were drawn to it in the first place. You might stay with it later on for yet another reason. The path is the goal; meditate, and see.

If you'd like a "bottom line," meditate as an ongoing training in the Four Noble Truths.

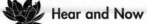 **Hear and Now**

> "Simply practice meditation in order to live a better life, or even just to live a good life, whatever meaning that holds for you. Or, meditate as a means of learning how not to be afraid—of death, or of all the insignificant concerns that paralyze your innate ability to live fully. Meditate to activate creativity. Meditate to recognize the value of the truly good things in life: friendship, honor, respect, compassion, and love."
> —Ajahn Sumano Bhikkhu

Viewless View, No Thought, Effortless Effort

Because meditation's not a prepackaged program—but, rather, an intimate engagement with life itself—we end where we began, with the subtle but sturdy realm of viewpoint. It's good to have a sense of where you are now and where you want to be. To get there, the best view is no viewpoint, empty of all views and no thought of enlightenment. Enlightenment *is* the ultimate goal. But it can't be reached, only found—not through grasping, but through letting go. Meditation reveals the delusions that have crusted over our true nature, and shows us how to appreciate its innate radiance. Yes, meditation might also clear your thinking, sharpen your concentration, deepen your compassion, elevate your wisdom, empower your intuition, make you psychic, and improve your tennis score. But you might rather think of these more as possible bonuses, rather than as goals. Enlightenment often happens the way accidents do. Practice makes us accident-prone.

The path itself is the goal. Striving after enlightenment is a setup for a fall. I say this only so you can easily recognize it and step aside, if you happen to fall into the rut. The true nature of mind is open, transparent, and boundless. So when limited self—blinded by opinions and views—seeks selflessness by saying, "*I want* (grasping) to *calm myself* (believing there's a tangible, separate, lasting self to calm, that can be switched on and off)," that only reinforces the illusory self that perpetuates suffering. It's like trying to lift yourself up while sitting on a chair. (Don't go there.)

Please don't meditate and build up a sense of self. ("I can sit full lotus, nyah-nyah.") Nor should you try to annihilate your self through meditation. ("Out, out, damned spot!") Or, slightly different, someone says "I want to calm my mind." *Question*: Where is mind? It's like asking to bring back a pot of gold at the end of a rainbow—the more you search, the further it gets. Trying to calm your mind often makes your mind only more restless, like a wild horse at the sight of a harness. The mind calms itself, as we'll see next. Effort can be effortless and light. Buddhist practice is continual, step by step and breath by breath. Whether sitting on a cushion or in a car, waiting in line or lying down, it's all practice. (You know what the man coming out of the subway said to the lost boy holding a violin case who asked him, "How can I get to Carnegie Hall?" He said, "Practice, practice!") And don't worry about having to start all over again. Why do you think they call it *practice!*?

The Least You Need to Know

- Practice means finding and staying on your spiritual path. It's not like music you practice to perform at some later date, but rather an act to put you in touch with the present moment. It's more like musical scales, which musicians practice daily, no matter their level of achievement.

- The best approach is to take a beginner's mind, a "don't-know" mind with no preconceptions or judgments.

- Everyone can find a place for practice at home. It's more important to practice daily than sporadically for great lengths of time.

- Altars are an option. If you bow to an image of the Buddha, it's to acknowledge, pay respect to, and nurture the buddha within you. Beads, a bell, and incense are also optional for meditation.

- You might find a teacher through interest in a certain school, or vice versa. When choosing a teacher, do some homework and listen to your heart.

- Understand that meditation isn't a means to an end, it is the means *and* the end.

10

Meditation: Base Camp

In This Chapter

◆ Basic meditation

◆ Body: posture, and stretches

◆ Spirit: conscious breathing

◆ Mind: letting it become quiet on its own

◆ Walking meditation and sound meditation

If you were to come away with only a few things from this book, one would be that *meditation is continual.* Here is a basic practice of meditation that's ancient yet as vital and viable today as it ever was, and adaptable to all circumstances: *Taste, and see.*

I liken meditation to explorers setting up base camp—it's home base, square one. Here you can be safe, still, at one, and enjoying and renewing your vision and vows during this pilgrimage called life. Welcome to Base Camp!

Home Base: A Basic Meditation

When a preacher says, "Now we'll have a moment of silent meditation," he knows he better mean just a moment, or else he'll be looking at anxious faces and hearing nervous coughs. For the rest of us, here's a brief sketch of a basic short meditation, adapted from a teaching by Zen teacher Norman Fischer. It has five parts, which are as follows:

1. Settling into conscious breathing

2. Counting breath

3. Discerning breath's subtleties

4. Emphasizing how your breath wants to be

5. Jumping off and just being with whatever's there (your life at the moment)

To begin, take stock of where you are. Check in with your mood and your body. Relax, notice your breath, and focus your awareness on that and that alone. Note in-breath (and only that) and out-breath (and only that). When you'd like, count 10 breaths this way: in-out counts as one. Try 10 conscious breaths, counting after the out-breath. You might also begin to notice a space in between. When information from your senses, feelings, and thoughts arise, note them, acknowledge them, and let them go, all within continuous and more spacious awareness. Keep returning to the breath, within awareness. If you wish, count 10 more breaths, this time making the count follow the in-breath. After developing concentration and calm this way, for 10 breaths, notice the subtlety in each breath: each with a beginning, middle, and end; some being smoother, some longer or shorter; and so on. After staying with just that attention for a while, stay with just breath and awareness, in the way they manifest at this moment. Go with the kind of breath that feels good right now. Emphasize it a bit. Finally, just stay with yourself in the present, with no props at all anymore. Just … this.

That's the theme. The rest is variations. I like to break it out as: body, spirit, and mind. Start anywhere; they work together. It's easy to remember: body, spirit, and mind as one.

Be a Buddha, Sit Like a Buddha (Just as You Are)

Our mind may not always dwell in the present moment, but our body sure does. So we can always start from (t)here: the here of "here and now." Meditation can be practiced walking, standing still, lying down, or sitting (that is, anytime). Sitting has a particular potency. Archaeologists in the Indus Valley (the Buddha's stomping grounds) have dug up small figurines in the seated, cross-legged posture of meditation dating back at least five millennia. That's a long time to be sitting. Sure, the sculptor might've been commemorating a sit-down strike or something. We don't know for sure; they didn't come with descriptive booklets. But just looking at them you sense a reverence.

In the full lotus, the classic meditation position, each leg's on the opposite thigh. In a half lotus, only one foot rests on the opposite thigh, the other rests on the floor or on the calf, and often with a pillow to support that knee. In the Burmese position, both feet are folded in front of your body, not crossed over each other, both knees on the floor.

Have you tried it? Seated, your body realizes you aren't going anywhere. The little alarm bells always on the lookout for dangers in the environment dim down and dwindle away. Your hands aren't manipulating any tools. There's nothing to say or do but sit and breathe, in the here and in the now. Subtler forms of attention can emerge. In the sheer simplicity of living, peace can be as simple and solid as that.

Knees slightly apart, you can meditate while kneeling. You can sit on your heels, a small bench, or your zafu on end. If you sit in a chair, see if you cannot rely on the back of your chair for support. Rely on yourself.

Ears over Shoulders: Basic Posture

The basics have stayed the same for millennia. You sit on a cushion on the floor, but a chair works, too. Your contact with the ground should feel like a stable tripod of feet-legs-knees and sit-space. To let your tailbone make contact with the ground, your pelvis might tilt, bottom forward. Then your entire spine is resting on the earth. Feel yourself sink down into this contact, and let your vertebra stack up, like a solid mountain upon the earth.

If your back is straight, breath and energy can flow freely the length of your body. If you tend to slouch, imagine a small ring's at the top of your head (where your hair meets your scalp) and a hook coming down from the sky, engaging that ring and gently lifting you up as far as your waist. Your lower back naturally curves in and your upper back naturally curves out. Your spine's erect and stretched, not hunched or scrunched.

Or think of sitting in a way that embodies dignity. Everybody knows that feeling and how to embody it. Rediscover it. Reclaim it. (You can practice throughout the day: think "sky hook"; think "dignity.")

Check it out. Your shoulders are back so your chest can comfortably expand. Your ears are over shoulders. Your shoulders are over your hips. Your nose is aligned with your navel. Your eyes are horizontal with the ground (don't squish the back of your brain, nor your larynx), but tuck your chin in, which lowers your head just a fraction. You might visualize the sky supported on your head.

Arms are away from your body. Your hands can rest on your knees, palms down or up. Now, test your position. Sway front and back, left and right. Get centered.

> **Hear and Now** _____
>
> "The state of mind that exists when you sit in the right posture is, itself, enlightenment. If you cannot be satisfied with the state of mind you have in zazen, it means your mind is still wandering about. Our body and mind should not be wobbling or wandering about. In this posture there is no need to talk about the right state of mind. You already have it. This is the conclusion of Buddhism."
>
> —Shunryu Suzuki Roshi

Giving Body Language a Hand: Mudras

As the motionless posture of our legs and feet sends a message to our brain that we're in a safe place, so, too, does the placement of our hands hold meaning. An etiquette book, for example, may tell you not to put your little finger out at a 45-degree angle when you hold your fork, so as not to appear "backstairs refined." All the Buddha's gestures (*mudras*) have meaning (nonverbal literacy), such as his earth-touching mudra. Fingers outstretched except the tip of the thumb and index finger meeting in a circle is the mudra of teaching.

Two basic mudras are *bowing* and the *meditation mudra*. Practice in company often formally begins and ends with bowing in. Bowing is a meditation, in and of itself, just by joining palms, a universal gesture of unity of spirit. There's a famous etching by Albrecht Dürer of two hands praying, as if by themselves. In the East, putting palms and fingers together can be a gesture of spiritual greeting, instead of shaking hands. In India and Thailand, you put your palms together at your chest and raise them to your forehead, often followed by a bow, still in that position—eyes and joined hands going outward and down to a spot on the ground equidistant between the greeter and the greeted. A bow can also be a quarter inch. However done, "palms-joined" says "the buddha within me salutes the buddha within you" (no separation). "Have a nice day."

This Is _____

Fingers aligned, palms join together for a **bow** (*namaste* [*namas* means to take refuge and *te* is "you," together meaning "I take refuge in you."], Hindu; *wai*, Thai; *gassho*, Japanese) is a Buddhist hand gesture called a **mudra** (Sanskrit for "sign" or "seal"). By outwardly imitating certain gestures, we can cultivate the inner state associated with them (means become ends; the path becomes the goal).

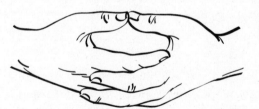

The cosmic meditation mudra.

In seated meditation, you can place your palms on your knees. Here's a mudra. If you're right-handed, place the back of your left hand on top of your right palm; lefties, vice versa. Thumbs straight, making contact at the tips, form an oval (resembling an egg from the front). Rest your hands on your feet, ankles, or thighs. This places the mudra below your navel, approximately level with a point—called *dan tien* in Chinese and *hara* in Japanese—considered a vital center (along with the heart region, in center of the chest, and the head). Many call this a central repository of life-force (*prana; chi*), carried through the breath. Concentrating on belly breathing, one shifts focus away from the head to the base.

Getting Down to Earth: Prostration

Prostration can be wonderful. Muslims do it five or six times a day. In Buddhism, it's a fluid yoga, starting with hands together, above your head. Then lower them to (1) the crown of your head, (2) your mouth or neck, and (3) the center of your chest (your spiritual heart). A half prostration takes kneeling, and touching the earth with hands and forehead. In full prostration, hands then slide forward, until completely lying down. Sometimes people then slightly raise their palms, while keeping heads down, before smoothly reversing the process to a standing position. It might look like abasement to a Westerner. Actually, as Venerable Sheng Yen points out, if you do it slowly, fully, and smoothly, and experience the movement, your body relaxes, making space for the mind to do so, too.

Prostrations are common in Chinese, Korean, Japanese, and Tibetan temples. Going for refuge takes three prostrations, reciting "I take refuge in the Buddha," "I take refuge in the Dharma," and "I take refuge in the Sangha," one for each prostration. Here we see prostration plus recitation plus visualization integrating body, speech, and mind.

Doing No Thing But *This:* How Relaxing!

There's a bit more to sitting. In the next chapter, you'll learn a Buddhist "body scan" technique for deep relaxation, but let's get a head start. (We'll start at the head.) Let each of your muscles relax, group by group, head to toes. Relax your scalp; relax your face; relax the sides of your neck; relax the back of your neck; relax your shoulders; relax your ribs; and relax your heart. Let your belly soften, and so on. All the while, notice your breath.

Did you know? There are about 300 muscles in your face. One way of relaxing all of them is by exercising just one. Give yourself the gift of a smile, like Buddha. You need only lift one corner of your mouth, slightly, like Mona Lisa. Breathe, and see how the smile feels. (Sometimes joy precedes a smile; sometimes a smile precedes the joy.) Thich Nhat Hanh has coined a nifty phrase for this: *mouth yoga.* He remarks, "Why wait until you are completely transformed, completely awakened? You can start being a part-time Buddha right now!"

Rest your tongue on roof of your mouth, or tip to teeth or inside upper lip. (*Mmmmm.*) What about the eyes? Seeing is really a very intricate, complex process. Closing the eyes is a common way to begin to relax. It frees us from all that information: the rectilinear borders partitioning space, and which includes seeming domination by objects, and the primitive back-brain alert-system, on the lookout in the environment. Closing your eyes directs sight inward instead. Eyes closed, we feel rounder and more boundless. Pitfalls to eyes-closed are possible hallucination or falling asleep. Once relaxed, you might reopen your eyes, perhaps still half-closed. If you're facing a wall, pick some spot just below eye level. When concentration wanders, return to the spot. An alternative spot is a space about three inches from your nose or a spot on the floor about a yard away. When in sangha, it may be a spot on the back of the person in front of you.

And that's all there is to it. You know the saying, "Don't just sit there, do something!" Well, Buddhists like to rephrase it: "Don't do anything, just sit!"

Opening Up: Warm-Up Stretches

Oscar Wilde once prayed, "Spare me *physical* pain!" We're only human, so we're bound to feel discomfort. Sitting regularly for as little as a half hour can be demanding of neck and knees, for example, two anatomic features that haven't changed a heck of a lot since we redistributed our weight from four legs to two. And when withheld energy starts flowing during meditation, it's wise to be bodily grounded. (I'm not suggesting that blue sparks will start flying out of the top of your head—yikes!) Pains often fall away on their own, just by being aware of their ebb and flow in the waves of our mindstream. But you're not inviting pain. So warm-ups can be a sound investment in a healthy, happy practice.

Please check out *The Complete Idiot's Guide to Yoga* for information on such poses as the Bound Angle, the Butterfly, the Cat, the Cobbler, the Cobra, the Cradle, the Downward-Facing Dog, the Hero, the Locust, the Lunge, the Supported Bridge, and the Triangle. See *The Complete Idiot's Guide to Tai Chi and QiGong* for warm-up exercises, excellent stretches before meditation. There are also Tibetan Buddhist exercises called *Kum-Nye* you might want to explore.

Yoga instruction in the sequences for such poses as the downward-facing dog (left) and butterfly (right) can help enhance meditation.

Why Not Breathe? You're Alive!

Body, spirit, and mind are one. *Breath* is another word for spirit. What could be more impermanent and insubstantial, yet vital and universal, intuitive, and effortless? After you become familiar with conscious breathing, it forms your base camp, so you can practice meditation throughout the day just by stopping to enjoy two or three mindful breaths, or even just one. We can always start here, and return here at square one.

Along the Path

The Sanskrit word for **breath,** *prana,* also means "universal energy" and "life-force," similar to a Chinese concept, *chi* (pronounced "chee," also spelled *qi*). The word *spirit* comes from Latin, *spiritus* and *spirare,* meaning "breath" and "to breathe." (Inspiration means breathing in.) Old Testament Hebrew and Greek words for *spirit, ruach* and *pneuma,* mean "breath" and also "wind" (merging within and without). In Hebrew and Arabic, *nefes* means "soul" as well as "breath." Buddha devoted an entire sutra (*Anapanasati*) to breathing, as a vehicle to enlightenment.

Conscious breathing may sound ironic. Yet it's an ever-present given in our lives upon which we can focus mindfulness: mindfulness of breath. As you may have noticed for yourself, breath unifies body and mind. Take a slow, deep breath, in and out. Notice how calm that feels. Try flutter breathing and notice the similar anxious feeling. Then do the math: we breathe an average of 17,250 times per day. To add consciousness to the process is a great gate for entering into awareness. Here follows three techniques to assist one-pointed mindful meditation via conscious breathing:

◆ Body awareness

◆ Counting breaths

◆ Mantras and gathas

See if just one might be especially interesting. Trying them all right now might be overkill.

Tips: This isn't yoga. That is, you're neither trying to control your breath, nor make it any different than it already is. Your job is to just watch it. It may seem like a paradox: controlling the breath to control the mind, without controlling anything, just observing. But that's the name of the game. Effortless effort.

And these are only tools. (The raft is not the shore.) Your meditation isn't about nose or tummy (not to mention the parameningeal epigastrum). Basic meditation is about letting body, mind, and breath get reacquainted, and seeing how these old friends work as a team.

Having a Gut Feeling That the Nose Knows

The nostrils and belly are two *body* areas that can help center your mind on your breathing—and help your breathing center your mind. (With either focus, you'll notice how breath affects your entire trunk.) As you breathe, focus on your nostrils. Plant your undivided attention there, like a sentry at the very tips of your nostrils. Mouth closed, notice your breath as a sensation of touch: cool, maybe even fragrant, coming in; warmed by your body going out. This single technique can be the crux of many entire meditations.

Or you might focus on your belly (a typical Zen approach). Maybe you've heard Stereotype 164 of Eastern meditation as being "navel-gazing." Actually, it's not the navel, but an area about the size of a dime, three or four fingers down from your navel (*hara* or *dan tien*). As Lama Surya Das points out, it's front-row center! If our nostrils are the gates, this might be thought of as the palace basement, the storehouse, the secret treasury. (Actually, there's a vital acupressure point right there.) Notice how the belly falls in, as breath falls away; how it opens, as the diaphragm pulls up and the bellows of the lungs expand, for breath to return, on its own.

> **Hear and Now**
>
> "This is universal. You sit and observe your breath. You can't say this is Hindu breath or Christian breath or Muslim breath. Knowing how to live peacefully or harmoniously—you don't call this religion or spirituality. It is nonsectarian."
>
> —Charles Johnson

Focusing on belly breathing may run counter to how you've been brought up. I was taught to keep my abdomen hard, military-style. "Hold it in," the expression went, and because body and mind are one, this applied to emotions as well; aren't they often called "gut feelings"? So it's not uncommon to see people trying to breathe deeply by expanding their chest rather than their bellies. When frightened, babies breathe in their chests, as if scared of contacting something overwhelming in their belly. Some people often carry this trait over into adulthood as a basic policy toward life. ("Uh-oh, this might make me breathe deeply: Houston, we have a problem.") Yet we see portraits of Buddhas (and Renaissance maidens) with curving bellies.

Staying focused, feel a natural softening of any hardness in your belly, breath by breath. Breathe *into* any tightness in your belly. *Exhale* any tension this might release. (*Ahh!*) You might find your breathing automatically fills your belly more than before.

If so, just notice it. If not, no sweat. Breath eventually deepens, slows, and calms on its own. Belly awareness can assist the process. This is the Buddha's way—providing the nourishment for our seeds of awareness to blossom into a lotus.

Let Each Breath Count: In-Out = One

Counting's another way to focus awareness on breath, and to keep your mind from wandering. Try this: *Calmly let your breath fall away in exhalation and say to yourself "one," then breathe in that "one." Breathe out again, and begin "two."* (Or breathe *in* on one, and count the exhale.) Don't think of anything else but your breath—just your breathing in, your breathing out, and a very quick, light count. At "four," return to "one" again. If your mind wanders, as it does, begin all over again, at "one."

Tips: If you can't make it all the way to four, you're not an idiot(!). Buddhist friends of mine, even after decades of practice, are still at four. And if you can make it to four, you're a junior Buddha. Try ten. But don't get a swell head about it; and remember, you're not trying to reach a goal—it's only practice.

You don't have to feel like a dummy to return to such simplicity as 1-2-3-4; these are basics of life. Buddhism's an opportunity for starting over. It's back to basics, a beginner's mind.

The key is this: whenever you find you've tarried or strayed, and return to the breath, you do so within awareness, again and again, within mindfulness.

Remember, too, your attention is on your breathing, not the count. And when you're ready, let go of these training wheels and just be conscious of your breathing, in and of itself. Simple as 1-2-3. Peace is every breath.

Consider conscious breathing as your base from which to set forth and explore, and to which you can come home. It's a gate to the place of center or centering you might hear about in spiritual circles. It's a *grounding* in something as indestructible as Earth. Invest in regular practice to maintain this base camp. Build upon it by adding five minutes to your practice until you're comfortable just sitting and *enjoying your breathing* for 20 to 45 minutes or so.

Vocabulary of Breath: *Mantras* and *Gathas*

Besides body awareness and counting, there are two verbal options for quieting the mind and refining awareness. *Mantra* (pronounced "mohn-trah") is another Sanskrit word that has made its way into everyday speech. ("*'Prioritize'* is his mantra.") A mantra can be a word or a phrase mentally repeated (or chanted aloud) to aid our focus. When we repeat the Buddha's name, we're remembering him and focusing on our own awakened energy. This can also dissolve our clinging to negative habit energy by substituting positive habit energy. Another technique for conscious breathing is mentally saying "in" while breathing in, and "out" while breathing out. Some people mentally recite "in-in-in" and "out-out-out" to emphasize the whole flow of each breath. *Tip:* It's quite okay if you find yourself breathing out a bit longer than you're breathing in.

A Buddhist *gatha* (pronounced "gah-thah") is a verse from a sutra or an individual's expression of spiritual insight. You might think of them as prayers, but they aren't necessarily expressed to any supreme creator deity. For example, here's a stanza in the Sutra on Full Awareness of Breathing:

> Breathing in, I know that I am breathing in.
> Breathing out, I know that I am breathing out.

Using that gatha as a conscious breathing tool, say the first line to yourself when breathing in, the second when breathing out. It's very suitable for a 20- to 30-minute meditation. You might make a mental shorthand to just the mantra "in" and "out." Keep your mindfulness on your breathing, not the words.

Embellishing it, Thich Nhat Hanh offers this marvelous gatha:

> Breathing in, I know that I am breathing in.
> Breathing out, I know that I am breathing out.
> Breathing in, I calm my body.
> Breathing out, I smile.
> Breathing in, I'm aware of the present moment.
> Breathing out, I'm aware it's a wonderful moment.

After you get the hang of it, you can use mental shorthand:

[In-breath] think "in" …	[Out-breath] think "out"
[In] think "calm" …	[Out] think "smile"
[In] think *present moment* …	[Out] think *wonderful moment*

Slowly, Slowly, Peace Is Every Breath

At first, you might not have even been aware you were breathing. Half the time, who is?! Gradually, you'll become more familiar with breath and its landscape. Your awareness becomes more discerning.

If a breath's long, just notice that fact. If another breath's short, just notice that. Some start out one way and turn out another. Notice how far one out-breath can seem to go. Also be attentive to how breath begins on its own, without your willing it. (Ta-Da!) Notice, too, how breath flows. Is it powerful or soft; shallow or deep? And there's a space in between breaths; notice that lull, too. In so doing, you're training your awareness to be more supple. The poet Emily Dickinson once called herself an "inebriate of air," but connoisseur of breath will do just fine, too. As Zen teacher Darlene Cohen observes, so much changes when we shift from a desire-based culture to a breath-based culture: we notice within each moment a greater range of possibility and a wealth of nuance and texture.

Breath is a tremendous tool for unifying body and mind as one. Put in a different way, Shunryu Suzuki Roshi gives us a marvelous teaching when he calls breathing a *hinge*. We breathe in, he says, and air comes into the inner world; exhale, air goes to the outer world. Inner world / outer world—both endless. Actually, there's but one world, the whole world. Breath passes through us like someone going through a swinging door. "When your mind is pure and calm enough to follow this movement," Suzuki continues, "there is nothing: no 'I,' no world, no mind nor body; just a swinging door."

As you learn to become more and more immersed in awareness of your breathing, one very interesting thing you'll notice is how not only your breathing, but also your body, feelings, and mind, will slow down—calming, deepening. You might experience a feeling of at-oneness, a sense of release, and pleasure. Maybe it will be a new kind of pleasure. If so, go with it. You deserve it. You've earned it by simply being. Meditation can bring not only peace but also great joy. (See for yourself why the Buddha's smiling.) True happiness is a mind at peace.

 Hear and Now _____

"'I am breathing in and making my whole body calm and at peace.' It is like drinking a cool glass of lemonade on a hot day and feeling your body become cool inside. When you breathe in, the air enters your body and calms all the cells of your body. At the same time each 'cell' of your mind also becomes more peaceful. The three are one, and each one is all three. This is the key to meditation. Breathing brings the sweet joy of meditation to you. You become joyful, fresh, and tolerant, and everyone around you will benefit."

—Venerable Thich Nhat Hanh

Turning Off the Radio: Quiet Mind

Body, breath, and *mind* interplay in conscious breathing. And what is mind? It's like a mirror across which things pass without ever penetrating or remaining within it. Put a flower in front of it, we see a flower. (Our eyes never directly contact a flower.) Besides this clarity, it also is capable of conceptualizing: it sees "a rose" as well as a flower, compares it to other roses, wonders whether they would smell as sweet by any other name, and so on. So mind can wander and be focused.

"Turning off the radio" is Robert Aitken Roshi's phrase for extraneous conceptualizing; mind wandering. Of course, in the decades since he coined it, the analogy has become only more apt. That is, we've become a soundtracked culture, with music to study by, drive by, walk by, those cell phone conversations you wish you hadn't overheard, and less and less chance for us to have big ears for the amazing sounds of nature all around (our own life music, and the spacious silence with which it's interwoven), within and without. Quieting the mind is very basic. It's a gentle shushing of our roof-brain chatter. Our built-in, automatic mental radio talk show twitter fades off into the background, if we just let it. Let go. Let be. *Question:* Does it ever shut entirely off? Misconception 97 is that Buddhist meditation is about becoming a blank—nihilism. (*Click!* OFF.) No, and (Misconception 98) you don't drift off and away, elsewhere. Nirvana's not only now (or never) but clearly here (hear, hear!).

Our base camp of meditation makes available the solidity and clarity we need to be aware of and allows us to let go of our inner monologues and dialogues. Observing instead of reacting, we can see how our mind creates an illusory sense of life and self. So we don't change the world; we change our minds, and we notice our world has changed, too. Because mind is capable of such wonders, why not get to know your mind?

Leaves from the Bodhi Tree

Contemporary Cambodian Buddhist patriarch Maha Ghosananda tells of a young monk who studied diligently, every day. But he grew upset that he couldn't learn everything, and soon couldn't sleep or eat. Finally, he came to the Buddha and asked to leave the order. "Please," he said, "there are many teachings and I can't master them all. I'm not fit to be a monk." The Buddha told him, "Don't worry. To be free you must master only one thing." The monk begged, "Please teach me. If you give me just one practice, I will do it wholeheartedly, and I'm sure I can succeed." So the Buddha told him, "Master the mind. When you've mastered the mind, you'll know everything."

Being aware of our breathing, we become aware of our mind. Here follow three tips for optimal mindfulness.

Infinite Soundscape: Hear the Here, of the Here and Now

The idea of silencing the mind can be a kind of stereotype. Meditation's not a sensory deprivation tank, though even there you'd still hear your body. So don't be surprised to find meditation accompanied by the gentle drums of your pulse, the lilting flute of your breath, and the hum of body-mind's nervous system, all along for the ride.

Here's a simple exercise with natural sound you can practice anytime, anywhere. It's especially good in beginning silent meditation. Stop and *listen* to the life where you're living, 360 degrees all around. Appreciate *where* you are. (A study of cell phone conversation finds the majority is about "I'm over here, and heading over there.") Be *here*, now. What sounds near? What's far? And in between? Bearing witness, don't label the sounds, just hear them as they are. You might hear the jagged yawp of a bird, the corkscrewing siren of a passing fire truck, or the rumble of a window shaken by the wind. Just hear what you hear. Without reacting. Passing cars might be more soothing than you'd expect, more like ocean waves (expressing the contour of roads). Let go of your prejudices and preconceptions, and listen. And notice how sounds overlap in curious, unrepeatable rhythms! All they mean is that you're here, and now. Let whatever comes to your senses during meditation awaken you to that fact. And continue to enjoy your breathing. Notice the sound of your own breathing. Lastly, notice too the space in which it all occurs, silently ( ). Notice how your mind is always aware, whether there's sound or silence, and how continual awareness seems to grow.

You can always appreciate this unique symphony of life, moment to moment. (Stay tuned for encores.) Meditation on the natural music of sound (*plink!*) and silence ( ) cannot only expand your awareness, but also make it more centered, concentrated, and discerning. What often keeps us from this grounding is an inner narrator, labeling sounds (and sensations, thoughts, and feelings) and fading away when we shift attention from everything being our personal story, to the more expansive reality of What Is—things as they are, in and of themselves, in a state of continual becoming and seemingly without limit. You might treat all your senses, feelings, and thoughts like this. Notice the space between and silence around them; they diminish as the spaciousness of continual awareness seems to silently grow.

Notice What You Notice: Mind Quiets On Its Own

Quieting your mind is like calming your breath. You're not trying to make that happen. Your job's just to breathe and observe. Observing your breath and all its qualities, it tends to calm and slow, by itself, slowing and releasing. Thoughts come and go. Just observe them, too—but don't invite them to sit down with you for tea. Unattended, they'll go off on their own merry way. ("All conditioned things have their arising, and their passing away.") Like clouds, thoughts evaporate, and the blue sky looks bigger. You might imagine your meditation a mountain, and thought-clouds parting and dissolving when they touch it.

Be like a mirror or a mountain lake, reflecting whatever passes before it. Tibetan Buddhists suggest watching your thoughts the way an old person on a park bench watches children at play, without thought as to which kids are yours. Your thoughts aren't necessarily you. By being aware of them, but not identifying with them, they recede. Dzogchen teacher Lama Surya Das suggests: "Don't let your mind bother you and don't bother your mind."

Take a Kindly Attitude Toward Your Mind

Why not treat your mind as a mother would her own child? Have compassion for yourself. Smile at habitual scenarios (again, "mouth yoga"). By just letting be, being compassionately aware, habit energy lets go its grip. Remember the first Noble Truth. You're not alone in this. There'd be no doors without walls, so don't bang your head on them (as we all tend to do). Be kind to yourself!

As you learn compassion for your own baggage, you'll have it for others. But we often forget that compassion for all beings includes ourselves. If you can't be kind to yourself, who else can you be kind to?

The Path Is the Goal: Walking Meditation

"Slowly, slowly, step by step, each step is a meditation, each step is a prayer." Perhaps one reason I love Maha Ghosananda's saying so much is because I love walking meditation and so I know it as literal footsteps. Walking meditation is often an opportunity to stretch after sitting. (In Zen, it's usually done for five minutes in between stretches of sitting. Theravadins also enjoy it in between sittings, for more like 20 minutes.) In and of itself, it can be a marvelous and very powerful practice. It is said that, after Enlightenment, the Buddha's next meditation was walking, getting up and taking mindful steps around the bodhi tree, grateful for its having sheltered him during his long night. Having experienced total transformation, he put it into action. Walking meditation can lead to enlightenment no less than sitting meditation.

Indoors or outdoors, find some place where you can walk without obstruction or interruption. A backyard will do, as will a quiet street, a big emptyish room, or even a hallway. The idea is to go in a circular path, clockwise. Your hands can be at your side.

Or you can form a cosmic mudra (which is what I do). Some people join their palms in a gassho. Others make a fist with the left hand and cover it with the right hand, holding them to their navel or hara. Still others join their hands behind their back, like a bird with folded wings. Here, too, assume a posture that embodies dignity. And don't forget mouth yoga.

Your assignment's to be aware of your breath *and* your motion (lifting a foot, placing a foot, setting a foot down). And see, too, how your mind interplays as you do so. I know of two paces. Slowest, is one breath per step (in, left; out, right). That slowwwwww. Visualize you're a king or queen, making a decree with each step. Or visualize yourself as a lion or lioness, walking so slowly. Or visualize a flower blossoming or a fresh breeze arising from every step.

Along the Path

It's thought that when primates first stood, that freed their forelimbs (wow! a whole new world). So, brains expanded to meet that challenge. (Note which followed which.) Thus dawned the human species, the only species comfortable on two legs. In the mere act of walking, of being bipedal, we can reclaim an ancient wisdom hidden just beneath the whirl-a-gig surface of our ever faster-paced world. Walking literally creates the world, *our* world, step by step.

The slow pace, for 20 minutes, can be really refreshing and healing. Another way is self-paced. Walk slowly as you breathe normally. Note how many steps you take per breath, and stay with that. Count steps as you do so. Maybe 1:2—or 2:2 or 3:3—for in-breath, and the same on exhalation. Later, you can experiment with an extra step, to breathe in or exhale more. Some people say "in" with each step during inhalation, and "out" during exhalation (in-in-out-out; four steps). Or some say "peace-peace-peace." Others use gathas, one line for each breath. As Dharma teacher and Zen gardener Wendy Johnson was practicing walking meditation one day, she found herself mentally saying to herself, "Walking … on the … green … earth" (for four steps, breathing in), "each … step … is … peace" (*breathing out*). (She says the words came up to her through the soles of her feet.) Or try one syllable for each step, such as "fresh breeze blows" or "lotus blooms," for three steps. PureLanders might say "Am-i-ta-bha." Whatever you try, just coordinate your breathing and your walking, even and flowing; and coordinate that with your count and your half smile. (This all may be subtler than trying to walk and chew gum at the same time, but in being done proves much more fun.)

I know for me, each step is a pilgrimage … a going forth and stepping out into the unknown, embracing the entire universe, and recognizing oneness with whatever's at hand, realizing it … feeling the earth coming up, meeting my foot, a kiss from my soles to my toes … an ever-new discovery of harmony, gratitude, calm peace, and quiet joy … the feeling of having arrived … the only destination there ever is: the present moment, our true home. Plus, it's a really nice body massage! But that's just my attempt to verbalize my own general experience of it. Try it a few times, and see.

Here are some tips for walking in mindfulness:

♦ Notice what you notice. Don't get attached. Kiss the joy as it flies. (The orange-green iridescence on the wings of flies buzzing around some dung on the mosaic of the ground is no less perfect than dawn sunlight tingeing cloud tips with gentle gongs of peach incense.) Practice equanimity.

♦ If you're distracted, look at the ground a yard or so ahead, or the back of the person ahead of you in a group.

♦ Walking meditation is like dancing—you're not trying to reach any particular spot. (There's no destination. You've already arrived: in the here and in the now.) Step by step, peace is every step.

♦ By taking just one peaceful step, you're affirming peace in the world is possible. Don't just imagine it. Be it.

> **Hear and Now** _____
>
> "People say that walking on water is a miracle, but to me, walking peacefully on the Earth is the real miracle. The Earth is a miracle. Each step is a miracle. Taking steps on our beautiful planet can bring real happiness."
>
> —Thich Nhat Hanh

Q-Tips and Lotion: From a Beginner's First-Aid Kit

A teacher and sangha are the best medicine for hindrances you may encounter along the Path. Meanwhile, here are eight tips from my unofficial manual of Standard Operating Procedure (SOP):

1. Remember the Middle Way: the guitar string neither too loose nor too tight. Stay focused, but don't try too hard.

2. Mind-wandering is natural. Noticing how it strays and returning to breath (over and over again) all take place within mindfulness.

3. Sometimes people feel a bit dizzy meditating. Add an extra beat or two to your exhalation. Exhaling more than you inhale rids the body of excess carbon dioxide.

4. If you're going around in circles, try this: Take a slow deep breath, filling your lungs and then your belly. Then slowly let it all out, belly then lungs. Repeat twice more. Now return to your practice.

5. Only you can practice; no one will do it for you. But watch out for treating Buddhism as an off-the-shelf "self-help" therapy: otherwise, it can be just another way of building up or consolidating the ego (me, me, me).

6. Don't look for results. Don't try to "get" anything out of it. Subtle and gradual changes are just as good as dramatic and sudden. If a friend should remark you seem calmer or happier lately, you're on the right track.

7. Being kindly to yourself, you'll find yourself seeing more kindly connection with others.

8. You can't step into the same river twice (not even once!). Don't expect today's meditation to be like yesterday's or tomorrow's.

All the tips and tricks are just tools. After you get to the other shore, set down the raft of skillful means, and proceed. So, now don't just do something—just sit! In the immortal words of Lama Surya Das: "Meditation is a way of being, not just one more kind of doing."

The Least You Need to Know

- Meditation's like that center referred to when people speak of being centered. Integral to wisdom and conscious conduct, mind training is a key to continual practice.

- Posture matters. The body isn't evil, or to be escaped. Our body is a temple.

- Breath is a natural interface between body and mind, and it is always available. Conscious or mindful breathing means being aware of your breathing and nothing else.

- You're not trying to control your breath, or your mind. Just be aware. Stopping to just be aware can calm your breath and your mind.

- Quieting the mind doesn't mean turning into a stone statue. Trying to banish thoughts and control your mind only creates more thoughts and a restless mind. Simple awareness can clear mental clutter and sharpen your mind.

- More than mere stretching, walking meditation is a powerful practice.

- Take a friendly attitude toward your mind. Everyone encounters difficulties. Learn from others' wisdom about common hurdles in meditation.

Look Within: Insight Meditation

In This Chapter

◆ Stopping and seeing: tranquility and insight

◆ Noting: the hallmark of emotional intelligence

◆ The body scan: a total tune-up

◆ Element meditation: cosmic interconnection

◆ *Metta* (loving kindness): the basis for compassion, joy, and equanimity

Now that your Meditation Base Camp is all set, we'll look into four major schools of practice. If one resonates with you, try it out. The matter at hand is life—your life. Buddhism is only a lens for that. (Don't get attached to the tool or the word.) "Buddha" is but a word for True Happiness. It's your birthright … your true nature … your own buddha nature.

Various Theravada teachings coalesce in the West to make available the path of Insight Meditation (*Vipassana*). It teaches us tranquility and looking deeper. Compare your life, your mind, and your heart to a forest lake surrounded by hungry animals in the bushes. The wind can only ripple the surface, not the whole body of water. When the lake is calm, it can mirror whatever passes before it. If someone were to toss a stone in, we'd see it fall way down to the bottom. It's not about making a wish as the stone sinks; it's about looking within … looking deeper.

This Is

> **Vipassana** represents one of hundreds of resources available in Theravada that embrace the entire Pali canon of sutras and commentaries. Relatively free of metaphor or ceremony, with informal teacher–student relations, and translated into Western idiom (often with eclectic borrowings), it's become the most popular Theravadin "import" in the West.

Stopping and Seeing Deeply: Calm Concentration and Deep Insight

Vipassana means "clear seeing," with a connotation of looking within. Of course, life is all around, without and within. But when we experience something for ourselves, then whatever insight is born of it can take root and ripen in our own life. It entails stopping, cooling out, and investigating. In so doing, one connects with an unbroken teaching lineage extending back to the historical Buddha. Remember, among his last words were: "Be a lamp unto yourself." Look within and work it all out for yourself. No one else can do it for you. So a Vipassana teacher acts as your friend along the Path, more mentor than master. To earn accredited lineage as a Vipassana teacher, there's a review process by a senior patriarch, but it's not necessary to study under him (or her) for long periods of time; a number of teachers can recommend a student for advancement.

Insight Meditation includes experiential, present-moment, compassionate inquiry into the nature of self, finding it impermanent, interconnected, and unstable. (Before exploring such meditation, we might clarify here an interesting point about the Marks of Existence. These factors of impermanence and interconnection might seem to cause us dukkha, but also, at their core, are beyond duality, and are thus free, so are also nirvana. So we might say either dukkha or nirvana are a mark of all existence, depending on our view.)

Meditation, as noted earlier, along with effort, turns on the spokes of concentration (*samadhi*, Sanskrit; *samatha*, Pali) and mindfulness (*sati*); or if you prefer, tranquility and insight. Thus far, our base camp has emphasized the first: *stopping* (developing one-pointed concentration, calming, or finding tranquility).

Stopping is a very good practice, anytime. It's not unusual to feel buffeted around willy-nilly, like a pinball. The word for our world's pace is *Faster!*—all the more reason to stop from time to time. For example, next time you see a stop sign, welcome it as a reminder to return to the present moment. Feel bone and blood and breath. When you hear a bird or see a child who awakens your heart, consider it life calling you, a chance to practice stopping on the fly. Stop, sense your breath, and check in with the Here and Now (bowing is optional). Stop whatever you think you're doing (hatching a plot, say) and call home. Our true home, the here and now, is the only home ever available to us.

Stopping is akin to the Buddha's renunciation. It implies cessation of grasping. Our body–spirit–mind can do wonders, if given the chance. Breath releases. The mind relaxes. Energy recharges. We're solidly grounded in where we are, with space to reflect What Is. So with stopping and calming as a base, we can look within. This is *insight*. It's not baseless, abstract conceptualization; rather, we notice what's presently real. For instance, consider our breath. What's more impermanent than breath, ephemeral as a sigh? What's more interconnected than breath, as we breathe in the exhalation of plants and trees and nourish them with our out-breath? How unsatisfactory to try to cling to breath, and how liberating to simply let breath flow on its own. How unsubstantial, yet vital. It's limitless, flowing, and free. So, too, are we.

Such experiential present-moment mindful insight (Vipassana) refines our ability to analyze, discriminate, and discern. Just as we note the qualities of our breath's dimensions, textures, and nuances, so, too, can we discern the same in our life. Just as one-pointed concentration on breath lets the mind rest and be still, so, too, can our mind develop marvelous clarity, penetrative depth, and subtle analysis. Recalling the life of the Buddha as a teaching, we're reminded how he used his own life to understand the meaning of life itself. After he renounced (stopped) both his over-sensual and over-ascetic practices, his senses became more focused and more in the present. With mindfulness, he was able to concentrate on each aspect of every moment, which led to insight into the Three Marks of Existence and the Four Noble Truths. Having discovered that the human mind shapes our world and how we respond to it, he used his own mind as a key to fathom the nature of mind itself. So, too, can we.

 Leaves from the Bodhi Tree _____

Hear the lovely word *sati* ring in the names of two sutras central to Vipassana: *Anapanasati* and *Satipathana*, Mindfulness of Breathing and The Four Establishments of Mindfulness (body, feelings, consciousness, and the objects and contents of consciousness; the Three Dharma Seals apply to each).

Using our own life as our laboratory, with the focused beam of mindfulness, we can look deeply at the Four Noble Truths and the Three Marks. To break a destructive habit, for example, we can examine karma with calm clarity, contemplating the root of our daily actions and their results. As Burmese Vipassana teacher S. N. Goenka says, "The whole process is one of total realization, the process of self-realization, truth pertaining to oneself, by oneself, within oneself."

Samatha and Vipassana, together with diligence (effort), function with the rest of the Eightfold Path, but consider how they work in tandem, as a duo. In the sutra commentary called *The Establishment of Truth* (*Chengshilun* or *Satyasiddhi*), samatha is compared to a calm meadow, and Vipassana to planting seeds there. With samatha, you can get a grip on weeds; with Vipassana, you can cut them away, from the roots. If samatha is like soaking beans in water, Vipassana is like cooking them.

Those are basics of Insight Meditation. Here follow four common techniques and meditations (tools and medicine) from along the Vipassana Trail: (1) noting, (2) the body scan, (3) element meditation, and (4) metta. Regarding these, the Buddha's own words are simple: come, try, and see for yourself.

Note the Itch Without Scratching

Meditation is applicable to all aspects of daily life. When we sit to meditate on conscious breathing, we're stopping and stepping aside from habitual affairs, letting go and letting be. What's wrong with mindfully scratching an itch? Nothing, but noting (the itch, and the urge to scratch) instead of scratching can discipline and refine our awareness, so as to recognize our habits and impulses without having to act upon them all the time, like a trained monkey dancing for peanuts. (Persian poet Hafiz likens it to a divine elephant with amnesia trying to live in an ant hole.) With insight and practice, the dinosaur-size habits of difficult emotions can dwindle to the size of little elves. Eventually, these habits might become the size of a mustard seed, which the least breeze could blow away from the palm of a hand.

The mindful practice of noting was popularized by Burmese teacher Mahasi Sayadaw (1904–1982). We've already briefly touched on it in the previous chapter: "noticing what we notice." It's not only a means of quieting the mind (samatha), but also a tool for insightful inquiry (Vipassana).

Try staying with breath through conscious breathing, and incorporate noting its details. Lightly, make soft, gentle mental notes of your breathing. As you do so, allow yourself to go into greater and greater detail, while staying in a tranquil, meditative state. For example, be aware of and note the phases of your breath: "air fragrant at nostrils … air filling nostrils … belly expanding …" and so on; or however it seems to you. See if noting might open up conscious breathing so you can concentrate on it even more, and see if that makes you even calmer and more lucid.

A clear stream might look motionless, until we place a little leaf on the surface and *Zoom!* it sails off. So, too, does meditation show us our mind's transparent currents. When your mind wanders, as it will, just make a mental note of that. It's all part of the continuous meditation. You might repeat a key word, like a friendly, subliminal mental bell. For instance, say to yourself, "mind wandering, mind wandering" (or "ripples, ripples" … on the quiet forest pool). And return your focus to the present moment. Always stay with the breath.

From a base of calm and peace, noting can help mirror your mind. For example, you might note when you're anticipating the future ("rehearsing, rehearsing") or analyzing the past ("reviewing, reviewing") rather than dwelling here and now. It's interesting how much of your life is invested in analyzing or anticipating. What tempting, un-satisfactory illusions of a substantial, permanent, separate self might such grasping and longing feed? Might you be happier if you let all that go? In other words, use whatever you note as openings for inquiry into your true nature, levers to return to Original Mind, your interrelation with What Is. As the saying goes, "Inquiring minds want to know."

Tips for Noting

Here are nine tips for noting, from along the Vipassana Trail.

1. You'll notice little dances of monkey-mind. Don't block them, just note. They're often twitters of "I like it," "I dislike it," and the more neutral "it's just okay." (Indifference can constrict us as much as grasping or fearing.) You might be sur-prised to see how much energy's dedicated to this dance of thumbs up, thumbs down, and shrugs—and to discover what a relief it is to no longer dance to their tune! Three generic mental Post-Its for this:

   ◆ "… attraction, attraction …"

   ◆ "… aversion, aversion …"

   ◆ "… neutral, neutral …"

2. See if you can phrase your notes without "I"—not "I am aware my fingers are tingling," but "fingers tingling." As you progress in your practice, you might fur-ther abbreviate the note to just "tingling."

3. As with basic meditation, noting's a gentle process. Use it with a light touch. Don't be someone who staples posters to lampposts with your noting. Just tap the moment gently with your mental Post-It, and move on. The idea's to note but not react. Pause, observe, and proceed.

4. Imagine each note is a drop of a secret-formula cleansing agent dissolving dirt and grime and polishing your pristine, shining buddha nature.

5. You might not have been aware of your mind at all, nor that you're not always living in the now. Mindfulness can be like placing a leaf on the surface of what looks like a calm, still stream, and *zoom!* the leaf sails off on a speedy current we hadn't seen until now. It's good just to be aware of this.

6. If your mind-wanderings seem to go on and on before you stop to note them, you might note, "mind wandering, mind wandering; three minutes" (guesstimate) or "mind wandering, on and on," and return to the present (conscious breathing).

7. Don't get embroiled in a running commentary, like a sports announcer. That is, don't comment on your noting, much less on comments like a pair of facing mirrors (reflecting each other endlessly), known as "infinite regress." Let it go. No need to narrate a whole chain of associations, which can never be reconstructed anyway. Just return to the breath.

8. Relax. Suspend judgment. Simply observe. Stay with and keep returning back to the breath.

9. Don't forget to eventually let go of noting, and enjoy choiceless awareness.

Training Heart as Well as Head: Emotional Intelligence

A popular spin-off of noting as a lever of mindful awareness and insightful inquiry is called *emotional intelligence*. It's a needed balance to a tendency to overemphasize our intelligence quotient (I.Q.), all head and no heart. Being aware of our feelings is superior to feeling without awareness, because our feelings—particularly difficult emotions—can pull us by the nose when we lack awareness. Here is one way to consider practicing emotional intelligence in difficult situations. Think of the red, yellow, and green lights at a traffic intersection. (1) *Red*. Stop. Be aware of problematic thoughts, emotions, or impulses as they arise, rather than being run by them. (2) *Yellow*. Slow down. Evaluate how, if at all, to respond to the situation. What are your options? Which will most benefit all concerned, for now? (3) *Green*. Test your insightful decision through action. If the outcome isn't 100 percent as you'd expected, accept it rather than start a whole new chain of difficulty. I've come to learn, for example, to sit on my initial impulse to respond to statements or issues that I know are problematic (to me), rather than feel I need to immediately reply. The problem usually proves to be my perception rather than any actual present threat. The greater my sense of urgency, the stronger the signal telling me to just hold back, wait, watch, and learn.

You can engage in noting all the time, 24/7, not just on a meditation cushion. Note while peeling potatoes or folding linen. In walking meditation, for example, try noting your movements as a continuous series of separate sensations. Be comfortable and go really slowwww, maybe one in-breath per step and one out-breath per step. Note: "left heel reaching out," "left heel touching down," "ball of left foot touching down," "right ankle automatically rotating upward," "toes of left foot touching down," "right knee bending," "left foot and ground in full contact," "right heel lifting up" … and so on. Directly perceiving walking, can you see its impermanence and its lack of any separate identity? Where is your walk but in each step? If feelings accompany any phase, such as fear of falling or gratitude for solidity, note them. If they reoccur, direct your mindfulness there and inquire if anything is associated with them.

Case in point: The other night, taking my evening walk over Russian Hill, I was experiencing an exceptionally intense nausea and stomachache. I caught myself saying to myself, "Aargh! I'm in pain! Ouch! I can't make it go away! Can't concentrate! I'm not going to make it! Doomed!" and so on. I was practically ready to cry for my mommy when I realized I hadn't noted any of it yet. So I shut up, stopped, got out of my own way, and noted the sensation: "belly aching, belly aching." And *Bing!* the feeling collapsed like a house of cards and vanished the way a television image does when a television set is shut off. In its place returned awareness of my stomach rising and falling with my breathing in the beautiful early spring night air, and I was able to feel each footstep again. As I walked, I inquired a little and felt my tummy ache as an accumulation of stress I hadn't faced (couldn't stomach). I was literally belly-aching about it, rather than facing it, accepting it, seeing it, seeing through it, and moving on.

So it's important to note feelings that come up, as well as to experience them. Buddhism doesn't ask that we ignore the fear or anger or anxiety of our emotional realms, but rather suggests that if they're experienced mindfully, they're no longer such threats. They no longer run us. For instance, imagine you're showing up for a basketball game and you hear somebody shout, "Hey, everyone! Pee Wee's here!" If that person sees you react, then he knows he has you. He has only to shout "Pee Wee" to make you lose your focus and miss a shot. But, if you feel the irk, note its root at your self-image, and evaluate how reacting would negatively impact your game, then you're not letting your feelings run you. Now you're being *emotionally intelligent*.

This is a tool for transformation, furnishing an essential distance and offering a way of smiling at unwanted habit energy and letting it go. Without nourishment, seeds won't grow. Calmly noting, you can get a handhold on worn-out habits and traits and illusions of ego, break them down, and let them crumble away as you relax into freedom. The little Post-Its of noting are like brackets placed around something, [like this]. These brackets enable it be dislodged, observed, examined, understood, and let go. No need to throw anything away—doing that would be too forceful, creating further karma to deal with further along. Noting lets you see what works for you, so as to nourish those seeds, and so as to not water seeds of what doesn't further. (*Question:* How many Vipassana meditators does it take to screw in a light bulb? *Answer:* Two— one to do it, and one to note it.)

The Chinese word for mindfulness. "Now," above; "mind/heart," below. Mindfulness brings our mind back to the present moment. Just one breath can bring body and mind together as one, in the now. (A block version of the word on the left, cursive in the middle, and an even more flowing version on the right.)

(*Calligraphy: Kazuaki Tanahashi*)

The Wisdom of the Body

Common Misconception 7,462: "Meditation is all so mental." *Au contraire!* Buddhism's an opportunity to integrate word, deed, and heart—body, spirit, and mind. Here follow two meditations grounded in the body's innate wisdom and its wide amplitude of sensations and awareness, full of emotional and spiritual resonance: (1) the Body Scan and (2) Element Meditation. These, and the following meditation on metta, are all presented as a kind of shorthand for you to try. If you like any, practice them with a teacher, in a group, sometime.

The Body Scan: A Whole-Body, Whole-Mind Clean Sweep

The first time out, start slowly. Once you get it, with practice you'll find a pattern. Once familiar with the pattern, you can even do it in a few breaths. You can also learn longer, more detailed versions.

It's done lying down, on your back. Your arms are at your sides, and your legs are uncrossed. Take a few mindful breaths, and then begin by directing your attention to the toes of your left foot. Continue conscious breathing and see if there are any sensations there. Imagine your in-breaths are contacting this focal point of your body, and your out-breaths are exhaling any tensions. As tension and emotions are released, note them doing so. Note, too, how your sense of yourself changes with them.

Contact the sensation, whatever it is, and move on. Notice the sole of your left foot. Don't visualize it, experience it. Stay with your breathing, and concentrate on your sole until you sense it. Continue working your way up until you've scanned your left foot. Then scan your right foot. See if there are any right–left differences.

> ### Hear and Now
>
> "Your body can sink into the bed, mat, floor, or ground until your muscles stop making the slightest effort to hold you together. This is a profound letting go at the level of your muscles and the motor neurons which govern them. The mind quickly follows if you give it permission to stay open and wakeful…. It's the whole body that breathes, the whole body that is alive. In bringing mindfulness to the body as a whole, you can reclaim your entire body as the focus of your being and your vitality, and remind yourself that 'you,' whoever you are, are not just a resident of your head."
>
> —Dr. Jon Kabat-Zinn, *Wherever You Go, There You Are*

Move up to your ankles, calves, knees, thighs, groin, pelvis, hips, and so on. Note areas of tension or pain. Note areas of pleasure or bliss. Note neutral areas. Take time when you scan your head. Note any tension in your jaw, and let it release. The same is true for your chin, back of your neck, lips, tongue, palate, nostrils, cheeks, eyelids, eyes, eyebrows, forehead, temples, and entire scalp.

Finally, concentrate on the tip of your head, where your hair meets your scalp. As you do so, feel your entire skeleton. After a minute or two, move your attention beyond the tip of your head, to a point a few inches beyond your head. From that spot, let the focus of your awareness vanish into space.

How do you feel compared to when you started? Did you note particular areas as reservoirs of tension or emotion? Common speech reflects this awareness when we say someone's carrying the world on their shoulders, or when we say life can be a pain in the neck, and so on. Four key emotional reservoirs are the hips, navel, chest, and throat. Aligning our lower back to make contact with the ground thrusts our hips out, sometimes releasing withheld anger. The hara center (defined in Chapter 10) is below the navel and can have a warm, strong, centering emotional influence. The center of our chest is our spiritual and emotional heart, the reservoir of dark, tight sorrows as well as bright, expansive love. And, as messenger for expressing our feelings, our throat might feel tight or open, perhaps holding tears or song. Noting enables us to be aware of the twisted ropes and grasping knots within our body that keep us from flowing freely, as well as the humming energy capable of elevating our spirits. It can help us examine what we're holding on to or what we think we're holding on to, because what's clutched is often not present in the here and now, but rather buried in our body like heirlooms in attic trunks. The scan is a good way to smooth out knots we've tied ourselves into.

This awareness is also very useful when in the thick of a seemingly dangerous emotional situation. First, we can defuse any sense of danger by noting it. Rather than saying to ourselves, "Oh no, end of the world, this is it," we first note the alarm: "feeling angry," "feeling defensive," or whatever. Then we note where the feeling "lives" in our body. By noting "constricted chest," or "lightheaded," the sensation can dissipate. And the blockage can yield insight.

Meditation's not about becoming an emotional zombie. Rather, it's an opportunity to (1) root out unwanted feelings and habits, (2) water the seeds of good habits and feelings, (3) establish and maintain the ability to have an awareness of choices, and (4) choose *wisely* (rather than feel overwhelmed or react unthinkingly). Buddhism's about our whole body being one with our whole mind and heart. As we'll see next, that includes the whole cosmos.

Hear and Now

"When the surf echoes and crashes out to the horizon, its whorls repeat in similar ratios inside our flesh.... We are extremely complicated, but our blood and hormones are fundamentally seawater and volcanic ash, congealed and refined. Our skin shares its chemistry with the maple leaf and moth wing. The currents our bodies regulate share a molecular flow with raw sun. Nerves and flashes of lightning are related events woven into nature at different levels."

—Richard Grossinger, *Planet Medicine*

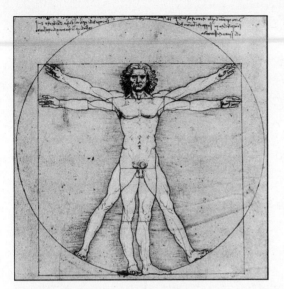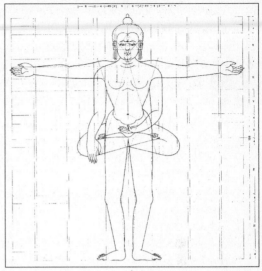

It's perfectly rational to stop and meditate. Our words "reason" and "rational" (of a sound mind) come from "ratio" and "relation." "Meditation," similarly, comes from a root for "measure." Both figures above measure the universe in human scale (macrocosm and microcosm), each differently. On the left, Da Vinci's person reaches outward to encompass the circle (infinity, eternity); on the right, the meditator draws inward, becoming a kind of circle.

Where Is Self?: The Answer Is Elementary

Here's an exercise that unites you with the whole universe. (Welcome home.) Meditation on the elements enables you to experience firsthand how what you're accustomed to calling "me" is a limited and isolated concept, and to experience a more freely unlimited and a more deeply interconnected reality. You can be at one with the process of nature. It's a guided meditation first taught to me by Vipassana teacher and author Wes Nisker.

Practicing basic meditation, consider your contact with the earth as you sit. Sink into that space. As Native Americans affirm, "The earth is all we have." You can never fall off. Feel that vital connection as a solid body, all the way down to the structuring of your bones. Consider how you depend on earth's minerals, right down to the very clay in your marrow. (*Question:* does this body belong to you?) From that feeling, next consider water. We're 75 percent liquid. Such fluidity is our internal transportation system, making us cohere. Consider your blood, sweat, and tears (sounds like the name of a rock band!), your urine, mucus, bile, and the fluid in your joints, flowing like rain and rivers. (Can you ever hold on to this watery self?) Consider how the salinity of our metabolism is that of the sea. Feel how the sea runs through your veins and lymph, all over. Like the tides, we're affected by the phases of the moon. Now consider your wateriness as the realm where life on earth evolved, and staying with that gooshy awareness, see if it's different than your usual sense of identity.

> ### Hear and Now
>
> "In meditation we can actively cultivate a sense of our coemergence with the elements and atmosphere, cellular life and sunlight, plants and animals, sentience—the whole evolutionary shebang. I have found that a deep calm and clarity and a sense of belonging can arise when people experience themselves in this way—as perfectly natural."
>
> —Wes Nisker, *The Big Bang, the Buddha, and the Baby Boom*

Then notice the air you're breathing. Consider how air covers the planet, filling all spaces, everywhere. As you breathe in, notice how you don't have to will it; your lungs naturally expand and contract with the universe. Feel the vital air-rhythm of which we're all a part. Notice how you can't hold on to it; you can only let go and let be. As you breathe in, consider you're inhaling the out-breath of trees and exhaling the in-breath of the grasses. Feel that impersonal continuity, and be one with spacious air consciousness, beyond self. Now, just like the air you breathe, the fire that fuels you isn't yours (it's a perpetual loan, like the idea of self). Through chlorophyll, we literally eat the sun. Consider how our internal campfire maintains a steady 98.6 degrees of warmth. Consider how all the chemical combustions and electrical impulses in your cells—your energy—is due to the loan of fire. This, too, is more than your usual sense of "Me." Lastly, for a moment, consider awareness, or conscious energy; it's elemental: awareness is as an element co-emerging with the complex interbeing of other elements.

So who are we, really? Our true nature, our buddha nature, is no different than nature, or nature's awareness. From such we emerge, to which we always return, and truly are.

Medicine for a Healthy Heart: Loving Kindness (*Metta*)

How's your heart? When we say someone has a good heart, we don't just mean blood pressure. Qualities associated with good-heartedness are openness, empathy, generosity, loving kindness, compassion, and wisdom. This next meditation is all about massaging that heart. If you find too much dullness in your world—or depression, anxiety, fear, or anger—this might be of interest. Really, you gotta have heart.

Sublime States: The Four Brahmaviharas

Metta is a central Vipassana meditation, and is itself one of four sublime states. It is said that a man who worshipped Brahma (God) came to the Buddha and asked, "How can I remain sure I'll be with Brahma after I die?" The Buddha answered, as always regardless of class or creed, in a way this man could understand. Because Brahma is love, the Buddha taught of opening the heart. Thus he spoke not of a hereafter but of the divine dwelling in our own hearts, called *Brahmavihara*, which can be translated as "sublime state," "divine dwelling," "heavenly abode." The realm of the sacred is right here, and is immeasurable. Abounding in an endless supply, Buddha points to four such splendid states, or energies: (1) loving kindness, (2) compassion, (3) joy, and (4) equanimity. Living with them and in them, our hearts grow as wide as the world.

It's interesting to note how Buddhist wisdom locates each as close to but different from less skillful energies. That is, each of the four states has a "far enemy," the clear opposite of the quality. And each has a "near enemy," somewhere in between the two. The near enemy is like a toxic mimic, a deceptive substitute we settle for instead of the real thing. A near enemy reinforces our sense of self and separation and so can slide us into the far enemy. For example, sentimentality inherently implies clinging; pity implies feeling superior or fear.

The Four Sublime States (Brahmaviharas)

Virtue	Near Enemy	Far Enemy
Friendliness/love	Sentimentality/selfishness	Ill-will/hatred
Compassion	Pity/grief	Contempt/cruelty
Appreciative joy	Glum boredom/cynicism	Envy/jealousy
Equanimity	Apathy/indifference	Resentment/greed/aversion

Metta translates as "loving kindness." Compassion (*karuna*) is the ability to feel *with* someone, instead of feeling something *toward* someone, and is thus a bit more active than metta. Appreciative joy (*mudita*) is the spontaneous response of gladness and rejoicing at the good fortune or success of one's self or others. (The media gossip industry, hanging on the careers of stars, is mock mudita.) Equanimity (*upekkha*) is nonattachment, even-mindedness, and balance, and may be the closest of the four to enlightenment. Its synonym in Hindi, *tatastha*, is like one who sits on the bank of a river watching the waters flow. Each can be cultivated in practice, first on a cushion in meditation, then in daily interaction in the world.

Things Go Betta with Metta

Vipassana teacher Gil Fronsdale's definition gets right to it: "Most simply, metta is the heartfelt wish for the well-being of oneself and others." Begin with yourself. Open your heart to yourself. Focus your mindfulness on your feelings about your happiness and general well-being. Maybe you feel pretty good about yourself but feel a bit vulnerable or even fragile about certain issues, such as health or financial security. Now wish yourself well-being, saying to yourself what seems appropriate. Most common is: "May I be well. May I be happy. May I be safe and secure. May I be at peace. May I thrive."

Give yourself a gift of metta. Think kindly of yourself, saying "May I be well," and visualize yourself as being well. Then move on to wishing "May I be happy," and picture a happy you. Then, move on to wishing "May I be peaceful," and envision yourself at peace. It's as if you're harnessing this natural metta force, beaming it onto yourself, and visualizing the result. Rather than beaming pure, clear-light metta, you're varying the metta, as if using a different hue each time. Wellness, happiness, and peace—it's all metta.

> ### Hear and Now
>
> "Just as a mother guards her child with her life, her only child, just so should you, too, cultivate boundless heart toward all beings. Let thoughts of loving kindness for all the world radiate boundlessly, into the sky and into the earth, all around, unobstructed, free from any hatred or ill-will. Standing or walking, sitting or lying down, as long as one is awake, one should develop this mindfulness: this is called divine abiding here."
>
> —The Buddha

Stay mindful of your heartfelt intentions. If they bring up positive feelings, amplify them; unify positive feelings with your intentions as you silently repeat your words. After opening your heart to yourself, send metta to others. Try these five stages:

1. Yourself
2. Those near and dear
3. Neutral people
4. Problem people
5. Everyone

Near and dear ones can be family, friends, teachers, and even pets. May they be well, may they be happy, and so on. A neutral person might be the postman, a bus driver, the truck driver who brings groceries to your corner store, or an unseen neighbor. May they be well, happy, and so on. Now that you're breaking the barriers between yourself and others, you come to problem people: people who have a problem and people who are a problem to you. A problem person could be someone with an illness, a rival, an enemy, or someone you just don't like. This might seem to take stronger metta, but it's the same kindly attitude that is calling for you to open your heart that much more.

Then you might visualize all the people you've sent metta to as if they're all together, and send them all metta, equally. May they be well, may they be happy, and so on. From there, you can send metta to everyone in the building, on your street, in your city, in the nation, on the continent, and on the planet. The heart knows no limits.

Tips for Practice

Having been blessed to practice metta on a retreat (a treat!) with Sharon Salzberg, I can attest that a teacher can guide you through the long form of the various phases of metta. Practicing with a group of people, you feel metta in the air. Sometimes positive energy can bring up negative, and so it helps to know you're not alone when facing a difficult phase. Meanwhile, until you find a sangha near you, here are a few tips:

◆ You're not showering your loving kindness on the people in your mind's eye, or wringing their necks with it. Rather, with the same quick, light touch of noting, you gently tap them with the thought and then move on.

◆ Before sending metta to a new group of people, picture them very well in your mind's eye. When you pick neutral people, think of people in your life for whom you have no particular emotions, no charge, one way or another. It's important to really make contact; otherwise, you might tend to rush to problem people, those with whom you're having difficult relations, or even enemies. Rushing in wouldn't be skillful; it would only reinforce the separateness you feel between you and the other person(s).

◆ One way to approach sending metta to your enemies is to see it as being the same as sending metta to your own inner enemies. That is, sending metta to yourself, you're embracing your problems and shadows as well as your accomplishments and lights.

◆ Metta isn't confined to a meditation cushion, but is also something to be carried out in word and deed, as we write and speak, and in our daily actions.

Metta makes a swell companion to mindfulness. One mindfulness motto is: "If you hold yourself dear, watch yourself well." A metta motto might be: "Take a kindly attitude toward yourself." (Who will you be kind to, if not your own provisional self?) Make best friends with yourself (your mind, your heart, and your life). Then extend that compassion. We're all in this sandbox for saints together.

May *you* be well, happy, and at peace! Much metta.

Hear and Now

"If we hold on to our humility, if we let go of our egos and stop clinging to whatever it is we're clinging to, we'll find the wonderful surprise that behind all that gunk is a natural kindness, a love for everyone and everything that we never thought we had. And if we let ourselves act from that place, we'll discover a kindness without limits and an unutterable peace."

—Geri Larkin

The Least You Need to Know

◆ Vipassana (also known as Insight Meditation) is the most popular form of Theravada in the West. It's scientific, as its insights are obtained through personal observation, open for testing and replicable by anyone.

◆ Insight Meditation teaches how to observe and learn from our own immediate experience, using calm concentration (*samatha*) and analytic inquiry (*Vipassana*). It enables us to see, understand, and realize our interconnectedness, impermanence, and liberation from suffering (nirvana).

◆ Four meditations are noting, the body scan, the elements, and metta.

◆ Vipassana applies to body, heart, and mind, and isn't limited to sessions on a cushion. It is a continuous meditation, integral throughout our daily lives. (Start with breath.)

12

Gate to the Source: Zen

In This Chapter

- ◆ Zen: meditation
- ◆ Lineage: a continuum of teaching
- ◆ Using words to go beyond words: koan, mondo, and turning phrases
- ◆ Mahayana perspectives

Who are you? What is meditation? What is your life? These questions are at the heart of this dynamic practice known as Zen. What is Zen? It's inexpressible, yet it must be expressed. But wait: all the books, all the websites, all the seminars—none have fully revealed the Ultimate Zen Truth, ever, until now—which, in a *Complete Idiot's Guide* first, I'm going to tell you right here. And it is this:

(And you can quote me. Verbatim.) So now that I've told you what you already knew (no?), what else is there to say?

> ### ✿ Hear and Now
>
> "When Buddhism first came to China it was most natural for the Chinese to speak about it in terms of Taoist philosophy, because they both share a view of life as a flowing process in which the mind and consciousness of man is inextricably involved. It is not as if there is a fixed screen of consciousness over which our experience flows and leaves a record. It is that the field of consciousness itself is part of the flowing process, and therefore the mind of man is not a separate entity observing the process from out-side, but is integrally involved with it … The practice of Zen is to experience the overall [flowing] pattern directly, and to know one's self as the essence of the pattern."
>
> —Alan Watts, *What Is Zen?*

Zen: A Practice Without Any Particular Practice

Zen means "meditation," and "the awakening associated with meditation." (The path is the goal.) Relying on intuition, Zen might seem mystic, but it's really not mysterious. It's playing baseball to play baseball, not swinging a bat around. It's a vast sky, without limit. It's your life. It's your true nature. It's all this, every day.

> ### This Is
>
> Zen (*dhyana* [*djana*, from which we get *gnosis*, Greek for "knowing"], Sanskrit; *chan*, Chinese; *son*, Korean; *thien*, Vietnamese) literally means "to meditate": it is meditation and the fruit of meditation. In Zen, a head teacher is usually called *roshi* (venerable teacher); in Chinese, *shifu* (pronounced "see foo," literally meaning "father teacher"); in English, Zen master. Its direct, nondual, intuitive approach clears away habits of mind so one can see one's true nature, one's buddha nature.

Slow or Fast: The End's the Same

Zen traditionally comes in two popular flavors, *gradual* and *sudden*. The goal of both, enlightenment, is instantaneous and independent of whatever means of facilitation. In the gradual school (*Soto*, Japanese; *Tsao-tsung*, Chinese; aka *Silent Illumination*), there's only one technique—if that—called *zazen* (sitting meditation) or *shikantaza* (precisely nothing but sitting). Its motto is: *"To be a Buddha is to sit like a Buddha."* This doesn't mean by sitting you'll become a Buddha. (Were that so, I'd be writing *The Complete Idiot's Guide to Frogs*, who indeed spend all day long sitting.) Rather, in sitting, completely sit. Be at one with it, all of it, and nothing else. Be aware of body and mind in stillness, and you can enjoy not having anything to do but be. Thus, you can recognize and enjoy your Buddha nature and your capacity for awareness and awakening. And, as you go about your day, you can realize how integral the awakened mind is with *all* aspects of everyday life. This is a technique of no technique: meditation as *choiceless awareness*. It's not about any single posture or meditation, but rather continual mindfulness. It's being fully engaged with the myriad instances of whatever's at hand: brushing teeth, eating, feeling irritated, folding linen, entering a room, and sitting, each done all the way through.

The sudden school (*Rinzai*, Japanese; a.k.a *Koan Study*) prizes sudden illumination, and adds *koans* (pronounced "koe ahn") as focal points of meditation. Koans are seemingly illogical riddles, like "Two hands come together in a clap. What is the sound of one hand?" Another example is this saying of Hui Neng: "Show me your original face, before your mother and father were born!" A koan is not a riddle. It doesn't call for a solution (it's not a math puzzle with an equation waiting in an answer book); rather, it is a personal breakthrough, a flash of enlightenment. *Aha!* (*Ha ha ha.*)

In the West, the two schools are often blended, the specific recipe depending on each temple. Some Zen groups might also have elements of Theravada (as is the case in the tradition of Venerable Thich Nhat Hanh) and/or of Pure Land. Vajrayana practices called *Dzogchen* and *Mahamudra* are cousins to Zen. (Same mountain, different approaches.)

The generic meditation in Chapter 10 is formless enough to serve as a home base for zazen, particularly the final part: jumping off from any technique into choiceless awareness, Buddha mind.

Here, even practice, the idea, or any framework that colors and preconditions can be counterintuitive. This is challenging. For example, if you still consider yourself a part-time Buddha, would that be like holding down two jobs? Even if so, you could sit in the boss's chair right now (it's empty). Why be a Buddhist when you can be a Buddha?! There's nothing to attain. You *are* It. Your everyday mind is *already* Buddha mind, so … every day is a good day!

The Gateless Gate: You're Already There

The Way of Zen is easy and wide. Come on in. Every session begins and ends with the same simple rituals. Even if you don't know the drill, it's easy to clue in. Everyone takes off their shoes before entering the meditation room, called a *zendo*. You sit a stretch. Then you might walk, and then sit some more. Next, someone shares their understanding, giving a little Dharma talk. Tea and cookies, afterward (optional).

You can just show up—no introductions necessary—as often as you like. If you ever decide to take refuge there, then you'll have a one-on-one interview with the teacher. If asked, "Why have you come to study?" be honest. "I don't know" can be just as valid an answer as "To attain enlightenment." You might find your teacher answering, "Me, too." But if your inmost intention sounds like self-improvement, or some other way of getting off to a bad start, your teacher will clarify the practice. (*Genjo Koan*, in the Foreword, is a good model.) After initiation into a sangha, you visit your teacher for one-on-one chats, called *dokusan* or *sanzen* (going to Zen). Periodic meditation retreats last up to one week long, called *sesshin* (gathering mind).

In this chapter, we'll explore three aspects of Zen: (1) teachers; (2) koans, and so on; and (3) some Mahayana elements encountered in Zen as well as in Pure Land and Vajrayana. But please remember, Zen (which is to say Buddhism) isn't found in books, CDs, catalogs, websites, or incense. It's found in how *you* realize it in your life.

The human realm is part of an unbroken continuum of nature. (See the fishing boats?) So, too, is the embeddedness of each of us within essential buddha nature. (Notice, too, the unpainted patches? Such blank space represents evening glow and still waters, and the inexpressible vistas of the human mind, space as emptiness, and the universal mind.)

(*Mu Chi (1210–1280), Southern Sung Dynasty, Evening Glow on a Fishing Village (detail), Nezu Art Museum*)

Zen Teaching: Direct from the Buddha

Zen emphasizes a student–teacher relationship, as well as life in community. It's a great dance, as two people work intimately together for one awakening of mind, within sangha. As you diligently put your effortless effort into this School of Awakening, your teacher provides necessary challenge, support, and checks and balances, and mirrors your progress with the compassionate wisdom and clarity of Buddha Mind itself.

Study with the Buddha. Not just by text or even somebody's example alone. Learn from your own experience. Zen teachers encourage students to see their own mind as Ultimate Mind. For instance, asked by a student, "What is the right way to contemplate and realize the truth?" Chinese Zen master Zhaozhao (778–897) stood up and said, "I have to go to the bathroom," started walking off, but then paused midstride and said to the student, "You see, even a simple thing like this, I have to do on my own. No one can do it for me."

Leaves from the Bodhi Tree

If you take refuge in a Zen sangha, you're often given a woodblock lineage tree. (It's not a universal practice.) At the top of the scroll is a circle representing the Buddha. Below him, there's Kasyapa. Like a family tree, the genealogy branches out and down, until you get to your own roshi. Below your roshi, there's a circle, representing you. Sometimes, in the margin, there's a red line, extending directly from the Buddha to you.

With living Zen teachers now active in the West, we can see not only how essential the teacher is in Zen, but also how each teacher brings to it his or her unique temperament and emphases, over the course of their life, along with that of the sangha. This provides a chance for us to consider an important theme in all schools of Buddhism. *Lineage* carries the past to the future, through the present moment. Many Westerners, drawn to Zen as a kind of free-range spirituality, overlook the fascinating crucial vitality of lineage. Some think of Zen's lineage within Buddhism, for instance, in the same breath as Sufism within Islam and Hasidism within Judaism—as iconoclastic spirituality without the shackles of religious doctrine or dogma, emphasizing each person's innate powers of directly accessing the sacred. True, yet isn't that exactly what the Buddha did within the Hindu culture of his time?

We noted in Chapter 4 how important continuity is in transmitting a coherent body of doctrine and discipline. Well, for all its seeming wildness, Zen is quite meticulous about its own formal lineage, to preserve the vehicle itself (Buddhism/Zen) and to ensure each practitioner is getting the real deal (awakening mind, also known as "Buddha") without personal bias or distortion. Yet there's no barrier to the Gate to the Source, where you'll find legendary ancestors (formerly called "patriarchs") mingling with contemporary teachers and students, in a lineage of innovation. (Contemporaries and ancestors are rubbing elbows here in these pages, in this very moment.)

The First Zen Ancestor: Buddha's Flower and Kasyapa's Smile

It is said the first transmission of Zen took place spontaneously. It was on a day when the original Sangha was on retreat. Everybody gathered on Vulture Peak for the day's Dharma talk. The Buddha came out, sat on the peak in peace and at harmony with everybody and everything, and said nothing. Then, for all to see, he held up a flower from a nearby bouquet. That's all. (*Silence.*) Suddenly, a star student named Kasyapa broke into a smile. The Buddha could see Kasyapa really got it. End of sermon.

Thus it is said the Buddha transmitted Dharma to Kasyapa, the first Transmission of the Lamp. What did the Buddha teach and what did Kasyapa understand? The inescapable impermanence of reality? The flower's mutual interdependence with the whole universe? (Only the Buddha and Kasyapa could know, being of One Mind.) From this encounter (a flower and smile) comes a traditional summary that's kind of a Pledge of Allegiance of Zen:

- Special transmission outside orthodox teaching

- Not dependent on words

- Direct pointing at mind

- Seeing your true nature, become Buddha

The First Ancestor of Chinese Zen: Bodhidharma

Flash forward. In the remarkable transmission of Buddhism from India to China, we hail Bodhidharma, the Buddhist name of an Indian prince who went East to China in 526 to teach the Dharma. That year, Emperor Wu, a supporter of Buddhism, heard Bodhidharma had braved the three-year Spice Route trek to get there, and invited him to his court. CNN wasn't there, but the meeting reportedly went like this …

Emperor Wu: "I've had temples and monasteries built in my realm, and commissioned translations of Buddhist scriptures. Tell me, what merit have I accumulated for myself thereby?"

Bodhidharma: "None whatsoever." (He didn't reprove the emperor and say that charity that brags is merely self-aggrandizement. Nor did he preach that in true generosity there's no giver, no gift, and no giving. Rather, he was very Zen about it.) "None whatsoever."

Emperor Wu (flustered, but persisting): "Well, then—please tell me, sir, what's the highest principle of Absolute Truth?"

Bodhidharma: "There is no Absolute Truth, only utter emptiness."

Emperor Wu (at the end of his rope): "Listen, just who do you think you are!"

Bodhidharma: "I don't know." (So saying, he stood up and walked out.)

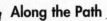

Along the Path

> Bodhidharma's famous "I don't know" to the Emperor is characteristic of Zen, which urges us to think no-thought, beyond thinking, to not know, to have a don't-know mind or a beginner's mind, to bear witness. A Japanese word for it combines mind (*shin*) below the character for no-thingness (*mu*). Mushin isn't mindless or heartless (you know, an idiot); rather, it means "getting out of one's own way" … "having no conception, much less preconception" … "not living in one's head" … "experiencing life in full participation."

Bodhidharma crossed the Yangtze River (separating north and south China), on—of all things—a single blade of grass (what a guy), and settled in at a temple in a northern province called Shaolin (*shao* pronounced "now"). There, he sat facing a wall for nine years. No, he didn't stare at a wall out of frustration because he didn't speak Chinese! Hardly. He was practicing (and teaching) … Zen.

Here's a portrait of Bodhidharma (Daruma, in Japanese): six brush strokes, plus some extra brush-wipes for his mat. But if you think it could be just anyone seen from behind, look again. That fierce determination, that no-bull presence, could only be …

(Wall-Gazing Daruma, by Daishin Gito [1656–1730], ink on paper, 25 inches × 10¼ inches, New Orleans Museum of Art, gift of an anonymous donor [79.220]).

The True Person Has No Rank: Sixth Ancestor, Hui Neng

Now, Kasyapa and Bodhidharma were both noblemen from the Indian subcontinent. But our next ancestor of Zen, Hui Neng (pronounced "hwee nong"), was allegedly born of a poor family. In fact, they say he was illiterate! (Who woulda thunk it!? And why not!?)

Flash forward to China five centuries after Bodhidharma, when Buddhism's really taken hold. Hui Neng gathered and sold firewood for a living. Delivering wood one day, he overheard someone reciting the Diamond Sutra (a popular scripture on emptiness and wisdom, requiring sublime insight more than lofty erudition). When he heard the phrase, "Awaken your mind without fixing it anywhere," he became enlightened, right there on the spot. This is really curious: no counting breaths, no mantra, no noting of the watcher and the watched, no six years of wall-gazing, no nothing! *Blam!* Right out of the box, *alikazam shazam*, he produced awakened mind out of nowhere. He attained *kensho* (a.k.a *satori*), "Oneness." He was awakened to the limitless immediacy of sunyata. His beginner's mind *was* infinite Buddha mind.

So what did he do? He hiked over a thousand miles to the Zen monastery up north, and knocked on the door. Hongren, the temple's master and current ancestor of Chinese Zen, opened the door and said, "Where are you from and what do you expect to get from me?" Hui Neng said he's only a humble man who has come a long way from the south who wants to pay his respects and wishes only Buddhahood. Hongren jeered, "Ha! An illiterate barbarian from the South! How can an illiterate barbarian from the South expect to become a Buddha?" Hui Neng replied, "Literate/illiterate, north/south, dualities don't concern the Buddha's way." "Hmmm, a wise guy!" Hongren thought to himself, admitting Hui Neng into the sangha and giving him menial duties, like anonymously pounding rice in a shed way in back.

Meanwhile, Hongren had been fixing to retire. He'd said the vacancy would be open for a Zen poetry competition, by writing a *gatha* (poem) to demonstrate intuitive understanding. Everyone knew Shen Xiu (pronounced "shen syew") was the shoo-in, so no one else tried. But Hui Neng asked someone to read to him what Shen had posted on the wall, a quatrain about our body being the Bodhi Tree and our mind a standing mirror we must constantly wipe clean of dust. "*Ha!*" Hui Neng thought, "This guy doesn't even know his own mind." He dictated his own, countering that quaint metaphysical poetry with his bold instant classic of nonduality, and posted it: *bodhi* (enlightenment) doesn't have trees, and this mirror doesn't need a stand, itself forever so pure that dust has nowhere to land.

Leaves from the Bodhi Tree _____

> Hui Neng was out for a walk when he came upon two monks quarrelling beneath a flagpole.
>
> "The flag is moving," one monk said.
>
> "No, the wind is moving," argued the other.
>
> So it went, as amongst two little kids, "flag," "wind," "flag," "wind," until Hui Neng stepped in.
>
> "Your mind is moving," he said, and walked away, leaving them both stunned.

I'm no literary critic, but Hui Neng didn't write a poem *about* mind, like Shen's; rather, he manifested Universal Mind that creates poems, actualizing truth in plain speech. Well, that night, old Hongren appeared in Hui Neng's little monastic cell, and bowed. Obviously, he knew who wrote the second poem. He transmitted Dharma to Hui Neng, mind to mind, and gave Hui Neng his ancestral robe as had been handed down to him. Then, an interesting twist: Fearing for Hui Neng's life, when Shen Xiu found out Hui Neng was now the Sixth Ancestor and not he, Hongren led Hui Neng out the back gate before everyone woke up and saw him off at the ferry, saying, "Lay low for a while, then teach Dharma a good ways away from here." So Hui Neng lived in anonymity for many years before starting his own monastery near the big port city of Canton (Guangzhou), later teaching thousands of people—but that's another story.

Mahayana: It's a Big Boat

We might pause here to note five Mahayana elements to our tales of Zen ancestors: (1) innovation, (2) devotion, (3) emptiness-based wisdom, (4) populism, and (5) skillful means. Every Zen student and teacher practices *innovation* in applying his or her own life to the teachings. Where Theravada is based on the Tripitaka, teaching here includes a degree of sacred story. Scholars today tell us Bodhidharma and Hui Neng were real people, but the previous stories are more legend than fact. Does that invalidate their teachings? As with mythic aspects in the life of the Buddha, the point is to engage in the stories' teachings as they touch our own realities today. This is a *devotional* aspect of the mythic dimension, a way of delving into teachings beyond intellect, taking them to heart and realizing them for ourselves. (We'll see another focus for the devotional impulse at the end of the chapter.)

The wisdom (*prajna*, Sanskrit) in these stories often draws on emptiness, emphasized more in Mahayana. If everything is empty of separate lasting identity, a silent flower is as much buddha as the Buddha. "Only vast emptiness," Bodhidharma tells the Emperor. He knew there's no One Final Holy Supreme Truth you can formulate in words. Once you've even tried, you've limited its infinite essence. "Awaken mind without grasping." Hui Neng won the robe of lineage by pointing directly to mind, beyond mere concepts of Bodhi Tree, mirror, and dust—he saw enlightenment as a concept being as illusory as ego, empty of any concrete, permanent, or separate identity, much less personal immediacy. Even the concept of trying to wipe a mirror clean of concepts is itself but another concept. Don't let anyone glue your feet to the ground, not even "Buddha."

Sacred story, devotionalism, and the compassionate wisdom of freedom from concept all helped Mahayana make Buddha's Way popular, accessible to a wide spectrum of people for whom Hui Neng might be seen as representative. (Some scholars have suggested he might have been of Hmong or Miao heritage, or even from as far south as Vietnam. He's certainly a fellow you might see sitting next to you, riding on the bus, going to work.)

A fifth aspect of all Mahayana traditions has been previously noted, an art of Dharma in action called *upaya*, "skillful means." We've mentioned this in the analogy of a Buddhist tool being like a raft to take us to the other shore (nirvana), whereupon we leave the raft behind. The Buddha Way is rich with such tools: the right tool for the right job and the right person. Besides sacred story, shikantaza and koans are further examples of *upaya*. Shikantaza uses no specific meditation as meditation (no method as method), so complete awakening might intuitively and spontaneously occur. Silent illumination. Similarly, a koan (as we'll see next) not only points to buddha nature, but also comes directly *from* buddha nature.

If Zen had a logo, this might be it. A circle ("enso," Japanese) universally implies completeness, or all. A Zen circle can also imply zero, sunyata, fertile void, true reality, enlightenment, no beginning/no end in all phenomena, no symbol whatsoever, the turning of the Wheel of Dharma, harmony, and womb. All in one stroke.

(Calligraphy: Kazuaki Tanahashi)

Awakened Speech: Expressing the Inexpressible

Question: if words can get in the way of our experience, and thus in the way of our realization of Zen, why are there thousands of books of Zen teachings, from its ancestors to today? *Answer:* A few centuries after Buddhism had come to China, it became such a scholarly study, splitting hairs over words in scriptures, that Zen opened the window to let in the fresh air of direct, immediate personal experience. In so doing, it developed its own body of text over the ensuing centuries. Common Misconception 199, debunked: Zen isn't about the abolition of words, in a kind of dumb or dumbed-down anti-intellectualism; rather, it involves true mastery of words (right speech, living language). Words have buddha nature, too. So the Zen student awakens with them, as we see next.

The Sound of One Hand: *Koan* Study

Zen practice is training in letting go of everything our mind grasps onto (preferences, opinions, concepts, and so on) to see our mind as it really is: inherently free and awake. But Zen is minimal in its techniques, demanding nothing less than leading a genuine life. There's nothing to be gained from studying a *koan*, any more than from sitting or anything else; in Zen, every instance is an opportunity to give it all we've got. It is authentic. There is nothing else behind it. It is complete in itself.

This Is _____

The Japanese word **koan** means "public notice" or "legal case." Just as a lawyer might refer to *Brown* v. *Board of Education* regarding segregation, so can each koan be referred to, illuminating a particular principle—such as Buddha holding a flower up and Kasyapa smiling, a teaching without words. Life's holding out a flower to us, but do we see it? All koans directly point at the mind. Their question is called *hua tou* (word's head, or mind before thought). There's an element of *paradox* (in original Greek, meaning "beyond thinking").

Typically, sitting in home-base meditation, in light-handed, one-pointed concentration, a Zen student might then practice shikantaza's choiceless awareness, or koan study. (Neither is really a further step; peace is every step.) A koan could be seen as both samadhi and vipassana: a point of concentration to still the mind, as well as a contemplative inquiry for insight. Yet koan study demands the practitioner really bore down deep. For instance, what does it mean that your original face, your Buddha mind, is said to be before your father and mother were born? Where do your mother's and father's nature and nurture end, and your authenticity begin? (Show, don't tell.) Then, too, father and mother seem to imply dualism, and the koan demands going beyond the dualism of the intellectual mind and the discursive patterning of language, sorting reality into subject and object, therefore and thus. But that's still not all. Father and mother also suggest our physicality, yet the koan speaks of somewhere where body and mind drop away. Even experiencing authentic oneness is not enough if there's no wonderment. And the inexpressible must be expressed. It's nowhere to be found and no way to be gotten to. Show me, the koan says. Show me who you really are. And in trying to *be* the original face, you realize you can't, and you can't help not to.

 Hear and Now _____

> "What's true meditation? It's to make it all—coughing, swallowing, gestures, motion, stillness, words, action, good and evil, success and shame, win and lose, right and wrong—into one single koan."
> —Zen master Hakuin (1686–1769), author of the koan "What is the sound of one hand?"

Zen deals with life-or-death issues. Yet as Zen became known in the West, koans became conversational topics removed from dedicated, intimate Zen study. From the outside, they might seem daunting, or they might seem to be wordplay—a riddle ("When is a door not a door?") or a logic puzzle ("I swear to you I'm a liar"). True, they use words to go beyond words … a kind of short-circuit to the linguistic wiring of habitual thought patterns … a shock, almost (like waking up and not knowing where or who you are) … a radical doubt or questioning requiring something deeper within us … to enable us to directly experience reality, unfiltered. For example, a Zen monk once held up a bamboo stick before some other monks and said, "If you call this a stick, you fall into the trap of words, but if you don't call it a stick, you contradict facts. So what do you call it?" (*Answer:* A monk went up to him, took the stick, broke it over one knee, threw the pieces into the room, and sat down.)

"What!?" (That's a koan, too!) A full koan comes with a story or situation, a saying or poem, and commentary. (For a taste, try Michael Wenger's commentary on a passage from Dogen's *Genjo Koan*, in this book's foreword.) The shorter form could just be a question—such as about original face, one hand, what is this—and is called a *hua tou* (pronounced "hwa du," literally meaning "word's head" or "mind before stirred into thought").

If you want, try adopting "What!?" as your own one-word koan. Asking "What is this?" focuses the mind, for calming concentration, and directs it in inquiry, turning the light of inquiry back on itself. Breathe in and then ask, "What is this?" Stay with the questioning with each out-breath. What is this that is breathing? Keep asking (not intellectually, but of your entire experience in this moment; not, "What is meditation?" but, "What is meditating?"). Ask again, further. What is reading? What is before reading? What is my life? Who am I? Stay with the question, "What … is … this?" Stay with the question mark. Stay with it through your day, your week, life-deep, life-long.

Koan contemplation is like the inevitable, necessary, real dragon in your path … or the young child who keeps asking innocent questions (why did we ever stop?!). It's not just something reserved for when you are perched on a cushion. You take your koan home with you. Wake up with it in the morning. Look at it in the mirror. Brush your teeth with it. Have breakfast with it. Take it to work. Bring it with you until you can't live with it, and can't live without it. When you've finally mastered your koan, congratulations: you're ready for all the others.

Leaves from the Bodhi Tree

Koans were compiled some 1,300 years ago, but their crazy wisdom lives on.

Consider the zingers of Samuel Goldwyn and Yogi Berra. Goldwyn was the "G" in MGM, an irascible movie mogul who drove Hollywood people crazy by barking such unarguable, twisted statements as, "A verbal agreement isn't worth the paper it's printed on!" A koan might ask, "Show me that paper." (Would you shake hands with me on that one? Or would you, like him, say, "Include me out!"?) When not playing baseball with the New York Yankees, Yogi Berra came up with such gems as, "When you come to a fork in the road, take it!" "No one goes there anymore—it's too crowded." "It's déjà vu all over again." and "It ain't over until it's over." Next time you're asked the time, remember how Berra replied: "You mean *now*?"

Why more than one koan? The *hwadu* "what is this?" was enough for Korean Master Kusan (1909–1983). Yet some 400 koans have been indexed over the centuries, out of about 1,700 in all. Each deals with particular phases of the Way. Primary ones, such as the sound of one hand, are designed to help tip the practitioner over the edge of fabricated, provisional self into immediate, boundless reality and realization of unborn, undying Buddha mind. Further koans can gauge how far the first breakthrough went, or assist further breakthroughs, lest a student go off illumined only to get caught in a lion's trap farther down the road. They can assist in differentiating within the realm of nondifferentiation, as well as in understanding the lives and teachings of forerunners, beyond the literal words. With koans, a teacher can guide a student through the Zen landscape of unimpeded interpenetration without limit, so you can appreciate all the roses along the Way. If you take on koan practice, you might pick the koan you'd like to work on, or be assigned one by your teacher. During dokusan, you'll be asked "How's your koan?" But koans can be appreciated in and of themselves. Pick one; it will eventually lead to all the others, full circle.

Dharma Combat: *Mondo*

Related to koan is a kind of question-and-answer repartee called *mondo*. When Bodhidharma had that wild conversation with Emperor Wu, that was mondo. Hongren's Zen poetry competition? Mondo! Hui Neng and the monks arguing about the flag and the wind? Mondo yet again! Zen master Shitou came along a generation or so after Hui Neng. Once, a monk sincerely asked him, "What am I supposed to do?" He replied, "Why are you asking me?!" The monk answered, "Where else can I find what I'm looking for?" Shitou replied, "Are you sure you lost it!?" The monk realized he'd already had what he most longed for: awakening.

The awakened language of Zen applies throughout daily life. (Watch what you say!) One Zen monk said to the other, "Hey, that fish's flopped out of that net! How will it live?" The other monk answered, "When you've gotten out of the net, I'll tell you."

 Hear and Now

> King Milinda said to learned monk Nagasena, "I'm going to ask you a question. Can you answer it?"
>
> Nagasena replied, "Please, ask your question."
>
> The King: "I've already asked."
>
> Nagasena: "I've already answered."
>
> The King: "What did you answer?"
>
> Nagasena: "What did you ask?"
>
> The King: "I asked nothing."
>
> Nagasena: "I answered nothing."
>
> —*Milindapañha*

It may sound like a Vaudeville routine ("Who's on first?" "Who's on second—I-Don't-Know's on first."). More apt might be two jazz soloists, exchanging riffs, no end in sight, dueling Dharma.

More Mind-Mirrors: Zen Mottos and Gathas

Along with koans and mondo, Zen also encourages *turning phrases* (to turn the mind) to promote and commemorate understanding, such as lines of poetry, sayings, and pithy phrases. The four-line Zen motto regarding Buddha holding up the flower and Kasyapa smiling is one example (in Chinese, just four lines of four words each). The quatrain from the *Genjo Koan* is another example. (This book is full of such slogans.) Here are but three very general Zen mottos.

"*Form is emptiness; emptiness is form.*" ("Is" could be translated as "is not different than." "Form" also includes phenomena, events, and things.) On a simple level, it's saying there is no shape that does not in its way manifest boundless energy, and boundless energy can only be experienced when bound by a form. In this, it's close to Einstein's theory of relativity. But as emptiness-based wisdom, it has further range. For example, think back to Hui Neng and the poetry contest. His opponent copied the traditional notion of dust as a symbol of sensation and the attachments they engender … and mirror as mind, with the sense that mind and sensations must be separated, sensations gotten rid of—whereas Hui Neng says there's nothing to get rid of, since mind and its sensations are one seamless emptiness. To experience our true nature is to experience the emptiness of our experience.

The turning phrase might also be used as the meeting of the particular and the universal, or suchness and emptiness. Consider an empty shoebox, with a lid. Closed, the amount of space it contains is very precise (form, suchness). Open the lid. How much space is in it now when its emptiness includes all the space outside, without limit, as well as inside? (So keep an open mind.) A shoebox can also be useful as a gift box, a place for sorting cards, and so on. (Don't get too philosophical, but don't get like Imelda Marcos, either, stuck on suchness.) So this phrase also embodies the Middle Way.

"*Not one, not two.*" Again, this is the Zen of the Middle Way. Michael Wenger calls it Buddhist math. To say everything is all One can get vague, like misty woo-woo. There's no One without the many. It takes yin and yang to know nondualism. But we're not insisting on dualism either. Neither *duality* nor *nonduality* are given any more weight than the other. We need them both. Not the Western Either/Or, but rather Both/And. With bowing, for instance, two hands come together in one gesture, with no separation between you, your act of bowing, and what you're bowing to. Not one, not two.

"*Chop wood; carry water.*" Sitting is just one form of meditation. Pay attention. With mindful awareness, every part of our day can be meditation. Washing a bowl, one can enjoy the warmth of the soapy water, and feeling the round circularity of the surface. So Mahayana being innovative, a contemporary practice has sprung up of composing gathas to celebrate mindfulness in everyday activities. Washing dishes, for example, can be likened to bathing the Buddha, cleaning the body of awakening. Before driving a car, one can remind one's self that when turning the key and pushing the pedal, the car will go faster, and so the senses will go faster—but one can vow that the mind will remain still. Zen master Robert Aitken writes, for instance, "When the children fight in the car I vow with all beings to show how the car doesn't move unless all of its parts are engaged." And "When I'm drawn to watch crime on TV I vow with all beings to smile at my own little drama and expose the killer of time." And with the "all beings" of his vows, we come to the capper of our brief Zen tour, the vast and vital Bodhisattva Vow.

Universal Participation: The Bodhisattva Vow

Last but not least, here's a text common to Zen as well as all Mahayana traditions.

- Beings are numberless; I vow to awaken them.

- Delusions are inexhaustible; I vow to end them.

- Dharma gates are boundless; I vow to enter them.

- Buddha's way is unsurpassable; I vow to embody it.

It's often chanted in English as a sangha. It has corollaries in Theravada tradition, such as metta meditation's all-inclusive compassion; the four lines could even be seen to parallel a deep reading of the Four Noble Truths. What traditionally sets the vow apart from Theravada tradition is the shift of intent, in the very first line: from the very outset, one's own practice is for the sake of all. A bodhisattva has an aspiration for nirvana, enlightenment, and an awakened heart (*bodhicitta*, Sanskrit), not for himself or herself but for the welfare of all. He or she will even defer complete nirvana until all beings are free of suffering.

 This Is _____

A **bodhisattva** is one whose being or essence (*sattva*) is enlightened (*bodhi*) with the wisdom of direct perception of reality and the compassion such awareness engenders. He or she renounces all rewards for personal deeds, dedicated to the enlightenment of all beings. An archetypal bodhisattva is *Avalokiteshvara* (*Guan Yin* [female], Chinese; *Kwannon*, Japanese; *Chenrezig* [male] and *Tara* [female], Tibetan), embodying compassion. Another archetype is *Manjushri*, embodying wisdom.

In a way, the Buddha affirmed this intent, this path, when he answered Mara's question, "Who are you to say you're enlightened?" by touching the earth, invoking all beings. He continued that bodhisattva path when he left the Bodhi Tree to teach for the rest of his life. This vow calls to us in the present moment, awakening our compassion, courage, and love, calling us to transform the afflictions we see around us, calling us to recognize a better world is possible.

This could be a giant step in your own practice. The Vow connects your practice with all bodhisattvas. On one level, that's all our ancestors, including your grandparents and parents, who cared for you above themselves, as well as such singular selfless historical figures as St. Francis, Gandhi, and Jane Adams. As Martin Luther King Jr. would say, until we're all healed nobody is healed. It also includes a pantheon of bodhisattva archetypes, personifications of primordial enlightened energy, our own highest human potential, such as Avalokiteshvara, Manjushri, and the Buddha. And the Vow connects your practice with all living beings, because all things possess Buddha nature. A tree, a rock, and a cloud are beings. During zazen each morning, I am not alone. I sit with all beings, vowed for enlightenment. This awakening isn't of a solitary soul, but rather one that finds its place within community, finding meaning in connection.

There's a seemingly koan-like quality to this, as well. How can anyone honestly vow to help *all* beings? The sheer idea is overwhelming and mind-boggling. But that's partly the point. The practice is just that selfless and all-encompassing. As Michael Wenger points out about the Vow, "You don't take it because it's doable. You take it to make it so."

With a smile of compassionate wisdom, Guan Yin contemplates the moon and its reflection in the water (is either any less real?). Here's meditation in an informal pose of elegant grace and royal ease.

(The Water and Moon Guanyin Bodhisattva, *eleventh to twelfth century, China, polychromed wood, 95 inches × 65 inches [241.3 centimeters], The Nelson-Atkins Museum of Art, Kansas City, Missouri [Purchase: Nelson Trust; 34–10].)* (*Photo: Robert Newcombe*)

The Least You Need to Know

◆ Like other branches of Mahayana, Zen emphasizes the Bodhisattva Vow. A bodhisattva's awakening is, from the initial intent, linked to the awakening of all beings. Bodhisattvas include embodiments of archetypal energies, such as compassion (Avalokiteshvara) and wisdom (Manjusri), as well as living personages (such as our ancestors).

◆ "Zen" means meditation, and "the fruit of meditation." Other schools also teach meditation. Some ingredients that make up the special Zen flavor are: immediacy, completeness, "not one/not two" (neither dualism nor nondualism are primary), authenticity, dailyness, selflessness, dedication, questioning, intuition, spontaneity, and humor (sometimes to the point of crazy wisdom).

◆ Zen emphasizes direct immediate experience, and is typified by a minimum of means. Its practice might be typified as choiceless awareness, koans, and …

The Way Is Easy and Wide: Buddha's Pure Land

In This Chapter

- Amida Buddha's vow to save all who call
- Buddhas, Buddha lands, and Bodhisattva deities
- Faith, vows, and practice
- Self-power and Other-power

We come now to the largest of Buddhist schools in the world. Flourishing in the West for over a century now, it's our oldest Buddhist tradition. Yet only recently has it been enjoying the attention it deserves.

The Way is easy and wide. Even the most blissful realm of ultimate transformation is available in the mere twinkling of an eye. There's a sixth-century Chinese saying that applies: "A ray of light into a room that's remained dark for a thousand years dissolves a thousand years of darkness." Here's a glimmer …

Remembrance as Practice

The Buddha welcomes all. The seeds of enlightenment are present within everyone's heart. The Buddha within my heart seeks nirvana; my Buddha nature seeks Buddha-hood. Yet long ago, to many common people, the original Way of the Theravada teachings seemed to be for monastics or the wealthy few, those with sufficient temperament, training, and time. What about servants of wealthy patrons of the Buddha, say, who might have glimpsed the Buddha in passing, but who wouldn't have an entire day free to themselves, much less three whole months? Oneness in sunyata is fine, but not with hungry mouths to feed. Well, another word for *mindfulness* (*smirti*, Sanskrit) is *remembrance*—remembering to return to the here and now; remembering our true nature, our limitless buddha nature.

> **Hear and Now**
>
> "There shall be no distinction, no regard to male or female, good or bad, exalted or lowly; none shall fail to be in his land of purity after having called, with complete faith, on Amida."
>
> —Honen Shonin (1133–1212)

Pure Land is simply about remembering the Buddha. It is a calling to mind, a taking to heart. To sincerely wish liberation, remember the Buddha, the awakener of mind and heart. This calling-to-mind and taking-to-heart is called *recitation* in Pure Land. Silent or spoken, when we recite Buddha's name, we're thus remembering him. Just hearing the Buddha's name is the same as hearing his voice, who calls us to awaken. His name embodies his awakening (Buddha), so invoking that name makes manifest his enlightening awareness—in which there's no separation between speaker and hearer. Through the Buddha's name, we can remember our own buddha nature (before our mother and father gave us a name), which is one with all things. Because our minds can conceive of Buddha through a word, our minds must indeed partake of the Buddha's mind. Our mind *is* Buddha's mind—one mind.

Consider the time of the Buddha. Thousands had seen him and felt his presence. Surely, just remembering him would bring calm, clarity, keen awareness, and open-heartedness. Over time, a full-blown path arose, about a century before Christ, and was then developed further by such Indian luminaries as Nagarjuna and Vasubandhu between the second and fifth centuries. But that's mere historical fact. Let's explore how transcendental themes enable us to deal with crucial personal issues in a way historical fact cannot. The historical and the transcendent dimension interpenetrate each other: so touch one deeply, you touch the other.

Say His Name, and You'll Be Free

Anyone who calls on Amida Buddha is taken to his Pure Land. (The path is the goal.) Known throughout East Asia, here's the marvelous story behind that amazing statement. (Note, as you hear it, how it echoes the Buddha's own story, as if he were telling of Enlightenment in figurative terms.) As the story goes …

… once there was the son of a king, who came to truly understand the suffering that's the human condition of us all. So compassionate was he that when he saw anyone suffer, he suffered, too. He resolved to bring everyone to a place beyond suffering. So he devoted himself to the Way, and eventually became the most excellent monk, known to the Sangha as Dharmakara (Storehouse of Dharma) for his living the teachings to the fullest. For example, he devotedly practiced the *paramitas* (perfections): generosity, patience, perseverance, conscious conduct, loving kindness meditation, equanimity, insight, and so forth. Well, as he came closer to nirvana, he made many vows, including (as you might have guessed) the bodhisattva vow to forsake Buddhahood if all beings could not attain it. (Even a wretch like me.) Should he attain enlightenment, he vowed to bring anyone who called on him to a world beyond suffering.

Well, after innumerable lifetimes (the fruit of much labor), he became one with timeless, infinite Buddha nature. The field of his awakening became known as *Sukhavati* (Ultimate Bliss, or Blissful Realm), a pure land. Dharmakara's Buddha name became *Amida* or *Amito*, combining *Amitayus* (eternal life) and *Amitabha* (infinite light). Any one name is enough to get you through the door: Amida. Amito. Just sincerely say his name. He'll hear you. This Buddha's our guy. Call on him. He'll see us across.

 This Is _____

> Rebirth in the Pure Land is hosted by the compassionate vows of Amitabha Buddha. *Pure lands* (also known as *Buddha fields*) are beyond realms of desire (our impure world), form (realms of lesser deities), and formlessness (realms of higher deities), as well as *samsara* (never-ending wheel of deaths and rebirths), but some are present *within* samsara. In the Pure Land of Amitabha Buddha, we study the Bodhisattva Path without hindrance. Depending on interpretation, we can be reborn there after death, or be reborn in the purity of our own mind, our own Buddha nature.

That's the story. In this chapter, we'll hone in on four key Pure Land elements: (1) *faith,* (2) *vows,* (3) *practice* (often called *cultivation*), and (4) *Other-power.* As we'll see, Pure Land is *devotional,* like the *bhakti* branch of yoga, linking the practitioner to life's sacred, inherent goodness. It fuses that devotion with recognition of the Buddha's *boundless compassion,* and with the Mahayana base of the wisdom of creative emptiness.

As preface, let's begin by clarifying pure lands, their deities, and merit, lest they stand in the way of the simplest of paths.

Not on Any Map: Buddhaland

The idea of a pure realm resonates in many contexts. Paradise, musician and performance artist Laurie Anderson tells us, is exactly like where you are right now … only much, much better. There's more to life than what meets the eye. Sometimes people sense another dimension. Some scientists (such as string theorists) posit our world as but one of a thousand million. And it's human nature to call upon spatial imagery for visualizing the nonmaterial. Consider computer games, depicting dark forces to engage in combat (dungeons, say, in worlds of doom). We've named a recent amorphous communications system a Net, a Web, just as we saw Indra's Net in Chapter 8 as a spatialized image for the unimpeded interpenetration of all things. We also speak of the mansions of the soul, again as if it were a place. Judaism, Christianity, and Islam all speak of the Kingdom of God, within and without. Pure Land is like that kingdom, using spatial imagery to help us discern what's formless and ineffable.

Themes besides space often bear similarities to Pure Land, in other creeds. Thomas speaks of Jesus being the light and the life, not unlike Amitabha's infinite light and endless life. Of course, the Pure Land might resemble Christian Heaven. Three points of distinction are noteworthy. First, Pure Land is traditionally a realm after death, but humanist interpretation speaks of its presence here and now. (Who says Heaven is up!?) In this, the Kingdom of God and Pure Land might match. Maybe we haven't realized yet that what we seek yonder is really right at our feet. We could be reborn into the pure land of our own mind—our innate, pristine buddha nature.

Moreover, Christian heaven is final. ("When you're dead, you're done.") The Pure Land, however, is a realm of transformation. Here we continue our practice, within perfected conditions. (Beyond the earthly dualism of father and mother, traditional language speaks of our being reborn inside a divine lotus.) Not quite nirvana itself, but it's very close. From that place, all the Buddha's teachings will be as easy as opening a fist … or a lotus.

Third, there's not just one, but myriad pure lands, like alternative parallel universes (Buddhaverses, Buddha lands)—each with a respective host, one and all manifesting Buddhahood. It is said that in addition to the historical Buddha, Shakyamuni Buddha (but one of thousands of Buddhas to have appeared on earth), there are trillions of Buddhas throughout the universe, all named Buddha. (Enlightened energy is just that perfectly limitless.) All are reciting the name Amitabha. (Salvation is as dynamic as that.)

🪷 **Hear and Now**

"Heaven. Now there's a thought. Nothing has ever been able, ultimately, to convince me we live anywhere else. And that heaven, more a verb than a noun, more a condition than a place, is all about leading with the heart in whatever broken or ragged state it's in, stumbling forward in faith until, from time to time, we miraculously find our way. Our way to forgiveness, our way to letting go, our way to understanding, compassion and peace."

—Alice Walker

Earthly Buddhas and Transcendent Buddhas

Each Buddhaverse is hosted by enlightened beings, transcendent Buddhas, almost akin to deities. In the time of the historical Buddha, deities were commonplace. A thought coming to someone was described as a deity visiting them. Thus, Mara the Tempter could be seen as a projection of the Buddha's own mind. Shakyamuni Buddha didn't want to be worshipped (thus saying "Be a lamp unto yourself"); nor did he want images made of him. Yet we've noted how Buddha images being made in Afghanistan became a growing practice. Nor did he teach about God or gods. Nevertheless, many patron donors of the original Sangha worshipped a pantheon of Hindu deities. Mahayana accommodated their longing for salvation and devotional taste for imagery and poetic myth (though Hindu Vedanta ultimately more fully satisfied such yearning and ultimately prevailed in India.)

So having immersed ourselves in the life and teachings of the historical Buddha, we now encounter the notion that Shakyamuni was but one of millions and millions of enlightened beings in myriads of realms. Each is depicted in meditation (usually seated, but sometimes standing) within their own particular paradise (pure land, buddha field, buddhaverse), in perpetual bliss, enjoying the truth they embody. These superhuman, transcendental figures may be seen as representing abstract aspects of Buddhahood, with various deities for the rainbow spectrum within Supreme Enlightenment. (Pure Land is devoted to Amibtabha; Vajarayana, as we'll see in the next chapter, enshrines myriads of such Buddhas.)

Actually, this is all usually second-nature to Easterners. And pure lands are vast enough to be open for interpretation. Some adherents worship transcendental Buddhas as actual cosmic entities. Another interpretation is that they're manifestations of supreme enlightenment, putting a human face on formless qualities, that we may feel greater kinship with them—conceptual entities representing qualities we wish to instill within ourselves, already within ourselves to cultivate. It's up to each sangha, each teacher, and ultimately each practitioner.

Venerable Heng Sure, one of the first monks born and ordained in the United States, explains:

> "Buddhas have realized the virtuous qualities, or essential goodness, of the Awakened Nature that we humans share with all beings. When somebody brings to fruition the virtue of their nature, they "wake up," and become a Buddha. By reciting the Buddha's name, we invoke the power of that virtue already latent inside us."

So for example, when you don't get angry and flip somebody off in traffic, then that goodness allows the pure land to come forward. Some consider their body the pure land, their mind Amitabha. Reciting the Buddha name, some concentrate on being mindful of their true nature. (Similarly, *samsara*, the cycle of rebirth, might similarly be seen from a humanist perspective as a continuum of karma within this one life.)

Whether the Pure Land is your sangha, or your own mind's field of awakening, an earthly realm or a celestial one, is up to you to see. When you visit a Pure Land sangha, you'll find members who think of Amitabha's Vow (to save all who call) in terms of deathbed assurance of rebirth in nirvana, and others who're open to deconstructing the Vow as myth, or sacred story. Story is a time-tested means of pointing to truths that must be felt, not analyzed—a way of using words to sidestep their inherent dualist tendency. Of course, what you wish to make of such stories is up to you. After all, Amitabha Buddha made his vow for *you*. (For a survey of transcendental Buddhas and such, please visit our website, Dharma Door, at word.to/deities.html)

The Pure Land Is Vast, with Room for Varied Emphases

Some Adherents Emphasize	Some Adherents Emphasize
Historical Amitabha, with arms to hold us, ears to hear us.	Amitabha as formless power of universe removing delusions of ego; infinite buddha nature.
Pure Land as afterlife, only reachable after death.	Pure Land not apart from this world; found in essential purity of mind.
"Other-power," outside assistance, granting favors.	"Self-reliance"; "other" seen as manifestation of mind.

> **Hear and Now** _____
>
> "When reciting the Buddha's name, gather your thoughts. Recitation originates in the mind and is channeled through the mouth, each phrase, each word, clearly enunciated. You should also listen clearly, impressing the words in your mind. Manjushri taught: 'Hearing within, hearing one's Nature—one's Nature becomes the Supreme Mind.'"
>
> —Yin Kuang (1861–1940), thirteenth Pure Land Ancestor

Transferring Merit: Instant Karma?

Not to look a gift horse in the mouth, but how is Amitabha able to make good on his vows? We can see it in a variety of interesting and instructive ways. The common answer in Buddhism is called *merit*. Simply put, it's as if there were a candle to Amitabha's light, growing brighter (not darker) as more and more people light their candle from that flame. To further appreciate merit, consider karma once more, the universal law of moral cause and effect, which the Buddha radically transformed from a determined fixity into an ethical process. In early times, it was thought of like a bank account. Everything we do generates debits and credits that link us to other beings. You help me out, I owe you. A settling of accounts takes place at death (one reason rebirth/reincarnation is an issue at all). Unless we could completely clear our karma once and for all, rebirth could continue indefinitely (samsara).

This brings up the question of motive (Right Thought). Back in the early days, people did good deeds to earn merit for a better rebirth next time. Easier to study the Way as a wealthy human in the next life than, say, a chicken. For some people, earning merit only built up selfish ego, greedy for merit, under cover of good motive. (Thus Bodhidharma's reply to the king's self-praise, "No merit whatsoever," hearing only a big show of ego.) The bodhisattva vow, on the other hand, selflessly directs the merit of any good karma we might generate as going toward the enlightenment of all beings.

So following meditation or a Dharma talk, Mahayana practitioners often dedicate any merit generated thereby to the well-being of all beings, plus maybe to a particular sangha member in need. (I dedicate any positive potential of this book to the development of your heart of kindness, appreciation, and love, and to all beings, that they may all become fully awakened; may all beings live in peace, with each other, and within their own heart.) Transference of merit works in a similar way (if only a mortgage were as simple). Amitabha had been called Storehouse of Dharma. So what happened to his storehouse of accumulated merit when he finally attained enlightenment? You might say he invested it, to create a fund, dedicated for everyone. (*Carte blanche.*)

Along the Path

"The world of things is really nothing more than a kind of reflex of people's deeds. An environment can exist only as long as there are persons whose karma compels them to perceive it. In the same spirit, one now claims that the merit of a Bodhisattva may be great enough to create a Pure Land not only for himself but also for others to whom he transfers it."

—Edward Conze

So Amitabha Buddha's karmic merit is so vast as to enable a purified realm for it all, a buddhaverse—and with such a limitless surplus of karmic merit that he could *transfer* it to anyone who asks, so they can join him. It's as if there is a rain cloud hanging overhead, but a strong wind could blow it away; his immense good karma can overcome a weaker one. Amazing, but then, to continue an economic analogy, any bank links up with all the banks in the world, in one huge banking system. So being one with Buddha means also being one with Buddha's infinite store of karmic merit.

Our karma, in effect, helps create our reality. If we sincerely open our heart-minds, and practice the Eightfold Path, we will tune in to Amitabha Buddha's karma as well, limitless blank karma, infinite possibility. With his enlightened karma comes the reality he's now living: his pure land.

Amitabha is joined in his pure land by two bodhisattva disciples: Great Strength and Avalokiteshvara. Here's one of 33 different ways of depicting Avalokiteshvara, whose head burst when beholding all the suffering of the world. Amitabha restored the head as nine new heads. The thousand arms are a result of the vow to help all beings.

(From Tibetan Mandalas, *International Academy of Indian Culture, Courtesy of Dr. Lokesh Chandra)*

> **Hear and Now**
>
> "On a single atom, there are as many Buddhas as there are atoms in the world, sitting in the midst of an ocean of his disciples. Likewise, the entire sphere is filled with an infinite cloud of Buddhas …. On each atom, there are as many pure lands as the number of atoms of the worlds. In each pure land, there are infinite Buddhas sitting in the midst of the disciples of the Buddhas. May I see them and perform enlightened activities with them."
>
> —Gandavyuha Sutra

We can also picture how Amitabha's vow works through another key notion, that of the unimpeded interpenetration of all things. Such a simple act as calling Amitabha to mind is immediately interconnected with the most profound, even inconceivable, of realms. (Remember Indra's Net?) Consider, for example, the empowerment of being one with a Buddha who is but one of many Buddhas … one of myriads of enlightened beings, themselves all Buddhas who have lived amongst us or on other dimensions, all teaching the Dharma, throughout time immemorial. Now imagine each Buddha accompanied by a retinue of Bodhisattvas, whose awakened Buddhahoods are dedicated for the sake of all beings. Each of these Bodhisattvas dwells in a particular transcendental realm (Pure Land/Buddhaverse) of his or her particular enlightening energy, where he or she is teaching the Dharma this very moment.

Here's yet another slant. Amitabha's pre-Buddhahood name was Storehouse of Dharma, Dharmakara. Shinshu scholar Soga Ryojin speculates Dharmakara is a mythic representation of *store consciousness*. When schools of Buddhism delineate grades of consciousness, store consciousness (*alaya*) is often seen as the ground of them all, the deep realm out of which factors of consciousness emerge.

And to advance one more dimension to this, Amitabha is a simple way of presenting the nondual realm of Buddhahood, our mind the same as Buddha's mind. If we consider consciousness as the screen upon which our senses play, then Mind is our awareness—of our consciousness, our feelings, the phenomenal world, everything. When Mind is aware of needless suffering, we realize our own mind is bound up with the needless suffering of all beings. And when our Mind is free of needless suffering, we realize our Mind as part of nirvana. So our awareness of Buddha puts us in touch with Buddha's awareness. Our awareness *is* Buddha. Our mind *is* Buddha's mind.

This Is _____

In Chinese, Amitabha Buddha is invoked Namo Ami-to-fo (pronounced "Nah Mwo Ah Mi Toh Fwo"). This recitation is called *nien fo* (contemplation, or remembering). In Japanese, Namu Amida Butsu; the recitation is called *nembutsu*. In Vietnamese, Nammo Adida Phat. *Namo* or *namu* is a form of deep homage, like "*In the Name of the Father.*" The name invokes the one upon whom we rely, in whom we take refuge. We can hear this in *namaste: namas* (taking refuge) plus *te* (you).

Hear and Now _____

"When reciting the Buddha's name, you should gather your thoughts together. Recitation originates in the mind and is channeled through the mouth, each phrase, each word, clearly enunciated. You should also listen clearly, impressing the words in your mind. Manjushri taught: 'Hearing within, hearing one's Nature—one's Nature becomes the Supreme Mind.'"

—Master Yin Kuang (1861–1940)

Three Keys: Faith, Vows, and Practice

One doesn't become free just by rubbing some beads and mumbling some syllables. Dharmakara's great effort calls for reciprocal diligence on our part. As with Insight Meditation or Zen, persistent dedication creates a kind of groove for us to enter. It's as simple as someone who keeps a picture of their beloved in their wallet, and looks at it from time to time: where we might only see a person, they see something else entirely.

The Pure Land path asks just three things of us: *faith, vows,* and *practice.* We must have faith: in ourselves, in the benefits of a pure life, and in the existence of the Pure Land (be it the Kingdom of God, the beloved community, or paradise now). We must make vows to follow the Bodhisattva Path and enter the Pure Land. And we must diligently practice our vows and the Eightfold Path, cultivating and following the teachings, cherishing their virtue, and nourishing our seeds of awakening heart and liberated mind. Together, these pave the path to our entry into the realm of Awakening.

Serene Faith: The Way of a Dewdrop

Faith needn't be blind. The Third Noble Truth requires faith, based on understanding the previous noble truths. It's a confidence and trust, faith in possibility, or a letting go (knowing one can't fall off a mountain, say). It's faith in our experience, through our littlest recognitions: that mind can quiet of its own, that needless suffering can diminish, and that life is essentially good. We can have faith in our interconnection with all things. Faith here isn't blind. Faith is heeding the Path, ever at hand.

The Vow of Compassion: Even Butterflies Hear It

The essential compassion of transferring merit helped universalize the Buddhist path. (Actually, you and I are enjoying its benefits right now because this is why movable type was invented: so people could generate and dedicate karmic merit by spreading the Dharma; more copies, more merit.) Enlightenment is a totally new way of sharing our common life, and dedication of merit is one logical outcome. When we pray for someone, this is, in effect, our aim: to transfer merit. So it's only natural that people would want to call upon Guan Yin or Amitabha to transfer a little merit.

Buddhism is implicitly about oneness rather than isolation, so a key factor here is that the petitioner's perspective shares that of the bodhisattvas—for the sake of all. As reciting and hearing Buddha's name become one with what that name means, the cultivator might be drawn to the bodhisattva vow as by a magnet, for the sake all beings. More than a matter of a possible miracle or two, the recognition of the boundlessness of the bodhisattva's compassion embraces and eventually transforms a person's entire being, everything on earth, and beyond. With one simple, seemingly sideways step, the Pure Land path crosses a barrier steeper than the Himalayas: the eighteen inches between our head and our heart.

 Hear and Now

> "We surround all men and all forms of life with Infinite Love and Compassion.
> Particularly do we send forth loving thoughts to those in suffering and sorrow; to all those in doubt and ignorance; to all who are striving to attain Truth, and to those whose feet are standing close to the great change men call death, we send forth oceans of wisdom, mercy, and love."
> —Jodo Shin-shu benediction

The Nonpractice of Practice: Cultivating the Dharma

Where other Buddhist paths might seem like those of an ant climbing the alps, Pure Land resembles a boat sailing downstream, *with* the wind—a log rolling downhill. The Pure Land schools live up to the name of their collective branch, Mahayana (Great Vehicle), in welcoming rich and poor, man and woman, monk and nun, young and old, saint and sinner. We mortals might better appreciate universal compassion, or boundless love, by considering how much more it can save a bad person than a good one.

Pure Land's like an ocean, buoying up everybody. It can provide deathbed reassurance of a blessed afterlife, and it can be a general, moment-to-moment panacea throughout life. No arcane metaphysics to study. You don't have to shop around for a teacher, a roshi, or a guru. Go straight to Amitabha, who's vowed to save everyone, even the lowest of the low, and who accepts you just as you are.

Practice in Pure Land is often called *cultivation:* cultivating our awakening, our own seat in Amitabha's limitless Pure Land. The Community of Mindful Living, in the tradition of the Venerable Thich Nhat Hanh, enjoys a greeting that goes like this: "A lotus for you; a Buddha to be." It's good for letters, but also bowing in, with palms together in *gassho* (without knuckles pressed together, a gesture of "presenting a lotus"). Here are some Pure Land lotuses for you, a Buddha to be.

Giving Chants a Chance: Recitation

All the schools of practice in this book engage in chanting, also known as *recitation*. In East Asia, monastics typically recite the *Amitabha Sutra* and the Buddha's name every day. Some monks take as their personal practice the recitation of the Buddha's name up to 10,000 times a day or more. Here in the West, laypeople get together (on Sundays, usually) to study Dharma and recite together (plus enjoy community activities), perhaps with monastics.

Like song, recitation is a wonderful congregational practice, as well as a personal one, and Chinese and Japanese temples are very convivial. If you're a newcomer, you'll be most welcome; many sanghas are already very diverse. "Namo Amitofo" and "Namu Amida Butsu!" are common greetings. I've been to some that furnish sutra recitation booklets transliterating Chinese for English-speakers. If you get lost, the person next to you will usually notice and kindly point in your book to where everyone is. (Actually, *not* knowing the meaning of the words can be a good practice, too: selfless nonattachment, receptive faith, compassionate heart. I find my throat can choke up when my mind is trying to grasp the words rather than letting my heart sing. A practitioner has compared it to listening to opera without understanding the words, just letting the sound flow over and through one.) Whatever sutra they're reciting, it's a wonderful practice to join in the chant. A serpentine melody spontaneously emerges while every syllable is pronounced, taking on a life of its own. (Zen and Nichiren, on the other hand, prefer a kind of monotone.) Whatever the temple, a good tip for chanting in a group is to be neither too soft nor too loud—just blend in. At Shin service, they listen deeply to a Dharma talk, and then chant nembutsu. Then people hang out together, often over some home-cooked vegetarian food. (I love those persimmon ginger cookies!)

At home, you might start and end a day with a few minutes of recitation. Take refuge in Amitabha's vow. Try this gatha: "Namo Amitabha Buddha of Infinite Light." (*Namo* [in-breath]; *Amitabha* [out-breath]. *Buddha* [in-breath]; *Light* [out-breath]. Short form: *infinite* [in-breath]; *light* [out-breath].) Count: In + out = one breath. Practice in groups of ten, with a mala to keep count. As with basic meditation, don't alter your breath. If you practice with one heart, unconfused, one mind, single-minded, you'll find yourself getting quiet, coming present, centering down, grounding. Over time, you might notice the arising of meditative awareness and one-pointed concentration, and awareness of a mindful, nondiscriminating, spacious state of light and peace. You might be entering the state of mind realizing the Pure Land in this world.

For busy people: Set aside just a bit of time for your morning and evening. Visit your domestic breathing room. Join palms, bow in. Inhale 3–5 seconds; exhale 9–15 seconds. Recite as you exhale: *harmony*, in the morning; *gratitude*, at night. (Do this syllable by syllable; hear the bell in each syllable). The sound of the last syllable extends until the end of exhalation. Then bow your a head a bit and stay with the feeling for a couple breaths. Harmony waters the seeds of cooperation with others, being patient and calm. Over time, the seeds will blossom into an understanding you could call wisdom (Amitayus). Gratitude counts your blessings, watering the seeds of grace. Seeds of compassion will blossom (Amitabha). They cross-fertilize each other. Eventually, collapse the two words into one: Amitabha.

No matter whether aloud or silently, recitation can be a mindfulness meditation to recite anytime and anywhere, while washing the dishes or driving the car—while doing something repetitive, or doing nothing. You can recite before and after sleep, and even during. Scientists now concur with Buddhists that in one split second the mind conceives of literally thousands of thought formations. For most of us, they're mostly irrelevant fragments: "… blue, a new car, corn, yesterday, sale …" and so on. Recitation replaces ten thousand scattered thoughts with one good thought. How good to redirect our habit energy away from the constantly turning wheel of illusory roof-brain chatter, and to redirect it toward our aspiration for awakening, through the majestic, virtuous name of the Buddha, the primal vow of Amitabha. It's a good habit.

Exercise: Recite "Namo Amitabha," "Om Amitabha," "A-Mi-Ta-Bha," or even "Bud-Dha."

The Mind's Eye: Creative Visualization

The *Meditation Sutra* invites a personal visual creation of the Pure Land. It also invites mental contemplation of the 32 distinguishing marks of Amitabha. He's inconceivably vast. It is said that there's a white hair in between his eyebrows, which alone is five times longer than the tallest mountain in mythology, Mount Sumeru, which is about a million miles above sea-level. So don't sell yourself short. Think big. Think, for example, of Amitabha's purple eyes, deep and clear as the four great seas. Expand your mind. Think of the light streaming from his body, in a nimbus of 48 rays, one for each of his vows (set forth in the larger Pure Land sutra, *Infinite Life Sutra*).

Another approach is to recite Amitabha's name while facing an image of him—at home, with a portable altar, or even with a wallet-size picture. In *contemplation by image*, you might concentrate on that white hair between his brows. You might see it emit a ray of light, traveling to the ends of the universe. (Amitabha, you'll recall, means infinite light.) Within his light, you can imagine Buddhas and Bodhisattvas without limit, teaching and practicing the Dharma. You might smell heavenly perfume (such as the nectar of compassion) wafting from the Pure Land. Listening, you might hear its celestial music in the wind through the trees.

Pure Land Zen, Zen Pure Land

The first temple in Japan practiced both Zen and Pure Land. Then in the twelfth century, parishes had to register, identifying themselves with a single practice. (They could switch, but they could not practice both.) In China, however, schools often dovetailed, such as between Pure Land and Zen (Chan).

Try this: Meditating on the name of the Buddha, notice the space in between the two syllables, *bud dha*. It is the spacious, nameless, formless, perfect blank of infinite possibility. (Koan: "What is that?!")

Or try this: During seated meditation, think "budh" on your in-breath and "dha" on your out-breath. Then, when you feel yourself in samadhi, seeing clearly and deeply, ask yourself, "Who's reciting the Buddha's name?" Keep asking as you continue recitation. Ask further: "Who's asking, 'Who's reciting the Buddha's name?'" You might find your own mind, the Buddha, and all sentient beings are one. There is no separation. We're reciting (remembering) our own original Buddha nature. These are examples of Zen practice within Pure Land.

A mutual practice of Pure Land with Zen (*Nien-fo Ch'an*, in Chinese) provides a fail-safe, for example. If you don't crack the koan part, recitation will still earn you a seat in the Pure Land anyway. Moreover, the two can cross-fertilize each other. Where Zen ropes off extraneous, shallow thought with the koan, using the poison of words as the antidote to the poison of our egocentric, dualist responses to the world, Pure Land uses conceptualization to transcend conceptualization. The turning point in Zen koan study is the raising of "Great Doubt" (deep questioning); in Pure Land, the turning point is the experience of "Serene Trust" (the trust as shown by an autumn leaf, letting go, or of a dewdrop falling).

 Hear and Now _____

"This medicine is the 'Calling upon the Name of Amida,' and is wrapped up in the six syllables Na Mu A Mi Da Butsu.... For this medicine no money or special wisdom is needed. All one has to do is recite the words with your mouth.... Here indeed is a pivot of fundamental power."

"Do I hear you say, 'Too easy'? 'Such wares are intended only to deceive old men and women.' Many doubt their efficacy and ask of the wise if there is not some other way more suited for clever people. And Sakyamuni pointed straight back at the heart of man and said that within one's heart there is to be found the true Buddha nature."

—Zen Master Hakuin (1685–1768)

A period of recitation during samadhi or Zen meditation can dissolve the barrier between subject and object as effectively as koan practice or just sitting. That is, the mind that's the *subject* reciting the name, and the awakening Buddha that's the *object* of invocation, are really one. "My reciting Buddha's name is his very voice which calls me." Reciting the Buddha's name can thus be its own kind of koan, and continuous meditation. In Pure Land, this is often called "real mark" recitation, because it goes beyond marks or any attachment to distinguishing characteristics, and instead relies on your true nature, your buddha mind.

Practicing "No Practice": Other-Power, the Power Beyond Self

In Japan, the founder of Pure Land (*Jodo*) practice was Honen (1133–1212). In 1207, nembutsu chant was banned, exiling him and his disciple, Shinran (1173–1263). Now neither a monk nor a lay practitioner, Shinran came to a radical approach (Jodo *Shin*, or *True* Pure Land). The idea so far had been that faith in the Vow would bring a person to the Pure Land. But, Shinran argued, that's as if the Pure Land (or enlightenment, or buddha nature) is a reward, rather than a *fait accompli*, already given, thanks to the Vow. Amitabha has not only already guaranteed our ticket to his pure land, but we arrive without traveling. It's a done deal. (Now carry it on.) After initially taking refuge in Amida, recitation of his name need be done only in gratitude—like saying "thank you." Recitation with any expectation would only continue our delusion of self. Once we realize our true identity is no different than Buddha's, and that it has always been thus, there's nothing else to realize, except gratitude, and seeing how illusion has kept us from awareness, and vowing to relieve the needless suffering of others.

This is a very interesting reading of Right View and Right Thought. Outside of following the Eightfold Path, meditation or any "practice" whatsoever is to immediately set up the least breeze of separation and selfhood, stained with the taint of discriminating mind and separation. Using one's own ego, or self-power (*jiriki*), to try to overcome itself is like trying to grasp a bar of soap with wet hands. The harder you try, the farther away the goal really gets. Trying to will our own enlightenment only imprisons us in our own self-centeredness. All we can do is surrender to Other-power (*tariki*), which is Amida: unthinkable timeless being. Putting left hand to right, in gassho, Other-power meets self-power in full embrace, with nothing extra left over.

Other-power may sound way too simple, but simple ain't always easy. You've heard it's easier to give than to receive. Well, giving requires self-power; receiving, Other-power. Upon honest self-examination, you might agree you may have difficulty sometimes truly receiving: to listen, to accept, to let be, to let go, to surrender. Other-power's more challenging than you might first think—and sublime, and utterly natural.

"Clear seeing" in Shin is not so much seeing the unbounded nature of reality; rather, it is clearly seeing the human predicament: an awakened sense of our own limitations, a fiercely honest awareness of our own shortcomings or failures (a verboten word to many success-driven people) … that each of us might have tried to clamber up a 10,000-foot pole to grab a slice of some of that tantalizing enlightenment pie up at the top … and even felt some kind of spiritual pride at how much progress we were making on our way up to that prize, only to slide back down, realizing ultimately how much we were only patting ourselves on our back, self-congratulatory. What fools we mortals be! My English-language dictionary has pages of definitions all beginning with the prefix "self-," so it's no wonder that self-centered Westerners are in no less need of the power of selflessness.

One might be inclined to liken recitation to the concentrative stillness of samadhi, and meditation on the meaning of recitation to the insight of Vipassana, except we need to avoid the trap of dualism. Recitation, rather, becomes a mirror in which we can see our self-centeredness as well as our buddha nature. I might recite nembutsu and feel good about myself for doing so, but this is still foolish self-satisfaction—what

Professor Takamaro Shigaraki calls "no better than an ornamental or armamental accessory to our life." As a practice of nonpractice, mindfulness in everyday life does come about here. For example, here I'm already awakened by the primal vow, but *ow!* I bumped my head (hopefully not on somebody else's). So I stop and consider where my attention was directed (two places at once?). This path of inquiry can take me through the Buddhist teachings (noble truths, paramitas, brahmavirharas, and so on) and on through to the central realities of infinite light (wisdom, or pure feeling) and eternal life (compassion, or immeasurable love). Realizing the Way is really true, I might then recite nembutsu in gratitude. *Aha!* Thank you, Power Beyond Self!

Pure Land can be likened to a transcendent leap … sideways! We'd been like worms inside a dark stick of bamboo, climbing up and ever up, when all the time we could have just bored a hole at any point, and—*zip!*—climb out. Horizontal liberation! We're already as enlightened as we are. Shin asks us to look at ourselves in the plain light of day, just as we are, and be grateful. And try to live up to that truth through study of the Middle Way, listening deeply to our Dharma talks, and learning in community with our sangha. Actually, the pure land of Amida very much resembles the monastic Sangha, while we ourselves hold down jobs and raise families.

 Hear and Now

"We realize true gratitude when we are awakened to the fact that the foolish being who fails in being compassionate is the very object of Buddha's compassion."

—Reverend Ken Tanaka

Hear and Now

"The true nembutsu totally jolts and upturns *myself*, mercilessly exposing my present reality before me and causing great pains to my inner self. While the nembutsu was my own choice in my earnest efforts toward Buddhahood, at the same time it begins to severely criticize and negate what I am…. Then the nembutsu transcends myself to become the nembutsu of non-effort, and the nembutsu itself begins to say the nembutsu … no longer the nembutsu I say, but that which is only heard, coming from some place beyond myself…. In the true nembutsu, therefore, I choose to call the Buddha's Name, and yet at the very same time, the Buddha is calling me."

—Professor Takamaro Shigaraki

Surrendering to nondualism means allowing ourselves to receive the compassion of all the Buddhas, appearing to our limited perception as acting upon us as "Other-power." Actually, Amida transfers not only his merits (his incredibly wholesome karma surplus transforming our personal self-destructive karma), but also his enlightenment: his nondualist, infinite mind, which is one with the Compassion of All the Buddhas. It's that simple, but maybe you wish a nudge of more clarification ….

Shinran anticipated the charge of dualism, and so stipulated the goal was "to be free from any form of calculations." Elsewhere: "What is called Other-power is the same as saying there's no discrimination of This or That." Self- and Other-power only seem dualist to our limited, dualist perspective. Both participate together inseparably in a reciprocal I–Thou relationship without bounds. The Vow is akin to saying, "The Kingdom of God is within you." Actually, the divine is everywhere, but we need to experience this subjectively to understand, from our perspective: it is within *us*. It's like the person who stopped in the midst of devotional prayer and said, "Wait! Who am I, this mere insignificant speck, to even dream the immeasurable source of creation would hear my tiny thin voice within the inconceivably vast cosmos!?!" Taking it further, however, the person realized that because (by definition) God is everywhere, the Sacred thus dwelt within his very own heart, so it then became perfectly natural to pray.

As it's said in Tibet: "To understand all that *Buddha* means is to understand all of Buddhism." Namo Shakyamuni Buddha! Namo Amitabha Buddha!

The Least You Need to Know

◆ Pure Land is the largest and simplest school of Buddhism. Temples in the West (some being the oldest in North America) have been largely of Chinese or Japanese heritage, but are growing diverse.

◆ The Enlightenment of Amitabha Buddha creates a pure land, a field of awakening, a state beyond suffering, to which he will bring anyone who sincerely calls upon him. His bodhisattva vow mirrors that of his followers, who likewise dedicate their practice for the sake of all beings.

◆ There's no one school of Pure Land. Interpretations vary from traditional to humanist.

◆ Pure Land can dovetail with other schools, except in Japan where it became single. Jodo Shin concentrates on recitation of Buddha's name—not as practice or meditation, which is seen as only self-power, nor in petition (also ego), but in gratitude.

◆ In Chinese, recitation of Amitabha Buddha's name (called *nienfo*) is *Namo Amitofo*; in Japanese (called *nembutsu*), it is *Namu Amida Butsu*. No matter how you say his name, if you're sincere, he'll hear. (Om Amito!)

Chapter 14

Diamond Way: Tibetan Buddhism

In This Chapter

- Tantra
- Foundations and initiations
- Teachers
- Body–speech–mind as one
- Ritual and symbol

Vajrayana is the last classical tradition of Buddhist practice to reach Western shores. That's curiously appropriate because it preserves what it considers the final teachings of the Buddha. Here, wall we've learned so far is recast in yet another light, equally radiant.

Some speak of three major schools of the Way of the Buddha: Theravada, Mahayana, and Vajrayana. Another possibility is to speak of Vajrayana as Mahayana with a tantric twist. Decide for yourself.

Tibetan Buddhism in 500 Words or Less

Tibetan Buddhism (*Vajrayana*) may be the most complex of schools we're surveying, yet this brief chapter will give you a good handle. At its core, as in all Dharma pathways, is the compassion and wisdom of the Buddha, enlightened energy, unbounded awareness, and ultimate liberation.

This Is

Tibetan Buddhism is part of the **Vajrayana** school. *Vajra* means "diamond," so Vajrayana literally means "the Diamond Path." It is as indestructible and multifaceted as a diamond with crystal clarity, and it is the supreme of its kind. Within Vajrayana are four main schools: Nyingma, Sakya, Kagyu, and Geluk. Vajrayana merges Theravada and Mahayana elements with a Buddhist adaptation of an ancient Hindu yoga (*tantra*), and it incorporates shamanic elements of Tibet's pre-Buddhist *Bon* religion. It's arguably the most complex, and complete, branch of Buddhism.

Vajrayana recapitulates the entire development of Buddhism in India, with further modifications called *Tantra*. Vajrayana includes the base-camp practice of samatha–vipassana, as in Insight Meditation (calming mind and seeing clearly into reality), as well as the meditation-without-meditation of Zen (called *Mahamudra* and *Dzogchen*). Fond of debate, Vajrayana engages in analytics no less discerning and rigorous than Theravada. There's another similarity between Tantra and Vipassana in that both paths view obstacles to our meditation as levers into insight. And its broadly compassionate embrace is no less devotional than in Pure Land.

From a Pure Land perspective, we've also glimpsed at how buddha nature pervades every atom of the universe. So now we can appreciate tantra telling us, "Because everything has potential buddha nature, it's thus all suitable for practice. It's all *stuff* … all sacred … use it!" One example maybe you've seen: Tibetan prayer flags. These bright red, yellow, green, blue, and white squares of cloth with Buddhist prayers printed on them are strung out where the winds can spread their merit. That's tantric. You'll find the Mahayana perspectives we've already covered: the Bodhisattva Vow, emptiness (sunyata) as well as selflessness (anatman), sacred story, deities, and upaya (skillful means). In sum, imagine we're climbing up a mountain in search of healing waters. It can take us lifetimes. Tantra takes us there quickly, but instead of saying the water's all the way at the top, it asks us to dive off from a certain height, out and on down into the clear deep lake of enlightening transformation. Ready to take the plunge?

Tantra: The Thread Through the Tapestry

Tantra is defined as "weaving," as well as "continuum" and "system." So, this path continues Theravada and Mahayana practices with the thread of tantra running through them all. It's a systematic weaving of truths both outer and inner, self and other, and personal and cosmic; and it's a threading beyond to ultimate, complete, innate enlightenment, with the continuity of sunyata present at all levels. Don't worry about trying to grasp it all in one sitting (actually, don't grasp at all!). Tantra recognizes the interdependent, interwoven nature of reality (one sample of a fabric can reveal its overall pattern). The primal energies eternally shaping the cosmos also mold each of us. Each practitioner is treated as both a unique individual and as part of an infinitely interpenetrating matrix of all being.

> **Along the Path** _____
>
> Texts unique to Vajrayana are called *tantras*, as opposed to *sutras;* yet both words have similar meanings ("to weave" and "to sew," respectively). And our word *text*, from Latin, also means "a weaving." Some mystics *read* the world as their sacred text. Tantra interweaves an individual's personal life with the Buddha's Way. And it's a yoga (a word akin to religion, literally retying), yoking the sacred with the mundane and wisdom with compassion.

An interesting historical example of tantra is relevant in our introduction. When Padmasambhava was trying to bring Buddhism to Tibet in the eighth century, and was encountering the native deities of the Bon religion there, he did not wage a crusade on them. Rather, he incorporated them into the Tibetan Buddhism pantheon, where they're known as protectors. He didn't try to purge or cleanse, eradicate or purify. He worked with What Is, in transformation. That's a tantric approach.

Honor the Resistance: Transformation Yoga

Besides Padmasambhava and prayer flags, a more personal perspective is gained in seeing how tantra deals effectively with difficult emotions. (You got some? Sit by me!) Seemingly baser energies are energies nevertheless. So we can skillfully use them. Rather than suppress or disassociate from them (which would be the mistake of asceticism), tantra recognizes they, too, contain buddha nature, capable of purifying their own destructive tendencies. Where our mind reacts with confusion or dissatisfaction, that's where work's available, and where power already exists for transformation. For example, from the limitless, formless perspective of sunyata, it only appears that someone cut you off in traffic. They were only making a left, albeit maybe less than skillfully. So why did you take it personally? If you honked in anger, did they make you do it? Who controls your mind but you?

Along the Path

> Tantra can be likened to the philosophy and practice of alchemy. Alchemy transforms matter into spirit, as symbolized by changing lead into gold (comparable, here, to Buddha nature). Like the tantrist, the alchemist sees the Buddha nature in everything—even bird dung, as if it is really gold but is just sick and needs healing. (Of course, gold can't be changed into gold, just as our buddha nature already is Buddha.)

Here, a tantric slogan might be: "Honor the resistance." In that traffic moment, the one making the left turn is your guru, awakening you to one of your neuroses, your juicy spots, if you're willing to see yourself honestly in the plain light of day. Normally, our soft spots are where we build a hard shell for protection, which also keeps us numb, overprotected, rigid, and thus set up to be even more vulnerable to be hurt in the bumpy road of life. In such recognition, tantra doesn't equate the ego with original sin (as if it were the source of our separation from the nondual garden of bliss), but rather reconnects it to its base, the basis of all things, in the innate goodness of the heart.

Faced with the ego's toxic fires, tantra "fights fire with fire," using those energies to loosen the shackles of ego. What if, rather than honking and creating a chain reaction of bad karma, you generated instead a garland of compassionate metta for all beings in traffic here and everywhere, all tender radiant human beings like you, all wanting to just go along but needlessly suffering, all while ensconced in miracles of mind-engineering (cars) fueled by our common ancestral karma (fossil fuel), each holding the wheel of dharma in our hands!? There's an echo here of how the brahmaviharas have near and far enemies, in which boundless mind manifests less skillfully. There's a wise precision within anger, if skillfully transformed (capable, for instance, of discerning the compassion within passion). You might try reflecting upon this sense of tantra in your own daily life. Honor the resistance. Rigdzin Namkha Gyatso Rinpoche asks, "If you hate those who harm you, with whom will you practice patience? Those who harm you do you great kindness. Who can give you perfect patience? (So precious.) Your worst enemy."

From a broader perspective, tantra weaves together our devotional impulses, analytical skill, and meditative intuition, within a complete system of universal and personal reality—all in a full-course physio-psychic menu, interlinking body, speech, and mind.

From that perspective, we'll review five interwoven threads: (1) tantric foundation, and more advanced stages of initiation (empowerment); (2) the role of the teacher (guru) linking your path to the Buddha's; (3) how fully tantra engages body, speech, and mind, as one; (4) realms of poetry and myth, ritual and symbol; and (5) the path as the goal, as we'll see here … with a tantric twist.

Vajra and bell. The small ritual scepter, called a vajra *in Sanskrit (dorje, Tibetan), is a weapon against ignorance. It represents upaya (the compassionate use of skillful means, or method; the masculine principle). It might be hand-held by a deity, who might also hold a ritual bell (ghanta) in the other hand, representing prajna (perfect wisdom, or emptiness; the feminine principle). Together, the two represent perfect union.*

(From The Encyclopedia of Tibetan Buddhist Symbols and Motifs *by Robert Beer, © 1999, reprinted by arrangement with Shambhala Publications, Inc., Boston, www.shambhala.com)*

Foundation and Initiation: All Good Medicine

When you see the seated Buddha holding a bowl, sometimes it's a begging bowl, but other times it's a medicine bowl, in which he has every form of medicine there is, with just the right prescription for what ails you. Tibetan Buddhism offers us a full pharmacopia of healing medicine, with something there for everyone. There are preliminary teachings and practices, and advanced tantric practices involving initiation, called *empowerments*—all aimed, ultimately, at continual openness and a good heart. You could learn the preliminary, *foundational* stages (called *ngöndro* [pronounced "nundro"] or *lamrim*, though they are not identical) in several months, but they might take years to practice well. Some people spend their lifetime at foundational practices, while others eventually move on to empowerments; Tibetan Buddhists might say it boils down to personal karma. Enlightenment can come with just one prostration. Step by step, the path is the goal.

Step by Step: Basic Stages Along the Path

There's an emphasis, from the get-go, of enabling the practitioner to realize his or her own mind as buddha mind by personally retracing his or her career through Theravada, Mahayana, and Tantra (in that order, which just happens to be how they're laid out in this smart person's guidebook). This system of stages threads each practitioner from Theravada self-disciplined awareness to Mahayana compassionate awareness to totally enlightened awareness—in a process appropriate to his or her individual temperament.

One basic meditation is on how, out of all possible life forms, being born a human being is the best opportunity to realize the seeds of enlightenment are within all beings, though with a human birth also comes foibles. Death and impermanence are preliminary meditations, as are samsara and karma. Rebirth here is seen more as "interbirth," to use a word coined by Zen master and poet Gary Snyder. Indeed, we all continually give birth to each other. (Recall, here, Element Meditation.) All beings are as precious as our mother (or grandmother, or ancestors). So we have a compassionate bond with all beings. The Four Brahmaviharas (Boundless Minds) are practiced, opening the heart to the fullest dimensions of equanimity and love, and from the perspective of the bodhisattva, for the sake of all beings.

Foundational practices also include remembering kindnesses of others, disadvantages of self-cherishing, advantages of cherishing others, exchanging self with others (*tonglen*), developing *bodhicitta* (the compassionate aspiration to attain enlightenment for the sake of all beings), guru yoga, and identifying with sunyata rather than ego.

Consider, for example, *tonglen* (giving and receiving). Here, you take in the sadness and suffering of others and give them back your own happiness and capacity for nirvana. You might visualize someone's problem (anger, poor self-esteem, illness, and so on) as a black smoke. Then, inhale it into the diamond of your heart-mind where you see its innate radiance vaporize the black smoke *(Pffffsstt!)*. Exhale the radiant innate bliss of your pure heart-mind, visualized as a white light upon them and the whole universe. Now that creative visualization has become a popular spiritual practice in the West, many often associate light with inhalation and toxins with exhalation, but the reversal is instructive. Setting the pain of others before you unloosens the clenched fist of personal ego (whose personal desire for enlightenment thwarts itself by the inherent selfishness of such desire), generating instead *bodhicitta*, the altruistic desire for enlightenment for all beings, and transforming yourself as you help others. Because suffering is born of a constricted heart, self-cherishing and self-absorbed, taking on suffering expands one's heart, so as to take it all in.

Though tonglen can take a whole book to properly explain, it can be summed up with a one-sentence slogan: "Practice sending and taking with the breath." As such, it's part of a twelfth-century collection of such slogans called *lojong* (know how, mind-trainings, or mind changers), training the mind by changing habitual attitudes and reactions. Several contemporary teachers from both East and West comment on these traditional teachings, yet another aspect of Vajrayana reaching a wider populace. Sample slogans include:

- ◆ "Work regardless of outcome."

- ◆ "Find the consciousness you had before you were born." (The unborn nature of mind is pure awareness.)

- ◆ "Be grateful to everyone." (Thank you, friend! Thank you, enemy!)

- ◆ "Drive all blames into one." (Not, "Beat yourself up over everything," but rather, "What is blame?" When it arises, don't bite the hook!)

Generation and Completion: Meditation Buddhas (*Yidams*)

The purpose of the techniques just mentioned are for recognizing buddha mind as our own mind. Such joining and unifying are what the word *yoga* means. Another such yoga in Vajrayana is known generally as *deity yoga*. Here's how it works. Awakening bodhicitta establishes the basis of union. Our aspiration for buddha mind, for the sake of all beings, is the Buddha's own mind. Then comes unifying our mind with a buddha deity generated in meditation through visualization, a meditation buddha. There are two primary stages, *generation* and *completion* (with details to follow further on). A teacher initiates a student in the particular figure called a *yidam* (a deity, bodhisattva, or even historical figure) he or she has chosen especially for the student, a manifestation of Buddha chosen to match the yogi's personal temperament or need. This meditation buddha is enthroned on a lotus in his or her particular pure land, called a *mandala*.

A drawing of a mandala is like a two-dimensional blueprint for a three-dimensional visualization. A meditation buddha deity is pictured in the center, at the pinnacle of a pagoda-like pyramid shape, with narrowing ascending levels. It's like Pure Land visualization, with one's present environment being identified with the pure land. Along with a particular meditation buddha in a particular mandala, the student repeats the buddha's particular *mantra* and *mudra* (hand gesture). This is the *generation stage*. In the *completion stage*, the practitioner visualizes himself or herself *as* the meditation buddha, no longer separate, facilitated by the initiation of the guru manifesting that buddha energy for him or her. Eventually, one can visualize one's self as a buddha within a mandala, eyes-open as well as eyes-closed. Afterward, the buddha in a mandala is visualized as dissolving into and no different than emptiness.

This Is

A **mandala** is a circular form that can represent the world of phenomena, as well as realms of consciousness and pure lands of bodhisattvas and deities. Mandalas can be made up of rice or colored sand, or painted on scrolls (called *tangkas*). They can be temples, such as Borobudur in Java and Samye in Tibet, or three-dimensional yarn sculptures. They resemble other cultures' primeval cosmologies and mind maps, such as the *medicine wheel* and the *labyrinth* (without a spiral walkway).

Connecting with a Teacher: Guru Yoga

Vajrayana has texts (all the sutras, plus tantras), but it's an oral tradition. It's also a devotional path, and your teacher (*rinpoche*) becomes the focus of that energy as the living embodiment of the Buddha taking you through the Buddha's own path. The guru has been compared to how a magnifying lens concentrates and harnesses light, enabling it to kindle fire; here the light is Buddha's enlightened energy, available in a way the guru feels appropriate to the student's needs, the epitome of skillful means. Tantra can be challenging, affecting each person differently, so you need your teacher's wisdom and compassion to personally guide you through.

This Is

A Tibetan teacher can have many names, besides mentor, preceptor, and spiritual friend. **Rinpoche** (pronounced "rin-poh-shay," meaning "greatly precious") is akin to the Japanese *roshi*. *Geshe* (pronounced "geshey") or *Khenpo* is like a scholarly Ph.D. Individuals believed to be intentionally reincarnated (including the Dalai Lamas) are designated *Tulku*. A *lama* has often completed three-year training. Sometimes Tibetan Buddhism is mistakenly called Lamaism, somewhat akin to calling Christianity "Reverendism." (And a llama is like a small, woolly camel.)

This relationship is often sparked by an amazing sense of affinity ("when the student's ready, the teacher appears"). A guru is considered more important than a parent, because while your parents raise you in one lifetime, your guru takes you through all your lives and brings you up in the most profound way. Utter devotion is requisite because he or she represents your own buddha mind and inner teacher, as well as the Buddha's teachings, connecting you to the lineage.

Some Westerners have been known to take more than one teacher, but traditionally it's just one. A rule of thumb is to spend up to three years before making a commitment to a Tibetan Buddhist teacher (in Tibet, 12 years)—the bond is that intense. Sogyal Rinpoche once pointed out that Americans want to hear why they should do something before they go and do it, while Tibetans go ahead and do something, then their teacher will tell them why they did it. There are a number of similarities to Zen in this intimacy of teacher and student. For instance, just as the teacher isn't waiting for any correct answer to a koan, but rather your answer, when a guru gives you a particular mantra for meditation, the secret may not be solely within any particular mantra so much as within your own response to their power.

 Hear and Now _____

"Buddhists ... call the mentor 'spiritual teacher,' and 'spiritual friend,' as a close friend, not an absolute authority. This emphasizes how you have to free yourself, develop your own enlightenment. No one else can do it for you. But in Tantra the sort of transference relations to the teacher is very important. You spend twelve years to investigate such a central figure. You don't jump into receiving teachings from the first teacher. Not initiatory teaching."

—Robert Thurman

Open Secrets: Empowerment

Pssst! Listen! Do you want to know a secret? Vajrayana is often labeled "esoteric," meaning Not For General Consumption. Actually, Vajrayana wants everyone to be a Buddha; it's just that tantra is not to be tried at home alone. Anyone can practice Pure Land, say, but transmission of the tantric teachings formally begins during a special ritual of initiation (empowerment), following the foundational preparation yogas. (These days, in the West, with some teachers, transmission might also take place in ordinary conversation, or by a mere gesture. [*Thwonk!*] You never know.)

Esoteric Tibetan practices, unchanged for more than a millennium, are now reaching bookshop shelves, for sale to anyone (*Priceless Treasure:* only $19.95). This can be somewhat similar to "plastic shamans" promoting a sweat lodge purification ceremony without any grounding in the path of indigenous spirituality of which it's but a part. (Mindfulness, on the other hand, can be practiced completely independent of

Buddhism.) Vajrayana practice is grounded in preliminary preparation (ngöndro), initiation (*Abhisheka*, Sankrit; meaning "consecrating," anointing," or "watering"), and personal empowerment.

The mantra *Ah*, for example, can symbolize the entire *Heart Sutra* and *Diamond Sutra*— all of Buddhism in just one syllable! But initiation by a teacher is required to understand and practice. Actually, these secrets aren't the kind of cloak-and-dagger mysteries they might sound like. Having worked for years as a secretary, I'm proud to say the word *secretary* means "one who keeps the secrets." So has the Tibetan lineage faithfully preserved these precious teachings. Make no mistake, Vajrayana isn't a members-only secret society. Rather, it unlocks deep mysteries only to those adequately trained, and only from those in the lineage. An appliance won't work unless plugged in, and a guru provides that current, charged with a direct connection to Buddha juice in the here and now. Otherwise, to continue the analogy, scrambled radio waves are passing through us this very moment even though we may not have a set to tune in. ("More when we come back … and now *this*!"). Not having a set is equivalent to not having been initiated; something's there but it won't work in practicality.

Leaves from the Bodhi Tree

A visitor came upon a small crowd of Tibetan Buddhist monks. Their attention was riveted upon a single priest sitting on a platform. He joined them, watching this priest. When the ceremony of watching was over, he asked one of the monks what had happened. The monk told him that the priest had demonstrated the power of levitation. "But I didn't see him levitate," the visitor told the monk. "Oh," the monk said, smiling. "Then obviously you didn't receive initiation for the ceremony beforehand."

There's no secret to Vajrayana's deity yoga, whose ultimate goal is that the yogi will recognize his or her mind as Buddha mind. We've prepared the ground in seeing Amitabha's transformation from a devoted monk to a bodhisattva to a transcendental Buddha in his own pure land. Widening the frame, we can see Amida Buddha as but one in a pantheon or cosmic parade of particular transcendental figures, each a certain aspect of the Buddha's Supreme Enlightenment. Even with a humanist approach to deities, demystifying them would never detract from the distinct realities they represent. Scholar Georg Feurstein calls them "practical energetic presences," and notes how there's no clear boundary between their being "intelligent energy, personified symbol, and … divine background." If you prefer a convenient handle, you might think of them as aspects of the Buddha's Enlightenment, thus aspects of the same ultimate reality of which we all partake, and aspire to be aware of.

> **Hear and Now**
>
> "Now I will tell you something about the Secret School. It's not that mantras are secret. The Secret School is the efficacious response which comes from *your* recitation of mantras; I can't know your response. I recite mantras and have my efficacious response, and you do not know of it. This is 'no mutual knowing.' The ability and power are unfathomable and unknown, and are therefore called the Secret School. It's not the mantras themselves, but the power of mantras that is secret. This is the meaning of the Secret School."
>
> —Venerable Tripitaka Master Hsüan Hua

Tantric Weaving: Body, Speech, and Mind as One

Vajrayana practice engages and integrates body, speech, and mind, as we'll now explore. Taking refuge can engage *body* (prostration), *speech* (recitation of a refuge prayer), and *mind* (concentration on a meditation buddha). Similarly, we've observed visualization (a trait of Amitabha or of his pure land) and recitation (of his name) in the previous chapter; just add prayer beads to count recitations while visualizing, and you're integrating body, speech, and mind. Now, that's really cooking! One by one, let's look at each.

> **Hear and Now**
>
> "The fault that I always found in Western philosophic logic is that it doesn't have an ultimate courage in questioning whether the self exists. It starts with that assumption. Now if you take this logic to its absolute extreme fearlessly and question that, then you have a pure logic, and you can start building castles that have meaning on that basis, which is what the Tibetans have done. It's questioning the very basis of all reality, all existence, and the self itself. All phenomena."
>
> —Richard Gere

The Wisdom of the Body

The Buddha broke with the asceticism of his culture, but asceticism is deeply embedded in world civilization. You often hear the human *body* denigrated as a vessel of filth because sin (the Fall) is linked to the human body. A Puritanical impulse can be heard, no less, in some Buddhist camps. The body's naturally inclined to desire, to which we get attached. But our body's also a temple, and tantra embraces the body and its desires as potential for transformation and enlightenment. *Mudras*, for example, are ritualized hand gestures, integrating the mental and the physical. Emulating a particular gesture of a buddha deity further imparts their energy to us, physically (much in the way that smiling, or mouth yoga, awakens happiness).

Similarly, as in mouth yoga, sometimes *prostration* precedes the devotional impulse, rather than vice versa. Vajrayana perfects it to an art. 100 prostrations per day is one set; 100,000 times is another. Given the stubbornness of the ego, and how ingrained its habits are in the body, many tantric rituals are practiced 100,000 times. (*Question:* How many Vajrayanists does it take to screw in a light bulb? *Answer:* One, but they do it 100,000 times.)

Indeed, as a Himalayan school, Vajrayana is a *yoga*. A specific example is its attention to the energy centers along the spine called *chakras* (genitals, belly, heart, throat, and head) also found in other yoga systems; here, each chakra is associated with its particular meditation buddha. Plus, the body has *channels* (akin to acupuncture meridians), *winds*, and *drops;* these are pathways for circulation of subtle energy (similar to *prana* in Hindu yoga—and *chi* (*qi*) in *chi kung* and *tai chi* in Taoist yoga). Emotions also travel here and can get tangled up, constricting energy flow, especially at the level of the heart. Once these energies are recognized, liberated, and flow freely, they, too, transform into one's own original buddha energy. Just as Theravada says, "Nirvana now!" so does Vajrayana say, "Enlightenment in this very body."

Speech Vibrations Can Set Great Things in Motion

We've observed *recitation* as a means of stabilizing the mind, of providing a mirror for insightful inquiry, and of calling upon the universe's primal energies of enlightenment through the compassionate vow of Amitabha. Tibetan practice has a treasury of such sacred speech, called *mantras*. One etymology of the word *mantra* combines the Sanskrit root *man* (to think) with the suffix *tra* (tool) to mean "a tool for thinking." It could also be read as *man*, from *manas* (mind), and *tra*, from *tranam* (protection), *tra* itself meaning "to emancipate." The most famous Vajrayana mantra, "*Om Mani Padme Hum*," loosely translates as "the jewel in the lotus." One of the most purely musical, mellifluous, is that associated with Tara, a feminine buddha of compassion: "*Om Tara Tu Tara Turey Soha*."

Just as pictures predate words, so do the depths of oral culture present a continuity extending back much, much further than the reaches of written literacy. For instance, some one-syllable mantras are believed to have intrinsic power, in and of themselves, such as "*Om*." Hindu religions consider "*Om*" an eternal primeval vibrational frequency (sort of like the dial-tone of the universe). Pronounced "Ahhhhwwwwmmmmmm," a more phonetic spelling might be A-U-M. *Try this:* Take a good breath and let your exhale express itself in an "Ah." Then, let it lengthen out with "U." When you near the end, seal it with "M." (Try it three times.)

In Vajrayana, "Om" can manifest the Buddha's many bodies. The syllable "*Ah*" manifests the Buddha's speech, source of all sound. "*Hung*" manifests Buddha Mind. (It's also spelled H-U-M, but it's pronounced a tad like a funk singer grunting "hunh!") Upon initiation, reciting this three-syllable mantra with one-pointed concentration bestows the blessings of the body, speech, and mind of all the buddhas. Thus, after settling into tranquility meditation, a practitioner might meditate for fifteen minutes on the mantra "*Om Ah Hung.*" (Eventually, five minutes would be sufficient.) Recite "Om" to yourself while breathing in. In between breaths, concentrate on the center of your chest (your spiritual heart) and recite "Ah." On the out-breath, recite "Hung."

Seeing with Your Heart-Mind's Eye: Visualization

Creative visualization is a powerful tool for transforming the *mind* and *heart*. Some advanced physicists have speculated the universe is made out of photons (quanta of electromagnetic radiation). So when we visualize something (such as a peaceful beach), even though the image we conjure up in our mind's eye might seem purely subjective, it actually participates within the universe's interconnected net of light (Indra's web, again), causes and conditions interpenetrating. Actually, of all our five senses, our brain invests most of its sensory activity in visual information. Thus, people often close their eyes to meditate, to quiet the roof-brain chatter. Thus, too, we speak about knowing in terms of sight (*illumination*, en*light*enment), and wisdom as light. (You see?)

Visualization is an everyday phenomenon of which we're seldom aware, yet with vast, untapped potentials. Think of the name of a movie star, and you're also visualizing them; meaning, we think through visualization. Or think of your best friend out with someone else (illusion), and you're visualizing—feeling through visualization. And when you catch sight of someone you know on the street and it turns out to be somebody else, that's visualization coloring the way we interact with and even construct our world. Vajrayana asserts that we're not only continuously visualizing the world without being aware of it, but that we are also grasping onto and collecting mental impressions, using our preconceptions and interpretations as a filter. So creative visualization can enable us to bypass our habitual, automatic critical consciousness (which looks but does not see) to access our innate, alert ability to really see. Visualization enables a suppler, more discerning awareness of different grades of perceptions: undivided concentration, consciousness awareness, meditative awareness, boundless "naked" awareness, and the innate nature of our unconditioned mind. This quality of seeing as awareness is as brilliant, perfect, and pure as … a diamond.

Here is an image for visualization. Manjushri embodies the wisdom (prajna) of all Buddhas. He is holding the flaming sword of nondual wisdom in his right hand, symbolic of cutting off ignorance. This wisdom is not the kind of knowledge one gains from books or lectures, but wisdom born from insight into the nondual nature of reality, or emptiness. Usually Manjushri is holding a book in his left hand (the Prajnaparamita Sutra *on emptiness) or a flower upon which the book rests. In this particular form of Manjushri, created by the artist for a special sadhana (tantric meditation) for students of Trungpa Rinpoche, he holds a vase containing the nectar of immortality, symbolizing the undying nature of non-dual wisdom.*

(Drawing: Sanje Elliot)

As another example of integrating body, speech, and mind, we can extend the "Om Ah Hung" mantra to our mind's eye. In Vajrayana, the written word for each syllable has its own visual symbolism. You'd visualize a diamond-colored "Om" at the crown of your head, so that your body might be merged with Buddha's enlightened body; a ruby-colored "Ah" is at your throat, merging with his enlightened speech; a sapphire

"Hung" is at your heart (the center of your chest), merging with his enlightened mind (heart). Additionally, you can meditate on "Om" as the Sangha, "Ah" as the Dharma, and "Hung" as the Buddha. The great Tibetan teacher Naropa said, "My mind is the perfect Buddha, my speech is the perfect teaching, my body is the perfect spiritual community."

The central deity of this mandala is Jananadakini, a goddess with three heads and six arms. She is surrounded by eight goddess assistants. A guardian sits by each of the four gates.

(From Tibetan Mandalas, *International Academy of Indian Culture, Courtesy of Dr. Lokesh Chandra)*

What about mind-wandering? There's a three-part cartoon by Alex Gregory that nails the habit. First, we see a man wearing a tie, working at a computer; in the thought-balloon above his head, we see a golf club about to hit a golf ball perched on a tee. Then we see him in a golf cap and sports clothes, about to tee off. Now in his thought-balloon, there's the body of a naked woman. Next, we see him embracing a woman in his bed, while in the thought balloon we see … a computer. All the while, he has a blank look. The skillful means of yoking body-speech-mind in tandem can transform idle mind-wandering into constructive mind-wandering. If your mind naturally wanders off while reciting a mantra, let it wander: it will alight onto visualization. If it gets tired of that, you can do some prostrations—each shift of focus allowing the very tendency of the mind to wander to propel your practice, transforming butterfly mind into innate buddha mind. And here, yet again, being on the path as second nature *is* the goal.

Skillful Means of Ritual and Symbol

Taking refuge is universal in Buddhism. In Vajrayana, even this has its special yoga. Along with the Triple Gem (Buddha, Dharma, Sangha), Tibetan Buddhists take refuge in a very personal way, called the *refuge tree*. At its crown, you visualize your guru as a manifestation of the Buddha. And you visualize your guru there with all the gurus of your guru's lineage, and their sanghas, back to original Buddha. That's for a start. Along with that, you might visualize all the deities and bodhisattvas, and their guardian deities, their teachings, and their sanghas. And so on, down to your family, friends, worst enemies, and animals—standing or sitting with you or looking at you. Vow your going for refuge will help all of them. This is accompanied with appropriate prayer and prostrations.

From this, you might say Vajrayana has an emphasis on ritual (though even Zen can get pretty ritualistic, too). This isn't necessarily a bad thing. Generally, ritual connects a person or group with an idea, belief, knowledge, or power. For instance, people of every spiritual tradition give thanks for food. Furthermore, as we become aware, we notice how much of our behavior is habit energy, personal ritual unconsciously done. Just as Pure Land recitation replaces one perfected thought for 10,000 samsaric ones, Vajrayana adds visualization and bodily yoga. There's a dedication meditation before, and a dedication of merit afterward. And there are dozens and dozens of rituals. So Vajrayana's medicine bowl holds an abundant variety of tightly integrated rituals to clear away the obstruction of our automatic, knee-jerk, ingrained responses so our Buddha nature can fully manifest.

Indeed, tantra uses our own habit energy to transform itself. You could say it teaches us a very good habit: not doing anything out of habit. Quoting the *Sutra of Great Approximation*, Bokar Rinpoche suggests that, when opening a door, we can wish, "May the door of profound reality open." Walking, we might wish, "May I progress on the path of Awakening." In a car, we might wish, "May I ride the horse of diligence." Upon arrival, we might wish, "May I arrive at the city of Nirvana."

These are similar to mindfulness gathas we've already seen in Theravada and Zen, though with greater emphasis on symbol. Tibetan Buddhism is rich with symbolic images, phrases, and stories—similar to how koans, alchemy's private "language of the birds," and symbolic biblical texts such as The Songs of Songs all provide grist for the mill of a teacher's tapestry of interpretive commentary. An insight is found in the roots of the word *symbol*: from Greek, it literally means "to pull or draw together," similar to yoga as yoking, or tantra as weaving (as opposed to diabolic, meaning "tearing apart"). There's even an element of sympathetic magic (*sympathetic* meaning "fellow feeling") in realizing our kinship with the primordial innate wisdom within all things: the infant purity of dawn, a diamond dewdrop in the heart of a rose (the jewel in the lotus), the cascading waterfall of nectar (the nectar of compassion) … a whirling ring of fire, a small golden key … and so on.

The Gate to the Trail: The Path Is the Goal

Now you have a handle on Tibetan Buddhism, though I may not have even scratched the surface—another reason why it's called the Diamond Path. Only a diamond can penetrate another diamond. (Only mind can know mind.) I'll just add a road sign pointing toward the end of the road. If you follow through and are empowered in tantra by a teacher, he or she will reveal for you a glimpse of the goal, so you'll have something to work for, a flash of clear-light naked-awareness with which to begin each practice. Scholar Bernard Guenther likens the process to a heat-seeking missile. Once it locks onto its target, they're one; although the fusion's off in the future, the contact begins here and now.

As I suggested at the opening of this tour of Vajrayana, at the heart of it is direct root connection to enlightened energy and infinite goodness, limitless choiceless compassionate awareness and highest wisdom, and ultimate liberation—sometimes called here the highest yoga (*ati* yoga), Dzogchen, or Mahamudra. It's sometimes taught from the beginning and sometimes at the end. In the end, it matters not if you find out that the secret was that there was no secret (I'm not telling, because I don't know!). Be thankful when you've finally found out—and send the rest of us a postcard, from the summit of your mandala. Have a good journey!

The endless knot (shrivatsa, Sanskrit; dpal be'u, Tibetan) harmoniously weaves motion and rest, simplicity and profundity. Symbolic of interdependence, interpenetration, and interbeing, tantra has no beginning, no middle, no end. Like the Buddha's wisdom and compassion, it's infinite.

There's a saying that the Dharma is excellent in the beginning, excellent in the middle, and excellent in the end. This is reminiscent of the Christian saint who once said everything between here and heaven ... is heaven. In his *Song of Mahamudra*, Tilopa (988–1069) explains:

> "At first a yogi feels like the mind is tumbling like a waterfall; in midcourse, like the Ganges, it flows on, slow and gentle; in the end, it is like a vast ocean, where the lights of Child and Mother merge into one."

With Tibetan Buddhism we complete our tour of four major schools of practice in the West. But, really, the Buddha taught but one truth differently, depending on his listeners. Note, he didn't teach different things to different people. Dharma rain falls equally. Big trees soak up more, while saplings are happy with a sprinkle. (And each time, the rain nourishes a little more than before.) It's all One Dharma, without division and without location. Hinayana, Mahayana, Vajrayana—all are Dharma-yana. The Way of the Way. May you be safe on your journey, be truly happy, and thrive. May all beings be well.

The Least You Need to Know

- The most recent major traditional school of Buddhism to awaken the West, Tibetan Buddhism (Vajrayana) claims the most evolved teachings of the Buddha, and the most complete: vast, yet step by step; intellectually rigorous, yet devotional.

- Migrating from India to Tibet, Vajrayana is the only Mahayana school that didn't pass through China first. Vajrayana could be seen as Mahayana Buddhism with a tantric twist. Tantra represents a late development within Buddhist practice in India.

- Tantra requires initiation, and places great importance upon the teacher–student relationship.

- Tantric ritual engages body, speech, and mind, through such means as prostration and *mudra*, recitation of *mantra* (such as "Om Ah Hung") and invocation, and visualization of deities within mandala.

Part 4

Buddhism in Action: Applications in Everyday Life

We're at the midway point in our guide book. Having presented you with a map, an understanding of the vehicle, and knowledge of the rules of the road—the wheel is in your hands.

So why not put the pedal to the metal? And where is there to go? Well, there's nowhere the Dharma doesn't make inroads—with fascinating back roads.

Up ahead, you'll see how the everyday illuminates Buddhism, how Buddhism illuminates the everyday, and how the interaction can illuminate your own path ahead—every day.

Having toured living Buddhism, let's explore Buddhist living. Here are several points of interest, along the Way.

Chapter 15

Bringing It All Back Home: Relations

In This Chapter

- ◆ Relation is continuous
- ◆ On love, and other difficulties
- ◆ Marriage and parenting
- ◆ Living our dying

Nobody's an island. (Not even an island's an island, joined at its land base to all the other islands, beneath the sea.) We are always in relation. In our encounter with 10,000 things, we are continually awakened to our relationship to our original nature. Here, we'll review a life cycle of relations, everyday relations intertwined with our ultimate relationship: limitless, luminous True Self. Our lives are life itself, yet each time's but once. Here's a short survey of various phases of being one family in this life: through love, marriage, parenting, and death … to make room for life yet to come.

The Way of Relation: Interrelation

The Buddha and his followers pioneered the monastic lifestyle. The majority of Western practitioners today are pioneering a way within the secular lifestyle of a householder, where plenty of opportunities arise for spiritual realization through worldly relation. We're always in some kind of relation (if you don't think so, try missing a couple of payments on your credit card). There's no identity but in relation. Realizing our interdependence, we attain greater intimacy with life. So, we ask ourselves, "Am I in right relation?" Mastery no longer becomes a matter of ego, but rather skillful means: seeing, realizing, and fulfilling the Dharma of each situation; interbeing with whatever's at hand, as True Self. (I'm sure you can relate.)

 **Leaves from the Bodhi Tree**

> Here's a simple meditation, in which we can realize how our own family ties reflect our interconnection, our lack of separate self. Put your hands in front of you, palms down. Notice the shape of your fingers and knuckles, the patterns of your veins and skin. See how you feel about your hand. Looking at your hand, generate and send loving kindness to yourself. Now, see your mother in those shapes and textures, and see how you feel about her. Send her loving kindness. Now, see your father in your hand, and see how you feel about him. Send him loving kindness. Turn your hands over, join palms, and thank them for this meditation. Dedicate any good karma generated thereby to their well-being.

Who Will Ever Really Know and Love You More Than You?

Love: is it ever easy? It seems the most natural thing in life. We came into life through a father and mother, so we too naturally seek a mate. A common difficulty is in romantic love, really biting the hook. It can be a surefire set-up for disappointment. ("Dear Abby: How can I go on living?") As translator, poet, and freelance mystic Coleman Barks points out, "Western love ... is identifying with an idea that can't quite be consummated. It's *Romeo and Juliet*. It's the lived-out love that doesn't quite get shown." It's an assortment of chocolate-flavored dukkha waiting in a pretty, red, valentine-shaped box. (Not that I'm knocking chocolate, but it sure can be an addictive rush.) We so hope someone else will make us totally happy, will ultimately fulfill us. When they don't, we lick our wounds and seek someone else to alleviate the suffering; that is, to perpetuate it. (Been there? Done that?)

How to step outside the samsara of needless suffering, into freedom? One way to true love is by going beyond mere passion, through true compassion. See the powerful Other that rejected us as just another bumbling, confused sentient being like ourselves, likewise groping to deal with ignorance, fear, anger, and attachment. Going past identification with a situation (or our interpretation of a situation), compassion allows us to feel unconditional love for ourselves just as we are, as a whole human being, containing the entire universe. Metta practice begins with ourselves. We first practice unconditional love and compassion for ourselves, finding joy and equanimity in ourselves, before we can extend it to others. The bodhisattva vow unites us in compassion with all beings, including oneself. The practice leads us into interrelationship with the myriad manifestations of our true nature, rather than any seemingly fixed, lasting, separate, conceptualized Other. Then, when we are complete in ourselves, we can express our love for all through the love of another.

Along the Path

There are no dictates in Buddhist ethics about homosexuality. The fifth precept would apply here, too: being aware of the consequences of sensuality and sexuality, and not causing another or ourselves pain through breaking the bonds of trust. Gender (not the same as sex), like self, can be seen as a construct: of no permanent, independent, substantial identity.

Recently, I saw some cute ideas for Buddhist Valentine's greetings by Suvarnaprabha being passed around the Internet: "I can never extinguish my thirst for you." "I love you neither more nor less than I love all beings." "Let's you and me interpenetrate Reality." Sounds like a wiser alternative to blind romantic passion to me. Buddhist practice provides wise support for the work required to create and maintain an intimate relationship over time. For instance, it readily accommodates the demand for "giving someone space." Space, like silence (sunyata), is ripe, invaluable, and open.

Emotional intelligence applies to all our relations; certainly love as no exception. Surveying a trying emotional landscape through mindful meditation won't necessarily result in any greater solution than being able to come back and calmly and clearly say, "Here are the emotions that a certain situation arouses in me" (rather than trying to issue commands: "Don't do such-and-such!"). Knowing you're working toward a common direction, you can be direct with each other and state, "When you do *that*, it makes me feel like *this*."

Love puts the third precept into focus, deep listening and loving speech. Thich Nhat Hanh recommends a few mantras. Saying, "Dear, I am here for you," can open both your hearts. Here is a gratitude mantra: "I know you are there, and I am very happy." When you sense your beloved is hurt, why not say, "When you hurt, it hurts me, too"? When you sense your beloved is happy, why not say, "Your joy makes me glad, too"? (Wouldn't you, in similar situations, enjoy likewise?) Listen to what your beloved says and also to what your beloved is not saying, and open your heart.

Can you be a mindfulness bell for your beloved? When you see your beloved's mind wander, why not invite them back to the present moment by saying, "Is it just me or is it getting colder?" Or "Doesn't the air taste fresh?" This isn't necessarily to push them away; instead, it invites them to join you at the base camp of the here and now, whence all roads depend.

If two beings come together, aware they're spiritually complete in themselves, then living together they'll find how their temperaments can be quite different, yet recognize themselves in each other. It's an everyday cosmic dance of yin and yang ("not one, not two") complementing and balancing each other. A relationship can be a two-person sangha: two people, interbeing. "Whenever two people gather in my name," the Buddha said, "I'll be there." The commitment of love, here, is to the mutual intimacy of realizing we're all interconnected, through just this one person accepted as all people. Now that's a pretty good vow.

Mindfulness Vows with Your Beloved: Marriage

Marriage isn't a specifically Buddhist ritual, per se. A Buddhist priest can perform a legally binding ceremony, but isn't acting as a divine intermediary ("… by the power invested in me by Almighty God …"). Zen teacher Charlottte Joko Beck notes, "When we're married, we're not married to each other, but to the true self." In such union, a bride and groom affirm together their vows of refuge in the essential Triple Gem and the precepts; additional vows might affirm the continuity of life and the importance of understanding and mutual respect. Vowing to honor and cherish each other, which they already do, they're vowing also to honor and cherish their committed relationship and their practice. It's marvelous for two particular people to be coming together, walking the same marvelous path together.

Mutuality of bride and groom permits either to divorce if need be and also remarry, without stigma. They're not breaking any Buddhist vows, which they still hold sacred, still holding unconditional love for each other and staying on the path. When two practices each support each other, two can build well. If one is Buddhist and the other isn't, the dance is just as interesting. ("Hi, honey, I'm home! Guess what? I just spent seven days looking into my mind!")

Leaves from the Bodhi Tree

Here's a tale in which a wife's no less wise than a husband. A Tibetan arrowsmith named Saraha asked his wife to make him some radishes. He then meditated for 12 years nonstop. When he arose, he asked his wife, "Where are my radishes?" His wife replied, "You think I'd keep them?" He huffed and said he'd go off to the mountains to meditate. She responded: "A solitary body doesn't mean solitude. The best solitude is when the mind is far from names and concepts. You've been meditating for 12 years, yet you still haven't gotten rid of the idea of radishes. What good will it do to go to the mountains?" He realized she was right, and so abandoned names and concepts, and ultimately attained enlightenment.

Nobody Does It Better

Love invariably invokes the fifth precept, the importance of having an ethical basis for dealing with sexuality. But, as Suzuki Roshi once pointed out, the minute you say "sex," everything is sex. (Considering how many days he spent sitting before a blank wall, I'm willing to take him at his word.) Contemporary life offers up as many options for escaping the prison of a separate self as there are light bulbs in Las Vegas, with sex at the top of the come-ons. Sex sells. Of course, it's natural. Sex shapes the blueprint for how we get here and perpetuate ourselves. That's a powerful energy to tap into. So sexuality can be awakening, but also samsara, a sweet illusion. The Buddha knew, hardly a virgin himself. He'd not only fathered a child, but he'd also dallied daily with his harem of 500 concubines before he went forth.

Humans seem to be the only species who engage in sex not only for its regenerative aspects (producing children), but also for its generative aspects. It can generate not only pleasure, in and of itself, but also intensely shared feeling capable of transporting one out of one's self. Thus, it can be sacramental, but also a potential threat to the whole house of cards called ego, set up as a separate self. In the latter case, ego sometimes pulls back and reasserts itself, resulting in sexual power politics of dominance and submission—at its worst, sexual abuse. In Buddhist sexual relations, it still takes two to tango, and it welcomes the dance of yin and yang.

 Along the Path

The Western concept of sexuality might be summed up by Plato's analogy of a sphere that seeks wholeness after division: the union of two incomplete halves. In **Buddhist sexuality,** two wholes can come together and experience something larger. Tibetan Buddhists say that orgasm is a glimpse of sunyata. Asian terms for sexuality imply natural processes, such as "cloud-rain," evoking the union of heaven and earth.

This exquisite, nearly life-size Mongolian Vajrayana bronze is a purely symbolic representation of the tantric union of polarities called yab yum *(father/mother, Tibetan;* maithuna, *Sanskrit). Here Samvara and Vajravarahi dissolve selfhood in mutually appreciative, enlightened contemplation, their union of compassion and wisdom inducing unsurpassed bliss.*

(Zanzabazar [1635–1723], Sitasamvara with His Consort [White Samvara; *Mongolian, Caghan Demcig], Late seventeenth century, Gilt bronze, 21½ inches [54.5 centimeters] × 13¼ inches [33.8 centimeters], Chojin-Lama Temple Museum.)*

Some still misconceive Vajrayana as bursting with spiritually condoned eroticism. This is to confuse Buddhist tantra with tantric sex therapists. In Vajrayana, images of meditation deities paired with their consorts in sexual embrace are symbolic. The male represents active compassion through skillful means (upaya); the woman, wisdom (prajna). To be understood only in the deepest, most sacramental sense, such allegorical imagery is a bit akin to The Song of Solomon and Christian mystics who seek union with Christ the Bridegroom in ecstatic communion. Bear in mind the Vajrayana practitioner visualizes and identifies with both deities, thus unifying the energies they each represent, and identifying with the emptiness at their inmost core.

Awareness of the impermanence at the heart of life can have its own eroticism. Thai meditation master Ajahn Chah (1917–1992) once confessed that when he'd walk in the forest in his early years as a monk, every sensation gave him an erection. Viewing everything as sacred, eccentric Zen master Ikkyu (1394–1481) wore his monastic robes to the brothel.

No matter the school of Buddhism, the path calls forth an openness to relations beyond costume or mask—the capacity for naked awareness, if you will. And with commitment, the literal nakedness of two human beings can be a sublime occasion for experiencing and expressing love, a sacred trust, sought and found in the everyday bliss of a reciprocal relationship.

Mama Buddha, Papa Buddha, and Baby Buddha (Parenting)

A baby's not automatically born Buddhist, per se, even if he or she looks like a little Buddha, serenely smiling through all that juicy baby fat. It's up to parents to offer dharma seeds to their children and let them decide for themselves. Father, mother, and child all share True Nature. Consider, for example, the testimony of Patricia Ikeda Nash:

> "We are all, fundamentally, made from our mother's bodies and their love. Each night before going to bed, my son sits on my lap and presses his ear against my chest, listening to who I am, remembering. I gaze into his face, listening to his breath, remembering the night after he was born. Quiet and wakeful, we looked at one another for a long time. I felt as though his newborn body were the gateway to an immense tunnel filled with a crystalline ladder spiraling backward in time, containing the genetic and karmic essence of all our ancestors, and extending back to the first life form. How it shone! At that moment I understood the rightness of human life continuing itself, and despite the darkness that surrounds us, our capacity 'to enjoy life, living in honesty and strength.' I was contained within my baby, and he within me, a resonant abode of many voices."

Parenting as Practice

You can learn so much in raising kids. The strict schedule of parenting is comparable to monastic discipline; parenting adds the test of a child's stream of interruptions wearing down the ego. But a child can also be a dharma teacher. Little kids can live so intensely in the present that just witnessing them is like hearing a bell of mindfulness, awakening us to come home to the marvelous present moment. And watching your own bald little baby grow that first hair, cut teeth, and sprout up like a beanstalk is quite a lesson in accepting impermanence.

Kids are also a natural at beginner's mind. Questioning everything, just think of their letters to God. ("Dear God: If you are in my heart, don't you get bloody?") So, in their way, kids can be exacting little Zen masters, demanding a parent be fully present to whatever comes up, and testing the parents' ability to deal with fear, anger, bodily needs, and the whole soap opera of life *(The Turning Wheel)*.

Family Sangha and Dharma for Kids

How do you teach a child Buddhism? Teaching kids to be kind doesn't need a label attached, such as Buddhism. Likewise, learning to observe the breath needn't be religious. (It's so easy, even a child can do it!) *Tip:* If you keep the meditation short, they have a simple, good experience.

As the Buddha taught, so can we: by example. When people complain their kid won't sit still, do they themselves ever sit still? When they do, their kid will notice. When a kid sees a parent meditating, and sees how calming and refreshing it can be, they'll want to try it too. And when we're mindful of our difficult emotions, we're less likely to pass their charge along to our kids. We practice as a sangha. Whether it's a parent or child riding out an emotional storm, by going to the family breathing room, ringing a bell of mindfulness, and sitting quietly beside a flower, the whole family can hear the bell and practice stopping. In a word, as Thai teacher Sulak Sivaraksa affirms, "When even one member of the household meditates, the entire family benefits."

Teaching by example, a child learns to value what a parent values. A child familiar with mindful sitting, for example, can sit by a parent who's meditating in the family breathing room, and practice just being together. If our kids join us when we meditate, we have an opportunity to be happy together in a very intimate way, quite different from sending our kids off to a Sunday school, for someone else to nurture their spiritual evolution.

Besides having a common breathing room, family sangha can come together at a home altar. Bowing in, in the morning, a small child may enjoy making an offering of generosity to the Buddha—some fruit, or a cookie—forming a nice bond. Another family ritual in which a kid can play a role is giving thanks for the meal. If you chant, chant with your kid, whether formally, or cleaning the house together or out shopping. When they enjoy how calming it can be, they might sing the melody to themselves. Other Dharma family practices include visiting a hospice, going on nature walks, celebrating Earth Day, and hugs. You might also consider teaching kids yoga, so the lotus position won't be so much of a stretch.

There's no set way for teaching Buddhism to kids. ("Paints mandalas within the lines; meditates well with others.") Being a mindful parent means listening for when a child wants to be taught a particular lesson, attuned to when they need to enter into the parents' practice, and able to frame it for their child's particular level. Everyday life situations can be teaching opportunities. For instance, children can be taught to care for others through the example of how they play with their own possessions. Learning to appreciate the kindness of others is a good model for understanding interdependence and compassion.

Along the Path _____

A classic body of Buddhist children's literature is the *Jataka tales* (birth stories). Originally written in Pali, some are based on India's most ancient folktales. They're framed as tales of the Buddha and his followers' past lives (karma). Like today's cartoons, they feature talking animals. Each tale has a specific theme, such as the spirit of forgiveness, the importance of correct view, the value of generosity, and so on. Many familiar tales, such as those by Aesop, originate here.

Ever since Western-boomer Buddhist publishers became parents themselves, you can find Buddhist books easily available. Along with the life of the Buddha and his basic teachings, the precepts can be a core curriculum for kids. Guidelines for conscious conduct can show kids how they must define for themselves their Do's and Don'ts, as who they are and will become, and how that can't ever be taken away from them—a major rite of passage. As kids go through tweens, teens, and young adulthood, it means so much for them to be able to talk about difficult emotions without being judged. This leads us to another key skill … E.Q.!

What's Your E.Q.?: Emotional Intelligence, Revisited

We touched on emotional intelligence in our chapter on Insight Meditation. It's invaluable for parents and children. One guy who grew up in a Buddhist household remembers that he never heard his father say, "Don't push your brother!" but rather, "Think about your state of mind when you push your brother." And that stuck with him, gently initiating him into mindful awareness. The Red–Yellow–Green Light exercise is just as appropriate for kids as for us.

Hear and Now _____

"When we teach our children, we focus on technical skills, on computers, on math, on content, on intellectualism, which are divorced from the human heart. In fact it is the paradox that our skill in working with emotion is a far greater determinant of our success, let alone our personal happiness. That of course is the paradox of modern education. We have focused on the wrong things."
—Daniel Goleman

When Daniel Goleman wrote *Emotional Intelligence* in 1995, he could track down fewer than a half-dozen school programs in America teaching the ability to manage feelings and relationships. Five years later, there were hundreds of such programs (sometimes called Social and Emotional Learning [SEL]) in tens of thousands of schools. New research has revealed that the centers of the brain regulating emotions continue to grow into adolescence, rather than stopping after the first years of life as previously thought. In fact, they're the last parts of the brain to fully mature. So for example, 10-year-old girls who've had difficulty differentiating between feelings of anxiety, anger, boredom, and hunger might risk developing severe eating disorders when they're 12 and 13 years old. Paying attention to self-awareness and adapting to social relations over the full course of a child's school years not only promotes emotional and social maturity, but has also been proven to help prevent depression, addiction, violence, and suicide.

Welcome to the Club: Rites of Passage

Every path has its *rites of passage*. Our ancestors were very wise in creating such rites, initiating a new generation into the community and its ways. They understood how an adolescent male, suddenly seething with hormones, can be very dangerous. Without such rites, young men might wreak violence on the community itself, as seen today in youth gangs and youth violence. Our society does not invest in them as wholly as our ancestors did. As Bo Lozoff, director of the Human Kindness Foundation, succinctly puts it, "Life is deep but the national lifestyle is not." Commercial teen "girl culture" is an example of a superficial substitute for maturity with possibly dangerous consequences.

Buddhist culture has its rites of passage, equivalents to confirmation or bar/bas mitzvah. In Tibet, children are given a herd of yaks to tend, to acknowledge their growing independence. In Southeast Asian countries such as Thailand and Myanmar, a young man becomes a Buddhist monk for at least three months, usually after high school. He may return to the monastery at any point in his life. It is thus shared culture of the community at large.

Western Buddhism can learn much about Buddhist parenting, rites of passage, and education from Pure Land congregations which span several generations. Predominantly white sanghas began incorporating day care into the practice in the 1980s, and family practice days and rites of passage ceremonies have since evolved. In Boulder, the Tibetan Buddhist Shambhala Center has a rite of passage for which children prepare themselves by studying such Buddhist arts as archery, flower arrangement, and poetry. During the actual ceremony, children and parents bow to each other, vow to be kind to themselves and to others, and exchange gifts representing childhood and maturity. Children are our future, and thus they're our teachers as much as we are theirs.

Hear and Now _____

"Listen. Giving birth is like starting a fire: the father's the flint, the mother's the stone, and the child's the spark. Then, once the spark touches the wick of a lamp, it will continue to exist through the secondary support of the lamp's fuel. When that's exhausted, it flickers out.... Since the parents too have no beginning, in the end they, too, will flicker out. Everything grows out of the void from which all forms derive. If you let go of the forms, then you reach what's called 'the original ground.' But since all sentient beings come from emptiness, even the term 'original ground' is only a temporary tag."

—Zen priest Ikkyu (1394–1481)

The Great Matter: Who Dies?

Whether we're married or single, enlightened or not, it's a fact that eventually our life must make way for more life. But human nature doesn't readily accept that fact of nature. Here's the final lesson in learning to no longer grasp: letting go of life itself. Since we'll examine engaging with the death of others in our last chapter, let's explore here our own personal relationship with the Great Matter.

The Buddha's answer when asked what happens after death: [*silence*]. It's our living that's primarily the point. We cannot truly know life without death any more than joy without pain. The Buddha did say, "Just as the elephant's footprint is the biggest footprint on the jungle floor, death is the biggest teacher."

Like birth, our relationship to death implies all other relationships. For example, sex peeks at us when we consider death. You probably wouldn't think of death as part of "the facts of life" (although people whisper about death and shield children from it as if it were sex). The fact is if it weren't for sex, we might never face the mystery of death. Consider, for a moment, that if we still reproduced by cell division, one cell dividing into two, two into four, and so on—instead of Harry meeting Sally and later bringing up baby Harry Jr.—we'd have MaryLou becoming Mary *and* Lou. Billy would become Bill *and* Lee. (Imagine what weird family reunions all that would make.)

If we look at death as part of life's transformative, sexual embrace, we see simply one thing becoming another. (Who dies?) A caterpillar becomes a butterfly. (Has the caterpillar died?) An infant becomes a teenager. (Has the infant died?) A breadwinner becomes a retiree. A strong parent becomes a frail being, lying in a bed, sipping nourishment through an intravenous tube. Just as impermanence marks our relationships, so, too, does it mark our own phases, a messenger of the impermanent, illusory nature of self. (Who dies?)

This Is _____

Our culture distances us from death through vocabulary. A funeral *home* (where no one lives) is now a *chapel*. A *mortician* is now a *funeral director.* He sells *caskets,* not *coffins.* A corpse is viewed in a *slumber room,* and isn't *embalmed* but *prepared.* And *filling up a grave* with earth (not *dirt*) is now referred to as *closing the interment space.*

Along the Path _____

Animals do not bury their kin. Humans cover them up. Yet a traditional Tibetan funeral custom is *sky burial.* The corpse is taken up a mountain, dissected, and left there to be recycled in the wheel of life, generously offered up for the benefit of other living beings. The vultures who feed are considered embodiments of tantric deities (*dakinis,* "sky dancers"), and offering them human flesh is considered a virtue because they might otherwise capture and eat small defenseless creatures.

To ask what is death is to ask what is life. Rather than ask about what happens after death, can we even say what happens right now? To ask yet another related question, how can we face our own lives, and the death of others within our lives, if we don't face our own deaths? One answer is, "Die before you die." Awaken to your original face, naked awareness, which is unborn and undying. Then you'll be ready when your time comes. Nobody said it's easy. There's no right way or wrong way; there's only one way. You might think you messed up your entire life, but you'll always die perfectly.

Die before you die. Then, when your time comes, you can be present during your final moments, without going into a panic (such as, "Oh no! Did I leave the stove on!?"). If you get it right this time, this lifetime, then you can spend the rest of eternity doing absolutely *nothing* really well.

One of the West's first discoveries of Tibetan Buddhism was through the translation of *The Tibetan Book of the Dead,* whose title is literally *Liberation Through Hearing in the In-Between State.* In addition to its ceremonies for death and a kind of travelogue of realms after death, it contains meditations that can be conducted within this life. Life is a continuous stream of moment-to-moment deaths and rebirths. They have an illusion of continuity, the way Christmas tree lights can appear to move, but essentially it's all empty of form. We begin to see this when we notice various in-between states (*bardo*, Tibetan), such as in between breathing out and breathing in … falling asleep and waking up … in between thoughts … in between words …

Thinking about her own death, Buddhist teacher Geri Larkin decided she'd like all her friends to gather at her funeral to write poems about her, string them all together, and tie them up in a tree for the seasons to weather. How about you?

Exercise: Take some time to visualize your own death. See what holds you back … what frightens you … what would make you most happy. Explore your feelings. Let the truth of death overcome your fear of death. Include your death in your life. Discuss your funeral with your loved ones, just as if you were talking about buying a house. Let the reminder of death motivate your efforts to live each moment.

> **Along the Path**
>
> In India, the sight of death is public and commonplace. When Tibetans are dying, they're cared for by the whole community. China sets April 5 aside for visiting graves. In Korea, it's harder to avoid going to a funeral than a wedding. In Mexico, there's a serious but celebratory Day of the Dead, dating from Aztec times. They say, "¿Isn't today a lovely day to die?"

Try this: Live for twenty minutes as if you'd just been told they'd be your last. Then try this tomorrow, and the next day. Try living like this for an entire day, a week, a month … Like they say, life isn't a dress rehearsal. This is it. No curtain calls, no encores. No forwarding address. Live the words of the epitaph you'd like to leave behind as your exit line. Then, the stone slab will be merely extra.

The Least You Need to Know

♦ Buddhism isn't an escape from human relations. We're always in relation. Nonmonastic practice can thus be all the more challenging, and rewarding.

♦ Buddhism provides insight into the slippery slope of romance. When a couple shares a commitment to Buddhist practice and to each other, sex can be a natural, sublime expression of love. Buddhism can provide a strong framework for marriage based on sincerity and trust.

◆ A family can be a sangha, laypeople rather than monastic. Parenting is about learning as well as teaching.

◆ The final relationship is confronting your own death, integral to living a meaningful life.

Chapter 16

It's Not Just a Job, It's Life Itself: Right Livelihood

In This Chapter

◆ Defining success and measuring wealth

◆ Price or value

◆ Job or livelihood

◆ Workplace as sangha

◆ Our being in constant relationship has many faces

In the rankings of the top, personal issues of average everyday life, being loved is often tied with being a success. A Buddhist response to both realizes that being loved and being a success both mean little without *being*. Everyone has a relationship to commerce, and the voice of Buddha is heard here, too—again due to the majority of its Western practitioners holding down jobs in the workaday world, rather than living monastically (redistributing other people's money). Here, too, are plum opportunities to realize living Buddhism in the moment, and thus define for ourselves Buddhist living.

What's Religion Got to Do with Work?

The spiritual nature of work is not dependent upon religion, but religion can color our outlook. The American work ethic, for example, is based in part on Calvinist theology, which says if you're not a worldly success then you're not destined for heaven; but success is no reason for slacking off, because you'll only know if you've been chosen for paradise after your life is over. To contrast that with Catholic culture, I remember trying to post a letter at noon during my first day in Venice, Italy. Doors were closed except those of churches and cafes. So people dropped in to a cathedral to be reminded that their immortal soul is saved, then celebrated paradise on earth by hanging out over some cappuccinos in the plaza with everybody else. Eventually, work resumed as usual. After all, doing nothing can get to be hard work.

How do you define success, and satisfaction? Beyond a certain level of financial security, more money doesn't necessarily bring happiness. So we're happier to realize when enough is sufficient. Consider how, when Asia faced an economic meltdown in 1997, the Buddhist nation of Thailand mobilized Buddhist values to turn things around. For example, after restructuring, Siam Cement Group, the largest national company, reported its greatest profits in 35 years. The overall program, known as Sufficiency Economics, has global implications. As King Bhumipol defined it: "Sufficiency is moderation. If one is moderate in one's desires, one will have less craving. If one has less craving, one will take less advantage of others. If all nations hold to this concept, without being extreme or insatiable in one's desires, the world will be a happier place." The pursuit of happiness isn't exclusively Buddhist. We don't know why Thomas Jefferson inscribed it in the Declaration of Independence, yet we note the Buddhist kingdom of Bhutan measures its contemporary national wellbeing not according to its Gross Domestic Product (GDP) but rather its Gross National Happiness (GNH). Maybe we all could use a little bit (well, a lot) of this mind-set here at home.

Price or Value: How Do You Measure Wealth?

If this chapter sufficiently defines true valuation (value versus price), then it might reward your livelihood. It only demands a small investment of time, after which it's up to you how you settle this account. To begin, how do you rate success? Consider the Buddha. Raised in a palace, he knew all that wealth could buy, and how it would never ultimately satisfy. After his years in a forest, with only the clothes on his back (one thin robe), he knew values apart from money. All the money in the world can't buy happiness, nor can having no money. The Middle Way looks to a mean between the quest for the greatest good and the thirst for the greatest goods. The Triple Gem is priceless wealth, and the Four Noble Truths help us define what's enough.

Have you considered money, in and of itself? Consider this: on one day (September 29, to be exact, in the midst of the financial meltdown of 2008), a trillion dollars left the equity markets—*Poof!*, evaporated. Where did it all go? Money heaven? The phenomenon underscores the Buddha's teachings. Whether on Wall Street or Main Street, money—like self—is a story, a fiction; it's really convenient sometimes, but it is also temporary, conditional, nonseparate, illusory, and an abstraction (you can't eat, wear, or go to bed in your money). You might take refuge in it, but only so far.

How do you measure wealth? Defining it in terms of satisfying your desires, there's never enough. The grasping self is never satisfied. Measuring itself against the world, it sets itself apart, a set-up for further cravings, aversions, and indifference. Typical measurements of wealth are inherently dualist: pleasure/pain; praise/blame; fame/shame; loss and gain. In your own outlook, notice whether you label economic and work choices in terms of success/failure, boring/exciting, work/play, me/them, and so on. When you do, examine the self-image that accompanies them. Then look deeper and imagine what goals might really satisfy your vision of life, based upon your unchanging Original Nature. While you're at it, you might round up what's been around your house unused for over a year and donate it to charity. Generosity is a wonderful way to massage the heart and make it truly happy.

 Hear and Now

"I remember how destitute I was when I first arrived in Taiwan, fleeing China during the tumultuous years of World War II.... Even though I did not possess many things, I felt most fortunate and content. When I went to the market before the break of dawn to buy vegetables for the day [for the monastery], the stars in the sky kept me company. Flowers and trees were there for me to enjoy. Roads were there for me to travel. I also had the opportunity to meet people from different walks of life. Though I possessed nothing, I had all the wealth the universe could offer me."

—Venerable Master Hsing Yun

The great trick is knowing when enough's enough, thus knowing a satisfied mind. Are you going to be lying on your deathbed, thinking the whole time, "I really should have spent more time at the office!"? It might sound kind of silly, but it happens. Like the romantic definition of love, measuring wealth or success in terms of money can also be a set-up for guaranteed frustration. It seems there's never enough. The Middle Way shows precisely what's enough. When I have three pairs of slacks, and I see a fourth in a store window, why should I buy it if I don't really need it? Status? Self-esteem? Security blanket? Whether metal coin, tinted etching, or plastic credit card, the convenient fiction of money often tells a story illustrating the Second Noble

Truth, craving, in its worst form: greed, with its flipside of fear (both predicated on the idea that there's never enough). Don't bite the hook.

A meditation in hard times might be to visualize abundance and scarcity in the manner of tonglen. Breathing in, visualize scarcity and all its attendant fears, as a black coin of sludge. As you inhale the blackness and it contacts your heart, instead of clutching at and constricting your heart, it is zapped by a ray of clear light from the diamond purity in your heart, your boundless love and natural generosity. This light dissolves the black gunk, *Pfffsst!*, leaving behind a thin white fume that dissolves as you exhale abundance. As with metta, practice first on yourself, your own fears of scarcity, your own limitless capacity for good.

To understand the cause of suffering is to simultaneously see liberation from suffering. Money, which can alleviate material suffering, can also symbolize nirvana. Never fixed, always changing, money can be like a freeze-frame snapshot of life's infinite web of interdependence. And money is, in and of itself, blank essence, like a blank check. (See how fertile a zero can be, when added to the end of your bank balance.) In fact, because a dollar hasn't represented a fixed amount of gold or silver since the 1970s, its value is now really whatever people say it is, thus it is truly a construct of mind.

Dissolving the needy, skinflint, tabulating self in the light of insight and compassion, we see our ultimate identity is limitless. Sunyata, selflessness, always discovers a fertile cornucopia of abundance at the heart of the universe, perpetually creating itself in boundless goodness. And when it is for the benefit of all beings, the universe seems even more glad to help out.

The motto "Small is beautiful" originated in the title of a 1970s book by E. F. Schumacher, with a seminal essay, *Buddhist Economics*, rallying for *sustainability*, *human scale*, and *decentralization*. Please consider if any might be applicable to you and where you work.

Are there limits to growth? As Gandhi said, "There is enough in this world for everyone's need, but not enough for everyone's greed." *Sustainability* can be defined by a motto enshrined in a precursor to the U.S. Constitution, namely, the Iroquois Confederacy: "In every deliberation, we must consider the impact of our decisions on the next seven generations." Sustainability has become a buzzword, along with "renewable" and "green," to build and work efficiently within the limits of our natural resources. Indeed, building mindful values into market operations, mindfulness becomes a key market driver. Such sustainability can generate secure profitability that can scale up for thriving success.

Lao-tzu suggests ruling a nation as one would cook a little fish. But when he and Schumacher say small they don't mean just size. Size matters, but so too does *scale*.

Typically, a sangha can be worldwide, but based in small, local communities. Similarly, Taiwan's remarkable economic success story is built mainly of small businesses. Many Westerners now opt for the home office. There, you might embrace work's inevitable karmic decisions as your own, not some corporation's, all visible on the table. "Down-shifting" can also enable working couples to work together rather than apart, maintaining intimacy throughout the day. And relatively small elements can scale up into rich complex systems, given an adequate structure.

Traditional business models use a hierarchical mode, maximum power filtering down from a centralized point. A *decentralized* model is more like a network of units creating power from the bottom up, a whole greater than the sum of its parts. The components add value to each other's services, and the inherent fluidity keeps it all adaptive to change. And such decentralized systems tend to be self-organizing. Certainly, this model is true for Buddhism, as a global, decentralized system, varying from sangha to sangha. Self-organization permits a group of people to remain small yet build complex webs of interactions, spelling robust opportunities.

 **Hear and Now**

"The Buddhist point of view takes the function of work to be at least threefold: to give a man a chance to utilize and develop his faculties; to enable him to overcome his ego-centeredness by joining with other people in a common task; and to bring forth the goods and services needed for a becoming existence."

—E. F. Schumacher, *Small Is Beautiful*

Work or Livelihood?

To encapsulate the History of Work in 100 words or less, we note our ancestors in the Garden of Eden didn't have to work until the Fall—then it was punishment. Work's gotten a bad rap ever since. There may exist human societies without war, such as the Senoi, but none without work. Yet work wasn't always a curse. Ecologist Ernest Callenbach estimates that for hundreds of thousands of years our ancestor hunter-gatherers might have put in a 20-hour work week, at most. Only with the shift toward an agricultural basis of society did work become a burden: repetitive, with variable yields, and necessitating armies to protect the surplus. With the rise of technology came the Industrial Revolution, and now we've been living through a Post-Industrial Era with no less ups and downs. For instance, living in a society in which debt has become commonplace, and highly leveraged, we might look to the Buddha's encouragements to set aside income and avoid debt.

There is a spiritual dimension to work, which the Buddha addressed during his Axial Age of rapid economic development and consolidation, called *Right Livelihood.* He warned about job descriptions that endanger others, or harm the ecosystem. It's no less true and challenging in our own age of economic development and consolidation, in which we're globally enmeshed with everybody else's karma. Being mindful of this is to see work as practice.

Jobs come and go. If you think only in terms of having a *job,* then you may not yet have found *work.* A job puts bread on your table. Work's what you do because it focuses and fulfills your deep needs and highest values. That's livelihood. It's not so remote an idea. These days, there are not only employment counselors but also livelihood consultants,. They assist clients in evaluating their beliefs and life goals, skillfully managing their time and money, and moving toward their personal purpose.

"Work like you don't need the money." That slogan comes from Satchell Paige, who also said, "I never had a job. I always played baseball." He'd discovered what Alan Watts called "the real secret of life—to be completely engaged with what you are doing in the here and now. And instead of calling it work, realize it is play."

Mindfulness is an evolutionary sport, and this is quite applicable at work, in all walks of life. Consider your average police force, stationed at the bottom rungs of society's ladder. Their workplace and job description can be such an intense pressure-cooker that the suicide rate is, alas, twice the national average. Yet after Thich Nhat Hanh led a meditation retreat for law enforcement officials in Madison, Wisconsin, he reported:

> Police officers learned to go home to themselves and release the tension in their body; release the fear, the despair in the mind; learn how to get in touch with the positive elements of life that are in them and around them for their nourishment and healing, so that they can better relate to their families, their colleagues, and so that they can serve better the people. They are called "peace officers," and they should be. They should have enough peace in themselves in order to do so.

Continuing the law and order thread, consider the high-stakes, high-stress path of lawyers. Here, dualism is the ruling premise: plaintiff versus defendant. And yet there's a growing number of lawyers finding the practice of law and the practice of the Way doesn't have to be an adversarial relationship. Attorney Steven Schwartz, for example, who works with the law program at the Center for Contemplative Mind in Society, has combined the practice both of law and of mindfulness. It brings him to continually see if he's in right relation. When he represents a client, for instance, he looks at the sameness and the difference between him and them as a fundamental koan. "Seeing the sameness between me and the client inspires me," he says, "to use the difference impeccably. It ceases to be work, and becomes an opportunity."

Federal Trade Commission attorneys taking a mindful break on the Mall in Washington, D.C.

(Photograph: © David Burnett/ Contact Press Images)

 Leaves from the Bodhi Tree _____

In Tibetan lore, a plain cobbler named Camaripta begged a Buddhist monk to teach him the way of the Buddha. The monk suggested he transform himself as he changed leather into a shoe: identify his attachments and conceptualizations (the roots of bondage) with the leather; place it on the mold of friendliness and compassion (two immeasurables); pierce it with the awl of his guru's instructions (an instrument by which ordinary life is penetrated); then, with the thread of equanimity, sew together appearance and boundless reality with the needle of mindfulness; and, with the needle of compassion, clothe the beings of the world (in Buddha's body of the Dharma). Over time, the cobbler became a perfectly realized master (*siddhi*).

Bowing In to Work: Office as Sangha

Have you ever given yourself a mindful job review? What's your *internal* revenue? For starters, who's your boss, really? Nobody owns your mind but you. So honor the resistance, such as difficult co-workers or management: consider them as messengers as to the inevitability of dukkha. Your desires and choices, your satisfactions and dissatisfactions, they're all products of mind. Notice how your day goes, and where dukkha arises and where it ceases. See where ignorance, fear, anger, and greed still dwell, and where occasions arise for awakening of mind and opening of heart.

 **Hear and Now**

> "Real composure and real effectiveness at work come from being completely responsible and taking full ownership of everything you do. At the same time your heart is open and responsive. You are not easily knocked off center or fooled by your habits or narrow ideas. You are clear about your purpose, and at the same time you are not grasping for results."
>
> —Marc Lesser, *Z.B.A.: Zen of Business Administration*

Unclenching our heart, we work better. Giving each task your undivided, mindful attention, you'll find your energy's reinvigorated, not exhausted. One-pointed concentration gets more done in a day than if you begin by dividing tasks into those things you like and those you don't. Of course, every job has its monotony. But that can be used as a very good tool for generating one-pointed concentration, and thence mindful awareness. Notice when you work with full attention, a wide view, and when you feel constricted and blocked. With a stable mind, you can discern when it's getting stuck and bring it back to Original Nature.

Explore your space. Stake out your turf. Find breathing room. Where can you go to sit undisturbed? Where can you walk mindfully for ten minutes? And practice isn't confined to your breaks. Consider keeping an altar by a desk. Some people set up a meditation timer in their computer, and stop whatever they're doing to just take a few conscious breaths when it rings, every quarter hour. When you hear your phone ring, stop, notice your breath, return to your original nature, then see who's there, likewise breathing at the other end. Discover, within your work, The One Who Is Not Busy.

Buddhism's a minority religion, of course; certainly not a criterion on a job description. Yet everyone can appreciate its benefits without having to be on the Path. It's wonderful just to nourish your own practice at work and watch the quality of your work rise, and others' consciousness as well. As in a family, when even one person meditates, everyone benefits. If asked, you don't have to call it anything exotic, and thus set up separation. Mindfulness, emotional intelligence, and stress reduction are now part of the vocabulary. "Less stress" is universal

Zentrepreneurs and Tantrapreneurs: Three Case Studies

These days, it's less common to work in the same profession as our grandparents; moreover, it's not uncommon to change jobs during a lifetime. Siddhartha was offered a number of top jobs before he became the Buddha. First, he walked away from ruling an empire. Then, in the forests, he turned down plum teaching positions offered by supreme yogis of his day. Next, he stepped aside from his followers amongst the forest ascetics. Was he a continual failure? No, he followed his heart and all the rest followed. His life became his work, a life work still influencing the entire world.

What color is your parachute? Here are three enterprises that are striking examples of how Buddhism is finding its way in the West that may inspire your own livelihood.

Start with the Zen work ethic. In T'ang Dynasty China, Zen introduced the idea of monasteries being self-sufficient. No work, no eat. As Zen priest Norman Fischer puts it, "For Zen students there's no work time and leisure time; there's just lifetime, day-time and nighttime. Work is something deep and dignified—it's what we are born to do and what we feel most fulfilled in doing." At a Zen monastery, you'll find everyone working as part of a daily schedule; the higher the rank, the more menial the chore. Along with zazen, Dharma talks, and meetings with the teacher, the cultivation of work as spiritual discipline (*samu*) is one of the pillars of Zen practice. (And the most important place is the kitchen. Next to the head of the monastery, the cook is Number Two.)

With the beginner's mind of Zen comes a creative aimlessness, embracing intuition and serendipity possibly more beneficial than any prearranged scheme; some call it "controlled spontaneity." That's what happened at San Francisco Zen Center, America's first Zen monastery. They'd established their second monastery in the idyl-lic mountain forest wilds above Big Sur, California, property formerly run as a hot springs resort, and it supported itself by renting out the guest houses in the summer. Bread was served at student and guest meals and was offered for sale each day for guests to take home. After Ed Espe Brown's tenure as chef, whoever inherited the role of baker had to make, as Marc Lesser recalls, "25–30 each of three to four different kinds of bread, a total of 100–120 loaves, all completely from scratch."

So many guests were buying the bread that the Zen Center followed what was hap-pening right in front of their nose, rather than stick to any Five-Year Master Plan. They started their own bakery. That led, in turn, to a book of their recipes, Edward Espe Brown's *The Tassajara Bread Book* (1970), which became a shot heard round the world, sparking a national revival of homemade bread as well as of locally produced, organic grub (in turn, influencing and influenced by the "nouvelle cuisine" and "slow food" movements in Europe). So, in creating a business, they helped spark a national movement. (Tassajara still serves great meals for summer guests. Zen Center started a third monastery, in Marin, where they grow their own veggies. The bakery morphed into a thriving restaurant in San Francisco called Greens, known nationally via *The Greens Cookbook*).

Our second example illustrates how a small enterprise can take wings and thrive when following the Way—blending a spiritual mission and a social mission within a business mission. On the East Coast, a Zen meditation group led by a former aerospace engineer, Bernard Tetsugen Glassman, borrowed $300,000 in 1982 to open a small storefront bakery called Greyston, in the poor neighborhood of Yonkers. It would provide economic support for the sangha, and in a socially engaged way, by employing the unskilled and disadvantaged. Tassajara's bakery was an influence on their choice of a bakery, but they concentrated on gourmet pastries, enabling the company to stay competitive but small. Niche marketing.

Maintaining a don't-know, open mind, Roshi Glassman *became* the bakery, and bore witness to the suffering therein (the First Noble Truth). People didn't show up for work, or didn't have the skills. So Roshi Glassman and his wife, Sensei Sandra Jishu Holmes, rolled up their sleeves further and moved to be closer to their employees. He better understood why batter had been wasted, because people lacked such basic skills as not knowing how to properly measure. Workers sometimes didn't show up if addicted to alcohol or drugs. And he witnessed extended families living jammed together in tiny dwellings, like fish in a sardine can, or with no dwelling at all.

So as the bakery grew, the goal expanded to integrate personal growth and community development. It reached out to bring the chronically unemployed into its thriving workforce: people getting out of prison, or coming out of substance abuse programs, or off welfare rolls, or out of homeless shelters. One future Greyston employee had been unemployed simply because she couldn't leave her kids alone in her drugs- and violence-infested neighborhood.

Greyston began building a socially responsible mini-conglomerate, which they call a mandala, a combination of for-profit business with nonprofit social services, interfaith programs, and alliances with the community. As of this writing, the bakery employs 55 people and generates $5 million in revenues, which fund the nonprofit activities for the needy in the community, whether or not they work for the bakery. (The bakery isn't run as a charity, because the goal is to give people on-the-job training in a real business.) The nonprofit work began with a bakery training program that included "basic life and work skills." Then came Greyston Family Inn, providing housing and support, day care for kids, and job training and placement services. After that, listening to the new tenants of the Inn, Glassman heard the need for after-school tutoring for children, and classes for the adults on parenting and money management, and responded to those needs. Later a support community was formed for those challenged by HIV/AIDS. None of this would have happened had the bakery followed a preset five-year plan, and stuck to it. Instead, they've organically grown a model for other socially conscious enterprises. Here, "self-sufficiency in community" is the motto: realizing one's full human potential in the context of community. People matter as much as money. "This," they explain, "is a path from dependence through relative independence to an active state of interdependence." (And to update the success of Greyston, it's provided a model that has since proven scalable and is now thriving as a global organization, beyond the scope of this chapter, called Zen Peacemakers, integrating social engagement, interfaith study, and the arts.)

Our last case study starts with the Asian Classics Input Project. This nonprofit disseminates books of Buddhist thought, digitized and given away for free. In so doing, the project not only preserves vanishing cultural traditions, but also employs people who come from the countries where these books were written, often as refugees. It thus trains them in new skills for supporting themselves while saving the great books of their heritage. At-risk refugee teens and the disabled get an extra incentive: for every dollar they earn, another four are donated to a food fund for their village. All this is but one aspect of the parent organization, the Asian Classics Institute, now with many educational activities.

At the heart of this diamond mine of merit has been Geshe Michael Roach. "Geshe" denotes he's a scholar of Vajrayana, the Diamond Way; appropriately enough, from 1981 to 1995 he was vice-president of Andin International, specializing in diamonds. Begun with $50,000 in loans, when he left it turned over $125 million a year, employing about 500 people, which he attributes to managing the business and his life according to *The Diamond Sutra*. For the first five years he never told anyone he was a monk practicing Buddhist tenets at work; five of them were (1) tonglen (exchanging self with others; asking "what would help this person?"); (2) lojong (mind training; turning a problem into an advantage); (3) total honesty with everyone (good karma); (4) creativity; and (5) the bodhisattva vow. This last, key factor meant Geshe Roach, a monastic, never owned a penny, donating his salary, minus a living wage. He attributes his success to having a good attitude and being generous. Thus, he says he'd constantly be getting it and giving it away, and the happier for it.

Hear and Now _____

> "I love my work. It's very useful for a spiritual person to have a whole life around normal people. You get to understand the suffering that normal people go through—the stress that's involved in earning a living to feed your family. When I travel around as a big lama, no one criticizes me to my face. Everyone's always telling me what a wonderful person I am, and congratulating me on the things I do. But when I'm at work the boss screams at me. There's greed to deal with. There's the jealousy of my other vice-presidents to deal with. Your spiritual life gets challenged every few seconds. It's a laboratory for Buddhist practice which you don't get in a monastery."
> —Geshe Michael Roach

Whether you're chasing, choosing, or changing your work path, follow your heart and its compassionate wisdom. There's nothing to making money, if that's all you want to make. See how you can make your Way in the world. In sum, in work we see one of the great challenges, and opportunities, for practicing Buddhism in the West. See your work not just as an opportunity to practice mindfulness, but as mindfulness practice itself.

The Least You Need to Know

- Work is a fact of life. As an opportunity for practice, it can be a livelihood. As the Zen saying goes: "Before enlightenment you chop wood and carry water, after enlightenment you chop wood and carry water."

- Mindfulness practices can be beneficial to your work. Take three conscious breaths before entering a room or answering a phone. Practice deep listening.

- Be aware of people as well as products. In the human scale, size matters. Decentralization is another way to consider the work environment.

- Sometimes work calls for on-the-spot practice. A workplace can be sangha. Consider, too, the sangha of all those beings your work touches.

Chapter 17

Food for the Heart: The Meal of Life

In This Chapter

- Life as cooking
- You are how you eat
- Medicine for eating disorders
- The way of tea

Like our livelihood, food is sustenance, sustaining and nourishing us in every sense. Of all our relations in the world, what's a more basic living link? Plus, it's so colorful, fragrant, and tasty! Doesn't it truly engage body–spirit–mind as one? So how could food—its cooking and eating and growing—*not* be on the menu for an aware, awake way of life? Here follow a few thoughts on food … food for the heart. *Bon appetit!*

How to Cook Your Life

This ripe phrase is the title of a superb documentary film by Zen practitioner Dorris Dörrie about Edward Espe Brown, Zen priest and chef (as noted in the previous chapter). More than an analogy, it's factual. Consider, for example, how in Zen monasteries, the person of second most importance, after the abbot, is the chef, overseeing and orchestrating the creation of daily meals. *Instructions to the Chef* by Dogen, the thirteenth-century founder of Soto Zen, thus sit side-by-side with his classic *Instructions on Zazen*.

Along the Path

How a human being becomes a Buddha is not unlike how dough becomes bread. The recipe, cherished and passed along for future generations, is like the lineage and teachings of the Buddha. Given the proper conditions and care, it produces steaming hot bread, as fresh today as the first loaf ever baked. Its basics are quite simple, yet it varies according to the person and the circumstance (upaya); a bread analogy for American Buddhism, for example, might be the pop-up toaster.

Consider too how, as in living, you can start by drafting and sticking with a Grand Master Plan, a recipe, to shop for and follow step by step. But just as a raft is not the shore, the recipe is not the meal. The Dharma is not only the path but also the fruit of the path. The Zen approach is to take stock of what's at hand, and create with What Is. With curiosity and surprise, you meet and become intimate with the ingredients you're going to eat. And there are mindful meditations, for example, through your hands: chopping vegetables, say … "contacting" … "slicing" … "sliding away" … Then, without any far-off pie-in-the-sky goal (such as enlightenment), you get to enjoy the food you've made! Ed Espe Brown attests:

> "Anyone can do this kind of work. Whole worlds come alive. Entering into activity you find the world appears vivid with spinach, lettuces, and black beans; with cutting boards, baking pans, and sponges. While previously you may have hesitated or waited for the world to provide entertainment or solace, here you enter a world vibrant with the energy and devotion flowing out of your own being."

You Are How You Eat

You've heard the slogan: "You are what you eat." (Or, as comedian Darryl Henriques has modified it: "You are what you don't poop.") Seriously, consider that every seven years your body completely regenerates, all cells except bone, though even marrow is renewed. So the "you" of seven years ago is no longer here, except your skeleton.

And from where do you derive this new you? From the food on your table, which is, in turn, part of the life of the soil, the watershed, the clouds, the sun, the farmers, the truckers, the grocers … all there to be experienced at your table, an intimacy with life we too often let slip through our fingers, eating mindlessly rather than mindfully. Equally important: you are *how* you eat.

So for now, put your pyramid of essential food groups on the back burner as we explore not just food but nourishment, including a three-course survey of nourishing practices: (1) giving thanks, (2) mindful meals, and (3) dining as sangha. Plus, we'll look at the yin and yang of trends, some drops of compassionate nectar as to personal food issues, and a postprandial celebration of tea.

Thanks Giving, Every Day: Food Is Love

Every spiritual practice on this blue-green Earth blesses or gives thanks for food. Like bowing and saying Namu Amida Butsu, it can never be forced. Yet, we always have occasion at any meal. When in relation, it comes. (Palms come together, thank you, amen. Let's eat.) Actually, I find food tastes better if I stop to thank it. ("O taste and see.") I don't doubt scientists will one day find it is more nourishing thus. Cooks already know food tastes better when cooked with love. That's equally true for how it's eaten. Food is love.

Some spiritual traditions also give thanks after a meal ("Before, I was hungry; now, I'm not. Thank you."), thanks for the food before us, and afterward thanks for the food within us. To understand when enough is enough, and one is satisfied without being overfull, it helps to pause and begin from being centered, beforehand. It takes just a few breaths. Contemplating food before eating, in harmony and gratitude, is to consider and prepare for receiving food. Then it's a mutual interrelationship of proteins and lipids, with love and gusto. One traditional Buddhist meditation before eating is the *Five Contemplations*. A sketch of one version of it goes like this (please use whatever words feel appropriate):

1. **Regarding your food, consider all its ingredients, and all the moves they took to come from farm to fork.** How many different elements, farms, and innumerable labors come together in this one plate? Be compassionate for the suffering and joy of the farmers, the truckers, the grocers, and their meals. And be aware of those who have not. Consider the roundness or squareness of your plate as representing the whole universe, and the food within as its messenger. Everything is here. Contemplate your karma in this web of interbeing, and wish all involved be well and happy.

2. **Regard your meal and vow to be worthy of it.** Being worthy of your food means eating it mindfully. Contemplate this practice, and your practice in general, affirming that, even if you are already a Buddha, you can always stand a bit of improvement. Being worthy means your zeal, always giving it all you've got.

3. **Contemplate your food, and your mind, and vow not to be greedy.** Eat in moderation. Recognize there's a point beyond satisfaction where eating becomes greed. Also practice equanimity. Don't over-identify with personal likes and dislikes. Even if you're a vegetarian, you might eat meat if it's offered (such as ice cream).

4. **Consider your food as good medicine.** Nourishment means more than comfort, fashion, or pride. Notice food's *chi*, its life-force. Be mindful that food can promote health or illness. Contemplate how the wondrous medicine on your plate supports life and your practice.

5. **Vow to eat that you may realize the Way.** From considering food as a gift from the *whole* universe, to being a matter of *health*, it's only a hop to seeing food as *holy*. See your meals as an essential part of your journey of awakening. Contemplate the aim of spiritual, mental, and emotional evolution, accepting and consuming this food to accomplish it.

As the aroma of your meal wafts in your nostrils and you contemplate it in these five ways, join palms, bowing in to the food you're about to receive and all that you've contemplated. Like you, food has Buddha Nature, too: Artichoke Buddhas, Carrot Buddhas, Zucchini Buddhas …

Hear and Now

The farmer hoes his rice
in noonday glare;
I see his sweat pour
in huge drops down to the soil.
Ah! for the meal on your table,
are you aware
that each small grain
costs the farmer bitter toil?
—Li Shen (T'ang Dynasty)

An appropriate Buddhist after-meal prayer can be the Bodhisattva Vow. Another might be to generate and send metta. Here's a fine model Donald Altman includes in his book, *Art of the Inner Meal*, which you can modify however feels right for you:

May all beings be free from pain, hunger, and suffering. May all beings live long and be healthy. May all beings receive physical nourishment, well-being, and spiritual awareness through food. May all beings experience loving kindness and serve others with compassion.

Mindful Meals: The Taste of Nonself

Thanking the food opens the door to eating as practice. Or should I say "the process of eating"? Each mouthful can be a self-contained world, akin to the birth, growth, and flare-out of a galaxy. It takes slowing down … almost slow motion at first, as in walking meditation … coordinating conscious breathing, one-pointed concentration, body awareness, and mouth yoga. To practice even only the first few bites of a meal mindfully is to open the most wonderful dharma door.

Consider one bite. Imagine, for example, we're mindfully eating bread, communing with the spirit of grain. We might be noting a rainbow of sensations in just one bite: … "eye looking at bread" … "intention to eat bread" … "hand breaking bread" … "considering and visualizing ingredients and their origins" … "smelling bread" … "noticing salivation" … "hand lifting bread to mouth" … "looking at the bite, noticing its color and texture" … "closing the eyes" (perhaps) … "opening the mouth" … "lips taking bread" … "lowering the arm" … "tongue taking bread" … "mouth feeling texture of bread" … "appreciating the taste of the bread in mouth before chewing" … "front teeth chopping bread" … "molars grinding bread" … "flavor of bread" … "bread softening with saliva" … "bread releasing sweetness in mouth" … "bread mostly liquid, with little crumbs" … "bread all liquidy" … "taste disappearing" … "noticing impulse to swallow" …

Follow the flow of this one bite all the way through *after* being swallowed, and stay with the food and feel it traveling within. Supposedly, there aren't taste buds past your throat, but my tummy has a range of subtle messages it can send me, like "warm," "sour," and even shadings like "pepperminty." After that, do you remain alert to feelings? Do food sensations spark desires? Do desires create intentions in your mind? Does your mind act on intentions by causing bodily movements? Then, do you lift your hand again, out of habit? Or do you *intend* to do each action before you do it? Check it out. Take note. Be mindful. (*Try this:* At any meal, notice when you lay your fork down, and when you clutch onto it.) There are such spectrums and layers of sensation and nuance in just … one … bite.

Slowing down, it's easier to know when to stop. Actually, when we are attuned to our body, we might note something scientists call "taste-specific satiety." After a few bites of something, the taste buds' sensitivity to that taste dampens. That's why the first bite often tastes best, and why after feeling done with one dish you have plenty of appetite for something different. Once you recognize taste-satiety, it's easier to stop and still feel satisfied. Just as breathing naturally slows under the lens of mindfulness, so too does hunger dwindle away when eating mindfully. We discover we can make do with less. We're no longer feeding abstract desires (anger, boredom, insecurity). We're directly experiencing the miraculous reality of food, with each bite.

Leaves from the Bodhi Tree

Jack Kornfield teaches a meditation in which participants mindfully note the process of eating one raisin: it takes about 10 minutes (the time it takes to eat a salad). Likewise, Thich Nhat Hanh suggests a single orange as meditation: fully experiencing each slice, rather than peeling while eating. And Zen priest, chef, and author Edward Espe Brown has led a meditation on eating one potato chip, one orange slice, and one Hydrox cookie, each, "attentively in silence." His students have discovered that one potato chip wasn't satisfying (maybe that's why people crave more). Everyone loved the orange. And about half the participants couldn't even finish the Hydrox cookie! (See for yourself.)

The last bite—the last morsel, the very last crumb—can be as good as the first, and feel like a whole meal in itself.

Leaves from the Bodhi Tree

The Buddha once told the parable of a man walking across a field who saw a big tiger. He ran, and the tiger chased him. He came to a cliff. He caught hold of the root of a wild vine and swung over the edge. The tiger sniffed at him from above. Trembling, the man looked down and saw another tiger, far below, waiting to eat him. Meanwhile, two mice, one black and one white, came and started to nibble at the vine that sustained him. Just then, the man saw a strawberry growing within reach. He plucked it. How sweet it tasted!

From your *Complete Idiot's* Maître D', (me), here are four question areas, to assist mindful diners:

- Where and how do you find yourself objecting to mindful meals? (Does it sound boring? Does it go against cultural training? Do you miss food as escapism? Do you feel you have too much else to do? Do you not like the food itself?)

- Are you in the common habit of reading or watching television while you eat? If so, you may never really be fully eating and never really be fully reading, unless you've mastered the yoga of Undivided Attention of Doing Two Things at Once. (There's a bonus health aspect to refraining. Digestion and reading involve two separate but interconnected bodily networks. Trying to do both at once is only crossing and jamming those networks.) Just eat while you eat. Likewise, see if you can refrain from eating while you drive.

◆ (More common habits.) When eating, do you sit with the soles of your feet touching the earth? Do you slouch, or sit up straight? Do you lean down to your food, or do you bring your food up to your erect head? (You might think of any extra few inches it might take as bridging the gap between your heart-center and your head-center.)

◆ Did you know? Chewing each mouthful through to the end also has a health benefit. Mixing food with saliva begins the digestive process in your mouth, taking a load off other digestive organs.

Lifting an Elbow Together: Dine as Sangha

Eating mindfully in company is such a blessing. But according to some reports, as many as a third of American families don't eat together. It's interesting that countries with more eating rituals, like eating together, have fewer eating disorders. And eating together mindfully in silence can be communion, a way of sharing appreciation of being, and being together, in marvelous ways that words cannot express—even if only for the first few bites, then breaking the silence.

Even if you eat alone, eat as sangha: rejoice and join the universe in all the chemical transfers and emotional exchanges composing nourishment. Even if it's your one meditation amid a busy schedule betwixt life's bumpy roads, the oasis of a mindful meal can keep you on the path of peace … with all beings.

 Hear and Now _____

"The ritual of coming to the dinner table was once the very basis of community."
—Alice Waters

"Let the progress of the meal be slow, for dinner is the last business of the day; and let the guests conduct themselves like travelers due to reach their destination together."
—Jean Anthelme Brillat-Savarin

Slow Food: Time Well Spent

Whether you practice the ancient meditation of cooking yet, awareness of your food and how you eat is so elemental that the label "Buddhist" is almost redundant. Yet we might locate the mindful practices we've surveyed in a context of current trends, intertwining the transcendent dimension with the historical. In the previous chapter, we'd spotlighted the Zen of baking and cooking that sparked a national reevaluation of our eating habits. (It also led to such amusingly oxymoronic terms as "health food" and "natural food.") Riding in on that initial wave, the organic food movement has become a multi-billion-dollar industry, with a market growing by 20 percent each year. (*Organic food* is raised and processed without pesticides, irradiation, or genetic modification.)

In the latest wave, we might note a movement that began in Europe called Slow Food, begun in the 1980s in opposition to the encroachment of fast food and the faster pace it represents. In that, it reminds me of the ancient European motto: *Festina lente* (make haste slowly). But, it also brings to mind a Zen idea of Original Nature as connecting with The One Who Is Not Busy throughout all our actions. Slow Food also implies taking time to learn more about food. Indeed, one aspect of eating mindlessly is taking it for granted; and perhaps the easiest way to approach fast food is to know as little as possible about what it might contain.

I'm not pushing an agenda, only reporting, so you can pick and choose, and find your own Middle Way between extremes. Just think: for every recipe book published, someone else does a new diet book. Americans spend about $26 billion on vending machine food, yet $33 billion on weight-loss programs. Slow Food's natural swing of the pendulum may thus be worth noting. As much as mindful eating, it represents a deliberate approach to food. (When Thoreau said he went to live in the woods because he wanted to live deliberately, he probably had in mind the word's roots—*de liber*, "from freedom,"—as opposed to compulsion.) Slow Food emphasizes sustainability, small-scale, organic, seasonal and species variety, regional traditions, and of course leisure. Interestingly, critics who accuse Slow Food of being leftist, or self-promotion, fail to comment on the food itself. Fast food's here to stay, yet good quality, nutritious food could grow scarcer, given a growing world population, rising prices for food staples, and greater demand for meat and dairy (about half of the world's grain now goes to feed cattle).

Besides farmers, grocers, and restaurants, the Slow Food movement also consists of farmers' markets and Community Supported Agriculture (CSA) networks. (When's the last time you actually visualized a farmer's sunburned face and hands as you ate the food he grew?) Farmers can tell you exactly what they're selling, and cultivate varieties not found in stores. When's the last time you tried a Jonathan Spy apple, a Blenham apricot, or a Chandler strawberry? It was getting kind of critical with apples not too long ago, with practically only one red and one green on the shelves. At one time, there were 500 different kinds of apples in America. (Fortunately, there are seed savers.)

When you buy produce directly from a farm, you're taking home a fully realized buddha that needs little else; maybe a touch of steaming or baking, plus hearty, mindful appreciation. (If it's been in the refrigerator for two or three days, then you might need to fix it up a little, with a recipe.) Fresh food is an invitation to commune with a living spirit that needs no chaperone of sauce or spice.

Don't have a farmer's market or CSA near you? A community garden? How about a backyard patch or unused empty lot? What about the neighborhood school? (All are possibilities for a Buddhist entrepreneur.) Taking an active part in the life of nourishment and food security can also be an excellent way of opening the self to the selfless when dealing with personal food issues.

Do You Hunger and Thirst?: Food Issues

All living things hunger and thirst. Our appetite naturally intertwines tangible food and invisible happiness. We see this mutuality in the Chinese word for harmony, or peace: a seed of grain next to an open mouth. Similarly, the Catholic Eucharist unites the physical with the divine through the sacrament of consecrated bread and wine. Yet food can also represent conflict, and dualism. Even the Buddha had food issues, remember, pitting the material against the spiritual. He tried fasting his way to enlightenment, to probe and transcend the searing bonds of hunger hardwired into our physical makeup. Prior to that, he'd had his pick of the palace pantry. From these extremes of luxury and poverty, bingeing and craving, he discovered and taught a non-dualist alternative, the Middle Way.

> ### Leaves from the Bodhi Tree
>
> Zen priest Lewis Richmond remembers once serving food to his teacher Suzuki Roshi and a visiting Zen teacher. In mid-sentence, Suzuki reached over to Lew's plate, and popped into his mouth an olive pit Lew had left there, sucking on it as he spoke, until it was totally meatless, and casually replaced it. Elsewhere, another time, when asked what nirvana is, Suzuki Roshi replied: "Following each thing through to the end."

His first noble truth is about never being satisfied. The second noble truth likened this to an unquenchable appetite, a burning, consuming, ravenous hunger. Key here is that our discontent—our suffering, deeply rooted in our *cravings*—is not so much about the objects of desire (banquets or diet programs), but our attachment to them (our grasping). His third truth speaks of staying with what's present, which can be a delight (*sukha*, the opposite of dukkha, means "pleasure," or "bliss"). The fourth noble truth offers us timeless recipes for a diet of mindfulness. If the Buddha were to write a diet book, it wouldn't stress willpower (you can't will your enlightenment), but rather mindfulness as the key.

Mindful meals can help heal food issues. Weight Watchers has incorporated mindfulness in their teachings, though it's removed from the context of the Buddha's deep, compassionate wisdom teachings. By mindfully tuning in to the whole chain of mini-events, desire-as-craving-as-self can become transparent, seen as a kind of fictional device ("Wow, am *I* hungry!"), telling a story not present in the immediate situation (food as reward, identity, blame, shame, and so on). In truth, there's only a series of present-moment events, none with any intrinsic identity, and none like any other.

Mindfulness can enable us to recognize and understand the invisible levers of our intentions (for instance, eating as if fueling a machine, rather than nourishing the heart), the impermanence of our sensations (such as taste satiety), and the subtle inter-connectedness underlying our awareness. This latter aspect is underlined by relatively recent, remarkable, groundbreaking discoveries by neuroscientist Candace Pert, who finds that emotions link body and mind through the digestive system. In fact, our digestive system works like a second brain. Known now as the "enteric nervous system," the chemicals (such as peptides) and neurons in the sheaths of tissue lining the digestive system work as a single entity to learn, remember, and express many of our "gut feelings." Concentrating on belly breathing may not be such a strange idea after all.

Meditation: Please revisit the picture and caption of the hungry ghost in Chapter 5. Then, see if you can imagine your own hungry ghost. That is, if you're like me, you may harbor a hungry ghost (or two), and you may have been feeding it without much awareness. See if you can visualize yours. Can you give it a human face? (I don't give mine a name, just "That Old Hungry Ghost." But you can give yours a name, if you like.) As you go about your day, see if you and your hungry ghost can teach each other some Dharma. Some Buddhists set aside a small token of their food as an offering to the hungry ghosts. Some countries have a Hungry Ghost Festival (usually in summer), offering the ghosts gifts and entertainment. Consider setting aside one day of your own (July 15, say): Be Kind to Hungry Ghosts Day.

Looking around, it's ironic to note how in a land with such a relatively high standard of living, America also has such a relatively high number of people with food issues: hungry ghosts. We seem both stuffed and starved; overfed and undernourished. Consider the growing number of people who are suffering from obesity, ulcers, diabetes, irritable bowel syndrome, bulimia, and sugar craving, and those who are otherwise hung up about food. See if you can visualize and sympathize with the hungry ghosts of various food issues, and see the universal condition in them.

Leaves from the Bodhi Tree _____

In tantra, even eating disorders can lead to enlightenment. A master named Saraha chanced upon a glutton named Sarvabhaksa, writhing in pain because he couldn't find anything to eat. Saraha told him what a hungry ghost is, and the glutton asked how he could avoid such a fate. Saraha told him to visualize his belly as empty as the sky, all visible phenomena as his food and drink, and his appetite as a fire consuming it all. He did so until the light went out because he'd devoured the sun and the moon. Saraha then told him that everything he'd eaten was now nothing and to now meditate without food. Soon the sun and moon reappeared as he realized that appearance and emptiness are one.

Take Tea and See: The Tea Ceremony

Let's cap our tour by considering what mindful awareness might discover in just a few leaves of tea or beans of coffee. Many find a cup can enhance their sitting meditation. And a cup can be meditation in itself. This path has a venerable traditional ceremony, or can be appreciated by simply stopping for a moment to simply be what you truly are.

In China, Korea, and Japan, written records of tea and its traditions are intertwined with the introduction of Buddhism there. There's even a commonplace sacred story expressing the love for both, in the legend that during Bodhidharma's nine-year stint meditating facing a wall at Shaolin Monastery, he grew angry at his own dozing off. So, he tore off his eyelids and threw them to the ground, where they took root and sprouted up as tea bushes. Hence the eyelid-shaped leaves with invigorating properties.

America, too, has its tea karma, though many today may think of tea as, at best, a side-order beverage, usually served up in the form of a bag on a string, faintly resembling a mouse with a tail. The American Revolution had its roots in tea. It had been the national drink of England, featured in a ceremony known as "tea time." In the New World, colonial New York drank as much as all of England, and did so on into the early twentieth century.

Because Zen and Pure Land practice were lay as well as monastic, they suffused all aspects of Japanese culture. Of all Japanese arts, the tea ceremony is closest to being a total art form, like opera or High Mass, engaging body–spirit–mind as one. Guests might first become acquainted at the host's exquisitely landscaped and groomed tea garden. The ceremony proper is traditionally held in a simple, 10-foot-square tea room, a miniature Pure Land. It resembles a Zen monk's cell—a style which, in fact, highly influenced Japanese domestic architecture in general. The door is low, requiring bowing in. The floor's made of textured straw matting (*tatami*); the small, irregularly shaped windows with paper panes admit a subdued light. At the entrance, in a small alcove, is the only decoration, a flower below a scroll of Zen calligraphy. One stick of incense purifies the air. The only music comes from a bamboo water pipe dripping outside and the water boiling inside on a charcoal burner.

Hear and Now

"There are few hours in life more agreeable than the hour dedicated to the ceremony known as afternoon tea."
—Henry James

"If Christianity is wine and Islam coffee, Buddhism is most certainly tea."
—Alan Watts

"When tea is brewed with water drawn from unfathomable depths of the spirit, then we have truly realized the Way of Tea."
—Toyotomi Hideyoshi

Hear and Now

"The philosophy of tea … expresses conjointly with ethics and religion our whole point of view about man and nature. It is hygiene, for it enforces cleanliness; it is economics, for it shows comfort in simplicity rather than in the complex and costly; it is moral geometry, inasmuch as it defines our sense of proportion to the universe. It represents the true spirit of eastern democracy by making all its votaries aristocrats in taste."
—Kakuzo Okakura (1863–1919), *The Book of Tea*

The utensils and their arrangement catch the eye, and handling them pleases the touch. The cups aren't perfect porcelain but, rather, Zen pottery—unglazed at the bottom, often with a drop of glaze running down the side as a Zen "controlled accident." The fresh tea is a fine green powder, whipped into a "froth of liquid jade" as one Chinese writer put it, the color to be admired and the fragrance savored. Then: tea.

Top left: Garden of En-an teahouse. Design: Furuta Oribe (1640–1655), Yabunouchi School of Tea, Kyoto. Top right: Tea ceremony room. Konchi-in Monastery of Nanzen-ji Temple, Kyoto. Bottom: Ido-style tea cup. Koho-an Monastery, Daitoku-ji Temple, Kyoto.

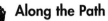 **Along the Path** _____

> "It was at once as if nothing at all had happened and as if the roof had flown off the building. But in reality nothing had happened. A very old deaf Zen man with bushy eyebrows had drunk a cup of tea, as though with the complete wakefulness of a child and yet as though at the same time declaring with utter finality: 'this is not important!'"
>
> —Thomas Merton, on having tea with D. T. Suzuki

Savoring a cup of coffee, espresso, or tea is now a global pastime. Nothing exotic. Cultivating a discerning intelligence, you can appreciate how tea has six tastes to savor: bitter, tart, sour, salty, spicy-hot, and sweet. Enjoying a cup of tea or coffee, you can practice element meditation: earth of cup, water in its drink, fire in its warmth, air in fragrant aroma, and the living, growing "wood" element of the tea leaf or coffee bean. Then, too, as the clarity of the initial cup or pot doesn't last, there's the chance to practice impermanence meditation. At minimum, it's the essence of meditation: a time to stop, practice undivided awareness of each moment, refine one's perception, and appreciate one's True Nature. And it's so much the better when celebrated in company. This is truly a door to the Dharma, as we can see in it its availability to all; this enjoyment itself has no door, no training necessary.

Cheers!

The Least You Need to Know

- Food is full of Dharma: teachings, and the fruit of teachings.

- Giving thanks to our food is a primary and universal spiritual practice. (It might also make food taste better.)

- Food awareness can mean mindful eating, as well as being well informed about ingredients and cooking.

- Even a simple pot of tea can be a meditation and a way of life, whose Dharma all can enjoy.

18

Everybody's Doing It: Buddhism and Popular Culture

In This Chapter

- The Way of Art
- Flower power
- The ultimate athlete
- Buddhist soul music
- Buddha at the movies

You don't need to seek out Buddhism in everyday life. In fact, to do so could mean to miss it entirely. Rather, Dharma is everywhere. Our challenge is to remain open to it anywhere, and realize awakening of mind anytime.

Awakening to the Dharma, we can find it anywhere. Thus far, in this half of our book, we've explored Buddhism in some of the fundamentals of our daily lives: relationships, work, and food. The cultural and social dimensions of our lives might seem less immediate, but they, too, hold Dharma doors to be found in the everyday, and are no less vital to our awareness. There's Dharma in fitness and sports, in backyard gardening, in the ever-expanding music playlist, and even at the movies!

The Way of Art = The Way of the Buddha

Culture is where we find it. It's whether we drink out of the bottle or a glass. It's our choice of clothes and the way we wear them. It's more than a matter of taste: it's our expression of our inexpressible aliveness along our path. No less than through the bells and cushions of formal practice, through such intangibles a Buddhist way of life becomes real. In this chapter and the next, we'll explore some of these instances, East and West, traditional and contemporary.

Each art we spotlight here underscores the boundless potentials of Dharma, applicable to each individual. In this variable applicability, we can see skillful means (upaya) as art, the Dharma made present through each person according to his or her background, temperament, and culture. Culture is ever-changing; the Dharma is unchanging, and is both teaching and fruit (path and goal).

We've touched on the tea ceremony, a living tradition in China, Korea, and Japan. The Japanese word for tea culture is *chado* (tea way), and in Japanese adding *–do* (way) to the end of a word indicates it is an art: for example, *chikudo* (bamboo way), *kado* (flower way), and *kyudo* (archery way). Another word for Way is Tao, which is also Zen. So we hear about Zen and the art of motorcycle maintenance, the Zen of changing diapers, and the Way of Pooh (as in Winnie, no pun intended). Indeed, where's the museum of things that *aren't* art?! Where's the temple of things *not* to worship?! It's all meditation, which is itself an art. Like the tea ceremony, Buddhism encompasses all the arts: applied, popular, and fine (the next chapter is given over to fine arts).

In a Buddhist sense, all arts are popular arts, because anyone is capable of awakening heart and mind. And the popularity of Buddhist arts in the West attests to its adaptability to our culture. Let's start by getting our hands in the soil. It's all about seeing the Way in our own backyard.

The Dharma of Dirt: Gardening

What is the spell gardening holds for so many? Surely, communing with and learning from nature must be counted a primary attraction. When we say original nature and buddha nature, it's the nature part that's our interface with the universe as co-emerging life.

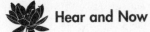

Hear and Now

"We are intertwined. Some bacteria sip nitrogen from the living air and fix it on the roots of host plants in plump pink purses of protein, while other bacteria consolidate sulfur from stone and render it available to our classic roses. And all the while, throughout solid ground where well-intentioned gardeners prune and pontificate on the surface, mycelial threads of a vast fungal network spread and radiate out in widening circles, attaching to plant roots for nourishment while fending off disease in the garden."

—Wendy Johnson

As always, there's Dharma in all the details, such as using weeds and waste as mulch to nourish our flowers—good models for not rejecting our own difficult, weedy traits, but using them instead as food for transformation. Gardening as a way of life can encompass growing our own food, encouraging us to grow our life as well as cook it. What better way to affirm and enjoy our kinship with all life? At minimum, gardening could mean cultivating a house plant or two. It needn't even be a pretty flower, but just ivy. Plant life draws us into the cyclic unfolding of the seasons, loosening our arbitrary schedule to attend to the organic time of nature, ultimate time. It teaches the interactions of the sources of life, and reminds us to pay attention. Everything changes. It's all interconnected.

Saying It with Flowers

We've noted how the Buddha's entirely wordless sermon was composed of a flower (compare to Jesus' "Regard the lilies of the field."). And we have the Buddha accompanied by flowers on altars, whether in temple or at home. A flower is a complete Buddha unto itself, making radiance with just the few ingredients it's given, a messenger of the entire cosmos. A few flowers on a table or altar bring the outside in, and draw the inside out. As Shakespeare says, "One touch of nature makes the whole world kin."

When I pass by flowers I've set out, I sometimes forget who put them there. I stop and admire them and wonder how I am any different. But I don't just stick flowers in a bowl willy-nilly. Arranging flowers, we find culture. Asian flower arrangements can be judged as masterpieces, no less so for being impermanent. The design is rather abstract, to convey the essence of the thing, and imply its potential (buddha nature). In a similar spirit are miniature trees in pots known as *bonsai*. They might seem thin or skimpy compared to the Western preference for abundance or still-life style. But such flower arrangements aim to look as if they are still growing, a skillful means in which each person can recognize their own essential buddha nature through direct communion. Pointing directly to mind, outside of words.

Seven chrysanthemums (an autumn flower) in a bed of pebbles, their stems bent and shaped to appear as a single plant. The design is triangular: heaven, human, and earth. Heaven is the highest stalk. Intermediate and somewhat diagonal branches are the human realm. At the base is the earthly. (The triad also correlates with Buddha, Dharma, and Sangha.) Next to it, a sketch of an imaginary arrangement reflects the latent elegance of design. Implicit, but only suggested, in photo and drawing is the space making the art possible ("emptiness no different than form").

(Chrysanthemum arrangement: Cynthis Lewis; drawing: Master Enkiduwasa Mori; collection of Beth Burstein)

You can find Shinto and Confucian symbolism in flower arranging, but the Buddhism was there all along. When Prince Umayada brought Buddhism to Japan, he sent envoys to China to seek cultural and spiritual guidance. One of these envoys, named Ono-no Imoko, eventually retired, living as a hermit priest by a lake. He was devoted to arranging flowers for altars. One of the early Japanese masters of the art describes the process: "Flowers should be placed in the container as one throws pebbles into a garden pool. It is done quietly and deliberately, and then left alone. To make changes is the sign of a novice." Priests of newly built temples came to him for instruction. Thus was born the first known school of flower arrangement, called *ike-no-bo*, meaning "hermit by the lake," which gave birth to Japanese flower arranging, *ikebana*.

It's interesting to note how something originally designed as decoration for altars became a devotional art in itself. You might consider this in Pure Land terms, in which meditation on a bodhisattva's pure land becomes as powerful as meditating on the bodhisattva itself. And this is, in part, what happened in Japanese gardening.

Ooh, Ooh, Ooh! What Just Five Rocks Can Do

One feature common to Japanese gardens has become associated in the West with Zen: sand and rocks. For one thing, a pond made out of granite gravel or sand was less expensive to make and maintain. They're called *karé-san-sui*, meaning "dry mountain water," itself a kind of koan. They became a common feature at the growing number of Buddhist temples as well as homes of the elite.

Like traditional Japanese rock gardens set amidst vegetation, karé-san-sui often imitate classical Chinese ink-brush landscapes. Flat-topped rocks look like brush-stroke mountains, and raked gravel or sand imitates waterfalls, rivers, and oceans (usually blank space in canvases). Overall, they might represent a pure land, or the river of life, or the progress of a monk's practice. Five qualities common to these gardens: asymmetry, simplicity, austere sublimity (lofty dryness), subtle profundity (deep respect), freedom from attachment (nirvana), and serene tranquility.

Detail of rock garden in Zhuiho-in Temple, Japan.

(Photograph: Frantisek Staud, www.phototravels.net)

The acme and enigmatic sphinx of rock garden art is at the Temple of Ryoanji (Peaceful Dragon), Kyoto. Fifteen stones are set in five groups across a horizontal bed of gravel about the size of a tennis court, raked horizontally and in concentric circles around the stones. (An interesting phenomenon is that you can never see all the rocks at once. You can only see, at most, fourteen at any one time. Turn slightly to take in the fifteenth and one other rock drops out of sight.)

The only literally living thing is a delicate native moss on the rocks (alas, recently drying due to climate change, here and at other temples), lending an atmosphere of mellow tranquility to the grounds. Some say the stones resemble mountain peaks jutting through clouds, or islands in the sea (like Japan herself). But the overall impression is more nonrepresentational, like the play of volume and mass in abstract art, an arrangement of stones almost random-seeming yet perfect, just so. Viewers are thrown back on themselves, inducing concentration that, as we know, can lead to mindfulness. A common impression people come away with is an indescribable feeling of both presence and spaciousness. It thus embodies the Middle Way between strict rules and utter naturalness—planned spontaneity, if you will. It's a fusion of both aesthetic and Buddhist doctrine: a monumental reflection of form being no different than emptiness, and of emptiness being no different than form. (*Tip:* If you visit, go when they first open to avoid the crowds. People often come again and again.)

Physical Culture Isn't Just Physical: Spirituality and Sports

The popularity of sports culture and fitness is attested to by all the people you see jogging past other people sitting around wearing baseball caps, both men and women. Attendance at sports events and gyms is on the rise in many cities, while churchgoing is on the decline. Yet we see an interface of spirituality and sports, extending far back to both ancient Western and Eastern civilization. Buddhism has key moves here, too, for personal fitness, team sports, and martial arts (which are art forms, too). So let's huddle!

Martial Arts Are an Art

Martial arts date back to pre-civilization. ("Hey, Joe, where ya going with that rock in your hand?!") But Shaolin Temple, in China, is a good candidate for Mother of All Martial Arts as we know them today. Located on Mount Sung, in Honan Province, legend has it that Bodhidharma settled here after his interview with the emperor, sitting zazen before a rock wall in a nearby cave. He learned that monks at the Temple either were falling asleep during meditation or were too restless to concentrate. He diagnosed them as being out of shape, and devised exercises for them (being from India, he probably included yoga), which later became the basis of *kung fu*. Shaolin Grand-Master Wong Kiew Kit finds Shaolin kung fu contains all the techniques of the world's martial arts today: karate punches, tae kwon do kicks, judo throws, aikido locks, wrestling holds, Western boxing's jabs and hooks, Siamese boxing's elbow and knee strikes, and Malay silate's twists and turns. (Note how many schools end in *-do*.) The sun of Shaolin shines on all martial arts today for having combined physical culture with moral character development based on spiritual awareness.

> **This Is**
>
> Kung fu (skill from effort) is a generic catch-all for numerous forms of Chinese martial arts, with myriad styles and sub-styles. Some are soft, redirecting an opponent's momentum and energy; some are hard, meeting force with force. Some work internally on *chi* (life force), such as *chi kung* (a.k.a *qi gong*, meaning "energy work") and *tai chi*, with their deep, slow, flowing movements; others are external and work on muscular energy.

Bodhidharma allegedly taught the martial arts to keep the Shaolin monks in shape to meditate, and to help them overcome that renowned enemy, fear, child of ignorance. Now, because bandits periodically raided the Temple, monks excelling in kung fu were designated to defend the grounds. Some were later enlisted into service by the emperor to save the throne from usurpers. This helped lead to the multiplication of Buddhist temples across China, with official patronage. And probably some came there to be monks to learn martial arts.

Flash forward. Martial arts grew noticeable in the West in the 1960s. Phrases like "Look within" crept into the vocabulary thanks to a television series called *Kung Fu* (created by Bruce Lee, but starring David Carradine). In 2001, the epic Taoist martial arts parable *Crouching Tiger, Hidden Dragon* swept the popular imagination, opening the door to a dozen other commercial Chinese martial arts parables. Eastern martial arts continue to enjoy a growing following in the West—except for the art of the sword, which was reserved for the warrior elite and is rarely taught solo today.

Bushido, The Way of the Warrior: Zen Swords and Arrows

We noted in Chapter 2 how the patronage of the samurai helped establish Zen in Japan. This warrior class had been in decline when Zen came along, and the samurai loved the fearlessness, immediacy, irreverence, intuition, and strict discipline of Zen, generously supporting it and devoting themselves to its rigors. And their military aristocracy was to remain in power for nearly seven centuries (until 1867).

The samurai shaved their heads like the Zen monks, donned Zen robes, practiced such Zen arts as flower-arranging and haiku, and learned Zen freedom-through-discipline: one-pointed concentration, dissolving the ego, and remaining present to the moment.

Indeed, for these soldiers who lived by their sword, swordsmanship literally became a life-or-death test of Zen attainment. When a samurai holds a sword, it becomes one with his purified heart, his *mushin* (no-mind). Without fixing it anywhere, his attentive mind flows everywhere—for any move that comes to his mind, his opponent will make a countermove, and so he'll lose the higher ground of original nature.

❀ Hear and Now

> "The mind must always be flowing. If it stops anywhere, the flow is interrupted and this is injurious to the well-being of the mind. In the case of the swordsman, it means death. When the swordsman stands against his opponent, he is not to think of the opponent, nor of himself, nor of his enemy's sword movements. He just stands there with his sword which, forgetful of all technique, is ready only to follow the dictates of the unconscious."
>
> —Takuan Soho (1573–1645)

One martial art the samurai practiced, which is a heck of a lot safer and more common, is *kyudo* (archery). (*Zen tip:* Keep your mind empty. Don't learn archery to learn Zen. You learn archery to learn archery. The Zen will arise along with it.) The Zen archer pulls back an arrow on an outsized bow, becomes one with the bull's eye, and an unwritten koan is answered … with a *thwack!*

The Ultimate Athlete: Go, Sangha! BE the Ball!

We all aspire to maximum performance, mastery, and perfection. When we select the Buddha as a model for our self-actualization, we realize the Buddha we wish to emulate is the Buddha within, our own buddha nature. Otherwise, we're only engaging in spectator sports. So, too, can the way of the Buddha train us to recognize and train our inner athlete, to go for the gold. The ultimate sport is not about outcome but how you play the game … and how the game plays you. (*Tip:* if you attend a gym, discover what happens when you focus on the interaction of your movement, breath, and mind, rather than watching television while going through the motions of a routine. Mindfulness can be a continual practice.)

The Middle Way in sports, as in daily life, means a Buddhist can remain alert in tranquility, and calm amid danger. Nate Zinsser, director of training enhancement at West Point, notes a middle way in his coaching. "The key, for Olympic athletes as well as weekend warriors, is to learn to juggle two contrasting disciplines. You have to be almost an obsessive-compulsive workaholic to get yourself ready to be good. But then you have to be this relaxed, Buddha-like Zen master, which allows all the stuff you have been training to come out." So an athlete and a samurai share with a classical pianist performing without a score, without even thinking of what note to play next. Did you ever throw something into a wastebasket, without thinking, and have it sink right in? But then you miss the shot the second time, because you thought about it too much? Buddhism helps foster and maintain that spontaneous, intuitive excellence. Athletes call it *the Zone*.

This Is _____

Sports buffs often talk about players entering **the Zone,** a mystical state of consciousness that seems neither physical nor mental … effortlessness amid tense exertion … as if playing in slow motion … perceptually sharp, keenly alert, with heightened concentration … almost as if being psychic. Such profound experiences, often commonplace to athletes, bear comparison to daydreaming, communion with nature, and spiritual contemplation.

In the Zone, it's all about being in the moment. Like the meditator, the inner athlete learns to break things down, breath by breath, one step at a time. This naturally means there's no focus on outcome, only on process. Golf legend Tiger Woods, who understands this well, acknowledged his Thai Buddhist mother, who trained him to understand the power of the mind. Once, he was on a winning streak that included the four most prestigious tournaments of the era all in a row. But on the golf course, right after winning the 2001 Masters Tournament, capping his achievement, he confessed he didn't realize the significance until it was all over: "I was so attuned to each and every shot, that I focused so hard on just that one golf shot. I finally realized I had no more to play. That was it. I was done. It was such a weird feeling. Then I started thinking, I had just won the Masters."

Team sports add the dimension of sangha, in which a coach can add the juice of Dharma lineage. Phil Jackson attributes his legendary success as basketball coach to two things: meditation and cigars. Seriously, in the competitive battleground of basketball, he vowed to create an environment of selflessness and compassion, and it's paid off. His work with first the Chicago Bulls, then the Los Angeles Lakers, combines an array of spiritual traditions. He's had Vipassana instructor George Mumford come in one week every month. Mumford begins by teaching how the Zone isn't a matter of self-will, but rather a by-product of awareness.

Hear and Now

> "Basketball is a complex dance that requires shifting from one objective to another at lightning speeds.... The secret is not thinking. That doesn't mean being stupid, it means quieting the endless jabbering of thoughts so that your body can do instinctively what it's been trained to do without the mind getting in the way."
>
> —Phil Jackson

Jackson has influenced such multimillion-dollar superstar egos as Kobe Bryant, Michael Jordan, Shaquille O'Neal, Scotty Pippen, and Dennis Rodman. His emphasis on teamwork as selflessness, compassion for each other's skills, and interconnectedness shows on the court. It's sangha in action. In the crunch of high-speed competition, a player can keep his cool and awaken to what's called for in each moment. Because of Jackson's trademark triangle defensive strategy, his players keep flowing. Win or lose, up or down, they cleave to the Middle Way and grow as a team. Their keeping at their best makes a direct link to the audience's best, so it's a joy to watch, even when the ball wobbles out of the rim instead of in.

The bottom line was laid out by Bodhidharma, back at Shaolin. Be it race-walking or sit-ups, tai chi or tae kwon do, swimming or bicycling, keep in shape! Form (training) is the key to emptiness (unlimited potentiality). Notice how meditation improves your physical skill, and how physical culture improves your meditation. It's a slam-dunk, double-eagle, rare-orchid, rock-solid, wisdom-eye home run!

Play It Again, Samadhi!: Musical Meditation

Music may be the oldest of human arts, requiring only a hand beating on a knee, or a lone human voice harmonizing with a forest. And it's perennially new, being created in the present moment—you can never capture it again, a presentation, making present. But it can be far more than a reminder of the present and its impermanence. Does the resonant quality of music mirror consciousness? Other living things have awareness, but we two-leggeds can be aware that we're aware, a kind of reverb. Perhaps you might wish to revisit the sound meditation in Chapter 10, and see for yourself.

Mindfulness exercise: Listening to any music, follow your breath, and note how the music moves it, taking us out of ourselves and bringing us back. Let your body and soul become one big ear. As a note bends, does your mind, too? Be one with the musicians and the music, feeling each note resonate in your heart. And with your hands in meditation, you offer silent applause of every moment.

In this section, we'll broaden your horizons. For example, I find Korean music invigorating once you get accustomed to its wonky asymmetric zigzag, like a dragonfly. To me, Vietnamese chanting, such as recorded by the monks and nuns of Plum Village, has one of the most soulful tastes on the planet. But the dharma has one taste. Like Willie Nelson once said, "It's all one song."

Giving Buddhism Its Chants

In and of itself, music is a mystery. Who knows where it came from: we do it anyway, even if only humming a little tune because we like to hum. Maybe we're serenading the microorganisms, or joining the music of the spheres (not so silly a concept, now that we know that matter is a form of vibration), or vocalizing the deep rhythms of life that surge in each cell of our protoplasm and throughout the galaxies.

Whether it's the *Heart Sutra*, or the name of Buddha, chanting solo or in unison as community we become conscious of being a part of something greater than ourselves.

There are numerous recordings of Buddhist chants in many languages, all good. If you haven't heard Tibetan multiphonic chanting before, check out the Gyuto Monks to get a sample of this unusual vibrational resonance. It's a tantric art of unification with universal energies. For one thing, the monks chant two octaves below C, a feat unrivalled in Western music. Such tones of low vibration travel farther and through more obstacles than high-frequency sound. Asian and African elephants communicate long-distance using this "silent thunder," and whales can communicate this way from Newfoundland to Puerto Rico (what might they be saying?). In such deep tones, you can hear overtones within a single note.

Plus, each monk can chant in three octaves at once. In effect, individuals are singing chords. Poet and Sanskrit scholar Andrew Schelling has described it as "craggy guttural prayer, like the sound of stones crumbling down a mountain precipice … comforting to hear as your own mother's voice, but above that, almost on wings, a distinctly audible angel's tone, sublime as its originating note is terrifying." Not knowing the words, you can chant along, intoning "Om."

Another popular timeless recording in this vein is *Chö*, a collaboration between guitarist Steve Tibbetts and Tibetan nun Ani Choying Drolma.

Blowing Your Mind the Buddhist Way

The oldest wind instrument on the planet may be the Australian didjeridu, a four- or five-foot trumpet of termite-hollowed wood, operating in the lower frequency range, with a continuous tradition dating back at least 30,000 years. Tibet has a similar-length horn made of copper, 10 feet long, said to represent the strength of the earth. It's often played with shorter horns representing the delicacy of the heavens, bringing these two forces into balance in the mind of the listener.

As the didjeridu is native to indigenous Australian spirituality, and the long horn is unique to Tibetan Buddhism, so is the Japanese flute called the *shakuhachi* native to Zen. Indeed, its art is known in Japanese as *suizen* (blowing Zen). Made from the root of thick, timber-strength bamboo, its sound is made by blowing perpendicularly across the end. Just as it takes time to learn how to sit Zen, or make one even, continuous line with Asian brush and paper, so it is with blowing one note on the shakuhachi: the hard-earned result expresses each player's distinct signature.

The sound is hauntingly like a voice and all its moods, but as with a rock garden, it is abstracted. It's evocative, as Debussy's impressionism for the piano can conjure fireworks, goldfish, dancing snowflakes, gardens in the rain, and so on. Listening to shakuhachi, I wonder where else have I heard the cry of distant deer, the voices of cranes as their young ones leave the nest, and distant thunder echoing within precipitous peaks?

There's a melodic line, but sometimes the notes seem placed at random, like rocks in a garden, or an act of nature, and with a pulse or heartbeat. Each note's variable, so the listener's mind slows down to pay due attention to each one, and, like good jazz, you're continually surprised to find where it's going next. Just like life. (There are several masters, Asian and Western, worth hearing. Tony Scott, the first American to record jazz in Japan, made a milestone recording in Tokyo in 1964, *Music for Zen Meditation*, substituting clarinet for shakuhachi, ushering in the New Age music genre. It's a real treat.)

Country 'n' Eastern, Soundtracks, and Other Joys

Western music has its fair share of Dharma ditties and such. I nominate Bach's "Pasacaglia and Fugue in C minor." Its tune is in the bass line, a cosmic cycle, and rather than emphasize melody (solo, ego) on top of that, it selflessly interweaves harmony and melody in continual meditation.

Have you heard of "country 'n' eastern"? It's country 'n' western with Eastern influences. For example, The Flatlanders from Lubbock, Texas, is composed of angelic tenor Jimmy Dale Gilmore, ex-circus rouster Joe Ely, and—my flat-footed favorite—Butch Hancock, composer of such mindful ditties as "My Mind's Got a Mind of Its Own," and "Just a Wave, Not the Ocean,."

To expand your horizons, I heartily recommend two more composer-musicians who've done double-duty with soundtracks: Kitaro and Philip Glass. Shelved under "New Age" somewhere between Enya and Yanni (say those two names together fast, three times), Japanese composer-musician Kitaro (meaning "Man of Many Joys") interweaves traditional Eastern instruments with electronic synthesizers in ever-unfolding soundscapes to heartily, mindfully hum along to.

Philip Glass plays with minimalist patterns made out of small, repeated fragments. He's described his musical composition and meditation like this: laying down a foundation, paying attention, putting in effort, and having the patience to repeat the same exercise over and over until you become the object of your attention.

So listen and you shall hear. Sing in the shower. Join a choir or a recitation sangha. Serenade the spheres. Stay tuned! Meanwhile, we turn next to the most totally resonant of art forms, one whose very nature mirrors consciousness ....

 Along the Path _____

> Lyrics with Buddhist overtones, intended or otherwise, include: Roy Ayers' "Life is Just a Moment," the Beastie Boys' "Bodhisattva Vow," Leonard Cohen's "Here It Is" and "Love Itself," Donovan's "The Evernow" and "The Way" (from *Sutras*), Ira Gershwin's "I've Got Plenty of Nothing," Butch Hancock's "Give Them Water," Robert Hunter's "Eyes of the World," k.d. lang's "Craving," John Lennon's "Imagine" and "Tomorrow Never Knows," Joni Mitchell's "Both Sides Now," Natalie Merchant's "Giving Up Everything," Alanis Morissette's "All I Really Want" and "Thank U," REM's "Everybody Hurts," Van Morrison's "Enlightenment," and Neil Young's "When God Made Me."

Mind Mirror: Buddha at the Movies

Looking back, the most popular art form the twentieth century bequeathed to posterity was ... movies! As mystic movie maven and filmmaker Stephen Simon says, "Movies are the most electrifying communications medium ever devised and the natural conduit for inspiring ourselves to look into the eternal issues of who we are and why we are here." So, of course, this has its Buddhist lights, and we can break that down two ways: film itself as Buddhist, and Buddhist films.

Now Playing: Film as Buddhist

Whatever's playing, I always enjoy the hush that settles in when the lights dim before the show. The sheer act of gathering together with fellow villagers for some storytelling around a campfire (the flickering lights and shadows on a movie screen) has primal roots, deep within the sacred. And film can, in and of itself, provide an apt model for our mundane consciousness—conscious *of* something, but what? Illusion, quite often. Plato once described the unexamined life in terms akin to sitting in a theater never aware of the projection booth where the images come from; instead, we take what we're seeing for reality. So it is, the Buddha shows, with the projections of our own minds, which we take as the reality of our experience.

This Is

Any permanent, substantial identity is a dramatic fiction. In ancient Greek theater, actors wore big masks called **persona,** the origin of our word *person.* In the Zen-influenced dance-theater called **Noh,** wooden masks even change expressions as the wearer shows them in different angles and shades of lighting.

Hear and Now

"… the metaphor of movie for life is an interesting one. The frames go by so quickly that we retain the illusion of continuity and are distracted from the light that shines steadily through each frame."

—Robert Aitken Roshi

"… If you want to enjoy the movie, you should know that it is the combination of film and light and white screen, and that the most important thing is to have a plain, white screen."

—Shunryu Suzuki Roshi, *Our Everyday Life Is Like a Movie*

There's a visual metaphor in Buddha's motto: "Come and see!" Vipassana: clear seeing into the nature of things. Burmese Vipassana master Sayadaw U Pandita notes that when we watch a movie, the process can be like Insight Meditation. Each has four phases: (1) appearance of object, (2) directing of attention, (3) close observation, and (4) understanding.

In Insight Meditation, (1) we focus attention on our breath, which leads to (2) discovering the rising and falling of the abdomen, followed by (3) noting the process and our feelings, and then (4) discovering special characteristics and how they actually behave, not how we think they do.

Watching a movie, (1) we focus attention on the screen, which leads to (2) appearance of characters and scenes, followed by (3) making out what's happening by observing carefully, and then (4) discovering the plot and appreciating the movie.

Cinema provides another metaphor for reality's Eternal Now. I remember once sitting behind a five-year-old and an adult at a matinee, and every 10 minutes or so the kid would ask the adult, "What's happening now?" The adult would answer, "Now they're getting to know each other." Or "Now they're going to get married." Or "Now they're on their honeymoon." If you think about it, every moment in a movie is (like life) always about "now." It is continuous present tense (even flashbacks and flashforwards). And this eternal nowness of time can be elastic: 10 minutes compressed into 3, or 3 stretched out into 10 (reminiscent of quite a few sitting meditations I've had).

Our minds are similarly elastic. A good analogy is seen in how movies are always breaking the ancient Aristotelian Unity of Time and Place (everything unfolding on stage in linear "real time," 1–2–3, all in one spot). A film opens space out like a jigsaw puzzle, constantly changing locations and points of view. So when we're engaged by film's space-without-particular-locality, we're also experiencing the limitless possibility of emptiness, and of our own mind, felt everywhere but nowhere to be seen.

Fiction films are usually a neatly patterned karma tale. For an interesting meditation sometime, buy a ticket to a movie you otherwise don't care about and walk in on the middle (at a multiplex this is easy to do). Then stay for the beginning up until you walked in. You'll see how everything that happened in the second half was a result of the characters' actions in the first half. (You can also try this at home, fast-forwarding into the middle, starting from there, then returning to the beginning.) See karma, study dharma.

Here's another meditation. Watch actors in group scenes when they're not saying or doing anything, and notice how they're compassionately making the other actors look good. Movies can nourish our own compassion. Typically, we hope it all turns out okay, and so identify beyond ourselves (which is what compassion means, feeling with), identifying with the other characters. And without compassion, we'd be aware we're sitting in our chairs the entire time. This is a secret part of the fun of watching movies: sitting there in our jeans and T-shirt, and at the same time being superstars, 33-feet tall, sliding back and forth between the two realms. ("*Great kiss!* Please pass the popcorn.")

If we stop to think about this further, we see that when we're engrossed in a movie, our ability to exchange self with others (tonglen) compassionately reveals the basic insubstantiality of self. It's all conditional. Late in life, Sir Laurence Olivier confessed acting didn't teach him to "get in touch with himself"; rather, it taught him how he had no idea who he was, really, having realized his heart's potential for being so many different people. Drama teaches that change of circumstances can change who we thought we were, slowly or in a flash. Like they say, there but for fortune go you or I.

Yet what film can ever duplicate what one can see on one's own mind screen as when settled on a cushion? This is particularly true in a visualization meditation (and whose intrinsic emptiness can be likened to a blank movie screen), and especially so in Tibetan Buddhism's delineating stages of vision, from the grasping of looking to the "naked awareness" of pure seeing. Cinema's painting with light pales beside the recognition that we are bodies of light, interbeaming and intergleaming on the luminous mandala of Indra's infinite net of light.

Is *Gone with the Wind* About Impermanence?: Buddhist Films

There isn't an Oscar for Spiritual Cinema, at least not yet. Themes include the nature of reality and identity and time, mythic quests, and the power of love. Within this unofficial genre, there are Buddhist films a-plenty, as testified to by the International Buddhist Film Festival. Their first call for entries in 2003 pulled in 300 films, from around the planet.

My personal all-time favorite is titled *Why Has Bodhidharma Left for the East?*, a koan that is asking, in effect, "What is the meaning of Buddhism (or life)?" "Is it worthwhile?" The film's not about Zen so much as it's about a Zen environment, on a remote Korean mountain. Like Zen, it's not descriptive but experiential, leaving the viewer to work on it. The *2001* of Zen Cinema, its decidedly non-Hollywood plot has very loose basis in a series of ten twelfth-century Zen poems with woodblocks, known as the Ox Herding Pictures. It took producer-writer-director-editor Young-kyun Bae seven years to craft this intimate spiritual epic, and it's deservedly made it to many an All-Time Top lists. The Director's Deluxe DVD was issued in 2007. G. G. says "Check it out!"

Leaves from the Bodhi Tree _____

> Some films of Buddhist interest include *The Razor's Edge* (compare the 1946 and 1984 versions), *After Life* (1998), *Caravan* (aka *Himalaya*, 1999), *Jacob's Ladder* (adapted from *The Tibetan Book of the Dead*, 1990), *Beyond Rangoon* (1995), *Enlightenment Guaranteed* (2000), *Samsara* (2003), *Milarepa: Magician, Murderer, Saint* (2006). Documentaries include *10 Questions for the Dalai Lama, Amongst White Clouds, Buddha Wild, Buddha's Lost Children, Into Great Silence* (2006); *Dharma River*, and *How to Cook Your Life*, (2007).

In this frozen moment from Why Has Bodhidharma Left for the East?, *one monk is asking another whether he should stay or return to the world. Or are we seeing him really debating with himself? A picture such as this draws from the pre-cinema magic of ancient woodblock prints.*

(Photo: Courtesy of Milestone Film & Video, New Jersey)

For more Buddhist films, please visit our website, word.to/films.html. Meanwhile, we can assist your navigating the field by distinguishing grades of Buddhism. There are distinctly Buddhist films, such as *Bodhidharma*. From Bhutan, there's *The Cup* (2000), about exiled Tibetan monks obsessed with World Cup soccer, the first film made by a Buddhist lama, Khyentse Norbu, who followed his debut with *Travellers & Magicians* (2003).

In many of the films of Yasujiro Ozu (*Early Summer, The End of Summer,* and so on), Buddhism's implied rather than explicit. A character doesn't experience a climax so much as undergo a subtle change that enables him or her to appreciate the suchness of things, each scene bearing equal emphasis. (The camera is often placed at the level of the belly of an invisible witness sitting in silent meditation in the foreground.) Akira Kurosawa commanded wider world attention, as with *Rashomon* (1950), in which a Buddhist monk hears one event retold from different points of view. Other spiritual classics from his lens include *Ikiru* (1953) and *Dersu Uzala* (1975).

Hollywood films can have unintended oblique Buddhist themes, such as *It's a Wonderful Life,* in which we see what life would be like if one single person hadn't lived, revealing how each person affects everyone else. In the cult classic *Groundhog Day* (1993), one man relives the same day 10,000 times until he gets it right. (You might see it more than once if only to figure out at what point his compassion really awakens.) George Lucas refused to specify whether The Force referred to by Yoda in *Star Wars* stands for the Tao, the Holy Spirit, Buddha-mind, or something else, nor whether Luke Skywalker's journey represented the Buddha's. After all, the motto in Hollywood has been: "If you want to send a message, use Western Union."(*Question:* is there a trade-off between message and violence?)

There are films in which Buddhist elements pop up like weeds between cracks in concrete, such as in the 1993 biopic about Tina Turner, *What's Love Got to Do with It*. Just one line in a movie can be undeniably Buddhist, such as in *Monsters, Inc.*, when Mike says to Scully (about Boo), "Oh no!, now that you've given it a name, you'll become attached to it!" Once awakened to Dharma, you can find Buddhist elements in, say, *Casablanca* (Rick choosing selfless generosity over romantic attachment). Video, of course, speaks the language of film. Millions have seen how Lisa Simpson could celebrate both Buddhism and Christmas ("She of Little Faith"), and the slyly satirical Buddhist episode of *King of the Hill* ("Won't You Pimai, Neighbor") is as cogent in its 22 minutes as many feature-length films.

Video and digital are lowering the bar to entry into moviemaking, including Buddhist filmmaking. Perhaps one day we, too, will have a Buddhist television channel as there is in Amsterdam and Korea. (I want my B-TV!) Meanwhile, I'll just wait … on my cushion, setting my mind screen up, and inquiring into what's projected there. (Please pass the popcorn.)

The Least You Need to Know

- Everything can be an art, and an expression of an awakened mind and heart.

- Gardening can be a Buddhist activity. In fact, the first flower-arranging school was Buddhist.

- A variety of martial arts can all be traced to Buddhist origins. Athletes and sports stars, already familiar with "the Zone," are finding Buddhism can add a winning ingredient to their training.

- Traditional schools of Buddhism have particular brands of music associated with meditation, such as shakuhachi and chanting. In the West, Buddhist influence can be heard in rock, country, and soundtracks.

- Film has analogies to Buddhist concepts, through such physical components as its projection and blank screen, and through its aesthetics, such as its eternal present tense. Besides film itself, there are also numerous films with Buddhist insights.

19

Awakening Ways of Seeing and Being: Dharma Art

In This Chapter

◆ Dharma Art

◆ Buddhist literature (reading and writing)

◆ Visual arts (contemplation and creation)

◆ Art as life, life is art

We've noted the emergence of Eastern spirituality in the West as one of the most important events of our century. It's plain to see in the arts. While religion and spirituality change incrementally, culture (for all its rare, timeless masterpieces) changes relatively swiftly, and so makes a good barometer. Seeing Buddhism adapting to our culture, we also see our culture adopting new influences. In so doing, we might deepen our appreciation of both Buddhism and art, as one.

Buddhism is an art (upaya), an art of awakening, wherever that awakening might occur, which is to say throughout all of life. Seen as Dharma, life is like a big library of teachings on awakening, where everything's free (in both senses of the word). Right down the street, The Buddha's Museum of

Art is always completely open for interpretation, 24/7, and is, in fact, a museum without walls. Isn't it marvelous? It all takes place within your heart.

Dharma Art: Opening the Eye of the Heart

When we use pictures and words, are we communicating? In this chapter, we'll track the traceless Way of the Dharma in pictorial and literary art—and also in life itself, art and poetry signifying not only picture and text, but also the indefinable heart of life and its human expression. We're not collecting images for a scrapbook to keep in a drawer. No, our goal is practical: to further develop our sense, begun in the previous chapter, of the art of awareness.

What is art? Consider the first recorded imagery, from the Upper Paleolithic: paintings of animals on cave walls and men and women with bird masks and bison heads, all expressing some deep transpersonal relationship with the universe. Quite possibly our Cro Magnon arts were part of proto-shamanistic ritual, culture and spirituality interfused from the very first.

From these back walls of our common past, selfless imaginative arts continued along in a long, unbroken continuity until the Renaissance in the West brought a shift of emphasis, focused upon the individual, the self. Flash forward to America, whose self-hood was founded on Puritanism and Calvinism, which purged pictures from the church and spread that austerity to everyday life. Then with the transformation of technology base came standardization and mass media. The telegraph, for example, was dedicated to messages of commercial or military matters rather than anything like devotional poetry, which withered away like a faded blossom. (*Dit-dot-dot dash* …)

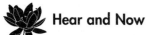

Hear and Now

"Zen students understand that the conclusion of Zen is daily life; but there is one more stage—that is Art."

—Sokei-an (Sasaki Soshin, 1892–1945)

Today, we're witnessing a revival of the spiritual in art—Renaissance II, perhaps. Just as the Renaissance drew upon classical sources from Greek and Latin, so, too, is our era being fertilized by classical Chinese- and Sanskrit-based cultures. To consider how many core trends of Modernism are indebted to Eastern spirituality, here are four examples: (1) emphasis on a decentered subject (nonself) and the environmental space surrounding, (2) meaning ("truth") giving way to a concern for construction (the composite nature of all things) and deconstruction, (3) subjective impression as well as objective expression (nondual awareness), and (4) movement away from isolation and the separate self (self-expression) and toward interrelation and process over product and fixity. Now, there's even art with no tangible, solid, permanent subject or object, by artists working purely with light, such as Richard Irwin and James Turrell. In all this, we can not only see how much of a Buddhist presence there is within art since Modernism, but also how much art itself has taken to the Way (whether or not it proclaims formal vows). Again, there are grades, and to the degree that art expresses and facilitates awakening, we can speak of the general influence of Dharma Art, which is in the air. Asian art scholar Ananda K. Coomaraswamy (1977–1947) suggests three working criteria to mindfully appreciate contemporary spiritual art:

1. Phenomenal (objective/outside world; "no ideas but in things")

2. Mental/Imaginative (subjective/inner world; "only the imagination is real")

3. Consciousness (spirit/mind; "everything is Buddha")

The first might be the painting of grapes so lifelike a bird might peck at them. The second might be a surreal or semi-abstract painting, such as Man Ray's image of gigantic red lips, floating above the horizon, formed of clouds at sunset. Marrying the two, you might get something seemingly ordinary, like the extraordinary birds of Morris Graves.

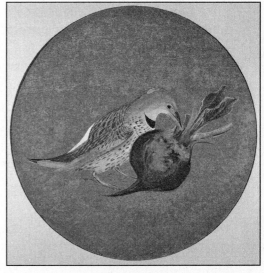

The painter uses a bird to speak for himself, and so for us. In the first figure, the bird's attention is riveted on the snail shell. (Anybody home inside?) In the second figure, seeker and sought are close together, of similar substance and shape as well as size. Neither drawn from life nor symbolic, there's nothing beyond the bird, beyond the snail, beyond the beet. Just this endless life, and thus, just so.

(Morris Graves. Bird and Snail, *sumi-e, 1950;* Bird and Beet, *pastel, 1979; Private collections.)*

Art is everywhere, like space or light or Buddha nature—but sometimes we need the Other-power of art's purified realm to remind us to look around (and within). We see life differently after looking through art's frame (or pages). In sharpening our perceptions, we refine our awareness. When we regard a painting or read a novel, our self-centered view loosens and broadens. Like Other-power, art can call us from our sense of a bounded, limited life to a purified realm. (Logic can only go from A to B, but imagination goes everywhere.) In so doing, art invites us to be on more intimate terms with our life. No mere spectator sport, such art calls us to personally seek its resonance within ourselves, merging audience and creator as one, in selfless, appreciative participation. Art and Dharma are both potentially a mindful mirror of the origin, workings, and ultimate experience of our own awakening consciousness. Such is the door of Dharma Art … and it's wide-open to your mere touch.

Life Is an Open Book, with Your Name on the Cover

To express the inexpressible is both completely impossible and utterly necessary. Words and The Wordless aren't mutually exclusive. Yes, Buddhism goes beyond words' inherent dualism, but it doesn't set up another dualism in its place, such as silence versus speech. Words have their place as skillful means, a form of practice, be it as mantra, koan, or "Please pass the salt." For example, we've dispelled the misconception that Zen, with its a-logical koans and silent illumination, is anti-literate. In traditional Zen, one commemorates a stage of awareness or enlightenment with a short poem, one's own or lines by another. Dharma Art encompasses mindful reading and empowering ways of writing. Whether you're reading or writing in this open book, it's always Page One … a blank journal … sacred text.

Some Picks for a Buddhist Reading Group: From Sutra to Haiku

The Dharma is potentially in any book. The obvious Square One to begin: books of Dharma teachings. Buddhist liturgy can reward as both practice and as literature. (In Korea, textual Dharma study is its own school of practice.) A life of the Buddha is a great start. Reading Theravada sutras, we get a picture of the Buddha as a real person. The *Heart Sutra* is so short, it can decorate the side of a teacup in Chinese, in its entirety; yet it inspires dozens of commentaries. (*Try this:* after studying this sutra for yourself, copy it out in your own handwriting on one sheet of paper, to post on a wall and contemplate.) The *Avatamsaka Sutra*, on the other hand, takes up three thick, heavy volumes. Scholar D. T. Suzuki is not sparing in his praise: "It is really the consummation of Buddhist thought, Buddhist sentiment, and Buddhist experience. To my mind, no religious literature in the world can ever approach the grandeur of conception, the depth of feeling, and the gigantic scale of composition, as attained by this sutra." More accessible, but no less inspired, is the Pure Land *Visualization Sutra*. Some texts, such as *The Way of Abiding* by Longchen Rabjam, practically read themselves. Zen's koan collections (*Gateless Gate*, for instance) and Tibet's *Lives of the Mahasiddhis* make for great summer reading or winter reading to curl up with (whose study can also be a matter of life and death). With his characteristic sharp wit and wise heart, Robert Aitken has written his own Zen tales, *Zen Master Raven*, with the talking animals common to both the Jataka tales and Native American storytelling.

Buddhism might seem bereft of romantic love, compared to such legendary couples as Krishna and Radha, Abelard and Heloise, Muhammad and Khadijah, Majnun and Layla, and Solomon and Sheba. Yet the world's first novel, *The Tale of Genji*, is an epic of intertwining tales of love and romance, and friendship and family, and was written by an eleventh-century Buddhist, Lady Murasaki Shikibu. So just because Buddhism invites us to look at ourselves without our storyline, it doesn't mean it doesn't appreciate a good tale. (In a curious update, Jakucho Setouchi, the twentieth-century Buddhist nun who translated *Genji* into modern Japanese, wrote *Tomorrow's Rainbow*, a young adult romance that rights a moral flaw she detected in *Genji*, publishing her first edition in 2008 … as a cell-phone novel.)

Like Buddhism itself, Buddhist fiction is emerging into its own in the West relatively recently. Early twentieth-century representations of Buddhism in fiction include Rudyard Kipling's *Kim* and Hermann Hesse's *Siddhartha*. Mid-century, Jack Kerouac followed *On the Road*'s overnight success with *Dharma Bums*. Soon after, J.D. Salinger published Hindu-Buddhist influenced *Franny and Zooey* and *Seymour, An Introduction*. A couple generations later, you can sample the diversity of contemporary Buddhist fiction in English from such anthologies as *Nixon Under the Bodhi Tree*, edited by Kate Wheeler, and *You Are Not Here*, edited by Keith Katchtik. Novelist George Saunders says fiction can be a way to access Buddhist teachings obliquely: "It's a way of thinking without thinking."

Besides the novel, other literary genres enjoy the Buddha Way. From H. D. Thoreau to Peter Mattheissen and Gretel Ehrlich, American naturalists have articulated the Dharma in such vivid, vital prose as *Cloud Forest*, *Snow Leopard*, *This Cold Heaven*, and *The Future of Ice*. Buddhist children's books naturally emerged upon the scene when so many boomer Buddhists began becoming parents; the first "prize" (a Caldecott Honor) went to Jon J. Muth's *Zen Shorts* parables. There are now Buddhist detective novels (a.k.a. mysteries), such as John Burdett's *Bangkok* series, Eliot Pattison's Tibetan series, and Jamyang Norbu's *Sherlock Holmes: The Missing Years* (a.k.a. *The Mandala of Sherlock Holmes*). Tsai Chih-chung with Brian Bruya brilliantly envision Zen koans and mondo as cartoons (like seeing a movie instead of reading the script) in *Wisdom of Zen* and *Zen Speaks,* and Osamu Tezuka retells the life of the Buddha as an epic eight-volume Japanese graphic novel (*manga*).

Along the Path

Contemporary American poets with affinities for Buddhism include Antler, David Budbill, Jim Cohn, Diane di Prima, Norman Fischer, Allen Ginsberg, John Giorno, Susan Griffin, Sam Hamill, Steve Hirsch, Jane Hirshfield, Lawson Fusao Inada, Robert Kelly, Joanne Kyger, Russell Leong, Louise Landes Levi, Peter Levitt, Jackson Mac Low, Michael McClure, Shiv Mirabito Denise Newman, George Quasha, Kenneth Rexroth, Albert Saijo, Leslie Scalapino, Andrew Schelling, giovanni singleton, Gary Snyder, Chase Twichell, Anne Waldman, Lew Welch, Philip Whalen, and David Whyte.

The rise of Ch'an (Zen) in China coincided with the heights of T'ang Dynasty poetry. Poetry, in and of itself, is the art of sacred speech, as seen in the Chinese word for *poetry*, literally meaning "temple of words." After all, didn't the Prophets, Jesus, Mohammed, and the Buddha all speak in pure poetry? (Not meant to be read the same way you would a cereal carton or newspaper.) This is immediately evident when reading the Buddha's *Dhammapada* (Way of the Dharma), written in verse. In our own time, a renaissance of spiritual, sacred, and devotional poetry is thriving (just think of Rumi, eleventh-century Sufi mystic, having become America's most popular poet for a decade)—and it has reflected strong Buddhist influences since the 1950s.

Of all genres of poetry, the most popular on the planet in the twenty-first century is the Buddhist format known as *haiku,* appealing even to those who don't otherwise "get" poetry. With origins in Japan (and thus Pure Land and Zen, as well as Shinto), its evolution into a world phenomenon parallels that of Buddhism, as each country adopts and adapts it as a native practice. A haiku lover might detect the influence of three primary streams intertwining in this growing practice: traditional haiku (Basho, Buson, Issa, et al.), contemporary haiku (local and international), and haiku by … kids. Because haiku really operate at the level of childmind, kids naturally write the best haiku of all. As we'll see next, haiku is a prime example of the democratic spirit of Buddhism: everyone has buddha nature; everyone can write haiku.

This Is _____

Haiku is a breezy, delicate, miniature impressionist sketch in words ("*Islands … shattered bits in the summer sea*"). An art of indirection, it juxtaposes two images, evoking a selfless moment for the reader to feel ("*A flash of lightning … and the jagged screech of a heron, flying through the dark*"). Haiku embody suchness ("*In the dark forest, a berry drops … Splash!*"). (Samples by Basho.)

Note for a Buddhist Writing Group: Empowering Practice

Writing and reading have an interdependent relationship. Like sides of the same coin, there's no me without you. As with Buddha nature, no special skill is required. To read, you don't have to be a Reader; to write, you don't have to be a Writer. To simply make a shopping list is to be a writer—and to write is to participate in the lineage of the most ancient of human technologies. Now, shopping lists aren't necessarily verse (what rhymes with orange?), but in the Complete Idiot's Guide School of Writing, even one word can be a poem. (Here's Cor Van den Heuvel one-word haiku: *Tundra*.) Words are Buddhas, too—which brings us back to haiku. Anyone can haiku.

Try this: Visit a spot of nature, as a "haiku hike." Bring a pocket notebook and pencil. See how many haiku you can write, on the spot. Jot down only short notes (if necessary), to go back over later. If with a group, share the haiku afterward. Contemplate Buddhist themes in your haiku (such as impermanence, interconnectedness, selflessness, compassion, suchness, and "Form no different than emptiness; emptiness no different than form").

To keep you on your toes, here are some haiku training tips. Be open and receptive to any unrepeatable haiku moments you might notice (notice what you notice). Say what you see. Be vivid (keep to "suchness"). Keep it simple. See how many words you can let go of. See the two elements in the situation and pare it all down to a short sentence, of seventeen syllables or less. See, too, if you can keep "I" out of the picture. Evoke a mood of selflessness. Leave it open for the reader to discover. (Show, don't tell.)

Haiku are the epitome of Dharma Art: spontaneous bells of mindfulness returning you to the wonderful present moment, opportunities to read the world as a text illustrating Buddhist truths about your own life, and empowerments for enriching contemplative practice. You can do this! Haiku can be very empowering. You don't have to even think about being a "writer" (just like you don't have to *be* "Buddhist"). Amateurs welcome! Haiku *are* beginner's mind. Over time, you might notice at least one haiku a day, every day: the trick then is to be mindful, stop, and note it. As you can see, it's a very mindful practice. Everyday mind is Buddha mind.

Whether I teach meditation or writing, the basics are often the same. "No one can teach this," I say. "It's about showing up, and being present when you show up." "It's easier to do it on a sunny day, than a rainy day: that dailyness! Applying the seat of the pants to the seat of the cushion/chair." Continual beginner's mind.

Everyone's a Buddha, whatever the school. Everyone's a writer, whatever the genre. Anyone can join the unofficial Buddhist School of Writing (a university that's the whole universe). To fully practice and enjoy its dharma, you might consider transforming the isolation of the craft by joining or forming a writing sangha. Here's a recipe for mindful writing in community, evolved over a decade of practice, by a group of veterans led by novelist Maxine Hong Kingston:

10 to 11 A.M.	Bowing in and meditation
11 A.M. to 1 P.M.	Writing in community
1 to 2 P.M.	Mindful lunch
2 to 3:30 P.M.	Reading our work aloud (and deep listening)
3:30 to 4 P.M.	Walking meditation
4 to 5 P.M.	Responses (loving speech)

A circle is the basic seating arrangement. A candle in the center of the group, beside a Buddha and some flowers, is optional. Designate a leader and a bell-minder: the leader introduces and facilitates the various activities of the retreat, and the bell-minder sounds a bell to mark them.

 Hear and Now _____

"Look at people! Remember your high school teacher told you to make eye contact? It means you're being sensitive to other people. It's caring about how words go out and back. Not watching is protecting yourself from intimacy, and criticism.

"Reading aloud is a good editing process. You'll feel if it's not comfortable in your mouth, or if rhythms are off. You'll hear it."

—Maxine Hong Kingston, leading a mindfulness writing sangha

Marrying the practices of writing and of mindfulness can result in something often resembling spontaneous Zen calligraphy, with words. (Many already know this process firsthand through keeping a journal, a good way of taming monkey mind, connecting with big sky mind, and opening the heart.) Millions of people are already familiar with the union of Zen and writing (Zen writing) first introduced in *Writing Down the Bones* by Natalie Goldberg. *Try this:* put pencil or pen to paper for ten minutes. Don't stop. Don't take your hand off the page. Ready? Go!

Opening the Eye in the Heart of the Heart

There's a Zen koan by Bodhidharma: "Show me your mind." (Where is this mind we want to calm? *What is it?*) And, *aha!*, we realize, like space, it's invisible, imageless, boundless. So how can anyone *show* buddha mind to anyone else? Likewise, images of the Buddha are only a representation of an experience (ours, his, alike; the person bowing to a Buddha and the image of the buddha bowed to are equally empty). Yet in Buddhism, there's visual art equal to Rembrandt and da Vinci, as mind-opening and heart-opening as it is eye-opening. Let's consider some examples from different schools.

Two studies in suchness, is-ness. On the left, a classic Chinese Zen brush painting of persimmons, each with its own distinct and unique shape, texture, and sheen. Each a buddha, placed just so. Each as fresh today as when painted. On the right, hotdogs by a leading contemporary American painter (familiar with the persimmons), each set in its bun with its own flair. Each perfect thus. The background in each: without horizon, empty. And, persimmon or hotdog, so subtly interdependent, it's hard to choose just one, seeing their relationship as well. (The persimmon that's not in a row, for example, calls attention to the poses of the other five.)

(Mu Ch'i, Six Persimmons [1269], ink on paper, 14 inches × 15 inches, Daitokuji, Kyoto. Wayne Thiebaud, Five Hot Dogs [1961], oil on canvas. 18 inches × 24 Inches, private collection, Copyright Wayne Thiebaud/Licensed by VAGA [New York, New York].)

Drawing Attention: Drawing the Buddha

Previously, we juxtaposed Tibetan chanting and Zen flute. The styles of the two cultures are an interesting contrast. The Zen practitioner wears black and gray so as not to distract. The temples are minimalist to allow the mind to relate to vast space. A simple bowl of miso soup might be accented by just one slice of scallion. Tibetans wear bright robes and cook spicy Himalayan meals. Their decorative sense tends toward the baroque, a sensual treat everywhere you look.

The West is only recently getting up to speed with the visual arts of Tibet, Mongolia, and Bhutan. I've included in these pages two reproductions of the amazing life-size bronzes by Mongolian master Zanzabazar. You can also get a taste of devotional tantric painting and drawing through the bell and vajra, and Manjushri, in Chapter 14. Have you compared the image of the Russian Christ and the Tibetan Buddha in our chapter on interfaith? They're not graven idols; rather, they're divinely inspired—two sides of the same selfless coin, each image fuses pristine, impeccable, analytical accuracy with rich, vivid, indelible, universal presence. Such freedom within strict guidelines hearkens back to pre-Renaissance arts in the West, when cathedrals and icons were completely anonymous works of devotion. As the West learns to appreciate such sacred imagery, Eastern and now Western teachers are training new generations of students in this art. British artist and teacher Andrew Weber compares drawing the Buddha to drafting a "spiritual map."

One more remarkable aspect of Tibetan art is worthy of mention. Museums now commission Tibetan monks to construct on their premises such painstakingly meticulous mandalas as the *Wheel of Time* (*Kalachakra*) … out of colored sand! Given how museums are repositories of permanence, everything with its neat descriptive tag, it's ironic that, in the end, the monks take the mandala outdoors and ceremoniously scatter their completed masterpieces to the elements, in affirmation of the interpenetration and impermanence of all things.

The Way of the Brush: Stroke by Stroke

Toward another side of the hall, as it were, is the ink-wash art of the brush. Here viewing becomes creative as the work invites our eye to imagine our own hand making its clearly gestural brush strokes. Looking at classical examples, you might remark, too, at how whole areas of canvas are left unpainted. They're not unfinished. What the West calls negative space becomes positive in the East. Look again at the landscape of the fishing village in our chapter on Zen. The unpainted areas evoke empty sky, and flowing river. (We can sense twilight mist in the paler grays, as boats and birds find homes for the night.) The Zen painter often uses space to evoke awakened mind (sunyata). (How do you show someone the sheen of the full moon, or of the enlightened mind, or of the awakened heart?) Our Bodhidharma, seen from behind, is made of the same stuff as the wall he faces: utterly blank, empty of any concept. (Don't know!)

This works like the pause in haiku between two images, or like a radio drama, relying on the audience's imagination to fill in. Michelangelo was asked, "How did you create David? He replied, "I took a block of marble and chipped away everything that wasn't David." Lao-tzu said a potter can't make a bowl from clay without empty space. (Thus, you must have space inside yourself, in order for anything to take place, such as peace.) As in rock gardens, haiku, and Zen itself, the space as well as the thing being pointed at must be intuited within your own heart.

Curiously, portrait here can become landscape, and vice versa. Bodhidharma can resemble a monumental mountain, a force of nature, appropriate to his towering place in Zen history. A river flowing through glowing hills can evoke human in-scape, rendering the invisible landscape of the heart-mind's lofty peaks and deep valleys, twists and turns. Imagine a landscape becoming a mental soundscape, letting your gaze meander and unfold the way you'd listen to music. Awakening your mind without fixing it anywhere, the Dharma artist will guide your awareness to the infinite and eternal in the immediate present, the picture right before your eyes. Here, the essence of the painter, the natural object, and the viewer become one mind. So a seemingly plain picture of a bird, or persimmons, can be taken on different levels: literal, figurative, and ultimate.

Consider, too, the very tools of the craft: rough brush dipped in hand-ground ink applied to highly sensitive, porous paper. When you see art students in a museum, copying a work in their sketchbook, they use pencil or pen, but seldom brush. That is, they're copying lines and forms, but, as Zen brush master Kazuaki Tanahashi puts it, "When you copy an Oriental piece of art, you attempt to copy the process—the posture, the way of holding the brush, the order of strokes, the way of putting pressure on paper, the brush moving in air, the breathing, feeling, and thinking."

Zen brush merges training and craft with spontaneity and awakened heart-mind. The Zen artist becomes one with her or his subject matter (be it a mountain, a river, or a mere circle), its essence poised on the tip of the brush. (Hesitate and the ink will blot and spread on the extremely fibrous paper.) With blank mind, facing a blank page, the artist takes the leap—like the total *whoosh!* of a samurai sword—and *Aha!* a single word, a single image, a single circle can be an unpremeditated discovery. (Like the first sip of tea. Like a koan's answer.) A red seal is an afterthought, the entire work being itself signature, an expression of the artist's unique mastery of selflessness.

Hear and Now

"In the Oriental calligraphic tradition, you are not supposed to touch up or white out a trace of your brush. Every brush stroke must be decisive; there is no going back. It's just like life. If each moment is our entire life, how dare we kill time? If each stroke is our entire breath, how dare we correct it?"

—Kazuaki Tanahashi, *Brush Mind*

The East Asian words thus brushed in our book are interesting in this light in that they're often pictures ("heart" as a picture of a heart). So reading involves seeing as a direct means of making meaning, rather than through deciphering letters representing abstract sounds (language made visible, words become art). And a reverse angle holds. Viewing classical Chinese and Japanese brush art, our seeing becomes a reading of the moment's brush mind, the *presence* in the present moment.

pine needling

Paul Reps, picture poem, from Sit In: What It Is Like *[Zen Center Press, 1975]*
Kazuaki Tanahashi, one-stroke painting, from Brush Mind *[Parallax Press, 1990].)*

Many of the words in brush calligraphy in this book were made for us by Kazuaki Tanahashi, who also made the *enso* (his signature circular stroke). Some of the backstory is interesting. Following a 15-year hiatus from making art, a friend gave Kaz some handmade cotton paper. "One day," he recalls, "without any definite intention, I drew a straight horizontal line across the center of a piece of paper. At the moment the brush would have moved to another stroke, something stopped me from adding anything. I had a feeling that what I wanted to express was all there—in the single line and in the space above and below. So I put down the brush.... As a calligrapher, I seemed to be stuck at stroke one."

Also capping off this section is a "picture poem" by an earlier Dharma Art pioneer, Paul Reps (1895–1990). Besides being America's first haiku poet, he was also a master of a Dharma Art called *zenga*. As we can see, picking up a brush, there's no difference between writing, calligraphy, and drawing. Fingers, hand, eye, heart, and mind go hand-in-hand in sheer intimacy, completely unselfconscious. We, too, enjoy how the artist enjoyed participating in the spontaneous expression of enlightenment. This very brush and hand are the body and mind of the whole universe. (*Next question:* might the art of the Zen brush hold true for brushing ... your teeth?!)

Art as Life: Life Is Art

In meditation, you can discover the source of all art. The wellspring of a fountain of images is present within you. Still, art's presence in our landscape is a sacred space (pure land). Dharma Art reminds us Buddha Mind is everywhere. Dharma Art pioneers slyly introduced new ways for the potentials of art to be found everywhere; in the every day. Maverick Allan Kaprow (1927–2006), who founded the art of the *happening* in 1957, proclaimed, "Not satisfied with the suggestion through paint of our other senses, we shall utilize the specific substances of sight, sound, movement, people, odors, touch. Objects of every sort are materials for the new art: paint, chairs, food, electric and neon lights, smoke, water, old socks, a dog, movies, a thousand other things which will be discovered ..." (Amen.) Here's one of twentieth-century art's still under-recognized gifts to us all. For everyone familiar with, say, Picasso, how many have heard of Marcel Duchamp, who went beyond "retinal art," to the mind behind the retina? In a characteristically French double negative, he said, "The only thing that is not art is inattention." Thus, he also announced, "The viewer makes it Art." So in 1913 he took a bicycle wheel, mounted it very neatly, upside down and free-spinning, on a white stool, and submitted it to the world as art. Thus was born a new art form, the "readymade," and with it the wheel of Dharma Art turned round to encompass life itself, as art. Rather than survey its many implications (from installation art and performance art, to digital sampling and clip art), let's zoom in on two more pivotal dharma artists, John Cage and John Daido Loori.

Soundscape Without Horizon

Smack-dab in the middle of the twentieth century, American composer John Cage invited us all to consider life as art when he premiered his concert piece entitled *4'33"* (pronounced "4 minutes, 33 seconds"). (Maybe you've heard this somewhere before?) The printed score is in three movements, and can be played by any number and combination of instruments … so long as they don't play a single note. The pianist premiering the work, David Tudor, sat down at the piano and played not one single note for precisely 4 minutes, 33 seconds. At that historic premiere, at the Maverick Concert Hall in Woodstock, New York, the back of the hall was open to the surrounding forest. During the first movement, you could hear the wind sighing through the trees. Light rain pattered on the roof during the second movement. And during the final movement, the audience whispered amongst itself, in counterpoint to the sound of other people exiting.

Of course, no two performances are alike. Furthermore, once it's performed, it never ceases. A soundscape without limit. The sound of nonself, the sound of silence; the sound of nonself. Ever now. Artists were no longer required to create timeless masterpieces. (Think of Rodin's *Thinker*, straining every muscle.) What a relief! Critics, grasping for labels, called this new approach "formless." But such art is shapely because mind and life are shapely. Just like that.

Leaves from the Bodhi Tree _____

> In 1946, John Cage learned Indian musical counterpoint from Gita Sarabhai, who told him that in her country the purpose of music is "to sober and quiet the mind, thus rendering it susceptible to divine influences." He later attended D. T. Suzuki's lectures on Buddhism at Columbia University for two years. The year before composing *4'33"* he visited Harvard's new soundproof chamber and was surprised to discover he heard his nervous system (high sound) and his blood flow (low). He realized the difference between noise and sound is awareness, or intention, and spent the rest of his life creating music without personal intention, to stimulate awareness.

Cage came to see music "not as communication from the artist to an audience, but rather as an activity of sounds in which the artist found a way to let the sounds be themselves." This could then "Open the minds of the people who made them, or listened to them, to other possibilities than they had previously considered.... To widen their experience; particularly to undermine the making of value judgments."

 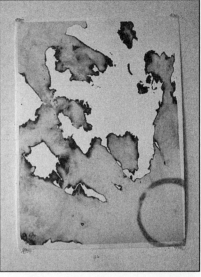

Printer Larry Hamlin with John Cage in the Crown Point Press studio, 1986. John Cage, Eninka 26, 1986. One in a series of 50 smoked paper monotypes with branding printed on gampi paper chine collé. Published by Crown Point Press. "Eninka" is Japanese for "circle, stamp, fire." These etchings were created by setting fire to newspapers, putting the fire out by running the press across them, laying a piece of special Japanese paper on top, and running that through the press. Then the paper was branded with an iron ring. (The circle echoes the Zen enso; see Chapter 12.) Utterly nonrepresentational, the work has a perfect naturalness of form, as of a pavement being painted by raindrops. Yet it was created under very controlled conditions: the number of newspapers, the duration of the fire, the placement of the ring, and the strength of its mark (its temperature) were all predetermined by tossing coins—"imitating nature in her manner of operation," as Cage liked to say, quoting Saint Thomas Aquinas.

(Photographs: Kathan Brown and Colin McRae)

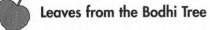 **Leaves from the Bodhi Tree**

In 1961, visitors to an art gallery were led by Yoko Ono to each piece of hers on exhibition there. For each work, she'd give them instructions. For *Smoke Painting*, for instance, the viewer was asked to burn the canvas with a cigarette and watch the smoke; the piece was finished when the canvas had turned to ashes. Many of her works are instructions, whose printed form she considers visual art, "painting to be constructed in your head," such as her *Lighting Piece, 1955: Light a match and watch till it goes out.* (The flame is never the same twice. And who watches?)

Photography: The Spirit of the Moment

With the rise of digital photography (plus framing and printing), it seems practically everyone's a photographer. I think photography may be the most widely popular "found art" practiced today, its subject invariably being "readymade." Indeed, with the emergence and widespread availability of photography in the nineteenth century, it was believed landscape and portrait painting would soon die out. The first commercially printed book of photographs (1844–1846), by William Henry Fox Talbot, bore a very telling title, *The Pencil of Nature*, as if this were life recording itself, a photograph of nature being nature's self-awareness. There's a growing number of Buddhist fine arts photographers with such vision today. Zen master John Daido Loori, for example, has scaled these heights, and come down the mountain, time after time.

Teaching, he might start his students with a koan; for instance, "Photograph a feeling of love you have for some person place or thing other than yourself and use light in such a way that light reveals the loveliness of your subject." The goal is thus to photograph something evoking that feeling, whatever and wherever it might happen to truly be. Only by proceeding with beginner's mind, with no preconceived notion of what or where that "something" might be, will the photographer discover it. Otherwise, the result will feel stilted, too, thought out, as if by an observer standing back rather than merging in intimacy. Only when a photographer feels the presence of the subject does a resonance occur between it and the photographer. Then, and only then, does the process begin. A certain relationship is discovered between object and light and eye, as fingers feel how the moment might wish to be framed. It's only once the mind has stopped moving that the picture can take itself, the camera photograph by itself, just as the brush can draw and write by itself. Next time you go out the door with a camera, you might pause and consider: can you photograph your Original Face (the face you had before your mother and father were born)? *Hint*: John Daido Loori calls his art "making love with light."

(Photograph: John Daido Loori)

The Least You Need to Know

- Dharma Art challenges perception and awakens heart and mind. Art and Buddhism cross-fertilize each other, as daily practice. Appreciation can be an act of meditation, no less than creation.

- Buddhism empowers writers as well as readers. Of numerous literary genres expressing Buddhism, haiku may be the most universal of our times.

- As art revitalizes its roots as a contemplative tradition, Eastern influences might be contributing to a second Renaissance. Modern art in the West reflects deep influences of Buddhism, such as in the opening up of the boundary between life and art.

Chapter 20

Life Within Us and Without Us: Buddhism and Science

In This Chapter

- New science reappraising old worldviews
- Fuzziness, chaos, and complexity
- Cognitive science
- Matter and mind

It's Nerdvana, for some. Of all our human endeavors, science can be one of our most powerful realms. Setting science alongside Buddhism, we can listen in on some fascinating dialogues: some world-shaking, some quite practical, and all reconfirming the wonder for which our eyes were made. Science can clarify, support, and refine our awareness in remarkable ways. Buddhism is, reciprocally, extending the reach and even the foundation and framework of science. (Of course, Buddhism is itself a science; in fact, it's a highly developed, ancient system of wisdom, transformation, and healing.) Here are some lab notes from the forefront of the science of lasting happiness. Test them out in your own life's research project.

New Western Science and Ancient Eastern Wisdom

Imagine Buddha, Einstein, Freud, and Darwin are having a conversation, and we can listen in. Well, that's partly what we're doing when we study science today, where their findings are still felt and are actively influencing each other. Buddha is bringing to the table a worldview that's extending science's grasp as well as grounding it in our human experience.

Astrophysicist Arthur Eddington (1882–1944) confessed, "Something unknown is doing we don't know what." (Verily!) With such candid beginner's mind, he also summed up science's newer approaches in 35 words or less: "We used to think that if we knew one, we knew two, because one and one are two. We are finding that we must learn a great deal more about '*and*.'" (No things but in relation.) This prompts us to begin by exploring current theory, before proceeding to recent practices.

To say a scientific revolution is underway might evoke an image of armed lab technicians in military berets seizing control of cyclotron laboratories in the name of the people. So it might be more accurate to call it a *paradigm shift*, a change in our pattern for considering reality. Was it coincidence that when science saw the universe as concentric spheres revolving around the earth, the model for society (paradigm) was a similar hierarchy, revolving around a king and his medieval court? Similarly, at the same time as Newton described atoms with fixed properties, Western democracy was describing citizens as autonomous entities with inalienable rights. So a paradigm shift is a change of foundational viewpoint (not unlike the beginning of the Eightfold Path, for many). And paradigms thus hold true for our daily lives as well as for science, so it's good to realize how deeply our basic assumptions (paradigms) color our notions of reality. (*Question:* In, on, and around what paradigms is your own life organized?)

This Is

A paradigm is a framework of ideas and tools that make up a worldview, a mind-set, an exemplar of reality. If you've only walked and then learn to ride a bike, you'll see the world in a new way. A **paradigm shift** takes time to be realized in society as a whole, affecting many walks of life as it does so.

Sometimes, we can only glimpse the shift of our era's paradigms, as we're intrinsically as caught up within them as fish within water. Just such a glimpse came in 1975 with the publication of a book by physicist and systems theorist Fritjof Capra, whose title heralded a shift of paradigm: *The Tao of Physics: An Exploration of the Parallels Between Modern Physics and Eastern Mysticism.* Elsewhere, Capra has continued Sir Eddington's "and"—seeking connections and interrelations rather than divisions and subdivisions.

Up to now, Western civilization's done a bang-up job of compartmentalizing life, reality so dissected and catalogued that our post-modern world seems quite fragmented. But now, this *mechanistic* point of view, breaking life down into parts and analyzing each separately, is giving way to a more *holistic* view that looks at how parts interrelate to form wholes and living systems (favoring *how* over *what*). As it does so, it seems to align more toward the Buddhist view. ("Everything changes; everything is connected; pay attention.")

The classic example of this turning point in science is Einstein's proposition that matter is energy, and energy is matter. It may be no coincidence that he was echoing a Buddhist principle: "form and phenomena have no unique identity beyond boundless energy; and boundless energy manifests itself to us as phenomena and form." Einstein had studied and admired the Buddha's teachings, "covering both the material and spiritual … as a meaningful unity," as he said, and thus able to "cope with modern scientific needs." It's as if scientists were finally crunching the numbers and doing the math from Professor Shakyamuni's previous findings. Similarly, Werner Heisenberg (1901–1976) discovered you can't simultaneously measure the location and direction of a subatomic particle, because the measuring tool enters into that equation. *Aha!* Interbeing in action: "this is because that is." That electron's there because I'm over here. Observation affects function. (Hence the need for Right View.)

 Hear and Now _____

"One finds in the realm of experience, essentially the same type of structure that one finds in the realm of elementary particle physics, namely a web structure, the smallest elements of which always reach out to other things and find their meaning and ground of being in these other things. Since this same type of structure is suitable both in the realm of mind and in the realm of matter, one is led to adopt it as the basis of an over-all world view."

—Henry Pierce Stapp

Newer discoveries in physics further confirm ancient Buddhist truths. For example, a hologram can create a three-dimensional mirage in midair; pretty neat! It's a sculpture made of light. Now, the really interesting thing is that if only half the negative is used, you still see the full image, just a bit dimmer. With a tiny corner, you'd still have the entire picture, in full, just dimmer still. That is, the entirety of information about the whole is distributed throughout the surface of the holographic negative. Remarkable. Any part leads to all the others and to the whole. This is the same as how any bead on Indra's Net reflects all the other beads. (A still unproven but interesting avenue of note, too, is Super-String Theory, which holds that this is but one of ten or so parallel universes. Stay tuned.)

As paradigms shift, they can affect everything from art to ego, from architecture to how you time your eggs. Here are three fascinating ideas from the changing paradigm, each with a new view of ancient Buddhist wisdom.

Paradigm Shift on Parade: Fuzzy, Chaotic, and Complex

The paradigm shift underway today includes science's basis on logic. Classical Western logic depends on Aristotle: "X" is either *A* or *B* (either/or). Something's either this or that, but not both. For example, electricity's either on or off; hence the Digital Revolution: software programming circuitry is all in ones and zeros, giving us everything from computers to cameras to cell phones. But with quantum physics' discovery of *complementarity*, science ran smack against the brick wall of Aristotelean dualism, and the limitations of its own vocabulary to describe what it saw as it broke through the previously inviolable atomic level. It was assumed that wave and particle were mutually exclusive. A test could prove light, say, is made of waves and not particles, while another test could prove light is made of particles and not waves. Physicists had to make up the word "complementarity" to discuss light being waves *and* particles (rather than call them "wavicles"; they'd never heard of the Middle Way—much less the old *Saturday Night Live* routine about New Shimmer, a new dessert topping that's also floor wax).

Hear and Now

"If we ask … whether the position of the electron remains the same, we must say 'no'; if we ask whether the electron's position changes with time, we must say 'no'; if we ask whether the electron is at rest we must say 'no'; if we ask whether it is in motion, we must say 'no.' The Buddha has given such answers … but they are not familiar answers for the tradition of seventeenth- and eighteenth-century science."

—J. Robert Oppenheimer

Toward the end of the twentieth century, a new branch of science opened shop in these grey areas, appropriately called *fuzzy logic*. Fuzzy thinking is ready for questions like "Growing a beard—or just not shaving?" Japan, at ease with the Buddha's Middle Way, initially gained about a five-year lead on the West in applying fuzzy logic. Today, fuzzy logic's programmed into cameras and thermostats, subways and nuclear power plants.

> **Along the Path** _____
>
> Buddhism trumps Aristotelean logic's either/or dualism (A / not-A) with the four-cornered logic (*tetralemma*) of its Middle Way philosophy (*Madhyamika*), as championed by Nagarjuna, who states: "Neither from itself nor from another, nor from both, nor without a cause does anything whatever anywhere arise." Thus we have (1) *A*; (2) *not-A*; (3) *both A and not-A*; and (4) *neither A nor not-A*. (Analyzing Nagarjuna's quote, you'll find he denies any and all four possibilities as being the sole truth.)

Chaos: There's Method in the Seeming Madness

Another relatively new science is *chaos theory*, studying the orderly patterns of what previously seemed merely grainy, pimply, pocky, seaweedy, wiggly, wispy, and wrinkled. (Sounds like they're studying my Uncle Melvin!) For example, a formula for plotting the seemingly random pattern of the outline of clouds matches a formula for the seemingly random pattern of coastlines. *Aha!* So how random is random, after all?

Chaos theory finds patterns in randomness, wildness … well, chaos. Such natural occurrences (cloud shapes, coastlines, mountain outlines, broccoli, ferns, and so on) can be mapped with a *fractal* (representing a fractional dimension, as between 1 and 2, or 2 and 3). This is interesting from a Middle Way perspective. What was once thought to be chaos can really be quite orderly, like the "controlled accident" of Zen: the way their gardens have an odd number of stones or trees because asymmetry looks more natural, or how a teacup has a drip in its otherwise perfect glaze. Wild splashes of paint reflect form (as my four-year-old cousin well knows); conversely, too high a degree of structure can ultimately be like goo (a warning to all control freaks).

Chaos theory upsets the paradigm of a clockwork universe of linear cause–effect relationships. Consider *the Butterfly Effect*, in which a single butterfly flapping its tiny wings in a Brazilian rain forest can cause a storm in Texas. It's possible because the essentially chaotic motion of the earth's atmosphere can amplify small disturbances into long-range, long-term behavior. A practical application is the realization that one outburst of anger, or small act of generosity, can ripple out in a whole domino effect, way beyond the seeming cause. (Everything's connected.)

A fractal can also reveal the orderly patterns of seeming chaos, in what's called their *self-similarity*. For instance, the jagged edge of just a chunk of cloud will be similar in shape to that of the entire cloud. An outline of a cauliflower bud has the same pattern as the whole veggie. This is true for mountains as well as coastlines, lightning, and ferns. Fantastic. Touch one part deeply, and you see the whole. Again, we see the web of interbeing in action.

Start with a basic fractal pattern (upper left square), inherent throughout nature, called a Mandelbrot-set. A small sector of it is enlarged (b), revealing a new sublevel, varying the underlying pattern. Isolating fragments further (shown here, six more levels) reveals an infinite series, infinitely connected, self-similar on all levels. Each is a phase of a continuum, itself embedded in a continuum, like beads on Indra's Net. As the Avatamsaka Sutra *states: "Each object in the world is not merely itself but involves every other object and, in fact, is everything else."*

(*From* The Science of Fractal Images, *Heinz-Otto Peitgen and Dietmar Saupre, editors [Springer-Verlag, 1988].)*

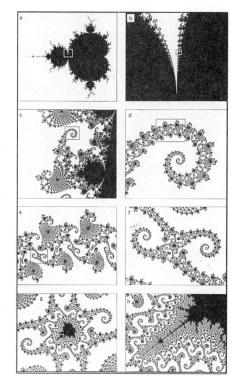

Complexity: It's Basically Simple

Based on chaos studies, *complexity theory* is a new multidisciplinary field. It observes what's variously called open systems, adaptive systems, and living systems (such as weather, traffic patterns, and ant colonies): large groups of simple individual parts in unpredictable interactions. A major finding is how, through complex interaction, components of a living system *self-organize*. Another word for this spontaneous creation of seeming order is *emergence*. It happens not despite the absence of any central plan or planner but, rather, in part because of such lack, such freedom (or sunyata, empty of any essential, intrinsic self); the "self" of self-organization (and self-similarity) is impermanent, unsubstantial, and interdependent (thus really nonself).

Because emergent behavior happens from the bottom-up, rather than top-down, it's scalable up or down (like the fractals of our illustration). The emergent illusion of reality (essence, self) depends on context, the level from which complex organization arises. Culture, for example, is the emergent behavior of social groups. A social group is an emergent property of the complex interaction of ordinary human beings. The miracle of any one human being is really a self-organization of cells … a cell being a self-organization of a complex interrelation of chemicals and conditions. (We'll return to the single cell in a bit.)

The ultimate example of a complex system is life. Matter is an emergent behavior of subatomic particles. Then some carbon comes in contact with a few simple, basic ingredients, and *Shazam!* it's alive. (Watch it evolve!) As it develops in complexity, feelings emerge. Out of feelings emerges consciousness. Besides consciousness (which can be nice), we've evolved the power of self-aware observation (nicer still). As Wes Nisker puts it so well: "Mindfulness is the opposable thumb of consciousness."

Buddhism, no different than life, can also be seen as a living system reflecting the complex interaction of simple units (Triple Gem, Four Noble Truths, Eightfold Path, and so on), dynamically evolving in interaction with each other, and with each practitioner and his or her environment, including other practitioners, and so on. We are thus complexity in action, with you at the center of the universe … interlinked with all of creation … everything and everyone else equally at the center of the universe … all moving unimpeded toward unlimited freedom. (Until you bump your toe and it's time to review the Four Noble Truths again.)

The Middle Way finds well-being (health) flowing like a fine river between the twin shores of formless chaos and firm organization. Right balance results in a complexity enabling living systems to grow and thrive with stability and flexibility, energy and adaptability. Next, we'll explore scientific inquiry that deals with interrelations of the nonphysical and the physical, such as "What is consciousness?" "Is there a mind–body connection?" and "Where'd I put my keys?"

Body Dharma: Holistic Healing

In the Buddha's day, medical knowledge was called *ayurveda*, meaning "science of life," a very viable ancient system still practiced today (Dr. Deepak Chopra being a well-known exponent, fusing it with contemporary medicine). It is said that as a prince, Siddhartha had studied Ayureveda but chose not to be a specialist. Instead, he became a general practitioner, in the widest sense. Having seen his teachings as good medicine, let's explore a little more of Dr. Buddha's approach to the process of healing as a practice. Interestingly, *medicine* and *meditation* come from the same Latin root (*mederi*, "to cure"). In Greece, around the same time as the Buddha taught, Hippocrates (the father of Western medicine) seemed in tune with the Buddha when he trusted the body's innate powers of self-healing and defined health as a harmonious interaction of factors. His fundamental oath, "Physician, heal thyself," echoes the Buddha's radical invitation for fellow seekers to investigate their findings using themselves as subjects. Yet the Buddha's methodology is in contrast with contemporary Western medicine, which favors a compartmentalized, linear, cause-and-effect model. Have a headache? Here, take some aspirin. (Of course, eventually you'll need to take three instead of two, then extra-strength, and so on.) And you might have to see a gastroenterologist (stomach doctor) if aspirin causes you a stomachache. I'm exaggerating, but what if your headache was caused by posture? (It's all interconnected.) As the Buddha pointed out, if the roots of disease aren't addressed, illness will only reoccur in innumerable forms.

As noted in Part II, the Buddha's approach is *holistic*. Such medicine (also known as alternative, complementary, or integrative) might begin by looking at underlying factors that can cause headaches, such as posture, diet, stress, and such escape valves from stress as alcohol. Moreover, it treats the *whole* person: body, spirit, and mind, as one. Thus Dr. Dean Ornish, for example, has reversed incidents of heart disease with a regimen focusing on consciousness, behavior, and diet. Generally, more and more, mindfulness meditation is becoming part of the general prescription for optimum physical health. The evidence speaks for itself (*res ipsa loquitor*). The Mindfulness-Based Stress Reduction program (MBSR), which Dr. Jon Kabat-Zinn established at the University of Maryland Medical Center in 1979, has now been adopted by over 400 health organizations, reaching tens of thousands of people. MBSR is being prescribed for all kinds of symptoms, many of which don't have easily identifiable sources, such as high blood pressure, heart disease, cancer, insomnia, infertility, premenstrual syndrome, and psoriasis, as well as depression, hyperactivity, and attention-deficit disorder. The high records of success include not only positive changes in behavior normally believed unchangeable, but also positive physical changes. Less stress *is* best.

Hear and Now

"These people have cancer, AIDS, chronic pain. If we think we can do something for them, we're in deep trouble. But if you switch frames of reference and entertain the notion that they may be able to do something for themselves if we put very powerful tools at their disposal, things shift extraordinarily."

—Jon Kabat-Zinn

Mind Science: Buddhist Psychology

As Einstein innovated our view of the objective world "out there," so did Sigmund Freud likewise transform our sense of the subjective aspects of life "in here." As without, so within. It's interesting to consider a co-emergence in the West of Buddhism and psychology, in tandem. After all, Freud and the Buddha both seem to say, "It's all in your mind." Moreover, they both offer a supportive, purified realm equipped with the tools for recognizing difficult emotions, looking into their origins, letting them be, transforming them, and letting go. Retranslating the Second Noble Truth's diagnosis of "grasping" as a "hang up," for instance, is a perfect fit between pop psychology lingo and Sanskrit. Just as a contemplative understands being *in* the world without being *of* the world, a practitioner of psychology recognizes ego (visible personality) without identifying with it, seeing how to *have* an ego without *being* one, or hanging on to one. (Just because you have a personality, doesn't mean you need to take it personally.) And though you might hear it said that anyone who takes up psychoanalysis ought to have their head examined, it's not a sign of defeat to work through still unresolved issues with a psychologist, even if one meditates.

 Along the Path

"Hold evenly suspended attention."
—Sigmund Freud
"Awaken the mind, without fixing it anywhere."
—*The Diamond Sutra*

Certainly, one of the great success stories of both holistic health and Buddhism's adoption by the West has been doctors and psychologists tapping into Buddhism's healing powers. Emotional intelligence and MBSR programs work without need of Buddhist vocabulary—nor of psychology's equally technical lexicon, for that matter. Yet there are places where the two traditions diverge as well as converge. For example, although Buddhism and psychology both teach the cessation of needless suffering, psychology would seem to stop there, while Buddhism continues on. While baseline normality's been the goal in psychology, in Buddhism that's but the beginning—grounding its view not on neuroses but rather on our boundless buddha nature, our great innate capacity for openness, trust, satisfaction, compassion, clarity, luminosity, and bliss. Emphasizing happiness rather than neuroses, this potential is now being widely explored in what's called the *positive psychology* movement.

Where psychology asks, "How can this script be changed?" the Buddha asks, "How are scripts necessary? How can consciousness itself be transformed?" A traumatic episode of the past is released when it's recognized that the self of that situation (the person abused or denied or withheld) no longer exists; yet, then what? Buddhist psychoanalyst Dr. Mark Epstein points out, "There is no true self waiting in the wings to be released." From beyond self, Ram Dass tells us, "Western psychotherapy rearranges the furniture in the room. Eastern techniques help you get out of the room."

> ### This Is
>
> *Compassion* is but one of several wholesome emotions not in psychology's dictionary. Another is **sukkha**. Just as there's no precise equivalent in our vocabulary for *dukkha*, so, too, for dukkha's opposite, a state of inner contentment and calm joy. Daniel Goleman defines *sukkha* as "a deep sense of serenity and fulfillment that arises in an exceptionally healthy mind." And through practice, sukkha (rather than a non-alienated functionality) can be the baseline of our everyday emotional life.

Lastly, oversimplification can be a mistake. It can be over-reductive to view Buddhism as just a therapeutic technique, a "self-help" tool to be manipulated for a predetermined end (like a drug). And, on the other hand, being a Buddhist isn't a license to walk away from feelings (or only note them, like a passive zombie); and becoming attached to meditation can be another form of narcissism.

Mind and Body as One: Cognitive Science

Hippocrates, Buddha, and Freud are still conferring. Meanwhile, let's next explore the Buddhist interface between body and mind. But what is mind? Can you show me your mind? (Is it your brain?) Modern Yankee poet Robert Frost once said, "The brain is a wonderful organ. It starts working the moment you get up and does not stop until you get into the office." Lately, however, we're witnessing the emergence of a very nuanced, complex, and useful sense of brain and mind working in tandem, with Buddhism often an interface, if not a paradigm, in a new multidisciplinary field known as *cognitive science*.

The current definition of *mind* echoes the Buddha: "mind is that which is aware." Some scientists now say "mind" simply represents the process of knowing, *cognition*, and isn't necessarily confined to the brain. Such mind is, as buddha nature is, potentially everywhere. A houseplant knows when it's dark and light, likes Mozart and Bach, and *minds* if it's not fed. Biologist Brian Ford notes how even a single cell shows certain intelligence. Amoebae, the so-called lowliest form of life, can pick up tiny grains of sand and cement them together to make lovely bell-shaped shells in which to dwell. Imagine, from there, how trillions of tiny cells self-organize to form the emergent behavior known as human beings. Complexity theory here is but one of many disciplines coming together like a Swiss army knife of various skill sets to give us the field of cognitive science. And the back story of its own emergence as a science is as interesting as its own research findings.

Hear and Now

> "The big breakthrough is to see mind as a process, not a thing. And the process is called cognition, which has given birth to the interdisciplinary study of cognitive science. The idea is that there is a process of cognition which is essentially the same as the process of life and implies that all living organisms are cognitive systems, down to the simplest cell."
>
> —Fritjof Capra

A prime barrier to brain-mind research had been the lack of a reliable *subject* on whom to conduct experiments. That is, Western science being dualist, everything has to be completely objective, and any subjective data ("introspection," in their lingo) was deemed off-limits—unreliable, untrustworthy, and impermissible. (How could you know, for instance, if a volunteer subject was really calm, or just lazy from having eaten a submarine sandwich?) Then came the convergence of two technologies co-emerging in the West: the sophisticated hardware for brain-scanning and brain–imaging, and the equally sophisticated "wetware" of meditators skilled in attaining, and sustaining, particular states of consciousness. Way back in 1967, Dr. Herbert Benson had to sneak Eastern meditators into his Harvard lab under cover of night—and found meditation lowered their heart rates by three beats a minute. They used 17% less oxygen. And their brainwaves showed more signs of theta activity, associated with entering sleep, though they remained awake. Three years later, he published his findings as a seminal book, *The Relaxation Response*, the title pointing to the existence of something as verifiable as the New World. Now the research continues in broad daylight, with more advanced equipment, a greater refinement as to meditation techniques and goals, and a multidisciplinary approach. Here follows six factual items, side-by-side, for your contemplative consideration. (Then we'll entertain some more speculative theory again.)

Item: The left and right sides of your brain are, indeed, different. The left hemisphere is verbal, linear, analytic, and critical; the right hemisphere is intuitive, artistic, nonlinear, and holistic. Wes Nisker spryly compares the difference to the evolution of traditional Western and Eastern thought. Science is the wisdom tradition of the West, the analytic left hemisphere, breaking things into separate chunks; wisdom is the science of the East, seeing parts interrelating as a whole. (In his analogy, the corpus collosum, joining the two, is "the global village.") So the goal here too is "East meets West."

Item: In a classic early study (1966–1970) by Akishige-Kasamatsu-Hirai, some Zen practitioners and a control group were exposed to a repetitive click. The control group gradually became habituated. Soon, their brain-wave activity no longer responded to the sound. The Zen adepts, however, emerged out of the meditative state with each click, fully registered the noise each time, and returned right back into meditation (like seamlessly getting off a meditation cushion to answer the door, then going right back to zazen). The study showed (1) the serene, alert awareness of Zen is consistently responsive to both external and internal stimuli, and (2) different practices can generate different shades of experience. A similar test with four Hindu yogis found their meditation remained undisturbed by loud banging or strong lights.

Item: Cognitive science has discovered how the portion of the brain that responds to physical pain (the anterior cingulated cortex) also responds to emotional pain. So, though the hurt feels different, the brain sounds the same alarm for emotional pain as for physical. As the first noble truth says, there *is* suffering. It's universal. (Quoting again from the crazy wisdom of Wes Nisker, "We're not being singled out for special punishment. We're not told why we're here, and are given just enough consciousness to know we're ultimately going to do that which we really don't want to do.") This finding also brings up empathy, which we'll explore further on.

Item: A 2007 report found when subjects saw an image of an angry face, there was increased activity in the brain's amygdala, a region of the brain capable of activating a range of biological systems to defend the body from danger. This response is so hard-wired it happened even when the photograph was flashed faster than a person can consciously see (subliminally). But by simply labeling the face as "angry" or "fearful" (rather than, say, "Harry"), the emotional response decreased. The tests reveal this is mediated at a region behind the forehead and eyes called the right ventrolateral prefrontal cortex, associated with thinking in words about emotional experiences, and also inhibiting behavior and processing emotions. So mindful noting can indeed help neutralize a difficult emotional charge.

Item: Meditation can actually change the structure and function of the brain. For example, meditators grow a thicker cerebral cortex, the outer layer of the brain—particularly in regions engaged with sensory integration and awareness, control and sustaining of attention, cognitive and emotional processing, and well-being. Researcher Sara Lazar notes this isn't due to passive relaxation: "Sitting and relaxing in front of the TV doesn't make your brain grow." And this cortical thickness is proportionate to the degree of meditation over a lifetime. Researcher Richard Davidson attests, "What we found is that the longtime practitioners showed brain activation on a scale we have never seen before. Their mental practice is having an effect on the brain in the same way golf or tennis practice will enhance performance." This marvelous pliability is called *neuroplasticity*—and it exists throughout one's lifetime. (You *can* teach an old dog new tricks!) You can train the mind … and change your brain.

Case in point: A study of Tibetan meditators found their brain waves showing higher gamma activity than normal, even before they began meditating. Their brains had a higher set point. (A set point is a baseline level; for instance, our brains have a set point beyond which our emotions can get beyond control.) The Tibetans proved meditation can reset their brains' set point. The seeming hard-wiring of the brain, then, isn't fixed by the time of adulthood, as was formerly believed. When they did go into meditation (samadhi), their gamma wave activity was off the charts, far higher than ever reported in any other test. Gamma waves are related to attention, memory, learning, conscious perception, and coordination of various brain functions, and are associated with higher mental activity and heightened awareness.

Along the Path

Tibetan monks have been furnishing a rich spectrum of "introspective subjects" for diverse experimentation. Vajrayana discipline represents millennia of intensive mind-science research. Within that tradition, tantric *mahasiddhas* (highest accomplishment) are accredited with an array of remarkable special powers. One recent scientific investigation correlates claims of a nectar of longevity produced in the crown of the head and which reverses aging, with the pineal gland's production of melatonin, stimulating stem cells in a process of regeneration.

Item: The natural tendency of the body to overreact to danger by creating inflammation is the culprit of a spectrum of illnesses (such as Alzheimer's, arthritis, cancer, diabetes, and heart disease). By stimulating the vagus nerve, meditation seems to dampen the inflammation response.

Question: What about artificially stimulating the brain, through prescription medication and biofeedback? *Answer:* While meds may work, they can also flood other parts of the body with chemicals. With biofeedback and meds, personal empowerment can be a factor (Right Effort). Bottom line, the meditator's goal is *altered traits*, not just *altered states*. This is reinforced by the discovery that nerves that fire together, wire together. So as molecular geneticist turned Tibetan Buddhist monk Matthieu Ricard reassures us, "Take care of the minutes, the hours will take care of themselves."

At this point, let's bring Darwin into the discussion. He and Buddha might immediately agree, "This body is not 'mine.' It has arisen due to causes and conditions." They might further concur that by recognizing aspects of our natural conditioning (such as the urge to cling) that prevent our full participation in the flow of life, we can merge into the life stream and further evolve to our best potential. To put a finer point on that last notion, Darwin uncovers how some of our genetic traits that have helped us survive the competition of species ("bloody in tooth and claw") can have ambivalent or negative downsides. Consider our evolved consciousness. Animals don't seem to whine about past or future, whereas we two-leggeds worry why we were never even consulted before we were born, is it fair, why us, and so on.

Item: Cognitive science finds our brain is evolutionarily wired like Teflon to retain negative impressions (to survive sudden danger), but lets positive ones slip by like Teflon (happiness not being a survival skill, apparently). Thus we also have to work to overcome our instinctual tendencies to negatively overreact. Don't bite the hook! Mindfulness is the opposable thumb of consciousness!!

Having a Gut Feeling: Neuroimmunology

Now that previously separated physiological systems are studied in interaction rather than in isolation, other interdisciplinary sciences are springing up. One thing doesn't change without transforming another. The new field of *neurocardiology*, for instance, studies how the mutual dialogue between the *heart* and brain influences each other's functioning; researchers view it as a "heart brain," much as Buddhists have spoken of "heart-mind" as interchangeable.

This Is

In the worldview of the Buddha's time, the **heart** was the seat of *prana* (energy), *ojas* (vitality), and *atman* (true self). Consciousness wasn't situated in the brain, but in the heart. Vedanta sage Ramana Maharshi located "the seat of the soul" in the sinoatrial node of the heart, which controls the heartbeat. In Buddhist texts, the heart is a sense organ, perceiving thought and feeling. We call that perception "mind" (*manas* in Hindi, meaning "heart"). It perceives dharma the way our nose perceives smell. Emotional balance occurs when we're in touch with our own emotions (heart) or the hearts of others. (So we don't exchange Valentine's Day cards with pictures of human brains on them, either.)

Other studies have shown meditation increases antibody response, thus boosting immunity. Such interactions are the subject of a new interdisciplinary field mapping new mind–body connections: *neuroimmunology*. Here, it's being discovered how emotions create chemicals *(peptides)* that operate throughout the body, not just the brain. We now know that stress causes the adrenal cortex to produce *cortisol* (an evolutionary "flight-or-fright" response), which lowers the immune system, which can lead to chronic fatigue and depression, in a downward-spiraling, negative feedback loop. Healthy activity, on the other hand, can stimulate the pituitary gland and hypothalamus to produce *endorphins*, chemicals that resemble opiates, with receptor sites throughout the body. So health and emotions create feedback loops, linking mind and wellness. Indeed, our immune along with our endocrine system is being thought of as a parallel neurology—"a chemical brain," so to speak. With mindful awareness, we can practice listening deeply to our body–mind's conversation, at the deepest levels, and enhance our health, constantly being reshaped … in the here and now.

This Is

Immunology is one of newest chapters in life science (physiology). Established in the 1950s, it studies how the body defines and defends itself. Now it's discovering how the immune system, the endocrine system (glands and hormones), and the nervous system act together, more like a network than as isolated systems. Thus, an even newer science of **neuroimmunology** has been born. Your health is bound up with your sense of who you are (and aren't), mind and body mutually influencing each other.

Beyond the Physical Dimension: Where Is the Mind?

"Show me your mind," a koan asks. Indeed, where is it?! Is it solid, like the brain? Or without fixed location, like space? (Or both!?) Pondering this, our gaze is drawn beyond the boundaries of the material realm, within and without … and beyond even the interrelations of the physical and the mental … to include the purely nonphysical, as well. This brings us back into the speculative, with which we began this chapter.

For instance, here's a Dharma gumdrop for you: because humans are capable of inquiry, and because we are one with the entire universe, does the appearance of us humans on the scene reflect the universe itself becoming conscious, self-inquiring, and self-aware? Consider too the question of morality. Is the universe amoral, or is it compassionate? (Or both?) If morality were a governing factor in scientific research, would we be witnessing such scientific wonders as the Pill … or the ecological nightmares besetting our planet? Yet recent research is revealing how important and deeply embedded empathy and compassion really are within the physical as well as mental realm.

We've noted empathy not just as a learned response but also as integral to our brain. Now consider *mirror neurons* (originally named "monkey-see monkey-do neurons"), by which the body interprets mere observation of an external event as actually happening to itself, such as the image of an angry face in the "noting" experiment. (Ever wonder why people laugh, scream, and cry watching images at a movie theater?) Mirror neurons actually register the same whether we're performing an act or watching someone else perform the same act. No difference, to the mind, between seeing and doing. The implications are broader than the power of visualization, as scientist Marco Iacoboni notes: "We are social because of our ability to imitate others, so that we can put ourselves literally in other people's shoes" (that is, we empathize).

Consider, too, the new field of *interpersonal neurobiology*. Here, Dr. Dan J. Siegel, for example, has shown how our empathic relationships are inseparable from the coherence of our mind and the organization of our brain. *Try this:* Visualize your brain by looking at your palm, folding your thumb over your fingers, and making a fist. The wrist corresponds to the primitive back-brain stem, in charge of survival. Your thumb is the limbic system, controlling emotion, learning, motivation, and empathy. Your fingers correspond to the neocortex (the right and left hemispheres, and so on), and the top of your middle and ring fingers can touch *both* the wrist *and* the thumb. In this latter region, the prefrontal cortex, we see our capacity to know ourself and empathize with others are inseparably bound together—regulating an array of functions, including attuned communication, the capacity to pause and center before acting, emotional balance, and extinction of fear. A healthy prefrontal cortex is associated with positive attachments to parents in early life, yet can equally be stimulated by mindfulness meditation throughout our lives. We could say this helps show how mindfulness enables us to become our own best friend. It also shows us, moreover, the virtue of sangha, of harmonious relationship and community, throughout our lifetime. This is another turning point, a paradigm shift.

What's wisdom without compassion? Until recently, our vision of what Eastern philosopher Alan Watts used to call "the skin-encapsulated ego" (the self) was as of a private DeLuxe Home Entertainment Center within the fortress of the isolated skull. This basic dualistic set-up, splitting observer and observed, has been pretty much the model in vogue for about five centuries, ever since French philosopher René Descartes said, "I think, therefore I am." It's led to great creativity, yet it has also been at the root of much alienation and despair. Only recently are we coming to realize our brain is a *social* entity, shaped and reshaped by contact with other brains.

> **This Is**
>
> A single **human brain** takes up 2 percent of the body's weight, yet requires about 25 percent of its oxygen. The number of states the brain is capable of at any given moment is 1 followed by a million zeros. It contains more cells (neurons) than stars in the Milky Way, and each has app. 1,000 points of interconnection (synapses) with other brain cells, 100 trillion such path-points in all, each firing from 1–100 times/ second, simultaneously, and with built-in feedback loops, enabling it to learn from experience and change its structure (neuroplasticity). Moreover, this adaptive process is dependent on interaction with other brains, from early childhood development on throughout life, thus confirming our inextricable and profound interdependence.

Which leads us to one final matter (pun intended). Just as my eye doesn't literally touch a rose, only its light, so too does the brain itself never really directly experience the world. Deepak Chopra compares the basic activity of our nervous system, its complex network of electrical impulses flashing on and off, to the illusion of lights seeming to travel around a Christmas tree, or images flashed 24 frames per second appearing continuous in a movie. So how do binary signals become an experience of the world … and where?

"Show me your mind." Werner Heisenberg observed, "Even in science, the object of research is no longer nature itself, but man's investigation of nature." This echoes the Buddha's parable of blind men researching an elephant, with the brain (or the galaxy) as elephant. Can science, itself an artifact of mind, show us the mind? Is the mind, and everything else in life, explainable in purely materialist terms: chemicals, DNA, wiring, computers, and so on? The experience of the sacred is not observable as is a brain lobe or a galaxy. Where is mind? We recall the Buddhist definition of mind as that which is aware. We've noted how even a single-cell amoeba is aware. And thus mind may be an emergent property of the complexity of all our cells. Cognitive science is finding mind's not located in just one place. This is coming closer to the Buddhist definition of mind as boundless, formless, and universal. This is backed up by an empirical realization common in meditation (as in focusing conscious breathing on the belly chakra): "Hey, I'm not in my head! Yet I'm still alive!!" (Until this point, some newbies might have a hard time with their breathing and attention, feeling perhaps like an oboist whose head's about to burst.) Moreover, it underlines the Buddha's advice not to grasp after a thing called self, nor any independent world outside such self that would thus come along with it (a package deal).

So rather than a static, fixed structure (such as a ladder or a chain), the newer paradigm is more of a network model: a network of networks operating through the checks and balances of feedback loops. (This is what the word "internet" means, of course: the internetworked network of networks. Thus, it's no surprise that humans should have invented it sooner or later; emergent behavior, perhaps?) In the network or *web*, there's neither center, nor top, nor bottom. Any node is defined by its relation to and interactions with all the others. It can survive failure of separate nodes because energy or information can reroute along many alternative paths. And when one node of the net attains a greater degree of knowing, the other nodes can bootstrap up, sharing that new complexity. As the Buddha said:

> As a net is made up of a series of ties, so everything in this world is connected by a series of ties. If anyone thinks that the mesh of a net is an independent, isolated thing, he is mistaken. It is called a net because it is made up of a series of interconnected meshes, and each mesh has its place and responsibility in relation to other meshes.

Indra's Net, the Avatamsaka realm, is becoming a scientific paradigm for mind and cosmos as one (the longed-for Theory of Everything?). We're each the center, continually in motion toward the center of a universe of interpenetrating centers. Indeed, the universe is looking more and more like a vast hologram in which we're each a body of light whose innate radiance is reflecting and interpenetrating with each other in one boundless, radiant, tenth-dimensional, rainbow mandala of interpenetrating diamond light. (Who knows.)

"Show me your mind." There's nowhere for it to be found … and there's no way to get there (a perpetual pilgrimage). Thus, a response to the koan might be: if there's no solution, then there's no problem. ("No matter, never mind.") Where is this mind that says there's a problem, anyway?! We've come here to our chapter's final frontier, touched in recent discoveries both in hard physics and biology: *nonlocal phenomena* (operating beyond the space-time grid). "Awakening your mind without fixing it anywhere" might imply mind is nonlocal. The Buddha never spoke about questions of mind versus matter (or God, or immortality), but his response might be evident in his turning the Wheel of the Dharma. Our mind encompasses the universe, which includes mind. We are inseparably the subject and object of our own study, person and world. Mind (even localized in a brain, such as yours or mine) is a part of a full-circle, endless-cycle feedback system interacting with the world (itself nonlocal). To clarify a bit, consider a couple examples of landmarks in nonlocality, so to speak.

In 1982, Alain Aspect conducted an experiment seeming to show how subatomic particles communicate with each other instantly no matter whether ten feet or ten billion miles apart. Instantly, here, means faster than the speed of light, which would pierce the time barrier (and the paradigm of logic that particle *A* cannot be particle *B*). Karl Pribram discovered memory is nonlocal, too. It doesn't seem to live in any one part of the brain (selective brain damage doesn't erase specific memories); rather, it is distributed much as an image is dispersed equally across a hologram. (Hence the phrase "holographic universe.")

Question: How is it animals find their way across incredible obstacles and distances? They cannot speak, yet Russell Targ, noted psychic and remote viewer (able to see objects and events not within the range of the five senses) tells us his ability is no different than what Padmasambhava taught: "Rather than rest in conditioned awareness grasping at meaning, naming, etc., dwell in naked awareness, independent of space and time." Clairvoyance simply means seeing clearly. To consider it hokum might also dismiss prayer—another paranormal realm of miraculous nonlocal phenomena, coming into medical recognition thanks to the seminal work of such doctors as Larry Dossey, who's amassed evidence from over 150 scientific tests, all positive, as to the healing power of prayer. Of course, rabbis, priests, imams, shamans, flocks of the faithful, and even some atheists have known this all along. Only, now it's being scientifically proven. (Nine out of ten doctors agree … when Buddhists generate metta, they're generating real metta!) When you're sick, pray—for yourself and others. And when you're not sick, pray—for yourself and others. Dedicate the merit of a meditation session to the health of someone in need. Try this gatha: *Breathing in, I heal myself; breathing out, I heal others.* Prayer works. Healthy skepticism is welcome: it's integral to the scientific method, and the Buddha's. Mind is timeless, boundless, universal, and healing. And it's quite ingenious, as well as curious. Marvelous. And all it takes is using your ordinary, daily life as its laboratory. As the Buddha says, *come and see.*

> **Hear and Now**
>
> "There is no matter as such! All matter originates and exists only by virtue of a force. We must assume behind this force the existence of a conscious and intelligent Mind. This Mind is the matrix of all matter."
>
> —Max Planck, Nobel Prize–winning father of quantum theory

The Least You Need to Know

◆ The Buddha's mode of thought applied the scientific method. But where Western science has centered itself on studying the interrelationships of matter and matter, Buddhists have studied the interrelationships of matter and matter, mind and matter, and mind and mind, as well as the nonself link between wisdom and compassion.

◆ New scientific findings confirm facts Buddhists have known for millennia, casting them in a new light. As science changes its model, or paradigm, it comes closer to embracing Buddhist understanding.

◆ Some new branches of science that harmonize with and illuminate Buddhism are fuzzy logic, chaos, and complexity; holistic health; psychology; and nonlocal phenomena.

◆ Buddha's application of the scientific attitude was unique for using the human mind as both subject and laboratory. This can be seen as a psychological process of analysis. Freud and the Buddha can work together for mutual benefit.

◆ Sometimes the benefits of Buddhist virtue, wisdom, and meditation techniques can become more easily and widely accepted when given a more generally descriptive name, such as "stress reduction," "mindfulness," and "emotional intelligence."

Chapter 21

Is Happiness an Individual Matter?: Engaged Buddhism

In This Chapter

- ◆ Engaged Buddhism
- ◆ Service
- ◆ Environmentalism, pluralism, and consumerism
- ◆ Peace

What is enlightenment? The answer's not in a book, but in your own life. Similarly, the meaning of "Western Buddhism" is not yet determined (it's up to us). And so, too, with *engaged Buddhism*. In ten words or less, it's Buddhism engaged in the realm of other people—the work on self as world, and world as self. Here, the second half of our book comes full circle, having begun with interpersonal relations, relating to the world as to a spouse or a lover or a family friend; that is, relating now to the world, as one would relate to one's self but on a larger scale.

I've phrased the path as a question, because if and how to practice in this way is all up to you. It's but one more option for living a fulfilling life, for being a whole person. May you find the possibilities interesting, if not engaging.

What Is Engaged Buddhism?

By now, I hope I've dispelled any misconceptions of Buddhism as emotionless, detached, otherworldly, navel-gazing nihilism. Renouncing greed, fear, and illusion doesn't mean walking away from the world of human relationships. A Buddhist, rather, joins a community of good friends and heads in a common direction. A Buddhist lives *in* this without being attached *to* it. Enlightenment isn't necessarily beyond the grave; it is in this very world. And our world, we find, is just as much in need of enlightenment as we are.

This Is

Engaged Buddhism is any practice of Buddhism to influence change in the world in creative, life-affirming ways, howsoever small they may seem. Mind and world are engaged as one. The phrase has been adopted by other creeds; *engaged spirituality* thus refers, similarly, to drawing upon a spiritual tradition for peace and social justice in action, and which actions reciprocally refer the participant to their own spiritual growth.

Hear and Now

"No man is an island, entire of itself ... / Any man's death diminishes me, because I am involved in mankind ... "
—John Donne

"All the happiness there is in this world comes from thinking about others, and all the suffering comes from preoccupation with yourself."
— Shantideva

Please don't get the wrong idea. Engaged Buddhism isn't obligatory to "being a Buddhist." Moreover, there's no program to be followed. (What a relief! And what a challenge!) Novelist and environmental author Peter Matthiessen has noted it's not New Year's resolutions; it's not politics. (Further relief. Yet American Buddhist Democrats might well get to know American Buddhist Republicans a bit better in the process, and vice versa.) And you won't have to feel like a lonely do-gooder, because you'll be practicing with all the others on this path, and for the sake of all beings. (Here is our final definition of *idiot*. In its ancient Greek roots, it means "private"; cut off from the world.)

Our responsibility to the world is simply our ability to respond. It's about looking out your window, going out your door, and following your nose. Old age, sickness, and death were "signs" that impelled Siddhartha to go out into the world to seek and connect with the ultimate meaning of life. You might well encounter similar "messengers" in your own life. If so, ask, "How can I be of service?" Consider that opportunity as practice: yourself and the universe as one life. Some typical areas of engaged practice are: service in hospitals, hospices, prisons, schools, and nonprofits; or working on the environment, race, human rights, gender, and nonviolence. You may come up with a new avenue tomorrow. At every moment, we're always engaged with the universe (through our interpersonal relations, through our diet, through our livelihood, through our thoughts and emotions, and so on); our road continually branches, with countless karmic choice-points at every moment, each a new chance to engage beyond self, with a warm heart. So this worldly Buddhism is but a further instance of life as a continual pilgrimage, one foot in the front of the other. As Dr. Ariyaratne ("Ari"), the Gandhi of Sri Lanka, says, "We make the road, and the road makes us." Up ahead, we'll explore the background, and then some examples.

 Leaves from the Bodhi Tree _____

> Ronna Kabatznick is a Buddhist practitioner who volunteered at a local soup kitchen, feeding needy people in her community. She found it literally nourishing for herself, which led to her idea that this would be a good way for people dealing with eating problems "to expand the ways in which they nourish themselves by practicing generosity and feeding hungry people," as she later recalled. She happened to be trained in these issues, having been a psychological consultant to Weight Watchers for nine years. Her experience at the soup kitchen (a lesson at a delicatessen) led to her forming an organization called Dieters Feed the Hungry, which eventually became a national movement, and included an infant formula drive.

A Brief History of Engaged Buddhism

Engaged Buddhism is already inscribed in the life of the Buddha. He didn't follow his enlightenment by remaining in the forest to simply enjoy the ubiquitous ambrosia of merely being. His turning the Wheel of the Dharma engaged his enlightenment with the world: *this* life, *this* suffering, in *this* world, *this* nirvana. And so he spent the rest of his long life engaged with the lives of his fellow human beings, from all walks of life. He also advocated householders (laypeople) be active in the political life of the times.

One criticism of Buddhism is that it's been around for over two millennia, yet the world doesn't seem to be any better off. Well, it all depends on your point of view. The Buddha renounced the privilege of raja-hood by which he could have commanded masses of society in one fell swoop. Instead, he set in motion a change of consciousness, based on freedom of individual choice. Thus, he didn't dedicate himself to overturning the caste system, but rather ordained people from all walks of life, one person at a time. Nor did he campaign against the inequality of women; instead, he initiated the ordination of women. He taught transformation on a person-to-person level, rather than through any programmatic social engineering (which might only perpetuate the same flaws, resulting in further social disequilibrium). Ending pollution, for instance, takes more than changing light bulbs: it's also about changing minds.

One cause of the downfall of the original Sangha in India was the failure of its monasteries to integrate with the rest of society. Yet, over time, other Buddhist leaders continued turning the wheel. Besides King Ashoka, Dr. B. R. Ambedkar springs to mind (also under-recognized in the West), who drafted modern India's constitution, grounding it in the democratic processes that Buddha embedded in his Sangha; challenged India's caste system (which even Gandhi approved), ordaining a half million Hindus like himself from the "untouchable class"; and is responsible for the Wheel of Dharma being on the flag of India today. And the work of Dr. Ari is being studied worldwide, not only for promoting peace within Sri Lanka's genocidal divisions, but also for his nationwide spiritually based, village-empowerment, community-service movement called Sarvodaya (which at one point had more of its own currency in circulation than the government's).

Leaves from the Bodhi Tree

In the fifth century, Buddhaghosa, son of a brahmin family from India, became a Buddhist and studied in Ceylon (Sri Lanka). He left us a record of what he was taught, titled *Visuddhi Magga* (*Path of Purification*). It begins with these striking words: "There's the inner tangle and the outer tangle. This generation is entangled in a tangle. And so I ask of Gotama this question: 'Who can disentangle this tangle?'" Ask yourself: are his words any less true today? How is your own tangle of self and tangle of world intertangled?

The phrase "engaged Buddhism" comes from Vietnam, largely through the work of Venerable Thich Nhat Hanh. His monastery preserved the Tea Ceremony (celebrating the joy of life) while jet bombers could be heard overhead, strafing the sky.

Practice couldn't be circumscribed by monastery walls. So he established a mini Peace Corps through which people could offer relief to the hungry and the wounded, and rebuild destroyed homes and villages. His monks and nuns, maintaining mindful awareness of breath and feelings at all times, practiced putting bodies into body bags as impermanence meditation. These occasions weren't considered even matters of choice, but rather integral to the practice, the Buddha's age-old practice of wisdom and compassion.

Engaged Buddhism grew in Asia. Soka Gakkai promoted nonviolent values opposed to the militarism in Japan that led to World War II. Thailand's ecology movement began with what are now called "environmentalist monks," ordaining trees in endangered forests as members of the sangha. And Dalai Lama XIV has been looked to by many not only as a spiritual leader but also for his engaged Buddhist worldview, a global "liberation theology." Engaged Buddhism is now growing in the West, as well, as seen in such groups as Amida Trust, Buddhist Peace Fellowship, International Network of Engaged Buddhists, and Zen Peacemakers.

Along the Path

> Martin Luther King Jr. reflects engaged Buddhism's influence in the West. In his nonviolent confrontation with the roots of injustice, Dr. King brought to bear his deep readings of the Gospels; of his own teacher, Christian mystic and activist Reverend Howard Thurman; of Mahatma Gandhi; and of Thich Nhat Hanh. Hear the lesson of interbeing in Dr. King's sermons when he speaks of our being tied together in an inescapable network of mutuality.

Engaged Buddhism seems to be taking shape as a distinct movement (if not branch) of Buddhism, as several factors coalesce. As engaged practice spread through Asia … … and simultaneously came West … at the same time, East and West were becoming more closely interknit … with social upheavals and environmental tragedies seeming more and more commonplace … and as younger generations would find engaged Buddhism good grounding for their commitment to a better world. Engaged Buddhism seems, too, a natural outgrowth of Western Buddhism's emphasis on lay, rather than monastic, practice. Here we can also appreciate Pure Land's Western traditions of Buddhist community involvement. It's also a natural interfaith phenomenon, as those who come to the Dharma from an Abrahamic faith are already instilled in traditions of social justice and prophetic spirituality (seeking divine meaning behind and within historical process). And this-worldly Buddhism also resonates with those who aren't meditators, per se, yet want to transform ignorance and affliction into clarity and peace.

Here, Buddhism can engage its insights regarding the self—a construct, without any intrinsic, permanent identity—with manifestations of self on a larger scale, in social constructs and relationships. They, too, bear the same three marks of existence (suffering, impermanence, and selflessness) and are liable to the same three poisons that confound us all (delusion, greed, and fear). Recognizing we're all one, there's no higher moral ground for the Buddhist. So, on the one hand, I'm called to action, to an engaged practice, by compassion, out of the needless suffering of which I can't help but be aware. On the other hand, I can't act against the welfare of anyone—even those who've caused others harm. There is no enemy. Good Guy versus Bad Guy doesn't further. Awakened heart can see all "sides" acting from their own wish for happiness. And I am as much responsible for the suffering as anyone else. That's a taste of such practice. In the rest of this chapter, we'll see some examples of the challenges and rewards of some common applications.

Service: One Big Circle of Giving

Volunteering at any charity or nonprofit can provide occasion for Buddhist practice. Serving others, we serve ourself; serving ourself, we serve others. From a certain light, volunteering might be seen as selfish, especially if the person giving is expecting thanks. In true service, there's the authenticity of mutual relationship: no "helper," no "helped," no "help." Something larger and deeper is taking place: a circle of giving. Buddhism grants us such intimacy with life: with our own life, the lives of those with whom we're in relation, and our interrelationship within the tapestry of life, greater than each and all of us.

Along the Path

Charity (*caritas* in Greek) is another word for love. In Judaism, there is a concept of *tikkun ha'olam*, "healing the world." Buddhism teaches the Bodhisattva Vow, taking refuge with all beings, affirming our interconnectedness. In the great Hindu epic, *The Bhagavad Gita* (*The Celestial Song*), Krishna speaks of *karma yoga*, a path to liberation through intentional action for the benefit of others, unattached to any outcome. These all provide frameworks for engaged spirituality.

Consider the homeless (or, as Charles Dickens put it, "the houseless"). More than money, I've found lending an ear can be an important donation, to listen and nonjudgmentally bear witness. There's Buddha nature within all the grime, behind the mask of story. There but for fortune go you or I. As one fellow once said as I was walking away after talking with him and leaving him with a quarter: "Hey, thanks! The money's nice, but thanks for stopping—I was beginning to think I was on Mars!" And how could I thank *him* for giving me an opportunity to practice compassion?!

Hear and Now _____

"It is my experience that the world itself has a role to play in our liberation. Its very pressures, pains, and risks can wake us up—release us from the bonds of ego and guide us home to our vast, true nature. For some of us, our love for the world is so passionate that we cannot ask it to wait until we are enlightened."

—Joanna Macy, *World as Lover, World as Self*

Service can have the marvelous effect of snowballing. A coming together of two dozen housewives and one Buddhist nun can grow to become millions of people. Today, when large-scale natural disaster strikes throughout the world, a grass-roots Buddhist humanitarian organization called Tzu Chi (compassionate relief) can have volunteers at work on the spot. It all started in 1966, when Dharma Master Cheng Yen, moved by the plight of the poor, encouraged 30 Buddhist housewives in Taiwan to set aside a penny and a half of their grocery money every day to establish a charitable fund. Tzu Chi today has 10 million members worldwide (including 59 centers in the United States). Whether their Dharma activity is international relief, medical care (for example, they maintain the world's third-largest bone marrow registry), environmental conservation, or community service, the goals are always of all beings being well and all hearts being filled with kindness, compassion, joy, and unselfish giving (the four immeasurable abodes, the Brahmaviharas).

Living Our Dying: Service in Hospices

Yogi Berra once quipped that he went to everyone's funerals so he'd be sure they'd all come to his. Of course, it's not being dead but the dying that's difficult (doubly so when it's covered over in our culture). But it's no surprise to find the Buddha at the bedsides of the dying. A Buddhist was once voluntarily taking care of a dying man. One day, the dying man finally asked the Buddhist why he was always so cheerful at his duties, unpaid and all for a perfect stranger. Without hesitation, the Buddhist smiled and replied, "I'm treating you the way I expect to be treated when my turn comes." (That's an engaged attitude.) Such impermanence meditation is becoming more commonplace in our society through volunteering in hospice work. A hospice provides comfort and support outside of a hospital setting for the terminally ill and their relatives. This allows the patient and his or her family to focus on emotional and spiritual care, so that medical concerns don't dominate the experience of dying.

The Buddha meditates while lying down during his para-nirvana (literally, "final" or "total extinction"). Even then, he continued to teach. Wouldn't it be a real honor to sit by his bedside and just be with him?

(Paranirvana Buddha., *sculpture by Loraine Capparell, glazed ceramic, 54½ inches × 43¼ inches × 1½ inches*)

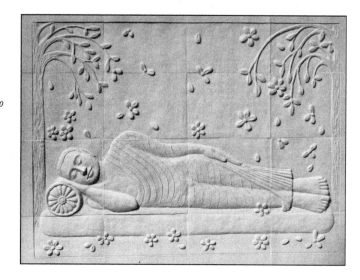

Hear and Now

"The process of growth is, it seems, the art of falling down. Growth is measured by the gentleness and awareness with which we once again pick ourselves up, the lightness with which we dust ourselves off, the openness with which we continue and take the next unknown step, beyond our edge, beyond our holding, into the remarkable mystery of being. Going beyond the mind, we go beyond death. In the heart lies the deathless."

—Stephen Levine, *Meetings at the Edge: Dialogues of the Grieving and the Dying, the Healing and the Healed*

Awakening of mind can occur anytime, such as while lending an open heart to a lonely voice, needing to be heard at least once in his or her life. Inquiring mind emerges in the silence of dying, as self dissolves and true nature is recognized. (Who dies?) Awareness is unborn, undying. In one hospice, a young volunteer asked each guest, "If you weren't here, where would you like to go?" Then he'd visit that place—the local piano bar, say, if that's what the person said. He'd bring a small video recorder, and he'd say to the people there, "You know one of your regulars is staying at the hospice and wishes she could be here at this piano bar right now. Is there anything you'd like to say to her?" Then, back at the hospice, being shown the video, the guest might recall and would talk about his or her whole life … and its whole meaning would unfold, resolving a work-in-progress.

Frank Osasteki, founder of Zen Hospice, says, "We take our elders and we shut them away in institutions, so that we won't have to bear witness to their pain or our ultimate destiny. What would it be like if we invited death in, if we offered it a cup of tea to get to know it better?" The motto at Zen Hospice is: *Stay Close, Do Nothing.* Zen priest Yvonne Rand suggests, "Just keep them company. Understand that sitting with a dying person is a great opportunity to stay with whatever you are accustomed to turn away from. It could be fear of pain, whatever. In being with the dying you meet your own edge." Hospice work is a powerful way to engage your Buddhist practice in the world around you, and within you.

Widening Horizons: Humanity Is Our Sangha

Race and gender are topics that can reveal new meanings from a Buddhist perspective. As noted, Western Buddhism wouldn't get past first base if it were for men only, much less pale males (of which I am one). Gender and race raise issues of passivity, vulnerability, and power (ego and its constructs), where Buddhism can get past a purely intellectual approach, to head and heart and hand as one. Clarifying and transforming these relationships means working for equality through Buddhist practice, and practicing Buddhism through work for equality.

Harmony of Diversity and Equality

To fully appreciate and understand what it means to be human, we might widen the horizons of our definition of "family." Like self, race, for instance, is a construct, an often too-constricting frame. Those who've explored the DNA of their family tree (genomic geneology) discover everyone shares a common ancestor in Africa. It's a good reminder of interbeing. Nobody's purely just one race, be they Afro-Cuban, Italian-Irish (Friuli), or Filipino (Asian-Hispanic). Everyone's a walking column of interraciality. We inter-are. We are all one race, the human race; our heart, one full circle turning.

So what to do when confronted by someone who labels you as "Other"? (Consider how it feels to be asked by a stranger, curious about your ethnic heritage, "What are you?") Buddha's medicine heals ignorance, ill will, and fear, whether one's own or someone else's. For people of European descent, Buddhism furnishes skillful means for awakening to and uprooting roots of racism within and without; for people of color, that includes internalized racism. And meditating on a retreat can bring up many things, such as an awakened connection with one's ancestors. What happens, for example, when people of African heritage contact the Middle Passage and the heritage of slavery stored in consciousness of deep memory? Engaged work here means dealing with what happens when the invisible is made visible, with understanding, dignity, and reconciliation. Spiritual liberation can coincide perfectly with the goal of social liberation: freedom.

> ### Along the Path
>
> The Rabbi of Messervitch once asked his followers to define being awake. One person said it meant being able to see the lines in one's palm. The rabbi said that didn't mean awakening. Another said it was being able to determine if a silhouette on a hill was a goat and not a dog. The rabbi said that still wasn't awakening. So someone asked him what being awake meant. "You're truly awake," the rabbi replied, "when you recognize all men as your brother, and all women as your sister."

Mothers, Sisters, and Daughters of the Buddha

Like race, gender can be seen both as a fiction and as a reality (emptiness is form). Engagement here can well extend beyond physical boundaries. Sakyadhita (Daughters of Buddha), for instance, deals with such issues as restoring the tradition of nuns in southeast Asia (women in the West now able to enjoy ordination), resettlement of refugee Tibetan nuns, the healing of the trauma of war widows, the wholesale slavery of young girls recruited or kidnapped into the labyrinthine Asian sex industry, and women's role in rebuilding war-shattered nations. True, some of these causes may seem to only have benefit abroad, but then they also give back to the well from which the water of Dharma has been drawn by the West.

The word gender refers to men and women. Nothing exists in a vacuum. The fifth precept reminds us that whatever our gender, we're always enmeshed in a web of male and female energies, requiring harmony to flow and function. It's refreshing to find sanghas with abbesses, and where I'm thus in the minority in terms of gender. This also engages me to extend my practice, how I view self, in my daily relations in the world. Whether you're a guy or a gal, gay or straight, you encounter gender gaps in everyday life. Upon examination, you might find a parallel between gender conditioning and ego: a construct we've accepted and identify with that keeps us from full intimacy with our lives. Being one of the few guys in a group of women also makes me all the more appreciative of feminine energy. A primary example, as we'll see next, is the matriarchal wisdom for caring for our environment, Mother Earth.

Along the Path

Molly Dwyers has catalogued male-female imbalances in terms of culture over nature, mind over body (or matter), life over death, the transcendent over the imminent, independence over dependence or interdependence, activity over passivity, order over chaos, objectivity over subjectivity, control over surrender, conscious design over spontaneous arising, clarity over mystery, reason over imagination, doing over being, competition over cooperation, work over play, private enterprise over public service, the professional over the amateur, the creative over the receptive, quantification over qualification, and the conscious over the unconscious, to name a few.

This lifesize sculpture of Tara is the feminine aspect of Avalokiteshvara, embodiment of compassion. Tara originates in the Himalayan regions, and has 21 different forms. In her compassionate omniscience, the palms of her hands and the soles of her feet have eyes. Her actions (represented by her hands and feet) are informed by the wisdom (eye) of understanding, upon which true love is based.

(Sitatara, White Tara; *Mongolian, Caghan Dara Eke; sculpted by Zanzabazar (1635–1723), late seventeenth to early eighteenth century, gilt bronze, 27⅛ inches [68.9 centimeters] × 17⅝ inches [44.8 centimeters], Museum of Fine Arts.)*

Thinking Like a Tree: Green Buddhism

In the later stages of his career, Eastern philosopher Alan Watts (1915–1973) was available for speaking on two topics: Buddhism and environmentalism. Sometimes, he'd give pretty much the same lecture for each, but would refer to his subject as mystical experience, or environmental awareness, depending upon the audience. Indeed, where does self end and environment begin? The question evokes both the paradigm shift implied in new sciences and in Buddha's teachings. We no longer see earth as that out of which the sun emerges daily, along the edge of the horizon. Since the Apollo missions, we've seen Earth entire, complete and complex. And we've become aware of the fragility of this gorgeous orb, and the enormous power we exert there-upon.

In the old Buddhist/new scientific view, we move away from seeing our environment through an anthropomorphic paradigm, with humanity separate from nature, as if we were custodians of nature as a warehouse of goods. Looking deeper, we're now seeing ourselves as embedded within a continuum, the web of life. An old Buddhist / new scientific spin on this view is *Dharma Gaia. Gaia* (pronounced "gaya," after the Greek goddess of the Earth) is the premise that the earth is herself a self-regulating entity, a living organism, a sentient being. Indeed, we might all well be part of one living being, herself possessing self-awareness, buddha nature. As has been said for thousands of years now, in the colors of mountains can be perceived the body of the Buddha (the awakening of life to itself); in the sound of water, the Buddha's voice. Buddha's Nature.

Hear and Now

"The entire range of living matter on Earth, from whales to viruses, and from oaks to algae, could be regarded as constituting a single living entity, capable of manipulating the Earth's atmosphere to suit its overall needs and endowed with faculties and powers far beyond those of its constituent parts."

—James Lovelock, on the Gaia hypothesis

Leaves from the Bodhi Tree

Here's a campfire game that Buddhist poet-ecologist Gary Snyder sometimes invites visitors to play with him when they visit his home in the wilderness of the Sierra Nevada mountains (with wood stoves for heat and photovoltaic cells for electricity). Describe the location of your house without referring to anything manmade. *Think:* Basin, range, watershed, flows, drainages. *Hint:* Where does your water come from? Where does it go when you're through with it? Are you in the sun or the shady slope? What grows around you? What doesn't?

Hearing the voice of nature, of Gaia, of Buddha, everywhere, can be marvelous, even for a city dweller. In my neighborhood, I'm aware of a tribe of wild parrots that fly west around 11 A.M. The migration of commuters outside my window is no less timely than of birds. At the office or in wilderness, we can always meditate on nonself elements of nature: the interbeing of the elements within our bodies; the pull of the phases of the moon; the communion we make with our food. Our conscious breathing can be literally and figuratively a breath of fresh air.

When our soil, our water, and our air are compromised, working to stem the tide isn't necessarily an altruistic duty. That implies sacrificing separate Self, for the "higher" interests of abstract Other. As activist Joanna Macy has put it, "It would not occur to me to plead with you, 'Oh, don't saw off your leg. That would be an act of violence.' It wouldn't occur to me because your leg is part of your body. Well, so are the trees in the Amazon rain basin. They are our external lungs. And we are beginning to realize that the world is our body."

Engaged Buddhism, then, might be seen as part of Gaia's immune system, the world healing itself. Environmentalist Paul Hawken locates the creative expression of engaged Buddhism as within what he considers the largest movement in the world, largely ignored by politicians and the media—spontaneous, unorganized, and from the bottom up. It's significant that Buddhist delegates of all schools from around the planet convened in 2009 (approximately the sixth such council in the history of the Sangha) to discuss how to heal our dear azure-blue ecosphere. If environmental information seems gross or too complex, it can be hard to study on one's own, much less respond to alone. Thus we see how on a practical level meditation helps heal burn-out, and sangha provides a mutual support system, for any engaged activity, of any bent.

And if still the light at the end of the tunnel should ultimately be turned off (to preserve energy?), so be it. Life goes on. All constructed things are impermanent, including human civilization. In deep time, our human moment is but a mere blip of evolving species adaptation ticking silently on the vast clockface of the Long Now. Meanwhile … let's consider how Dharma offers penetrating views on an elusive factor—fundamental to our well-being, as well as to how our general, current Way of Life impacts the life of Earth herself—called consumption.

What Would Buddha Buy?

"*Not too much, not too little.*" I wonder if the Buddha would like the Safeway logo, with its suggestion of a yin-yang, the Middle Way. I picture him there, with his own reusable grocery bag slung over his shoulder, talking to a shopper (a perfect stranger) about awareness ("Do you know where it comes from, and how it will affect the environment when you're done with it?"), and about making mindful choices ("Do you really need it?"). And he might smile to hear of the international Buy Nothing Day (November 28), a spiritual retreat amidst the frantic ramp-up to winter holiday shopping fever ("the Shopacalypse," as comic preacher Reverend Billy satirically refers to it—capitalism being, after all, our unofficial national religion). To Christmas shoppers, the Buddha might suggest: *Be the present.*

We recall how the Buddha's monasteries served as a kind of buffer zone between the ancient traditions of agricultural culture and the newly emerging market economy with its fierce competitiveness. Some see us as at no less of a turning point (a new Axial Age, for again turning the Wheel of Dharma). Without sustainability statistics nor solemn computation of your ecological footprint (measuring the pressure of your actions on the biosphere), Gandhi said it all: "There is enough for human need, not for human greed." And when it comes to greed—sad and sorry, mindless, grasping greed—the Buddha knows well this hook, with all its tempting lures, and beckons us, saying, "Come, sit by me."

The Buddha's critique of craving (and its resultant needless suffering) can pinpoint the precise mind-moment at which real pleasure morphs into abstract desire, the want to want—and, in our addictive culture, that exact same vital acupressure point is the target upon which America's current market economy capitalizes (pun intended). "Don't get hooked," the Buddha says. Don't bite the hook of craving illusion. Remember the hungry ghost, pictured in Chapter 5, craving more and more of what can never satisfy. Learn "enoughness."

With Dharma, a marketplace can be seen as a space in which to practice mindfulness, rather than mindless consumption (buying more than we think). Nothing exotic, we do it every day. In each ad and each potential point of purchase is a karma choice-point, the chance to practice wise compassion for the universal human condition: yours, a store's, a corporation's, and all the invisible intermediaries, all humans breathing together, liable to the same three marks of existence, three poisons, four noble truths, and the fourth precept (consumption) at varying levels of scale. The bodhisattva shopper vows to consider all beings, all creation.

It is possible to base contentment on being, rather than having. The temptations of buying that fourth shirt or new gizmo on display might be dwarfed by the real joy of creating more space in one's life by donating extra stuff for recycling. When tempted to bite the hook of despair over seeming lack, in one's life or in the world, try practicing generosity instead: it's hard to be greedily grasping when your arms are extended in giving. Reverend Billy energizes Christmas shoppers (and all consumers) with this motto: "*Love Is a Gift Economy.*" (Pass it along.)

Being Free Where You Are: Prison Dharma

As Sakya Jetsun Chime Luding reminds us, "The Buddha said that the place of practice is your own mind. It's not a physical place." Thus it's no surprise to hear of practice in prisons. As Lama Zopa Rinpoche says, "The real prison is being under the control of delusion and its action, karma." Suffering, and the cycle of violence, can be ended anywhere. And people in prison ("doing time") obviously have time for self-study, as well as karma to transform. Pure Land teachings ring clear here. If Amida Buddha hears a good person's call, how much more so a bad person: the compassion is greater.

There are now national networks for the Buddhist practice groups within prisons, where your volunteering could be time well spent. Besides providing pen pals, those engaged in prison dharma provide free books and correspondence courses, facilitate practice groups, and provide legal aid and post-prison support. Lee Lipp, the coordinator of San Francisco Zen Center's various prison projects, states:

> I hear the desire of many who are living in jails and prisons to find ways to relate to their suffering that can bring relief and new ways of being. Those of us who are "freeworlder" volunteers are so fortunate to be with those who are willing to express their suffering so clearly … fortunate to be in the company of those who are finding their path, just as we are—mahasangha [greater community] in dharma, no inside, no outside.

Three inmates begin a 10-day Vipassana session, up to 12 hours a day, giving up most of the daily privileges that typically define identity and dignity for prisoners. In a prison society where you have to always watch your back, just closing your eyes in a group setting can be a giant step.

(Photo: Anthony Pidgeon)

Heaven or hell can always be just one second away, all depending on your mind. In prison's violent environment, hell seems the easier choice. For men and women accustomed to failure, just practicing mindfulness can be a colossal victory. While mindfulness can't transform a criminal overnight, it can furnish a crucial turning point, providing tools for understanding and transforming karma; taking responsibility; detoxifying the poisons of greed, anger, and ignorance; and offering a model for leading a peaceful, rewarding life upon release—and never going back.

Sometimes a court case is required for Buddhism to be recognized as a religion for the context of prisons. (In the word "penitentiary," we hear the Christian implication of doing penance for sins.) Yet now that some prison guards and staff have seen the positive effects of Dharma, they welcome and even learn from the formerly strange-looking Buddhist teachers at their gates. Geoffrey Shugen Arnold Sensei, of the National Buddhist Prison Sangha, says, "Nothing you do can be singularly about yourself, and once you see it that way, everything changes."

> ### Leaves from the Bodhi Tree
>
> Buddhist chaplaincy is a recent form of engaged service. One seminal chaplaincy training program is designed to heal not only individuals but also environments and social systems. It thus applies the interface of Buddhism with complexity's studies of how behavior emerges at various levels of the scale. For its founder, Roshi Joan Halifax, it's the fruition of her work since 1979, when she began combining contemplative practice and social action in her trainings. Through her work in the prison system, end-of-life care, and the environment, she saw "chaplaincy was not only about serving those who were immediately suffering but also had to be directed toward institutions that fomented structural violence. Then with 9/11 and everything that followed, most terribly, the viralizing of fear globally, I thought: if fear can happen systemically, so can healing."

Buddhism's unique, engaged view—Right View, a freedom *from* the dualism of views—is reflected in extreme instances of prison punishment. At death penalty vigils, engaged interfaith spirituality finds common cause in the sanctity of human life. Where some demonstrators might see a kind of living Passion play taking place—the governor as Rome, the warden as Pilate, the condemned as Jesus, in a living parable of Good versus Evil—the Buddhist, bearing witness to and being the whole situation itself, with naked awareness rather than judgment, might see everyone as implicated equally in the execution, themselves included. Compassion is boundless.

Peace

No survey of engaged spirituality would be complete without touching peace: the inseparability of peace in our hearts, and peace in our lives, peace in our world; inside out, and outside in. Peace is practiced as the path itself, as well as the goal (the path is the goal), and is at the heart of all engaged Buddhist action. As Paul Reps once wrote, "Making a cup of green tea, I stop the war."

Hear and Now

"It is because of the practice of meditation—stopping, calming, and looking deeply—that I have been able to nourish and protect the sources of my spiritual energy and continue my work…. During the war in Vietnam, I saw communists and anti-communists killing and destroying each other because each side believed they had a monopoly on the truth. I was able to see that everyone in the war was a victim, that the American soldiers who had been sent to Vietnam to bomb, kill, and destroy were also being killed and maimed."

—Thich Nhat Hanh

Buddhism has been called "the gentlest religion" because no country ever went to war with another in its name. The Buddha came from a warrior clan, yet stated emphatically, "Hatred never ends hatred, only love." It's possible to practice peace in time of war, finding the Middle Way in a world seemingly at war with itself. Today, mindfulness is sometimes taught to soldiers before they go out, and to returning veterans struggling with post-war trauma. Myself, I've never lived in a world without war, yet I am also aware of peace within the world. Thus, mindful of interbeing, we might see peace as composed of nonpeace elements.

Spiritual and moral reasons aside, there may be good cause for nonviolence as often simply being the most effective means; for example, a study by Stephan and Chenoweth of 325 campaigns of resistance from 1900–2006 found nonviolence successful in twice as many instances as violent ones. Recall, too, the largest single demonstration on the planet in history took place for peace (February 15, 2003): might it reflect a paradigm shift underway? This might confirm Robert Aitken's likening engaged Buddhism to dropping oil in a glass of water. At first, there are just beads hanging in suspension in a column of water. As they coalesce, eventually one drop can change the whole picture: it's a glass of oil in which there's also water. *Slowly, slowly, step by step.*

Leaves from the Bodhi Tree

Ever feel pissed off and want to write an angry letter to Powers That Be? An angry letter only creates more hurt, and who wants to read it, anyway? ("Do unto others …") How about a Buddhist love letter, instead? It might begin acknowledging how wonderful—of all possible life forms—to be born a human being, and as such to be one in a seat of particular power, and to be able to use that power for the good of so many other people and life forms on the planet, so wouldn't it be nice if …

In a word, we are the world. As yoga teacher Shiva Rea neatly expresses it, in our spiritual path we can find balance to our relationship with the world, the Middle Way, through service:

> "If we feel a huge pressure to be heroes and saints, then we may miss some deeper work. It's really important to acknowledge that there are rhythms to *seva* [service]. Sometimes the most important service we can perform has to do with our own internal universe; that is, the seva of giving ourselves a deep healing or reorganizing our lives. This seva benefits ourselves, but it also benefits others because it allows us to have an even greater positive effect on the world. At the same time, however, I think that we all have to get engaged *now* because everybody on this planet has a duty to move toward a sustainable lifestyle. Whatever way we can—with balance—let's do that. Let's begin."

Peace is every breath.

The Least You Need to Know

- Our engagement with the world can be a fulfilling aspect of practice. Such practice is called *engaged Buddhism*, work on mind and world as one.

- Working or volunteering in hospices or prison education are examples of Buddhist engagement, mindful participation in community service.

- The Buddhist perspective toward the environment is a consciousness of and reverence for the interpenetration of all life and place.

- Issues of diversity can be understood, within ourselves and those around us, with compassion and healing. Reawakening and respecting the feminine in our lives concerns both men and women.

- Engaged Buddhism is nondualist, not dividing the world into enemies and friends. We're all responsible for the state of the world through our natural ability to respond. Engaged Buddhism is also nonviolent, changing the means to change the ends. So, as always, the path is the goal: "There is no path to peace; peace is the path."

Buddhism in a One-Page Book: Quick Reference

The Three Jewels

1. Buddha (The Awakened One)

2. Dharma (Buddha's teachings and all they pertain to)

3. Sangha (the practice, and the community of practice)

The Four Noble Truths

1. Life entails suffering (*dukkha*).

2. Needless suffering results from grasping, craving an illusion (*trishna*).

3. There's an end to needless suffering (*nirvana*).

4. The way to the end of needless suffering is the Path (*maggha*).

The Path

Wisdom	Ethics	Meditation
1. Right view	3. Right speech	6. Right effort
2. Right thought	4. Right action	7. Right mindfulness
	5. Right livelihood	8. Right concentration

The Precepts

1. Not killing	3. Not lying	5. No sexual abuse
2. Not stealing	4. No intoxicants	

Karma

You are responsible for your actions, words, and thoughts. Each results in a reciprocal action, word, or thought.

The Three Poisons

1. Ignorance
2. Greed
3. Ill will

The Three Marks of Existence

1. Impermanence (*annica*)
2. No abiding, substantial, separate self (*anatman*)
3. Dukkha/nirvana

The Vocabulary of Silence: A Buddhist Glossary

Trying to understand from words is like washing a dirt clod in muddy water. But if you don't use words to gain understanding, it's like trying to fit a square peg in a round hole.

—Master Yuanwu Keqin (1063–1135)

arhat   Worthy one. The ideal of arhatship in *Theravada* means having nothing more to learn, being free of cravings, attaining *nirvana*.

Atman   Hindu concept of a highest self, inherently one with the transpersonal, *Brahman* (Eternal Self). To the Buddha, the ultimate reality is *an-atman* (nonself), the absence of any identity or self-nature.

bardo   The state in between death and rebirth.

bodhicitta   The thought of enlightenment; the compassionate desire to attain full enlightenment for the sake of all beings.

bodhisattva   One ready for or who has even attained enlightenment yet has vowed to help all beings become enlightened.

Brahmaviharas   Divine dwellings or immeasurable abodes; *metta* (loving kindness), compassion, rejoicing, and equanimity.

Buddha   The Fully Awakened One, from the Sanskrit root *budh*, "to wake." One who is awake and capable of awakening others.

buddha nature   The capability to realize buddhahood; original nature, true nature, true self.

buddhism   A way of life in accordance with the Buddha's teachings; in the East, it is often called *Buddha-Dharma*, "Way of the Buddha," and is the enlightened way of things as they are.

Buddhist   A person who studies, realizes, and lives the basic principles of the Buddha's teachings.

compassion   Universal sympathy, sometimes expressed as the sincere wish to end the needless suffering of all beings, born out of recognition of the oneness of all things. Commonly expressed by *bodhisattvas*. Often paired with wisdom.

concentration   Buddhism has many words analogous to concentration. *Samatha*, "stopping" or "stillness," is a basis for concentration, and can yield tranquility. Used in conjunction with mindfulness and effort in the Eightfold Path, concentration is called *samadhi*, often translated as "one-pointed concentration," a single-minded attentiveness to doing what you're doing while you're doing it. This nondualistic state can be a basis for *dhyana* (meditation), thence *kensho*, *satori*, enlightenment, etc.

Dalai Lama   The Dalai Lama is both a religious and a national ruler. Dalai means "ocean," as in ocean of wisdom. Tibet had been ruled by Dalai Lamas since the seventeenth century, until the twentieth century. Dalai Lama XIV went into exile in Dharmsala, India, in 1959.

Dharma   The Buddha's teachings and the things to which they pertain (everything). Additional meanings: laws of nature, calling, path, righteousness, fruit.

dualism   Division of reality into oppositions (subjectivity/objectivity, self/other, etc.).

dukkha   Literal translation from Sanskrit is "a wobbly axle." Dissatisfaction, stress, suffering, anguish, caused by fixation on what is without a stable, separate, permanent reality. Recognition that life is a bumpy road.

emptiness   The state of being empty of any separate, substantial, lasting existence. (*Sunyata*, Sanskrit.) It is not anything. Rather than carrying a negative connotation, it implies no boundary, fertile void, openness, transparency, infinite potentiality. *See also* suchness.

enlightenment   Complete awakening, silent illumination (*see* satori); more practically considered in terms of enlightened action.

esoteric   Intended only for those sufficiently spiritually developed and properly initiated to grasp the true meaning; sometimes called "secret."

gassho   Palms of hands joined together in greeting, gratitude, request; often accompanied by a bow. (*Namaskar/namastey*, Hindu; *añjali*, Sanskrit; *wai*, Thai.)

gatha   A short poem or meditation.

hara   A node of energy (*chakra*, a "major acupressure point"), about the size of a quarter or a dime and located three or four finger-widths below the navel, considered one's true center—physically in posture, and spiritually as the central repository of *prana* or *chi* (life-force). (*Dan tien*, Chinese.)

holistic   Pertaining to a whole, such as a whole system or web, taking into account inter-relations of parts. (Originates from the same linguistic root from which we derive the words "healing" and "holy.")

insight   Seeing deeply, penetrating into the true nature of things, gaining understanding and wisdom. *See also* Vipassana.

interbeing   Interconnectedness, interdependence, the unimpeded interpenetration of all things.

karma   Universal law of cause and effect, not limited by time or space. It can imply rebirth, or continual perpetuation, and the means of liberation from such repetition (thus some speak of actions and thoughts as having good karma, bad karma, and no karma).

koan   A Zen meditation on a question or a story with a resolution that goes beyond rational intellect and common logic, such as, "All things return to the One; what does the One return to?" Sometimes it can be reduced to a very short question, called *hwadu*, such as "What is this?"

lamrim   Stages of the path in Tibetan Buddhism, leading to initiation into *tantra*.

Mahayana   Collection of Buddhist schools flourishing in northeast Asia, such as Pure Land, Zen, Vajrayana, and Nichiren.

mandala   Two- or three-dimensional diagram of cosmic forces, used for meditation; often depicts deities and their abodes.

mantra   Meditation practice using sound, syllables, or words.

meditation   One of three components of the Buddhist way, along with wisdom and ethics. More than a relaxed state, it's an activity of awareness, with various degrees of formal training available from a teacher, depending on the school. Meditation isn't confined to sitting; it is also practiced walking, working, and so on.

metta   Loving kindness, friendliness, goodwill.

Middle Way   Harmoniously navigating between extremes, not choosing opposing positions. The Madhyamika School of Buddhism recognizes relative truth and absolute truth, the latter being *emptiness.*

mindfulness   Intelligent alertness, being aware of things as they are, in and of themselves, and nothing else.

mondo   (Japanese) Zen question and answer, similar to koan practice.

mu   (Japanese) Nothing, not, nothingness, un-.

mudra   Postures and gestures often associated with a particular Buddha or an inner state of being; equivalent to speech, in preliterate cultures. In Vajrayana, they assist in visualizing a *yidam* (meditation deity).

mushin   No mind. Innocence, nondualist awareness, no-thought, beyond skill, beginner's mind.

nembutsu   In Pure Land Buddhism, recitation of the name of Amitabha Buddha. (*Namo Amida Butsu,* Japanese; *Namo Amitofu,* Chinese, in which case recitation is called *nien fo.*)

nirvana   Liberation, union with ultimate reality, state of perfection.

nonself   Absence of a permanent, unchanging self; selflessness. (*An-atman,* Sanskrit.) *See* atman.

noting   The mindful process of self-observation often used in *Insight Meditation;* observing whatever's passing through your body, feelings, thoughts, and consciousness, making a short mental note of it, and moving on.

Pali   Indian dialect derived from Sanskrit, in which the canonical texts of Theravada are composed.

paranirvana   Nirvana before/after death.

precepts   Ethical guidelines for conscious conduct.

pure land   A field created by a Buddha's enlightenment, in which he then dwells.

Pure Land Buddhist school   Also known as Amidism, this school emphasizes faith in and devotion to Amida Buddha's compassionate bodhisattva vows.

refuge   Taking refuge means appreciating, trusting, and relying on something.

samsara   The realm of endless cycles of rebirth into the same illusions, such as the idea that true happiness consists in satisfying ego, perpetuating the self.

samurai   The military elite who seized power from imperial aristocracy in feudal Japan, Kamakura era (1185–1333 C.E.). They appreciated and sponsored Zen for its fearlessness, irreverence, intuition, spontaneity, and strict discipline.

Sangha   Assembly, crowd, host. Generally, a Buddhist community of practice, or practice itself. More specifically, the Buddhist monastic order, arguably the oldest monastic order in the world.

Sanskrit   An ancient language of India, now used only for sacred or scholarly purposes.

satori   The experience of awakening or enlightenment. (Usually, satori is reserved for the Buddha; otherwise satori is often called *kensho*.)

sesshin   A Zen retreat, usually five to seven days in duration.

shikantaza   Zen practice of sitting just to sit; choiceless awareness, without techniques or subject.

skillful means   Teachings, techniques, and methods designed to further spiritual practice, varied according to the situation or the practitioner's temperament. (*Upaya*, Sanskrit.)

store consciousness   A Buddhist concept akin to the collective unconscious; the realm where karma accumulates, the soil where seed formations of future energies and essences to be manifested in phenomena are nourished. (*alaya vijñana*, Sanskrit.)

suchness   The immutable nature of things beyond all categories or concepts; their Buddha nature, with no boundary between perceiver and perceived; an aspect of emptiness.

sutra   Dialogue or discourse of the Buddha.

tantra   Originally a school of Hindu yoga that combined with Buddhism and native Tibetan beliefs. A distinguishing element of *Vajrayana Buddhism*, it's often characterized by its harnessing and transforming natural energies rather than suppressing them.

Theravada   Blanket term for Buddhist schools flourishing in south and southeast Asia, the most popular today being *Vipassana* (insight meditation). (Sometimes called *Hinayana*, which carries a disparaging connotation of "lesser, inferior.")

Three Jewels   *The Buddha*, the *Dharma*, the *Sangha*. (Also called *Triple Gem.*)

tonglen   A Vajrayana meditation of exchanging self for others.

Tripitaka   The Buddhist canon, recorded in *Pali*, including sutras, rules for discipline and conduct, and special teachings.

Vajrayana   The Buddhist school predominating in Tibet, Mongolia, and Ladakh, but also diffusing into China, Korea, and Japan. It embraces Theravadin and Mahayanan beliefs and adds tantric beliefs and practices, such as meditation with mantra, mudra, and visualization. A form of esoteric Buddhism.

Vipassana   Mindfulness meditation practiced in the Theravadin schools. Often taught as Insight Meditation in the West. Insight into the impermanence and lack of abiding, separate, substantial identity, leading to understanding of the true nature of reality.

visualization   Picturing an image in the mind's eye. In Buddhist practice, uniting with the energy symbolized by a particular visualization; then realizing its essential *emptiness*.

wisdom   Wisdom refers to insight into the true, nonself nature of reality, or emptiness. It is often paired with compassion. (*Prajna*, Sanskrit.)

Yidam   A meditation Buddha; a deity serving as focus of visualization in Vajrayana.

yoga   To unite (literally "to yoke"), such as yoking the mundane and the divine, integrating teachings and practice, combining learning and experience, and so on. (Note: The word *religion* similarly means "to bind.") Specifically refers to particular Brahmanic practices in India, but can apply to any spiritual path.

zazen   Total concentration of body and mind in an upright, cross-legged sitting posture; seated meditation. (Not separate from continuous, daily moment-to-moment meditation.)

Zen   A school of Buddhism emphasizing directly seeing into the nature of mind. The word derives from the Sanskrit for "meditation" (*Dhyana*), with a sense of the wisdom therefrom. (*Chan*, Chinese, where it mingled with Taoism; *Son*, Korean; *Thien*, Vietnamese.)

zero   This Buddhist glossary's final word … nothing.

From the Trees to Thee: Further Reads

When author Celeste West was the librarian at San Francisco Zen Center, she'd plant small, handwritten cards on a few shelves with apt mottoes she'd written, like: *Sometimes the best books are still in trees."* And *If a tree falls in the forest, does anyone read it?* Such reminders are indeed good, when standing in the company of ink-smeared dead trees (books), manifest as documents of Dharma thanks to the invisible labor of innumerable hands and minds, as found in a library, a bookshop, or your own night-stand reading stack. True, there's a venerable Buddhist lineage in the mere existence of books (the first printed book with movable type being Buddhist, predating the Gutenberg Bible). But I don't want you to be like a fitness book reader who never exercises, or a ladle in a bowl never tasting the soup itself. As Zen Center's founder Suzuki Roshi once explained, "Written teaching is a kind of food for your brain. Of course it is necessary to take some food for the brain, but it is more important to be yourself by practicing the right way of life."

Maybe a couple titles here might be right for you. I hope my annotations assist, and enrich your sense of the continual shaping of the Dharma in the West through books.

For starters, we turn to *the Buddha.* As we've seen, **the life of the Buddha** is a thread upon which is strung many teachings. The palms-joined favorite of many people is Thich Nhat Hanh's epic *Old Path, White Clouds*—not only for closely following ancient Pali sources but also for style and insight being in harmony with the spirit of the subject. There are, of course, dozens of other versions. Indeed, you can trace the evolution of Western appreciation of the Buddha through the range of his biographies. In Chapter 19, we noted Osamu Tezuka's epic graphic novel (cartoon *manga)* version; in Chapter 4, we observed the historical importance of Sir Edwin Arnold's adaptation as Victorian poetry ("*… looking deep, he saw … / How lizard fed on ant, and snake on him, / And kite on both; and how the fish-hawk robbed / The fish-tiger of that which it had seized; / The shrike chasing the bulbul, which did chase / The jeweled butterflies: till everywhere / Each slew a slayer and in turn was slain, / Life living upon death. … / The Prince Siddhartha sighed.*"). Five other literary retellings are noteworthy. Swiss author Herman Hesse (1877–1922) penned *Siddhartha* in 1922, but not translated from German until 1951, and ripening thence from cult classic to enduring chestnut. ("*Happiness is a how, not a what. A talent, not an object.*") On the other hand, few have ever heard of Robert Allen Mitchell (1917–1965), who had to drop out of Harvard's astronomy program when his family lost their money during the Great Depression, and spent the rest of his life impoverished in obscurity. Twenty years after his death, it was discovered he'd taught himself Pali and had written the elegant and moving book *The Buddha: His Life Retold.* ("*Now, very late that afternoon, just as the rays of the westering sun gilded the trees with a prodigal burst of glowing color, Gautama rose up like a lion bestirring himself and set out on the way back to his forest hermitage.*")

In 1955, Jack Kerouac (1922–1969) wrote a colloquial version titled *Wake Up*, unpublished until 2008. ("*Until recently most people thought of Buddha as a big fat rococo figure with his belly out, laughing, as represented in millions of tourist trinkets and dime store statuettes here in the western world.*") Also in 2008, Dr. Deepak Chopra published *Buddha*, a visionary historical novel vivid with his protagonist's inner conflicts, told with the compelling magic of a movie.

Tracing the **history** of the Buddha's teachings, two books I'd recommend are Edward Conze's *Buddhism, A Short History* and René Grousset's *In the Footsteps of the Buddha.*

The **interfaith** bookshelf thrives as dialogue continues, as in the pages of the anthology *Beside Still Waters: Jews, Christians, and the Way of the Buddha.* A milestone is Thich Nhat Hanh's *Living Buddha, Living Christ*, refreshingly unacademic and written from his heart. Following the Buddha's adage of "see for yourself," readers are invited to compare texts by the two master teachers side-by-side, in Marcus Borg's *Jesus and Buddha: The Parallel Sayings.* Martin Palmer's *The Jesus Sutras: Rediscovering the Lost Scrolls of Taoist Christianity* is an eye-opening look at China's initial reception of Jesus' teachings. And looking within Christianity's own traditions, Elaine Pagel's *Beyond Belief* is a fine introduction to the *Gospel of Thomas.*

The classic text in Buddhist–Jewish dialogue is Rodger Kamenetz' *The Jew in the Lotus,* based on the meeting of leading Jewish teachers and the Dalai Lama in India. On a more personal note, Sylvia Boorstein's *Funny, You Don't Look Buddhist* explains her practice within the context of her Jewish identity. On a practical note, for Buddhist-leaning meditation within Jewish tradition, check out Rabbi Alan Lew's *Be Still and Get Going* and Philip Slater's *Mindful Jewish Living: Compassionate Practice.*

Two bedrock studies in the **Vedic/Brahmanic traditions** are René Guenon's *Introduction to the Study of the Hindu Doctrines* and Heinrich Zimmer's *Philosophies of India;* a more recent study meriting inspection is *A Short Introduction to Hinduism,* by Klaus K. Klostermeier. Of several good titles, Michael Stone's *Inner Tradition of Yoga* is a fine introductory overview, and Frank Jude Boccio's *Mindful Yoga* is a good, practical bridge between yoga and Buddhism.

For the history of **Buddhism in the West,** Rick Fields' brilliant *How the Swans Came to the Lake: A Narrative History of Buddhism in America* is highly recommended. Of broader scope is Stephen Bachelor's *Awakening of the West: The Encounter of Buddhism and Western Culture.* For provocative philosophic commentary on the evolution of Dharma on our shores, also try his *Alone with Others.* And *Westward Dharma* is a definitive, scholarly survey edited by Prebish and Baumann.

I'm creating a category, here, which I'm calling **Western Buddhist memoir** (often with an element of travelogue). Standouts include *Accidental Buddhist* by Dinty Moore; *Wheel of Life* by John Blofeld; *Thank You and OK* by David Chadwick; *Questions of Heaven* by Gretel Ehrlich; *Buddha or Bust* by Perry Garfinkel; *Nine-Headed Dragon River* by Peter Matthiessen (the back-story companion to his *Snow Leopard*); *The Big Bang, The Buddha and the Baby Boom* by Wes "Scoop" Nisker; *Pure Heart, Enlightened Mind* by Christian Zen monk Maura O'Halloran (1955–1982); *Caught in Fading Light* by Gary Thorpe; *What the Buddha Never Taught* by Tim Ward; *Hard-Core Zen* and *Zen Wrapped in Karma Dipped in Chocolate* by Brad Warner; and *The Empty Mirror* by Jan Willem de Wettering (who also writes mystery novels). David Chadwick's monumental **biography** of Shunryu Suzuki Roshi, *Crooked Cucumber,* chronicles the creation of the Zen monastic tradition in America. Other pioneering titles are Sandy Boucher's *Turning the Wheel: American Women Creating the New Buddhism* and *Dharma, Color, and Culture,* edited by Hilda Gutiérrez Baldoquín. (The study comparing Eastern and Western mind-sets, referred to in Chapter 4, is in Richard E. Nisbett's *The Geography of Thought.*)

Considering Part 2 of our book, **Dharma: Truth, and the Way to Truth,** I recall Helen Keller's saying: "Although the world is full of suffering, it is also full of the overcoming of it." For a concise exposition of **the Four Noble Truths,** His Holiness the Dalai Lama XIV has published a book of the same name. For a full, active guide, I wholeheartedly recommend Philip Moffit's *Dancing with Life*. A classic title on the **Eightfold Path** is Bhante Henepola Gunaratana's *Eight Mindful Steps to Happiness* (the sequel to his *Mindfulness in Plain English*).

Of almost a dozen titles in English on the **precepts**—all good—consider Robert Aitken's *Mind of Clover*, Diane Eshin Rizzetto's *Waking Up to What You Do*, and the anthology *For a Future to Be Possible*. As to particular precepts, Philip Kapleau's *To Cherish All Life* makes a Buddhist case for vegetarianism. Alan Hunt Badiner's anthology of writing (and art), *Zig Zag Zen*, airs various sides of the debate regarding mixing drugs and Dharma. And Kevin Griffin's *One Breath at a Time* is a solid entry on awakening as sobriety, as can be found in the standard reference guide for the topic, www.buddhistrecovery.org.

For basic Buddhism introductions, I'm a fan of Noah Levine's inspiring and simple *Against the Stream*. Making clear the **fine points,** *The Heart of the Buddha's Teachings* by Thich Nhat Hanh is as good as it gets. *What the Buddha Taught* by Walpola Rahula is also universally admired and recommended. And the Dalai Lama XIV's *How to See Yourself As You Really Are* introduces understanding, meditating on, and realizing emptiness.

Last but hardly least in the Dharma Department are all the sutras. Inherent in the sense of the word dharma is that of teachings. Well, Buddhist teachings compose the largest body of sacred writings in the world. For a comprehensive overview, from Pali to Tibetan, try *The Eternal Legacy* by Sangharakshita (founder of the Friends of the Western Buddhist Order, and himself a prolific writer); he calls the documents he surveys "one of the most creative outpourings of spiritual energy known to human history."

The Dhammapada may be one of the most widely known and loved of all sutras, bringing us as close as possible to the historical Buddha's words. As with any such primary text, you might wish to browse more than one translation to get a feel, and make your study complete and personal. In Gil Fronsdale's translation, dharma is "experience" and samsara "wandering." But where his rendering cautions "*Speak or act with corrupted mind, / And suffering follows / as the wagon wheel follows the hoof of the ox,*" Geri Larkin's rendition of an urban American sangha, it's "*as certain / as the wheel of a bike that moves / when we start to pedal.*"

Putting the Buddha's Way into practice, through *Sangha* (our guide's Part 2), there are now supportive CDs as well books on beginning **meditation.** Rod Bucknell's and Chris Kang's *Meditative Way* covers the widest range, including sutras, classical and contemporary masters, and personal accounts. A complete collection of meditation practices from Thich Nhat Hanh is called (appropriately) *Happiness*. From the tradition of **Insight Meditation,** the sutras (*suttas*, Pali) are the original recordings of the Buddha's talks. Of primary interest is the *Anapanasati (The Four Establishments of Mindfulness)*, which includes the *Satipathana (Mindfulness of Breath)*. The *Anapanasati* is available in differing translations, with excellent commentaries from various teachers; for example, Analayo's *Direct Path to Realization*, *In This Very Life* by Sayadaw U Pandita, and *Transformation and Healing* by Thich Nhat Hanh. Readers wishing to experience more of the Pali canon might take a dip into *Thus Have I Heard: The Long Discourses of the Buddha,* translated by Maurice Walshe, and *The Middle-Length Discourses of the Buddha,* translated by Bhikkhu Bodhi; (besides being impeccable, you'll find the Buddha could be, at times, colorful, invigorating, and humorous).

A dozen leading Eastern proponents of Vipassana (Ajahn Chah, U Ba Khin, Mahasi Sayadaw, among others) all dwell in Jack Kornfield's anthology, *Living Dharma*. Jack Kornfield is himself a core founder of the Insight Meditation Society, whose teachers also include Joseph Goldstein, Sharon Salzburg, Sylvia Boorstein, Christina Feldman, Larry Rosenberg, Narayan Liebenson Grady, and Wes Nisker. (Try the latest, by any, to start.) I also recommend Stephen Levine's *Gradual Awakening*, a very fine mindfulness introduction (both firm *and* gentle). *Full Catastrophe Living* and *Wherever You Go, There You Are* are perennial favorites by Dr. Jon Kabat-Zinn, pioneer of mindfulness as a kind of stand-alone practice, with *Arriving at Your Own Door* as a newer entry. Ajahn Brahm's *Who Ordered This Truckload of Dung?* is a good intro to one of the brighter lights of a younger generation in the Thai forest tradition.

In the **Zen** zone, primary sutras are the texts of *Prajnaparamita* (Perfect Wisdom), mainly the *Heart Sutra* and the *Diamond Sutra*, but also the *Platform Sutra* by Hui Neng, which is the only text not ascribed to the Buddha yet given status of sutrahood. I'd certainly include Red Pine's rendition of the *Heart Sutra* for this gifted translator's close reading and insightful commentary. Flatfootedly, the most popular book of koans for beginners is Paul Reps' and Nyogen Senzaki's *Zen Flesh, Zen Bones*. For further study, you might try Robert Aitken's *Gateless Gate*.

And then there's the extraordinary thirteenth–century monk Dogen. There's no philosopher, teacher, nor poet quite like him. Three complete versions of his *Shobogenzo* discourses (96 in all) are now accessible in English: one under the guidance of Kazuaki Tanahashi, one via Shasta Abbey (online; free), and one by Gudo Wafu Nishijima Roshi. Taigen Dan Leighton and Shohaku Okamura have also given us Dogen's brief talks in *Dogen's Extensive Record*.

Of modern writers, everyone loves the timeless classic *Zen Mind, Beginner's Mind* by Shunryu Suzuki Roshi, recently book-ended by a companion volume, *Not Always So*.

Of course, there are as many different books as there are approaches to Zen. Other leading introductory titles are Robert Aitken's *Taking the Path of Zen*, Charlotte Joko Beck's *Everyday Zen* and *Nothing Special*, Cheri Huber's *Nothing Happens*, John Daido Loori's *Finding the Still Point* and *Art of Just Sit*, and Uchiyama's and Kosho's *Opening the Hand of Thought*.

For an introduction to Chinese Ch'an, I recommend anything by Sheng Yen; for Korean Son, ditto for Seung Sahn. For a really sweeping guide to Chinese Buddhism, I recommend Yin Shun's *The Way to Buddhahood*.

Pure Land cultivators study but three sutras: the *Amitabha Sutra* (*Smaller Sukhavati-vyuha*), the *Infinite Life Sutra* (*Larger Sukhavati-vyuha*), and the *Meditation Sutra* (*Amitayur-dhyana*). Plus, Pure Land shares with Zen an interest in the *Avatamsaka Sutra* (try Francis H. Cook's *Hua Yen Buddhism*, for an introduction). After 20 years' work, the collected works of Shinran are now available both in book form and online; Alfred Bloom's *Essential Shinran* is a good introduction. For Shin Buddhism, I also recommend *Bits of Rubble Turn into Gold* and *River of Fire, River of Water* by Taitetsu Unno, and *Ocean* by Kenneth Tanaka.

In **Tibetan Buddhism,** Dalai Lama XIV, Pema Chodron, Tarthang Tulku, Chogyam Trungpa Rinpoche, Lama Surya Das, Robert Thurman, and Thubten Chodron are but some of the leading, seminal teachers. Two engrossing autobiographies of lamas, *Lord of the Dance* by Chagdud Tulku and *Born in Tibet* by Trungpa Rinpoche, are informative and eminently readable. For a broad-brush, third-person panorama of Tibetan Buddhism in the West, Jeffrey Paine's *Re-enchantment* is fascinating. Kathleen McDonald's *How to Meditate* is a splendidly practical beginner's guide to Vajrayana. Looking deeper, I recommend a hefty pair by Reginald Ray, *Indestructible Truth* and *Secret of the Vajra World*; his anthology *In the Presence of Masters* is a very good survey of a range of contemporary teachers. Patrul Rincpoche's *Words of My Perfect Teacher* is an excellent foundational text. John Powers' scholarly *Introduction to Tibetan Buddhism (Second Edition)* is an invaluable reference.

With Dzogchen becoming a popular form in the West, more and more titles are available. For a really heartfelt, clear, and challenging exposition, try John Makransky's *Awakening Through Love*. Other titles in this tradition include: *Self-Liberation Through Seeing with Naked Awareness* by Padmasambhava; *Flight of the Garuda*, edited by Keith Dowman; *You Are the Eyes of the World* by Longchenpa; and *Vajra Speech* and *Painting with Rainbows* by Tulku Urgyen Rinpoche. A Mahamudra teacher deservedly reaching a wider audience is Thrangu Rinpoche, teacher of new Karmapa.

The second half of our book (Part 4) shifts focus from living Buddhism to Buddhist living; to **Dharma in everyday life,** starting with **relations.** Sandy Eastoak's anthology,

Dharma Family Treasures: Sharing Mindfulness with Children, was a lone book by the hearth for about a decade. It now has company, with such newer arrivals as *Buddhism for Mothers: A Calm Approach to Caring for Yourself and Your Children* by Sarah Napthali; *Momma Zen: Walking the Crooked Path of Motherhood* by Karen Maezen Miller; *Kindness: A Treasury of Buddhist Wisdom for Children and Parents* by Conover and Wahl; *Baby Buddhas: A Guide for Teaching Meditation to Children* by Lisa Desmond; and *Mommy Mantras: Affirmations and Insights to Keep You from Losing Your Mind* by Casarjian and Dillon.

David Riccho is a very gifted writer on relationships; try *When the Past Is Present* and *How to Be an Adult in Relationships*. For teens, there's *Just Say Om!* by Soren Gordhamer, *Wide Awake* by Diana Winston, *Buddha in Your Backpack* by Franz Metcalf, and *Silence and Noise* by Ivan Richmond. As to the Great Matter, consider *Who Dies?* and *A Year to Live* by Stephen Levine, and *The Tibetan Book of Living and Dying* by Sogyal Rinpoche.

Sun Tzu's *Art of War* and Miyamoto Musahi's *Book of Five Rings* brought Eastern consciousness to Western ways of **business.** One of the first books integrating Buddhism and the workplace was Claude Mhitmyer's anthology, *Mindfulness and Meaningful Work*. That opened the office door for such titles as *The Leader's Way* by Dalai Lama XIV; *Business and the Buddha* by Lloyd Field; *White-Collar Zen* by Steven Heine; *Putting Buddhism to Work* by Inoue and Williams; *Zen at Work* by Les Kaye; *Zentrepreneurism* by Holender, Stewart, and Fitzpatrick; *Work as Spiritual Practice* by Lewis Richmond; and, last but not least, *Z.B.A., Zen of Business Administration* by Marc Lesser. (When he ran Brush Dance, a publishing company, one of their best-selling cards said, "*If you think you're too small to be effective, you've never been in bed with a mosquito.*")

Naturally, as for **food,** you might seek cookbooks. As your maitre d', I've designated Edward Espe Brown as virtual head chef here, but I honestly can't single out any one of his titles because they're all well-worn and stained from continual use in my own kitchen: *Tassajara Cooking, The Tassajara Recipe Book*, and *Tomato Blessings and Radish Teachings*. Ditto for Deborah Madison's *The Greens Cookbook* and Anne Sommerville's *Fields of Greens*. I'm also quite fond of *Wake Up and Cook*, edited by Tricycle Magazine. Two titles that seem destined as bookends here are *Mindful Eating* by Jan Chozen Bays, and *Mindless Eating* by Brian Wansink. Of general interest is Michael Pollan's *In Defense of Food: An Eater's Manifesto*.

In 1948, Eugene Herrigel began a trend of books modeled on the title of his *Zen and the Art of Archery*. Indeed, the way of the Buddha *is* the way of **art.** *The Unfettered Mind* by Takuan Soho (1573–1645) is a seminal introduction to the Zen of Japanese martial arts. Had he known of golf he might have included it, but fortunately we can turn to *Zen Golf* (and the illustrated *Golf*) by Joseph Parent. and *Golf's Three Noble Truths: The Fine Art of Playing Awake* by Ragonnet and Moore.

With awakened eyes, Dharma can be seen (and read) almost everywhere. But to expand a bit upon the reading list already embedded in our chapter on **Dharma Art,** R. H. Blyth (1898–1964) blazed the trail in *Zen in English Literature and Oriental Classics,* ferreting out the Zen of even *Don Quixote.* Shakespeare is rich with Buddhism ("*A rose by any other name would smell as sweet.*" and "*So shalt thou feed on Death, that feeds on men, / and Death once dead, there's no more dying then.*") And, with or without sheep, Wordsworth at his best can be very Buddhist ("*To sit without emotion, hope or aim, / In the loved presence of my cottage-fire, / And listen to the flapping of the flame, / Or kettle whispering its faint undersong.*"). More recently, Norman Fischer brings a Zen perspective to the Psalms, in *Opening to You,* and to Homer, in *Sailing Home.* And I trust you'll enjoy my anthology *What Book!?: Buddha Poems from Beat to Hiphop* (five years in the making).

Besides *Dharma Bums,* three titles from the prolific typewriter of Jack Kerouac, emblazoned with his compassionate Catholic-Buddhist-Beat crazy wisdom, are *Scripture of the Golden Eternity, Some of the Dharma,* and *Visions of Gerard,* his intensely moving poetic memoir of his brother's death. Meanwhile, it will take time for due appreciation of the art of Maxine Hong Kingston's epic, *Fifth Book of Peace,* commemorating her fearless journey of mindful writing in community, and peacemaking. It seamlessly juxtaposes fiction with memoir (art and life) to create (or point to) something new (a literature of peace!); we've had so many works on war, thus far, what else is there yet to compare it to?

Science-fiction fans might well enjoy Kim Stanley Robinson's *Science in the Capital* trilogy (in the tradition of Ursula LeGuinn's *The Dispossessed*) continuing the author's interest in sustainability and Buddhism. Marc Laidlaw's futuristic science-fantasy quest, *Neon Lotus,* is spiced with an innovative and ultimately mind-boggling mix of technology and Tibetan Buddhism (prayer computers, thousand-armed robots, Bardo-scopes, and so on).

I always have an extra copy on hand of Frederick Franck's *Zen and the Art of Seeing* and *Zen Seeing, Zen Drawing* to give away; ditto, Paul Reps' *Zen Telegrams.* And Paul Discoe, another alumnus of Tassajara, redefines "house," in *Zen Architecture: The Building Process as Practice.*

On any **science** shelf, the classic book on paradigms is Thomas Kuhn's *Structure of Scientific Revolution.* Fritjof Capra followed his trail-blazing paradigm-shifter *The Tao of Science* with a number of titles, my favorite thus far being *The Web of Life.* A more practice-based text is *Buddha's Nature* by Wes Nisker. Three classics in the new interface of Buddhism and psychology are Daniel Goleman's *Emotional Intelligence* and *Working with Emotional Intelligence, and The Art of Happiness* by the Dalai Lama and Howard Cutler. Jack Kornfield spells out Buddhist psychology in sweet detail and with care-full insight, in *The Wise Heart.* Of possible interest, too, are Mark Epstein's *Going on Being,* and, for therapists, the anthology *Brilliant Sanity.*

Some leading, nontechnical authors in the field of cognitive science are Antonio Damasio, Michael S. Gazzaniga, Jonathan Haidt, and Marc D. Hauser. Sharon Begley has written a popular introduction to neuroplasticity, *Train Your Mind Change Your Brain;* Norman Doidge goes one step further, illustrating his points with fascinating case studies in *The Brain That Changes Itself.* And Daniel J. Siegel's *The Mindful Brain* reconfigures brain science, the way neuroplasticity reshapes old grey matter.

Of books from the Mind and Life conferences, *Destructive Emotions* has been a particular standout, reported by Daniel Goleman; B. Allan Wallace's challenging *Contemplative Science* is quite rewarding. Those with a science background might best appreciate the dialogue between Matthieu Ricard and Trinh Xuan Thuan in *The Quantum and the Lotus.* James H. Austin's *Zen and the Brain* and *Zen-Brain Reflections* can get techy, yet appeal to laypeople too, while Yongey Rinpoche Mingyur's *Joy of Living* is amazingly simple yet profound.

The Conscious Universe (Second Edition) and *The Non-Local Universe* by Robert Nadeau and Menas Kafatos explain quantum reality and its implications. Readers interested in the paranormal might enjoy Russell Targ's many works, including his memoir *Do You See What I See?* and his title on Buddhism (with J. J. Hurtak) *The End of Suffering.* Dr. Larry Dossey's *Healing Words* entered prayer into the scientific discourse in 1993; since, he's been prescribing such good medicine as *Healing Beyond the Body* and *The Extraordinary Healing Power of Ordinary Things.*

Three anthologies furnish a panorama of players in the terrain of **engaged Buddhism:** *Mindful Politics* edited by Melvin McLeod, *Engaged Buddhism in the West* edited by Christopher S. Queen, and *Engaged Buddhist Reader* edited by Arnold Kotler. *The New Buddhism* by David Brazier is a particularly bracing polemic, reinterpreting Dharma as a call to engagement, from a Pure Land perspective; such vigorous probing has more recently been matched by scholar David Loy's *Money Sex War Karma.* Two notable titles of prison Dharma are *Razor Wire Dharma* by Calvin Malone and *Finding Freedom: Writings from Death Row* by Fleet Maul. Satish Kumar's *The Buddha and the Terrorist* is a timely retelling from the life of the Buddha. Following Allan Hunt Badiner's watershed anthology, *Dharma Gaia,* some notable titles are *Buddhism and Deep Ecology* by Daniel H. Henning and *Dharma Rain* by Kaza and Kraft.

Besides Eric Schlosser's *Fast Food Nation*, two other classics are John Robbins' *Diet for a New America*, integrating health, compassion, and the environment, and Michael Pollan's *The Omnivore's Dilemma*, reporting as a citizen journalist on the interconnectedness of food. Two equally active anthologies reconsider consumerism: *Mindfulness in the Marketplace* edited by Allan Hunt Badiner; and *Hooked!* edited by Stephanie Kaza. In the spirit of "*Never again!*" Brian Victoria exposes the near total support of militarism in Japan by her Zen sanghas, in *Zen at War*. For further reading on all these topics, Donald Rothberg, author of *The Engaged Spiritual Life*, has compiled 200 engaged Buddhist titles online, in the Resources section of the Buddhist Peace Fellowship website, bpf.org.

In the ever-vital **miscellaneous** category, magazines and newsletters can be as important as the latest books for keeping up-to-date in any field. That's true here, too. In 1991, *Tricycle* successfully made its way to the national, glossy magazine racks, where it remains a touchstone in contemporary Western Buddhism. This was soon followed by the equally good *Shambhala Sun*, whose sister magazine *BuddhaDharma* is geared more toward intermediate practitioners. Other periodicals include *Inquiring Mind*, *Living Buddhism*, *Mandala*, *Mindfulness Bell*, and *Urthona: Buddhism and Art*. Plus, since 2004, there's an anthology of *The Best Buddhist Writing* of the year, edited by Melvin McLeod, always a pleasure to look forward to and refer back to.

So, in a word, the printed word continues turning the Wheel of the Dharma. You may even run across "Dharma books"—published for free as merit. There's no Buddhism in any of them (this one, too) … only fingers pointing the way … only what you take from them and make real for yourself. May you hear the Dharma, study its depth, and practice its loveliness. May you realize its true meaning.

Index

F

I

immunology, 329
impermanence, 102-103, 112
incense, 142
India
  death, 251
  expansion of Buddhism, 20
    Ashoka, 21-22
    camps/schools, 23-24
    destruction of Nalanda, 22
    Hinayana, 24
    Mahayana, 24
    Theravada, 24
  Hinduism influences, 38
    inheritances/contrasts, 39
    yoga, 41
Insight Meditation
  Body Scan, 174-176
  defined, 168
  Element Meditation, 177-178
  metta
    practice tips, 181
    sending to others, 180-181
    sublime states, 179-180
  movies, 292
  noting, 170-171
    emotional intelligence, 172-174
    origins, 170
    tips, 171-172
  overview, 168-170
  stopping, 169
integration of Western Buddhism into everyday life, 64
interbeing, 99-102
  defined, 101
  noticing, 112
intercausality, 102
interfaith awareness
  belief in a supreme being, 38
  Christianity, 44-45
  commonality within diversity, 36-37
  Hinduism, 38
    inheritances/contrasts, 39
    yoga, 41

Jubus/Bujus, 46-48
Muslims, 48-49
native spirituality, 49-50
Taoism, 41-43
internetworking of the Internet, 59
interpersonal neurobiology, 330
interrelation, 240
intimacy, 120-121
issues with food, 273-274
It's a Wonderful Life, 295

J

Jackson, Phil, 287-288
Jananadakini, 233
Japan
  flower arranging, 282
  Namu Amida Butsu, 210
  origins of Buddhism, 31-32
  Pure Land other-power, 215-218
  rock gardens, 283
  shakuhachi flute, 290
  suizen, 290
  tea ceremonies, 275
Jataka tales, 247
Jizo, 118
Jubus, 46-48
Judaism interfaith awareness, 46-48

K

Kabat-Zinn, Dr. Jon, 322
Kabatznick, Ronna, 337
Kagyu school, 33
Kalamas, 38
Kapleau, Philip, 53
Kaprow, Maverick Allan, 309
karé-san-sui, 283
karma, 39, 98-99
  movies, 293
  no-karma, 105
  noticing, 112
  transferring merit, 207-209
Kasyapa's smile, 188

Q

R

LOTUS SUTRA: Compassion highly emphasized

Avalokit svara = Embodiment of great compassion
    became Kuan Yin

metaphor
digging earth = getting rid of defilement — dig to
    Buddha nature

CHECK OUT
THESE BEST-SELLERS

More than 450 titles available at booksellers and online retailers everywhere!

Grammar and Style
978-1-59257-115-4

Word Search Puzzles
978-1-59257-900-6

Glycemic Index Weight Loss
978-1-59257-855-9

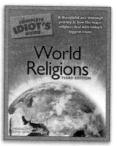
World Religions
978-1-59257-222-9

The Perfect Resume
978-1-59257-957-0

U.S. History Graphic Illustrated
978-1-59257-785-9

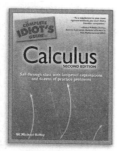
Calculus
978-1-59257-471-1

Positive Dog Training
978-1-59257-483-4

Personal Finance in Your 20s & 30s
978-1-59257-883-2

Organizing Your Life
978-1-59257-966-2

Learning Spanish
978-1-59257-908-2

Wine Basics
978-1-59257-786-6

Microsoft Windows 7
978-1-59257-954-9

Music Theory
978-1-59257-437-7

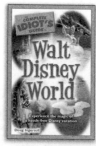
Walt Disney World
978-1-59257-888-7

ALPHA   idiotsguides.com